THE INNER LIVES OF MEDIEVAL INQUISITORS

THE INNER LIVES OF
MEDIEVAL INQUISITORS

KAREN SULLIVAN

THE UNIVERSITY OF CHICAGO PRESS
CHICAGO AND LONDON

The University of Chicago Press, Chicago 60637
The University of Chicago Press, Ltd., London
© 2011 by The University of Chicago
All rights reserved. Published 2011.
Paperback edition 2013
Printed in the United States of America

22 21 20 19 18 17 16 15 14 13   2 3 4 5 6

ISBN-13: 978-0-226-78167-9 (cloth)
ISBN-13: 978-0-226-10432-4 (paperback)
ISBN-13: 978-0-226-78166-2 (e-book)
DOI: 10.7208/chicago/9780226781662.001.0001

The University of Chicago Press gratefully acknowledges the generous support of Bard College toward the publication of this book.

Library of Congress Cataloging-in-Publication Data

Sullivan, Karen, 1964–
    The inner lives of medieval inquisitors / Karen Sullivan.
        p. cm.
    Includes bibliographical references and index.
    ISBN-13: 978-0-226-78167-9 (cloth : alk. paper)
    ISBN-10: 0-226-78167-4 (cloth : alk. paper)   1. Inquisition—Europe—History.
2. Catholic Church—Clergy—Psychology. 3. Catholic Church—Clergy—Biography.
4. Christian heresies—History—Middle Ages, 600–1500. I. Title.
    BX1713.S95 2011
    272'.20922—dc22
                                                                            2010024179

♾ This paper meets the requirements of ANSI/NISO Z39.48-1992 (Permanence of Paper).

FOR DANIEL PITT

At illi persecuntur et amant.

WALTER MAP

CONTENTS

	Acknowledgments	xi
	Introduction	1
1.	Bernard of Clairvaux: The Chimera of His Age	30
2.	Dominic Guzmán: Preacher and Disputant	53
3.	Conrad of Marburg: Zealot of the Faith	75
4.	Peter of Verona: Martyr of the Faith	99
5.	Bernard Gui: The Inquisitor as Performer	124
6.	Bernard Délicieux: The Scourge of Inquisitors	146
7.	Nicholas Eymerich: Toward the Spanish Inquisition	169
	Conclusion	197
	Notes	203
	Index	287

ACKNOWLEDGMENTS

I am grateful for the support I have received from my colleagues and friends in the course of writing this book. I am especially indebted to Deirdre d'Albertis, who read the entire manuscript and shared countless thought-provoking insights into these inquisitors over the years. Mark Lambert also reviewed much of the text and offered many valuable suggestions for its improvement. At different points, Cami Townsend, Roger Berkowitz, Peggy McCracken, and Bill Burgwinkle helped me understand what I was arguing in a new way. Marina van Zuylen, Michèle Dominy, and Leon Botstein provided encouragement at important junctures. The Bard Research Council funded a trip to various Italian libraries and archives, which was crucial for my investigation into the mysterious case of Carino of Balsamo. Many thanks, finally, to Randy Petilos, for his patient support of this project, and to Richard Allen, for his careful editing of the text.

INTRODUCTION

In his black cloak and white tunic, the inquisitor would approach the town on his mule, surrounded by his armed retainers, assistants, and servant. After he had met with the local priest and other officials, he would proceed to the church, where the parishioners would have been asked to assemble. In a loud, clear voice, he would preach to the congregation about the Catholic faith and about the heretics in the region who were teaching doctrines contrary to it. So dangerous were these heretics, he warned, that the pope and the superior of his religious order had authorized him to take action against anyone who had been converted to their creed or merely implicated in their sect, whether by attending their sermons, receiving them into their houses, or sending them gifts. Those who remained obstinate in their heretical beliefs would end up damning themselves body and soul, he announced, but those who repented of their errors would find the Church to be merciful. Over the next few weeks, in a closed chamber, he would receive those who wished to come to him and confess their sins in matters of heresy, with the assurance that they would receive a light penance. As a sign of the sincerity of their contrition, these penitents would be expected to provide information about other people's involvement in the heretical sect, so that they too could be brought back to the faith. Anyone who truly responded to the inquisitor's sermon, it was assumed, would seek to extinguish heresy, not only in his or her own heart, but in the Church as a whole.

After the grace period had come to an end, the inquisitor would summon those people who had been accused by the penitents and who had not yet come before him of their own will. Meeting with the inquisitor *in camera*, with only the notary and the two official witnesses present, these persons would be interrogated about their involvement in the heretical sects. They would not be told the names of their accusers or the nature of the accusations against them, and, as a result, they would be unable to confront these accusers or to challenge their testimony. Though, technically speaking, they were allowed to secure lawyers if they wished, these lawyers would be expected not to disrupt the proceedings by attempting to prove their clients' innocence, but rather to support them by urging their clients to confess their guilt and to welcome their penance. If there was sufficient evidence to think the accused parties guilty, despite their protests to the contrary, they could be tortured. If they later claimed to have confessed only to end the pain, they could be tortured again to determine whether their confession or their retraction was true. Under such conditions, the vast majority of accused parties would eventually confess their guilt, profess their repentance, and accept their penances, which would be heavier than those given to the parishioners who had come forth voluntarily. Even as the inquisitor relied upon the secular power to apprehend, imprison, and torture uncooperative heretics, he remained an ecclesiastic, who welcomed any confession elicited during the trial as, at least purportedly, the product of a change of heart.

When the inquisitor had finished considering all of the individual cases, he would organize a "general sermon" (*sermo generalis*) or, as it would later come to be called, an "act of faith" (*auto-da-fé*). As he had done before, he would call the community together in a public place and deliver a sermon against heresy, now on a raised platform with the local ecclesiastical dignitaries and the repentant heretics gathered around him. He would read aloud these penitents' confessions, would ask them to confirm their veracity, and would assign them penances, which would range from pilgrimages to nearby shrines, to the wearing of yellow crosses on their clothing, to imprisonment, perhaps even for life, on bread and water. At the end of this list, if necessary, he would announce the names of those who had refused to repudiate heresy, whether because they would not confess and abjure their errors or because, having already confessed and abjured them, they had relapsed and in doing so had proven themselves hardened in their heresy. As these impenitent heretics had abandoned the Church, he would declare, the Church was regretfully forced to abandon them in turn by releasing them to the secular arm. Because the Church does not kill or shed blood, the inquisitor would play no part in the next day's proceedings, when the civil authorities passed their own judgment against the heretics and burned them alive before the crowd.

While it is possible to determine the outer actions of the inquisitor, as a historical subject in the world, as this sketch has done, it is not possible to determine his inner thoughts and feelings in the same manner. We can know that the inquisitor traveled to a certain town on a certain date, that he tried people in this town for heresy, and that, as a result of his actions, some of these people were imprisoned or put to death, but we cannot know, let alone with any certainty, how he reflected upon what he was doing. Even if an inquisitor had left us an account, of his own hand, of what he thought and felt while functioning in this role, there was never any one, unified, self-identical experience that this account could purport to represent. The inquisitor may have perceived an accused heretic one way in the afternoon, when he was questioning him, another way that evening, when he was informing the bishop about his case, and still another way years later, when he was recalling his work as a judge to his confessor. From one hour to the next, from one trial to the next, from one stage of his career to the next, the inquisitor's thoughts and feelings and, even more, his perception of those thoughts and feelings, may have changed; at any one moment, he may have undergone multiple and conflicting sensations. Even if there had been a single, fixed inner experience that the inquisitor could describe in some such account, there is no way that its veracity could be confirmed. If he reported that he felt joy at having condemned a heretic hardened in his sin or sorrow at having failed to persuade him to repent of his error, we cannot know if he was telling the truth. His outer activities were public events, observed by other parties and at least potentially recorded by them as well, but his inner thoughts and feelings were private occurrences, observed by himself alone and hence incapable of being seconded. Unless we resort to our own speculations, based upon possibly anachronistic assumptions about the human psyche, what we know about the inquisitor we know from texts, yet texts cannot give us positive, verifiable knowledge about what someone experienced inside himself.

Though it is impossible to gain access to the inner life of the inquisitor as a historical subject in the world, it is possible, I would like to propose here, to gain access to his inner life as a literary subject in medieval texts. In his outer life, the inquisitor acted, and texts then represented, more or less accurately, what he did. When he arrested, interrogated, and sentenced an accused heretic, he performed deeds outside himself, which the final records of his investigations then aimed to portray. In his inner life, however, the inquisitor thought or felt, but whatever he was thinking or feeling was always already mediated by texts, that is, by discourses which were helping him to make sense of what he was already undergoing. When he arrested, interrogated, or sentenced an accused heretic, he experienced sensations which the texts he had encountered made recognizable and articulable. The literary inquisitor, inside the text, can never be assumed to be identical to the historical inquisitor, outside the text, but he provides us with as close a view as we can get of that inquisitor and, arguably, a closer view of him than that we could get if, by some miracle, we were able to meet him or even to be him. The discourses which would have been fleeting and inchoate in the mind of the inquisitor become stable and solid when they are written down. That which would have been diffuse becomes concentrated. Because it is only in the text that the inquisitor's thoughts and feelings achieve their fullest definition, it is only in the text that his inner experience is fully realized. In contrast to his outer life, the inner life of the inquisitor cannot be known as an objective fact, because it never was an objective fact, even to the inquisitor himself, but it can be known as a subjective fiction, because it is through such fictions that the inquisitor and his contemporaries made sense of his life.

If one considers the inner life of the inquisitor as he and his contemporaries depict it in their writings, one sees that it could take two forms. On the one hand, the inquisitor in these texts could imagine the accused heretic as someone whose identity is necessarily vague, indefinite, and subject to change. That man, seemingly so resolute in his heretical faith, may one day return to the Church. That woman, so long linked with the heretical sect, may go unnamed in the Book of Life, but this is a Book to which we have no access. While the inquisitor can ponder the witnesses' testimony and the accused heretics' own confessions, he remains uncertain about who these accused heretics are and, even more, about who they might one day become. On the other hand, the inquisitor in these texts could imagine the accused heretic as someone whose identity is singular, definite, and fixed. That man proclaiming the truthfulness of his heterodox creed is a damned soul, destined for hell. That woman, having once professed repentance of her errors, has exposed the falsity of this repentance through her relapse. From what these accused heretics' neighbors have testified about them and from what they have confessed about themselves, the inquisitor feels confident of his ability to determine whether they are innocent or guilty of heresy and, if guilty, whether they are capable of redemption or hardened in error. Whether the inquisitor in these texts understands the accused heretics' identity as defined by becoming or by being may not affect what he ultimately does, but, as we shall see, it does affect how long he waits before doing it, and the length of this wait is what makes all the difference.

CHARITY AND ZEAL

If there is one pattern in medieval accounts of the inquisitor by himself or by his peers, it is that he pursues heretics out of love, though he may understand that love as charity[1] or as zeal.[2] In the Gospel of Matthew, as all Catholic clerics of this time knew well, Jesus Christ declares that the first and most important commandment is "Love the Lord your God with your whole heart, and with your whole soul, and with your whole mind"[3] and that the second commandment is "Love your neighbor as yourself."[4] It is because they love God, such clerics thought, that they need to defend his teachings, as articulated in Scripture and as explained by Church tradition, and it is because they love their neighbor, they also thought, that they need to confront the heretic who is attacking those teachings. On one level, as we shall see, the inquisitor of these texts perceives the neighbor God wants us to love as the heretic himself. He is familiar with the Book of Ezekiel, where God declares, "I desire not the death of the wicked, but that the wicked turn from his way and live."[5] As he understands it, the Church must seek not to kill the heretic but rather to persuade him to reject his errors and return to the fold in order that he may be saved. On another level, however, as we shall also see, the inquisitor of these texts perceives the neighbor God wants us to love as what he sometimes called "the common people" (*vulgus*), that is, the passive, silent third party the heretic threatens to lead with him into damnation. Worrying that the Church might destroy someone who could have been converted and saved, he also worries that, by failing to destroy the heretic, the Church might enable him to ensnare others in his heresy. If clerics are to love their neighbor, as Christ bids them to do, the inquisitor in these works is sure, they must show charity toward the heretic, whom they strive to convert, but they must also show zeal on behalf of the common people, whom they strive to protect against the heretic's own efforts at conversion. While medieval texts about inquisitors may not have set charity and zeal into opposition as sharply as we will be doing here, they recognized them as two distinct forms of love, one of which may often look like hate.

Between the early eleventh century and the mid-twelfth century, when heretics were seen as resurfacing in Western Europe for the first time since Late Antiquity, the Church, in general, emphasized charity toward heretics. The bishops, who were at this time charged with preserving the spiritual well-being of their flocks, were unsure of their ability to identify heretics and as a result would hesitate to take action against them. They would initiate proceedings only after they had heard that certain individuals were teaching doctrines contrary to the faith. Summoning these individuals to ecclesiastical councils, they would question them and have them questioned by their colleagues. As bishops passively waited for cases of heresy to be initiated by witnesses' accusations, they passively waited for them to be resolved by God's deliberation. If they had reason to doubt the veracity of the accused parties' responses to their questions, they would oblige them to submit to "the judgment of God" (*iudicium dei*), whether by swearing their innocence over relics in a trial by oath or by withstanding the test of fire or water in a trial by ordeal. Even after they had identified heretics through these procedures, bishops were still unsure of their ability to identify heretics hardened in their heresy and as a result hesitated to release them to the secular arm. They did not arrest the renegade monk Henry of Lausanne until 1134, almost twenty years after he had begun spreading his errors throughout the Midi; even then, they continued to seek his redemption rather than his punishment and merely sent him back to a monastery—from which he soon escaped to renew his heretical mission. In those rare instances when heretics were executed during these years, it was more often than not at the instigation of the secular rather than the ecclesiastical powers. In 1022, for example, King Robert II the Pious of France had a band of so-called "Manichaeans" burned outside Orléans, and, in the 1160s, King Henry II of England had a group of "Publicans" branded, stripped, flogged, and cast out in the countryside outside Oxford, to perish in the winter weather. Mobs suspicious of what they regarded as "clerical leniency"[6] occasionally seized accused heretics from episcopal prisons and killed them before the bishops could conclude their proceedings. It may have been that, at a time when the Church perceived heretics as taking the form of eccentric individuals, like Leutard, Tanchelm, or Eudo of Brittany, or of small, isolated sects, like the "Manichaeans" of Orléans or Aquitaine, it felt less threatened than it would later and as a result less anxious to pursue harsh methods. Focusing not so much upon the common people as upon the heretics themselves, the bishops resisted treating these heretics as definitively and unredeemably guilty.

Between the mid-twelfth and the mid-fourteenth centuries, however, the Church turned from emphasizing charity toward heretics to emphasizing zeal on behalf of the common people.[7] In his 1184 decretal *Ad abolendam*, Pope Lucius III required bishops, not to wait for accusations against particular heretics, but to visit every parish in their diocese alleged to be infected with heresy at least once a year, to summon three or more honorable citizens of this parish to identify suspected heretics in their midst, and to compel these suspected heretics to clear themselves of these charges by trials by oath or ordeal.[8] Having obliged the bishops to become more active in initiating cases against heretics, the Church soon obliged them to become more active in investigating these cases as well. At the Fourth Lateran Council of 1215, it took advantage of the resurgence of Roman law and began to reject trials by oath or ordeal in favor of trials by "inquest" (*inquisitio*).[9] Instead of expecting God to reveal the truth about the accused party's faith through a miracle, ecclesiastical judges now took it upon themselves to discover this truth through their own reason, by examining witnesses and by interrogating accused parties. A trial "by inquest" (*per inquisitionem*) was a trial initiated, not by the accusation of a private individual, representing his or her interests, but by the informed decision of a public magistrate, and it was one resolved, not through God's intercession, but through that magistrate's own investigation. A trial "by inquest of heretical depravity" (*per inquisitionem heretice pravitatis*) was such a proceeding applied to matters of the faith. It was not until the 1230s, however, when Pope Gregory IX shifted the primary responsibility for such trials from the bishops to specially appointed "inquisitors" (*inquisitores*), most often from the newly founded Dominican[10] and, to a lesser extent, Franciscan orders, that the potential of these procedures was fully realized. Over time, these inquisitors were allowed certain judicial liberties,[11] including the rights to withhold the names of accusers and the nature of their accusations, in order to prevent their informants from suffering retribution for their testimony;[12] to proceed "simply and plainly, without the uproar and figures of speech of lawyers," in order to prevent the courtroom from becoming a scene of judicial theatrics;[13] and to resort to torture, if there was compelling but not yet conclusive evidence of guilt.[14] In addition to enabling its own ecclesiastical judges to function more actively and freely, the Church persuaded secular rulers to reinforce the power of their spiritual weapons with the power of their temporal sword. It may have been that, at a time when the Church saw heretics as taking the form of large, international movements like those of the Cathars (or Albigensians), the Waldensians, and the various heterodox offshoots of the Franciscans, it felt more threatened than it had felt earlier and as a result more eager to undertake severe measures. Focusing not so much upon the heretics as upon the common people, the inquisitors determined, not to await, passively and patiently, the conversion of individual souls, but to pursue, actively and impatiently, the protection of the social group.

    Wazo, the bishop of Liège in the mid-eleventh century,[15] exemplifies the charitable approach toward heretics, whom he regards as uncertain and unstable in their heretical identity and hence as capable of redemption.

Sometime between 1043 and 1048, Roger II, the bishop of Châlons-sur-Marne, wrote to Wazo, asking him what he should do with some heretics who had been discovered in his diocese and, in particular, "whether or not the sword of earthly authority should be directed against them, lest, were they not exterminated, 'the whole lump be corrupted by a little leaven.'"[16] In a response to Roger's letter included in the chronicle of Anselm of Liège, Wazo recalls the parable of the wheat and the cockle in the Gospel of Matthew, which, since the Church Fathers' struggles with heretics in the fourth century,[17] had been read as prescribing the Church's behavior toward these sectaries. In this parable, Christ describes a field which the master (that is, the Son of Man) has sown with wheat (that is, with good souls), but which the Enemy (that is, the devil) has then strewn with cockle (that is, with wicked souls). The master's servants ask him if they should go and collect the cockle, but the master replies, "Suffer both to grow until the harvest, lest perhaps, gathering up the cockle, you root up the wheat together with it."[18] Wazo reminds his colleague that it can be hard for humans to distinguish the cockle from the wheat and by extension heretics from Catholics. He warns them that there are heretics who, because of their "semblance of strict life,"[19] seem to be Catholics and that there are Catholics who, because of their natural pallor, seem to be heretics (who often adhered to a low-protein diet). The problem is not only that accused heretics may in fact be Catholics but also that, even if they are now heretics, they may in time become Catholics. Wazo asserts, "Perchance that harvest may disclose to be wheat some of those who grow as cockle in the field of this world, and it is possible for Almighty God to make those whom we now consider to be enemies of the way of the Lord superior even to us in that heavenly home."[20] On earth, Wazo recalls, Saint Stephen had been stoned to death by a crowd of Jews, whose coats were held by the future Saint Paul; in heaven, he conjectures, "The martyr apostle now rejoices to recognize as a superior apostle the one who once was his persecutor."[21] Like Paul, the heretic of today might become the Catholic of tomorrow, Wazo indicates, and, again like Paul, he might prove to be a far better Catholic than current members of the Church. Given that human beings are necessarily uncertain as to whether accused heretics are and will always be heretics, he advises Roger not to release the accused heretics of his diocese to the secular arm: "Let us not seek to remove from this life by the sword of secular power those whom God himself, Creator and Redeemer, wishes to spare."[22] With this reference to God as "Creator and Redeemer," he recalls that God created human beings and, after they had sinned, sent his Son to earth to redeem them. If the Church seeks to destroy the human beings God created and to condemn those he redeemed, it acts contrary to God's evident intentions, insofar as it withholds from human beings the charity and forgiveness God himself had shown them.

By stressing the heretics' uncertain and unstable identity, Wazo necessarily stresses their commonality with Catholics, whose spiritual state is likewise subject to change. He suggests that the master's servants, who sought to separate the cockle from the wheat, prefigure the Church authorities of today: "What . . . but the role of preachers is signified by the servants who wish to gather up the cockle when it appears?" And he suggests that Roger, who is considering "gathering up" the heretics he has apprehended, is one such Church authority. He informs his correspondent, "The fervor of spiritual zeal burning in your breast for souls deceived by devilish fraud shows that you are numbered among these servants."[23] While Wazo acknowledges that the servants' zeal may to some extent be praiseworthy, he proposes that their master's charity is ultimately more Christ-like. Echoing Ezekiel, he warns Roger, "Although we think [*putamus*] that we are exercising justice by punishing transgressors . . . , we judge before him who 'desires not the death of sinners' nor rejoices in the damnation of the dying but, rather, knows how to bring sinners back to repentance."[24] It is not that Roger would be exercising justice by destroying the heretics in his diocese; on the contrary, like the master's servants, Wazo writes, he would merely "*think* that [he was] exercising justice" by doing so. If, as we have seen, "It is possible for the Almighty God to make those who we now consider to be enemies of the way of the Lord superior even to us in their heavenly home," it is also possible for God to make us inferior to these alleged enemies in Paradise. Wazo thus compares our ignorance about the heretic, who may end up honored in heaven, to our ignorance about ourselves, who may ultimately not rank so high. Alluding to the harvesters (that is, the angels) who are said in the parable to come at the harvest (that is, at the end of the world) to separate the wheat and the cockle, Wazo writes of heretics, "Because it is indubitably proper for us to reserve such persons to the last harvest of the master of the house, for whatever he may command his harvesters to do about them, so also, for our part, it behooves us to await the harvesters in fear and trembling."[25] It is not that Wazo thinks that the heretics may turn out to have been right in their theological views and the Catholics wrong; rather, it is that all of us, both heterodox and orthodox, should exist throughout our lives in doubt as to whether we are in a state of sin or a state of grace and hence in anxiety as to whether we will be damned or saved.

Because the heretical other, like the Catholic self, is uncertain and unstable in his identity, Wazo concludes, in its encounter with the heretic the

Church must wait for him to repent, even if it must suffer in the interim. Christ provides a model for bishops' behavior not through his power but through his suffering. "In emulation of our Savior, who, mild and humble of heart, did not care to wrangle or contend, but rather to suffer abuse, shameful treatment, blows, and finally death on the Cross,"[26] Wazo writes, "we are commanded to bear with such things for a time [*interim*] in some measure."[27] As bishops, Wazo writes, they should follow him "who . . . knows how to bring sinners back to repentance through his patience and longsuffering."[28] On one level, Wazo is saying that bishops should not contribute to heretics' deaths because, as we have seen before, they should wait for them to convert. It is always possible that the heretics may return to the Church, he states, and, for that reason Roger should not hoe the field of the Lord, "lest [he] do this hastily [*immature*], lest it be done before its time [*ante tempus*],"[29] that is, before the heretics can experience such a change of heart. On another level, however, Wazo is suggesting that bishops should not contribute to heretics' deaths because, even if these heretics do not convert, these prelates will have cultivated their own personal virtue by waiting for them to do so. It is striking that, though Wazo states that bishops should bear with heretics only "for a time" and that they should refrain from taking harsher action only "hastily" or "before its time," he never indicates how long this period of forbearance should last or what should happen after it has elapsed. Without any such indications, it seems that the bishops should wait, not until a moment in time when they will be authorized to try these heretics, but until a moment outside of time when God himself will come to try all humans. Like Christ, "who . . . knows how to bring sinners back to repentance through his patience and long-suffering," Wazo hopes, bishops might be able to bring heretics back to repentance through similar endurance. Like Christ who bore such a terrible Passion, he suggests, bishops can bear the scourge of heresy during this period of abeyance. While Roger wants bishops to exercise violence against heretics, Wazo wants these prelates to endure the violence heretics perpetrate against them.

In contrast to Wazo, Thomas Aquinas, the thirteenth-century Dominican theologian, exemplifies the zealous approach toward heretics, whom he tends to regard as certain and fixed in their identities and hence as unlikely to change. In the parable of the wheat and the cockle, Christ seems to bid Church authorities not to uproot the heretics currently living among Catholics, yet, Aquinas argues, this is only because he fears that by eradicating heretics these authorities might accidentally eradicate Catholics as well.[30] If these authorities are able to uproot heretics without harming Catholics, however, Aquinas maintains, "This is not contrary to Our Lord's command, which is to be understood as referring to the case when the cockle cannot be plucked up without plucking up the wheat."[31] As justification of his belief that heretics can be and should be separated from Catholics, Aquinas cites Saint Paul's injunction (which Roger had also cited), "Know you not that a little leaven corrupts the whole lump? Purge out the old leaven,"[32] as well as Saint Jerome's advice regarding heretics, "Cut off the decayed flesh, expel the mangy sheep from the fold, lest the whole house, the whole lump, the whole body, the whole flock, burn, perish, rot, die."[33] He compares the heretic to leaven that can be cast out from a house, to a decayed limb that can be amputated from a body, and to a mangy sheep that can be culled from a flock, all metaphors which draw out the essential and unchanging nature of the heretic as heretic. It is not that Aquinas denies the possibility that the heretic might convert. Because the Church recognizes that a heretic may always return in his heart to the Church, Aquinas asserts, it is always ready to offer such a person the sacraments of penance and last rites. "In God's tribunal," he explains, "those who return are always received, because God is a searcher of hearts and knows those who return in sincerity."[34] In man's tribunal, however, Aquinas continues, those who profess repentance after a relapse into heresy are not received because human beings do not have access to men's hearts and as a result do not know if such professions are honest. Because the Church is never sure whether such a conversion has taken place or not, Aquinas continues, "It presumes that those who relapse after being once received are not sincere in their return."[35] Given this presumption, the Church does not bar seemingly repentant relapsed heretics from the sacraments, "but," he adds, "neither does she protect them from the sentence of death."[36] Like Wazo, Aquinas recognizes that we cannot always know whether the person consigned to the stake is in fact a heretic, let alone someone who will forever remain a heretic, but, unlike Wazo, he holds that we should err on the side of assuming that he is and will continue to be guilty as charged.

By stressing the heretics' certain and fixed identity, Aquinas necessarily stresses their difference from Catholics, who do not share their errors. As Aquinas sees it, "charity" (*caritas*) is that love which binds a man to his neighbor, based upon their commonality. Recalling Christ's commandments to love God and to love one's neighbor as oneself, he writes, "God is the principal object of charity, while our neighbor is loved out of charity for God's sake."[37] The person who loves his neighbor "out of charity" loves him, not for himself, that is, for the personal characteristics he happens to possess as an individual, but "for God's sake," that is, for the impersonal human nature he necessarily possesses as a fellow child of God. Though charity constitutes a binary tie, linking a man and his neighbor, this tie is guaranteed by the presence of God, whose connection to both human beings renders their affiliation possible. In contrast, as Aquinas sees it, "zeal" (*zelus*) is also that love which binds a man to his neighbor, but in such a way that it makes him hate all that is contrary to the well-being of that neighbor. "A man is said to be zealous on behalf of his friend," Aquinas writes, "when he makes a point of repelling whatever may be said or done against his friend's good."[38] It may appear that zeal arises from the intensity of hatred, insofar as it takes the form of an opposition to something, yet in reality, he maintains, "Zeal . . . arises from the intensity of love."[39] He explains, "For it is evident that the more intensely a power tends to anything, the more vigorously it withstands opposition or resistance. Since, therefore, love is 'a movement toward the object loved,' as Augustine says, an intense love seeks to remove everything that opposes it."[40] While charity would make a man love even a heretic because he loves God, with whom both the man and the heretic are affiliated given their common human nature, zeal makes a man hate a heretic because he loves God, whom that heretic stands to offend. "A man is said to be zealous on God's behalf when he endeavors, to the best of his means, to repel what is contrary to the honor or will of God,"[41] Aquinas avers. If a judge deals harshly with heretics, sending them to be burned, he makes clear, he does so out of a zealous love of God (or by extension the Church, which promotes God's will on earth, or the common people, whose salvation can be ensured only through the Church). In contrast, if a judge deals leniently with heretics, refraining from burning those who have relapsed into error, he writes, "This might be prejudicial to the salvation of others, both because [the heretics] would infect others if they relapsed again and because, if they escaped without punishment, others would feel more assured in lapsing into heresy."[42] When Aquinas speaks of human beings in general, he stresses the charity Wazo sees as uniting one man with a sinner "for God's sake," out of a recognition of their common nature in God, yet when he speaks of heretics in particular, he stresses the zeal he sees as dividing that man from the heretic, out of a recognition of the danger that a heretic presents to others.

Because Aquinas tends to imagine the heretic as fixed and certain in his identity, he concludes that the Church should not wait too long for him to convert, in order best to protect the common people from suffering.[43] Saint Paul had made clear that the Church should repeatedly admonish the heretic to repent of his heresy, yet he had also made clear that it should not do so indefinitely. The Apostle had written to Titus, "A man that is a heretic, after the first and second admonition, avoid, knowing that he that is such a one is subverted and sins, being condemned by his own judgment."[44] In ordering that the heretic be "avoided," Aquinas argues, Paul ordered that he be separated first from the Church by excommunication and then, if he still refuses to reconcile himself with the Church, from the world by death, and he did so because, "if [the heretic] is stubborn, the Church, no longer hoping for his conversion, looks to the salvation of others."[45] While the Church recognizes the value of an individual's life, Aquinas maintains, it recognizes even more the value of an individual's soul and, more still, the value of many people's souls. He writes, "If the presence of [bodily life] in one individual might be an obstacle to eternal salvation in many, we are not bound out of charity to wish such a good to that person; rather should we desire him to be without it both because eternal salvation takes precedence of temporal good and because the good of the many is to be preferred to the good of one."[46] It is true, Aquinas concedes, that, if our brother offends us, we should forgive him, as Christ recommends, "not . . . till seven times, but till seventy times seven times,"[47] yet, it is also true, he contends, that, if our brother offends our neighbor, especially by endangering his soul, or God himself, who created us, we should not be so clement. Christ bids us to forgive our brother so many times, yet, Aquinas writes, "These words are not to be applied to sins committed against one's neighbor or against God, for it is not left to our discretion to forgive such offenses."[48] He discourages Church authorities from bearing with heretics because, he believes, it is not these authorities but rather the common people, for whom these authorities are responsible, who stand to be hurt by them. It might be virtuous to allow oneself to suffer, he suggests, but it is not virtuous to allow others to suffer in one's stead.[49]

It is important to reiterate that, insofar as Wazo insists upon charity toward heretics and Aquinas upon zeal on behalf of the common people, the difference between these clerics is one of emphasis, not one of substance. Though Wazo discourages Roger from releasing the heretics of his diocese to the secular arm, he urges him to excommunicate them and to have this excommunication proclaimed to the common people, so that they may beware of them. He writes of these heretics, "They and those associating with them should be deprived of Catholic communion. Let it be officially and publicly announced to all others, so that, heeding the warning of the Prophet, they may leave their midst and eschew their most unclean sect, for 'He that touches pitch shall be defiled with it.'"[50] By the same token, though Aquinas encourages Church authorities to release heretics to the secular arm, he warns them not to do so until after these heretics have rejected two admonitions to repent. He affirms, "The Church extends her charity to all, not only to friends, but also to those who persecute her"[51] and, as a result, "she condemns not at once, but 'after the first and second admonition,' as the Apostle directs."[52] The two clerics agree that the Church should first attempt to correct the heretic through repeated admonitions and that it should proceed to exclude him from society only if these admonitions fail. Yet, while this difference is one of emphasis and not of substance, it is no less real and important. In the passages from Wazo and Aquinas we have considered, both clerics are responding to the same question—whether heretics should be allowed to live in a Christian society—and, despite the concessions they make to the other side, the one stresses the importance of waiting for the heretic's possible conversion, indefinitely if need be, and the other stresses the importance of taking action against the heretic, once one has waited long enough. Both charity and zeal were widely recognized as virtues throughout the Middle Ages, yet, as we see with Wazo and Aquinas, an emphasis upon the one could lead merely to the excommunication of unrepentant heretics and an emphasis upon the other could lead to their release to the secular arm.

As the Church as a whole shifted from stressing charity to stressing zeal, the consequences of this development became clear. For the more charitable sort of cleric, who is primarily concerned with saving the soul of the heretic, the heretic is another version of the self. Like the self, he possesses an interiority and hence can be viewed from the inside. He exists historically as a particular human being who became a heretic for particular reasons, such as his admiration for the seemingly virtuous lives of the heretics or his acceptance of their seemingly logical arguments. He is deemed capable of reason and as a result capable of dialogue and, potentially, of conversion to orthodoxy. Because of the heretic's rationality, the self engages with him directly, out of love of Jesus Christ, who, as we know from Matthew 18:20, is present when any two or three are gathered in his name. In contrast, for the more zealous sort of cleric, who is primarily concerned with saving people from the heretic, the heretic is an other, sharply distinguished from the self. As an other, he possesses no interiority and hence can be viewed only from the outside. He exists, not historically, as a particular human being, but eternally, as a minion of the devil, typologically, as a dragon, wolf, fox, or other beast allied with the devil, and eschatologically, as a forerunner of Antichrist, the precursor of the devil. Like these creatures, he is believed to possess an inherently wicked nature and to have become a heretic because of that inherent wickedness. As an other, finally, he is imagined to be incapable of reason and therefore incapable of dialogue or conversion, unless divine grace should transform his nature. Because of the heretic's irrationality, the self cannot speak *with* him, dialogically, but only *to* him or *of* him, monologically, for the benefit of God, the Church, or the common people. The self thus engages with this other only indirectly, out of love of these beings whom the other is seen to threaten. Once someone with whom the cleric identified before a third party, the heretic now becomes someone against whom the cleric defends the third party, with whom he identifies.

THE INDIVIDUAL AND HISTORY

But, the reader might be protesting at this point, when that inquisitor rode into town on his mule, he acted as he did not because of his own individual deliberations but because of the historical circumstances in which he lived. As we have seen, the procedures that this inquisitor used as he examined witnesses, interrogated accused parties, and judged the penitent and the impenitent among them had developed over the course of many years through the gradual evolution of Roman and canon law. And, as we have also seen, the assistance that the inquisitor depended upon receiving from the local lord, when he followed these procedures, was the result of an increasing collaboration between ecclesiastical and secular authorities over the course of much time. Whether the inquisitor devoted his energies primarily to persuading heretics to convert or primarily to protecting the common people against such heretics, this reader might contend, his actions must be the result not of his own, personal, moral decisions but rather of these impersonal, material forces outside himself. For such a reader, the image of the inquisitor as a solitary individual, arriving in the town and proceeding against heretics, with which we began, gives a misleading impression of what was really occurring during this encounter, when so many historical factors were informing how he acted. Yet, while it is true, as this reader may be thinking, that the inquisitor must be understood in relation to the historical circumstances under which he functioned, it is also true, I would like to suggest here, that he is never reducible to those historical circumstances and that that which is most interesting about him, especially, falls outside that grid.

Late twentieth- and early twenty-first-century historians of the Inquisition, including Christine Caldwell Ames, John H. Arnold, James B. Given, Henry Ansgar Kelly, Richard Kieckhefer, R. I. Moore, Mark Gregory Pegg, and Edward Peters, have emphasized, not the importance of the inquisitor as an individual, as nineteenth-century historians (including, most importantly, Henry Charles Lea)[53] had tended to do, but the importance of the historical circumstances which within which this individual functioned.[54]

Edward Peters acknowledges that the inquisitors were often "formidable,"[55] but he traces the impression they made not to their own characters but to a series of ongoing historical developments, including the increasing cooperation between ecclesiastical and secular authorities, the increasing severity of punishment in both ecclesiastical and secular courts, and the increasing effectiveness of the personnel involved in their tribunals. James B. Given, in his sociological account of the Inquisition in the Midi between 1275 and 1325, represents the inquisitors as developing new systems of documentation and new methods of punishment, but he identifies as the source of these developments not "individuals' consciously willed actions" but "a predetermined set of social, economic, and political structures,"[56] which provided the context for all such actions. Inquisitors pursued heretics in the way they did, he suggests, not because they decided to do so but because these structures oriented them toward this pursuit. John H. Arnold, in his account of the emerging confessional subject in the registers of the meridional Inquisition between 1240 and 1320, also explains why one should not attribute agency to inquisitors: "Rather than assuming an a priori 'individual' who has an interior sense of selfhood, possesses agency, and remains in some essence unchanged through the different cultural situations within which it finds itself, we might consider subjectivity as contingent and discontinuous, as something produced in different ways and with different effects by altering circumstances."[57] For Arnold, the inquisitor does not define himself as an inquisitor by summoning, interrogating, and judging accused heretics, whose trials he happens to record in his registers; rather, he is defined by these registers, which articulate the discourses he inhabits. Because these historians regard the source of the anti-heretical prosecutions of the Middle Ages as lying not in individuals but in the social, political, or textual structures these individuals inhabit, they devote relatively little attention to inquisitors, let alone to their psychological makeup, except as illustrations of discourses that extend far beyond themselves.

A recent debate prompted by R. I. Moore's work on persecution has highlighted the implications of emphasizing historical circumstances over individuals. In *Formation of a Persecuting Society: Authority and Deviance in Western Europe 950–1250*,[58] Moore argues that, beginning in the twelfth century, Western Europe ceased to be a society that happened to persecute certain populations, including heretics, Jews, lepers, prostitutes, and sodomites, and became what he calls a "persecuting society" defined by its exclusion of these religious and social minorities. In a new chapter in the revised edition of the book, Moore acknowledges that, in his effort to draw out the way in which attitudes toward heretics and other minorities evolved over time, he was obliged to stress the *enchaînement* of figures, events, and texts at the expense of the figures, events, and texts in and of themselves. Though he recognizes the value of both concentrations in the study of the medieval past, he writes: "*Formation* . . . is addressed almost exclusively to change over time."[59] Reviewing a collection of essays edited by Cary J. Nederman and John Christian Laursen entitled *Beyond the Persecuting Society: Religious Toleration Before the Enlightenment*,[60] Moore explains why he prefers to focus upon historical circumstances, especially in their change over time, as opposed to individuals, as this collection does. Though he praises the articles on Peter Abelard and John of Salisbury, he adds, "vividly as both essays illustrate the creativity and sophistication of their subjects, giants in any age, the question remains what wider conclusions we are entitled to draw not only about their world, but about the direction in which it was changing."[61] These two individuals may be of some interest in and of themselves, given their "creativity and sophistication," yet they would be of more interest, he suggests, if the analysis of their theories of toleration could be subsumed within "wider conclusions" about the time period in which they lived and the way in which that time period was changing. John of Salisbury's expression of disbelief in witchcraft in *Policraticus* 2.17, addressed in one of these essays, serves as a case in point. If one considers John as an individual, his dismissal of night-flying may seem impressive, but, if one considers "chronology,"[62] as Moore recommends that one do, this position becomes less remarkable. While John was able to make this remark with impunity in the early twelfth century, Moore observes, he would possibly have run into trouble for making it in the thirteenth or fourteenth century, and he would definitely have run into trouble on its account in the sixteenth century. If John is able to express skepticism about witches, it is not so much because of his own individual insight but because of the historical circumstances in which he lived, which allowed him to express and even in some way to entertain this view. However interesting an individual may be in and of himself, Moore suggests, the significance of his thought can only truly be established if it can be subsumed within a linear historical narrative.

While Moore argued for the importance of emphasizing historical circumstances over individuals, Cary J. Nederman has argued for the importance of emphasizing individuals over historical circumstances. In *Worlds of Difference: European Discourses of Toleration, c. 1100-c. 1550*, Nederman agrees with Moore that medieval society as a whole moved toward religious persecution in the twelfth century, yet he proposes that individual thinkers, including Peter Abelard, John of Salisbury, Marsilius of Padua, Nicholas of Cusa, and Raymond Lull, championed religious toleration.[63] Though Moore engages in little sustained discussion of individuals, let alone sustained analysis of the texts by or about them, Nederman devotes each of his chapters to close readings of texts by one or at most two thinkers, showing how each of them succeeds in balancing an adherence to one faith with an appreciation of a confessionally diverse world. As we have seen, Moore represents ideas, like John of Salisbury's rejection of witchcraft, as driven by ecclesiastical and secular institutions, which might define these ideas as orthodox at one point and as heterodox at another. In doing so, Nederman objects, however, that Moore "implicitly dismisses the power that ideas might have to drive ecclesiastical and secular institutions away from—as well as toward—the suppression of dissent or to aid in the redefinition of heresy."[64] While Moore holds that ideas, as developed by individuals, are the effects of historical forces, Nederman holds that they can be the causes of these forces as well. In contrast to Moore, who, with his emphasis upon large, historical structures, stresses one, single trajectory, leading from a kind of *de facto* toleration in the eleventh century to a *de iure* persecution in the twelfth and later centuries, Nederman, with his emphasis upon individual thinkers, stresses two simultaneous traditions, one tolerant and one persecutory. In their introduction to their collection of essays, Nederman writes, with Laursen, "Just as systematic persecution enjoyed its Catholic advocates, so did doctrines of patient correction and instruction and even of open debate find many supporters among those loyal to Rome. . . . On all sides, one can identify apostles of toleration battling with exponents of intolerance."[65] Instead of accentuating the conflicts *between* one historical period and the next, Nederman and Laursen accentuate the conflicts *within* one historical period. While Moore stresses the importance of history, especially insofar as it is undergoing a linear progression, Nederman and Laursen stress the importance of the individual, especially insofar as that individual complicates or resists any such linear progression.

To return to our inquisitor, it is true that he was to a large extent defined by the historical circumstances in which he lived. He was a Catholic, and, as a Catholic, he would have known, as the Church had long maintained, that "Outside the Church there is no salvation."[66] He would have believed that only Catholics, baptized in the Church and faithful to its precepts, have the opportunity to go to heaven and that all others—including heretics—do not have this chance. In addition to being a Catholic, he was also was most likely a Dominican or a Franciscan friar and, as such, would have subscribed to the pastoral mission of his order. As Ames has demonstrated, the prosecution of heretics, far from being marginal to mendicant spirituality, lay at the center of the friars' efforts to evangelize the common people.[67] Whether by preaching, by hearing confessions, or by reproving errors, the inquisitor would have seen himself as tending to the "care of souls" (cura animarum). A Catholic cleric and a Dominican or Franciscan, he was, finally, of course, an inquisitor, who was assigned the task of pursuing heretics, in accordance with what soon became an extensive body of literature, composed of papal bulls, the canons of Church councils, and the manuals of fellow inquisitors. Richard Kieckhefer and Henry Ansgar Kelly have shown that there was no "Inquisition" per se during the Middle Ages, that is, no centralized institution committed to prosecuting heretics, as there would be a Spanish and Roman Inquisition in later years,[68] but that the inquisitors, having been appointed by the papal office, were nevertheless expected to carry out their tasks in accordance with accepted procedures. As recent historians have emphasized, the inquisitor was molded by the society he inhabited, by the political organization in which he operated, and by the textual records in which he transcribed his activities.

Yet, though the inquisitor was to a large extent defined by his historical circumstances, I would like to suggest that he continued to be able to exercise a certain freedom within them. He was a Catholic, but it was he who decided to remain or, even, to become a Catholic and not a heretic. As we shall see, many of the first inquisitors, such as Conrad Tors, Raynier Sacconi, and Robert *le Bougre*, had been heretics before they became friars and inquisitors and were thus highly conscious of the theological options they exercised. Even inquisitors who had always been Catholics were regularly in conversation with heretics—occasionally highly educated, like themselves—and were thus regularly reminded that they could choose to interpret Scripture differently than they did. The inquisitor was typically a Dominican or a Franciscan friar, but it was he who decided to become a member of these orders and not, for example, a Benedictine monk or a secular priest. In selecting this order, he had selected, not the exclusively contemplative way of life of the monk or the exclusively active way of life of the priest, but the mixed way of life of the friar, which sought to bring the insights of Christianity to the common people by persuasion, if possible, and by force, if necessary. He may have been appointed inquisitor by the provincial of this order, but the provincial presumably perceived in him an aptitude, a motivation, and hence a desire to pursue heretics, which made him seem suitable for this position. There were Dominicans who served as inquisitors, but there were also Dominicans who pleaded with the pope to release their order from this responsibility. There were Franciscans who served as inquisitors, but, as we shall see, there were also Franciscans who participated in uprisings against the inquisitors and who were themselves burned as heretics. Even after he consented to pursue heretics, the inquisitor could choose to emphasize zeal or charity, condemnation or correction, the well-being of the community or the well-being of the accused party.

The history of the Inquisition may be the history of shifting social, political, and textual influences, but it is also the history of individuals, each of whom acts somewhat differently from every other individual, in a way that can never entirely be accounted for by the pressures upon him. Given that virtually all of the scholarship on inquisitors in recent decades has emphasized the historical context in which these individuals functioned, I will be attempting, not to dismiss that scholarship (to which I will allude, as necessary), but to rectify that imbalance by emphasizing the individuals themselves. Like Nederman and indeed like many recent scholars of history and literature,[69] I will be focusing upon a series of individuals as they are portrayed in their own writings or in writings about them. Instead of reading *into* the texts about these figures, relying upon external reality to make sense of their internal logic, as scholars often do, I hope to read *out of* these texts, postponing recourse to that external reality until I have first deciphered their internal logic. Though it is neither possible nor desirable to eliminate all the preconceptions one might have about how these individuals thought, based upon our understanding of that external reality, I will attempt, as much as possible, to bracket those preconceptions so that I can read these texts without their filter. Like Nederman, again, I will be striving to illuminate, not a historical trajectory into which these individuals fit, but the individuals themselves, who may or may not adhere to that trajectory. Wazo's interest in executions of heretics, when such executions were not widely being performed, and Aquinas's interest in arguments against such executions, when such arguments were no longer openly being made, do not fit within any linear, historical narrative about the development of heresy prosecutions, but they are nevertheless of interest precisely in their resistance to that narrative. As valuable as generalizations about historical developments may be, I hope that these generalizations do not force us to disregard the particularity of individuals who contradict them, or even to perceive those individuals as less interesting or less important as a result. While I regard the work of both Nederman and Moore as immensely valuable, I will be explicating the "ideas" of the figures I address and will be making no effort to draw out "wider conclusions . . . about their world [and] . . . the direction in which it was changing." By focusing upon individuals, we will see, not what Catholic clerics in general thought about heretics in the Middle Ages, but what it was possible for educated people to think about them in this time period, given the structures in which they lived. We may be shaped by the historical moment in which we live, but, within every moment, there are a range of positions one can take, and it is that that range of positions that I hope to articulate.

THE TEXT AND ITS CONTEXT

Still, the reader might be objecting, even if one were provisionally to accept that the inquisitor who rode into town on his mule acted as he did at least in part because of his own individual deliberations, the texts which inform us about him give us no access to his inner life and hence no access to those deliberations. We possess many medieval works about inquisitors, some, like inquisitors' manuals, composed by the inquisitors themselves, and others, like chronicles and saints' lives, composed by their contemporaries.[70] Despite their abundance, however, these works have not generally been viewed as illuminating their subjects' thoughts and feelings. Moore writes of medieval persecutors, for example, "Even when we can read their writings, we have no window into their consciences."[71] Daniel Ols similarly asserts, "One finds nowhere in the writings of the inquisitors a speculative reflection as to what founds and legitimizes their action."[72] Yves Dossat likewise concludes, "The personality of the inquisitors escapes us."[73] It is presumably because of the perceived inaccessibility of their inner lives that few studies have been devoted to inquisitors, as opposed to "the Inquisition," and that those studies which do exist have stressed the inquisitors' external actions rather than their internal motivations. A recent collection of "portraits of defenders of the faith" in Languedoc, for example, has provided a thorough description of the deeds of various inquisitors but limited analysis of their thoughts.[74] Yet, if scholars have understood medieval texts about inquisitors as telling us little about their inner lives, it may be, not because these texts keep silent on this topic, but because our preconceptions of what form an inner life should take and how we might gain access to it prevent us from hearing what they have to say.[75]

It is well known that, in order to read a medieval text (or, indeed, any text) properly, one must keep in mind the context in which it was created—that is, the genre to which it belongs, the author by whom it was written, and the purpose for which this author designed it—and one must interpret the text in terms of that context. Because inquisitors' manuals were drafted by and for inquisitors, they may be expected to represent the inquisitor positively and the heretic negatively. Because chronicles were usually compiled by Catholic clerics, often with the support of their monasteries or convents, they may be expected to take the point of view of the Church in its conflicts with heretics. Because saints' lives were typically composed by members of their subjects' orders or by their spiritual counselors, they may be counted on to promote their recognition as saints or the expansion of their cults. As all of these texts reflect the conventions of the genres in which they were written, it may be assumed that their depictions of inquisitors will reflect those conventions. And as all of these texts reflect the perspectives of the authors who came up with them—authors who occupied particular positions in society and hence who possessed certain interests—it may be assumed that their portraits of inquisitors will reflect those perspectives. If one truly wishes to grasp the inquisitor, it might be thought, one must study, not one text in and of itself, whose single point of view would entrap one in its subjective bias, but multiple texts, together, whose competing points of view will allow one to glimpse an objective truth in their interstices. One must read, in other words, not *in* these texts, but *between* them or *through* them.

It is also well known that in order to understand a medieval figure (or, indeed, any figure), one must keep in mind the tendency of texts to represent, not the real person we seek, but an idealized version of that person. Influenced by Karl Marx, Friedrich Nietzsche, or Sigmund Freud, we may assume that the inquisitor could not genuinely have pursued heretics for selfless, spiritual reasons, as medieval texts depict him as doing, but rather must have acted, consciously or unconsciously, for selfish and often material reasons instead. If an inquisitor prosecuted heretics, we may take for granted, it may have been for economic reasons, such as his hope to profit from the confiscation of heretics' property. It may have been for sociopolitical reasons, such as his desire to maintain or to aggrandize the Church's power, which was being threatened by the heretics' alternate doctrines and alternate ecclesial structures. It may have been for psychological reasons, such as his longing to repair the disorder in the external world, caused by religious turmoil, so that he might repair the disorder in his internal mind, caused by a childhood trauma or a dysfunctional family. If one hopes to gain access to the inner life an the inquisitor, it seems, one must read him empirically, as a historical, particular individual, in the service of his own needs, and not typologically, as the eternal, universal figure of the servant of God. Only texts which contrast the inquisitor's "real," private person with his "ideal," public persona, as modern autobiographies or biographies do, it seems, give the impression of intimacy and hence of access to his inner life.

As necessary as it may be to keep in mind the context in which a medieval text was composed, it is nonetheless true that much that is written about inquisitors cannot be accounted for by the genre, the author, or the assumed purpose of the text. An inquisitors' manual may be expected to represent the inquisitor positively and the heretic negatively, yet, as we shall see, it can at times represent these opposed parties in a similar manner. For example, a manual can depict the heretic as trying to deceive the inquisitor, and it can recommend that the inquisitor try to deceive the inquisitor in turn, citing the phrase "A nail is driven out by a nail" (*clavuus clavo retundatur*) to justify his trickery. Through its defense of the inquisitor's resemblance to the heretic, the manual thus recognizes the potentially troubling nature of this resemblance. A chronicle, composed by a Catholic cleric, may be expected to take the perspective of the Church, to which its author is affiliated, but it can also take the point of view of the town, the region, or the kingdom, to which he is no less connected. Though, as a member of the Church, the author may seem likely to support the inquisitor, as a member of these other communities, he can at times end up rejecting him. A saint's life may be expected to celebrate the strengths of the holy person in question, but it can also acknowledge his weaknesses, in a way that can seem contrary to its own purpose. Despite the assumption that texts written in different genres, by different authors, for different apparent purposes will give us different perspectives on the inquisitor they address, it often happens that the same portrait of this figure emerges from these varied sources. If one truly wishes to grasp the inquisitor, one must examine multiple texts about him, but one must also study each of these texts in and of itself, working out its internal complexities and contradictions. One must look for points of tension not only *between* texts but *within* them as well. One must read not *through* these texts but *in* them, ever more deeply.

As necessary as it may be to keep in mind the idealization which shaped medieval portraits of inquisitors, it is nonetheless true that this idealization may not have been as far from the reality of these figures as it may seem. As Jacques Lacan has proposed, in order to function in this world, a human being needs to project an ideal ego, that is, an idealized image with which he identifies himself. An inquisitor must imagine an ideal inquisitor—a judge who is just but merciful, strict but forgiving, zealous but charitable—who he would like to be; who, at least in part, he perceives himself as being; and who he would like others to perceive him as being. In questioning a heretic, in remonstrating with him to repent of his heresy, or in delivering a sermon before a general assembly, the inquisitor models his actions upon those of this idealized self-image. As integral as this ideal ego may be to a human being's sense of self, there is always a gap between the ideal ego and the self. The inquisitor imagines this idealized self, but he knows on some level that, as he aspires to emulate it, even as he acts in accordance with it, even as he identifies himself with it, it remains separate from him. He may for a time lose his temper with a surly heretic, he may for an instant doubt the veracity of a Catholic doctrine, he may in retrospect realize that someone he has condemned was innocent—all incidents that are described in the texts about the inquisitors—and at these moments he knows that he has fallen short of this ideal ego. Yet, though this image always remains apart from him, a dream to which he is always proving himself inadequate, the inquisitor cannot function without it. Even if he were the worst of all inquisitors—unjust, cruel, intemperate—he would still necessarily be acting in reference to a certain image of himself as inquisitor. There may indeed be a false, "ideal" inquisitor and a true, "real" inquisitor, but both are constitutive of the self, and the story of the inquisitor is the story of the interplay between these two constituent parts. Any effort to unmask the inquisitor as he appears in these texts, to read him, not typologically, but politically, economically, or psychologically, and to expose him, not as an eternal, universal type, but as a temporal, particular individual, would thus fail to recognize to what extent this figure's mask is inseparable from his face.

This study is literary in its approach to inquisitors, but it has historical consequences. It will be considering a series of Catholic clerics involved in the prosecution of heresy, but it will be aiming to define, not what these clerics were "really" like as historical subjects in the world, but how they depict themselves or are depicted by others as literary subjects in writings of this time. To put this in other words, it will be considering not the inquisitor but the figure of the inquisitor and hence not a positive history but an *imaginaire*. That being said, attention to the depiction of Catholic clerics involved in the conflicts over heretics in these writings may complicate in a constructive way our understanding of what these clerics were "really" like. As we have seen, the author of a text may be a Catholic cleric, a Dominican friar, even an inquisitor, yet, however much these various identities inform what he writes, he is never just this cleric, never just this friar, never just this inquisitor, but is always in addition an individual with views somewhat different from every other individual who falls into these categories. By the same token, the text may be a Catholic text, a Dominican text, even an inquisitorial text, yet, however much it is informed by these various discourses, it is never just the composite of those discourses. As crucial as it may be to apprise oneself of the context in which the text was written, if one allows oneself to see only that which one deems likely to have been articulated in that context—and not that which a close reading of a text reveals to have been articulated—one emerges with an impoverished view of the text and, by extension, an impoverished view of the context as well. This project is literary, not in the sense that it seeks to address the formal aspects of the texts it is examining, but rather in the sense that it seeks to address the epistemic structures around which these texts organize their worlds. As such, it can be said to belong neither to New Criticism nor to New Historicism but to a kind of New Humanism, which, though recognizant of the validity of late nineteenth- and early twentieth-century critiques of subjectivity, agency, and responsibility as natural entities, still insists upon the importance of these concepts as constructs in our own, day-to-day lives and in doing so, insists upon the importance of literary fictions in our historical existence.

While several different types of Catholic authorities were involved in the pursuit of heretics in the Middle Ages, only some of them will be considered in the following pages. Popes, such as Lucius III, Innocent III, and Gregory IX, played important roles in the prosecution of heretics throughout Christendom, as did papal legates, such as Peter of Castelnau and Arnold Amalric. Bishops, such as Bernard of Castenet, the bishop of Albi, Jacques Fournier, the bishop of Pamiers, and Pierre Cauchon, the bishop of Beauvais, played important roles in the prosecution of heretics in their own dioceses, both before inquisitors began to be appointed, when they held the primary responsibility of apprehending and trying deviants in the faith, and afterwards, when they continued to function as joint judges alongside these friars. Secular rulers, such as King Louis IX of France and Emperor Frederick II, signed legislation against heretics, and lords of lower rank assisted clerics in arresting such malefactors and, when necessary, in burning them at the stake. Though these ecclesiastical and secular potentates possessed institutional power to pursue heretics, however, it was not they but, interestingly, preachers and inquisitors, independent of such institutional power, who in the twelfth, thirteenth, and early fourteenth centuries emerged at the forefront of the campaign against such sectaries and in doing so transformed that campaign for ever after. While bishops, for example, could rely upon "ordinary" authority, grounded in standing episcopal courts, these other clerics relied upon an "extraordinary" authority, granted to them, for a certain time, by a papal commission. Functioning outside the ecclesiastical hierarchy, they thus represent what Moore terms the "new men" of the Middle Ages, that is, clerics who exercised power, not so much as lords with dominion over a particular diocese or monastery, but as educated men with command over fields of knowledge.[76] In the late fourteenth and fifteenth centuries, there would continue to be heretics (though now Brethren of the Free Spirit, Lollards, and Hussites), and there would continue to be Catholic clerics who opposed those heretics, but the inquisitors of this period tended to play a secondary role in prosecutions to bishops, secular rulers, or university masters, and for that reason they fall outside the scope of this project. The clerics we will be addressing here were all similarly situated in the Church, as outsiders to the ecclesiastical hierarchy they fought to uphold, and as such they can serve as legitimate bases of comparison with each other.

Out of recognition of the historical shift that occurred in the pursuit of heretics over the course of the Middle Ages, the following pages will consider chronologically a series of preachers and inquisitors engaged in this endeavor. In the twelfth and early thirteenth centuries, the Church sent preachers to the towns and villages of the Midi most affected by heresy, and these preachers attempted to persuade heretics to renounce their errors and Catholics to remain firm in their faith. In 1145, for example, Bernard of Clairvaux, the dominant figure of the Cistercian order, traveled throughout this region and warned his audiences to beware of heretical doctrines. Between 1206 and 1207, Dominic Guzmán, the future founder of the Dominican order, joined a dozen Cistercian abbots in preaching against heretics in this area. Catholic clerics refrained from prosecuting heretics during these years in large part because the secular lords of the Midi either would not or could not use the temporal sword to reinforce spiritual prosecutions. In the mid-thirteenth century, the Church began to send into the towns and villages of the Midi, Germany, Italy, and France inquisitors empowered not only to preach but to prosecute. Between 1231 and 1233, Conrad of Marburg, probably a secular priest, pursued countless numbers of accused heretics in Germany with a ferocity that led to his own assassination at the hands of knights allied with those he was prosecuting. Between 1251 and 1252, Peter of Verona, a Dominican friar, likewise pursued accused heretics in Lombardy and likewise met a violent death as a result. In the aftermath of the Albigensian Crusade, which had established the power of the Church to crush lords who tolerated heretics on their lands, both clerics exercised an authority to apprehend, interrogate, and judge suspected heretics that Bernard and Dominic had lacked. Finally, in the late thirteenth and early fourteenth centuries, the Church witnessed the full fruition of its inquisitors' prestige. Bernard Gui, the Dominican inquisitor in the Toulousain and the Albigeois between 1307 and 1328, and Nicholas Eymerich, the Dominican inquisitor in Aragon between 1357 and at least 1388, both took advantage of what was at that point a considerable body of canonical writing on the prosecution of heretics in order to compile voluminous manuals for inquisitors, synthesizing, glossing, and adding to what they had collected. It is a reflection of the historical shift in accepted ecclesiastical discourse that, in the eleventh and twelfth centuries, it had been possible to argue that the Church should not release impenitent heretics to the secular arm, but, by the thirteenth and fourteenth centuries, it was no longer possible to make this argument, and anyone doing so could be charged with impeding the inquisitors and, by extension, with supporting the heretics. If Catholic clerics appear to have been more charitable toward heretics earlier and more zealous on behalf of the common people later, it is, not because individual clerics changed, but, rather, because the historical structures in which they functioned underwent transformation.

Yet even as these pages consider these clerics chronologically, out of recognition of the historical shift that occurred in the prosecution of heresy during this time, they will also be considering them as juxtaposed pairs, out of recognition of the individual choices that these pursuers could still make. Both Bernard and Dominic were preachers, without authority to arrest, interrogate, or judge accused heretics, yet, while Bernard represents heretics, in his sermons and letters, as eternal types who choose heresy out of their own, irrational wickedness and who can thus be saved only through divine grace, Dominic represents them, in the words attributed to him, as temporal individuals who are induced to join these sects out of poverty or confusion and who can thus be saved through human appeals. So strong was Dominic's charity toward heretics said to be that, at one point, he planned to raise funds by selling himself into slavery in order to offset the generosity the heretics were showing an impoverished potential convert. Both Conrad and Peter were inquisitors assassinated on account of their work for the faith, yet, while the German nobility and clergy justified Conrad's murder, given the number of martyrs he had created through his persecutions, the Italian authorities deplored Peter's murder, given the martyr he himself became through his heroic end. So strong was Peter's charity toward heretics alleged to be that he was said to seek, not the vengeance of crime victims, which would be the assassin's death, but "the vengeance of martyrs," which was the assassin's conversion to a holy life. Bernard Gui and Bernard Délicieux were exact contemporaries, both mendicant friars in the Midi, both lectors familiar with theology and canon law, and both residents at times of their orders' houses in Carcassonne, but, while Gui became the most important inquisitor of his era, Délicieux became the most important antagonist of inquisitors, leading a major uprising against their power. So strong was Délicieux's charity toward accused heretics that he died in the prison from which he had liberated them, condemned by the inquisitors for his efforts on these accused heretics' behalf. However influential Eymerich's inquisitors' manual would become after his death, his prosecution of heretics was so opposed by the kings of Aragon (at times, with support from the papal office) that he was twice exiled from this kingdom. As we move from the eleventh and twelfth to the thirteenth and fourteenth centuries, it was no longer possible to argue that the Church should not put heretics to death, yet it remained possible to argue that the Church should not prosecute innocent Catholics, and defenders of accused heretics, like Délicieux and the kings of Aragon, made this case. It is precisely because zeal and charity were both respected as virtues throughout the Middle Ages that, even as the Church's emphasis shifted, individual clerics retained a certain freedom, expressed in different ways at different times, to stress either one over the other.

The seven clerics we will be considering are not all inquisitors per se, nor are the inquisitors among them necessarily "representative" of such clerics, but they are, I would like to propose, the most important figures in the development of the notion of the inquisitor, both for their own age and for our own. Bernard and Dominic were preachers against heretics, not inquisitors. By traveling throughout the Midi and delivering sermons against heretics, Bernard charted a path of activity that would be imitated by later Cistercian monks such as Henry of Marcy and the twelve abbots of the 1206–7 campaign. By joining the white abbots on this campaign, Dominic marks the transition between the efforts of these Cistercian monks and those of his own Dominican friars, who would be dedicated to preaching against heretics and later to judging them as inquisitors. While Conrad and Peter were inquisitors, they both functioned in this capacity for a brief time, during which the former was deemed remarkably vehement in his prosecutions by his contemporaries and the latter (to whom not one prosecution has been attributed) remarkably mild. Despite the brevity of their service, however, both clerics would be seen in later years as embodying the face of the Inquisition, whether that face be envisaged as religious fanaticism, in Conrad's case, or as religious martyrdom, in Peter's case. (In the sixteenth century, Peter would come to be recognized as the patron saint of the Spanish Inquisition.) Délicieux was neither a preacher against heretics nor an inquisitor but on the contrary a preacher against inquisitors, yet as such he stands as a fascinating foil to Gui, who participated in his trial. While Délicieux for a time emblematized a certain regional, Occitan resistance to the inquisitors, as is reflected in Jean-Paul Laurens' 1887 painting *L'Agitateur du Languedoc*, in which the defiant Friar Minor points accusatorily at his judges, Gui continues to emblematize the universal, Roman force of those judges, at least to readers of Umberto Eco's 1980 novel *The Name of the Rose*, in which the sinister Friar Preacher makes a cameo appearance. It could have been interesting to conclude this study by considering the fifteenth-century Dominican inquisitor Henry Kramer (Institoris), given that the early modern witch prosecutions, for which Kramer's *Malleus maleficarum* served as a principal handbook, flowed out of medieval heresy prosecutions. Yet it was even more interesting, I decided, to conclude by considering Eymerich, given that the early modern Spanish and Roman Inquisitions, for which his *Directorium inquisitorum* provided the cornerstone, also derived from this medieval tradition. By addressing not just inquisitors, let alone "representative" inquisitors, but a diverse assortment of clerics involved in the pursuit of heretics, we will be able to appreciate, I hope, not just who the inquisitors were, but what clerical models they evolved from; not just how they operated in their everyday prosecutions, but how they aroused the passions, both positive and negative, of their contemporaries; and not just how they justified their own actions, but how their peers found a language with which to oppose those self-justifications.

CHAPTER ONE

Bernard of Clairvaux: The Chimera of His Age

If our story begins with Bernard, the Cistercian abbot of Clairvaux (1090–1153), it is because he brings together in his person contemplation and action in a manner that would provide a model for the friars inquisitors who followed him.[1] As a contemplative, Bernard withdrew into a monastery and devoted himself to his personal salvation. The son of a Burgundian nobleman, he chose to join the recently founded Cistercians at Cîteaux rather than the Benedictines at Cluny, and in doing so expressed a preference for an order based in late antique eremitism, with its focus upon prayer, solitary meditation, and manual labor, over one enmeshed in high medieval feudalism, supported by tithes and tenants and preoccupied by its ministration to wealthy lay patrons. Toiling in the fields and woods of the Cistercian wilderness, he claimed to have learned the meaning of Scripture from the beeches and oaks around him, and his many mystical writings suggest that he experienced the union of God with the human soul. As a contemplative influenced by active virtues, however, Bernard felt compelled to seek not only his own improvement but the improvement of others as well. By the time he was twenty-five, he was abbot of the monastery at Clairvaux, which he used as a base for the expansion of the order. Though, at the time of his profession, the Cistercians' very survival was in question, by the end of his life he had helped to make them the dominant order in Latin Christendom, with 352 monasteries spreading across this realm, almost half of which were affiliated with his own house.[2] He praised the monastic life so eloquently that mothers were said to hide their sons from him and wives to cling to their husbands as he came near. Not only his order but the Church as a whole experienced the force of Bernard's personality. When two men were claiming the papal throne, it was Bernard who intervened in their dispute and ensured that Innocent II and not Anacletus II would be recognized as the true pontiff. When the Latin Kingdom of the East began to falter under Muslim attack, it was Bernard who preached the Second Crusade and inspired his contemporaries to undertake this disastrous campaign. A fellow Cistercian became Pope Eugenius III, but it was Bernard, from a shack at Clairvaux so humble it was said to resemble a leper's hut, who was said to rule Christendom during his reign.[3] Wherever Bernard went, he was lauded by some as a living saint on account of the many miracles he was said to have performed, even as he was denounced by others as a meddler and a humbug.[4] John of Salisbury observes these mixed reactions to the abbot, remarking, "He was 'a man mighty in deed and word,' with God, as some believe, and with men, as we all know."[5] It was Bernard's seemingly paradoxical combination of contemplative and active virtues that made him the imposing figure he became in many areas, including in the struggle over orthodoxy.

In the 1130s and 1140s, in an apparent development of the active side of his persona, Bernard established himself as the most prominent scourge of heretics of his generation. The masters of the cathedral schools, who were replacing the teachers of the monastery schools as the major educators of their time, aroused Bernard's anxiety on account of their excessively rationalistic approach to theology. Around Lent of 1139, Bernard was alerted to the errors in Peter Abelard's writings, and he met with him shortly thereafter to bid him to recant.[6] When the two men failed to resolve their differences at this conference, Bernard began to make his concerns about Abelard public, to which the latter responded by challenging him to a debate. At the Council of Sens, in June of 1140, Bernard began to list his perceived errors to the assembled ecclesiastics, but instead of responding to him Abelard left for Rome to appeal his case. In order to counteract Abelard's effort to exculpate himself, Bernard quickly sent a treatise against him to Innocent II,[7] as well as a dozen letters on the same subject to the pope and members of the curia,[8] and he succeeded in having him condemned for heresy. He pursued Gilbert of La Porrée, another master of the cathedral schools, at the Council of Reims in 1148 in a similar fashion.[9] Not only these wandering scholars, but the wandering preachers of the towns and villages, who had proliferated in the wake of the Gregorian Reform, caused Bernard worry on account of their excessively censorious approach to the clergy. The most notorious of these preachers, a onetime monk by the name of Henry of Lausanne, spread his doctrines in Le Mans, Poitiers, and Bordeaux before he was seized and brought before the Council of Pisa in 1135.[10] At this council, Henry renounced his errors and agreed to join the monks at Clairvaux, presumably as a result of Bernard's persuasion, yet, instead of retiring peacefully to this monastery, he escaped to Toulouse and its environs, where he began to proselytize again. Alarmed, Bernard wrote letters to Alphonsus Jordan, the count of Toulouse and Saint-Gilles,[11] and later to the people of this town,[12] warning them about this heresiarch. Finally, the clusters of ascetical heretics, nowadays often grouped together as "Cathars,"[13] who were being sighted at this time in different locales, disturbed Bernard, given their potential to offer an alternative creed to Catholicism. In the mid-1140s, he composed his sixty-fifth and sixty-sixth *Sermones super Cantica canticorum*[14] against these sectaries,[15] whom he identifies variously as "Toulousans,"[16] "Manichaeans,"[17] and "weavers."[18] Between May and August of 1145, he traveled throughout the Midi, preaching against the errors of both Henry and the "Toulousans" in Bordeaux, Cahors, Toulouse, Périgueux, and Albi, among other towns.[19] Though Bernard did no more than write and speak against heretics, his campaign against these masters, preachers, and ascetics would provide a precedent for later Cistercian and Dominican campaigns against heterodox populations.[20]

Despite the importance of Bernard's activity against heretics, the importance of his writings against these sectaries has tended to be dismissed by scholars. It has been observed that Bernard did not devote much of his corpus to this population. With hardly five references to heretics in each of the eight volumes of Bernard's collected works, Jean Leclercq notes, this topic was not an important one for him.[21] Moreover, those texts that Bernard did compose against heretics have often been perceived to be more rhetorical than substantive. G. R. Evans, for example, describes Bernard seeking to produce "a strong, clear impression" upon his audience,[22] rather than to represent heretics' doctrines in accurate detail. Dominique Iogna-Prat depicts Bernard as addressing heretics solely in "invectives, imputations founded on rumor, [and] judgments taken out of context": he writes, "For him, heresy ... should not be discussed; it is an abomination which must be brought to light and denounced."[23] Beverly Mayne Kienzle portrays him as using a rhetoric of "demonization ..., pollution ..., threat to the social order ..., and apocalypticism"[24] in his letters and sermons about these figures. In contrast to contemporaries like Peter the Venerable and Alan of Lille, Bernard has been seen, not as making historically grounded observations about heretics and their beliefs, but rather as imposing typologically based preconceptions upon them. Bernard's writings against heretics may admittedly not tell us a great deal about heretics, but, I would like to suggest, they do tells us a great deal about Bernard and especially about the way in which he reconciles his active pursuit of heretics and his contemplative, monastic existence.

As active as Bernard may have been against heretics, he consistently grounds his action in his contemplation, and it is the combination of action and contemplation that he himself sees as making him so zealous. It is because he is a contemplative, Bernard makes clear, that he is able to discern the diabolical otherness potentially present in the Catholic self and actually present in the heretical other. On one level, he suggests, heretics become heretics because they are confused people who mistake evil for good, given that evil does, in fact, often seem to be a good. In their confusion, they are essentially similar to Bernard's monks, who also long for sanctity yet also occasionally mistake where it lies. On another level, Bernard also suggests, heretics become heretics because they are wicked people who choose evil over good and who, by donning a fair-seeming guise, make this evil seem to be a good. With their inherent inclination toward wickedness, they are essentially different from the monks he usually addresses. Whether compared or contrasted to the Catholic self, the heretical other is, for Bernard, an essentially irrational, diabolically inspired force and, as such, can be redeemed not through rational arguments but only through divine grace. A Catholic cleric who hopes to turn a heretic away from his heresy should therefore attempt to do so, not by demonstrating to him the falsity of his beliefs, but by praying to God to illuminate him in the darkness in which he lives. While the pursuit of heretics was normally the task of active bishops and not that of contemplative monks, contemplative practice inspires Bernard to undertake this active role, he suggests, because this practice awakens him to an iniquity in these heretics that others do not fully appreciate.

MONSTERS

On one, charitable level of his writings, Bernard represents heretics as particular, temporal individuals who succumb to sin unconsciously and unintentionally, because they mistake evil for good, as any of us might do. In the sermons he addressed to the monks of Clairvaux (and, in their written versions, to monks at other Cistercian monasteries and to religious and secular clergy everywhere), he deplores the fact that Catholic clerics undertake theological study, pastoral ministry, or ascetical practices in the belief that these actions are good in and of themselves, without realizing that, if they fail to undertake these actions in a good way, they are not acting meritoriously. In the letters about Abelard and Henry and in the sermons about the "Toulousans," he deplores the fact that these heretics commit a similar error. So related are the temptations to which Catholic clerics and heretics fall prey that Bernard interprets the foxes in the Song of Songs, first, as "certain most subtle vices cloaked in the likeness of virtues,"[25] to which Catholic clerics are vulnerable, and, then, directly afterwards, as heresies or as the heretics themselves. Whether orthodox or heterodox, all are capable of going astray, Bernard argues, because all are capable of confusing their reason with God's revelation, their will with God's providence, and their vice with God's virtue, and the fact that this sin is the result more of confusion than of choice renders it no less wicked.

As Bernard sees it, it is because Catholic clerics are apt to rely excessively upon their own reason in theological investigations that Abelard has trusted too much in his intellectual powers. Bernard is writing, not in the context of a cathedral school, where masters were increasingly taking advantage of classical philosophy in their theological studies, but in the context of a monastery, where monks would not resort to Aristotle and other ancient thinkers until the 1230s.[26] Still, he knows that many monks, including William of Saint-Thierry, Geoffrey of Auxerre, and William of Champeaux, with whom he was in close contact, had been students or even masters at such schools and may still be attracted to this new learning.[27] In his sermons to his fellow monks, Bernard warns that they may lack self-knowledge.[28] He asserts, "If you do not know yourself, you will not have in yourself fear of God, nor humility."[29] The student who does not know himself does not know his inadequacy before God and as a result does not approach God with the lowliness of heart necessary for true knowledge of him. In contrast to this student, the bride of the Song of Songs, who represents for Bernard the ideal human soul, demonstrates the appropriate self-knowledge and as a result the appropriate humility when she asks of the Bridegroom, "Let him kiss me with the kiss of his mouth."[30] Bernard glosses this passage, writing, "The bride, seeking him whom her soul loves, quite rightly does not trust in her carnal senses nor acquiesce to the empty ratiocinations of human curiosity."[31] Because she knows herself, she knows that she will obtain what she desires not through her own, human capacities but only through divine grace, and she thus cherishes all the more the God who enables her to transcend her limitations. In his letters against Abelard, Bernard asserts that this master has succumbed to the lack of self-knowledge that threatens all clerics. Recalling Abelard's volume on ethics, *Scito te ipsum*, he advises, "It would be better for him if he knew himself, in accordance with the title of his book, and did not exceed his own measure."[32] Given Abelard's claims to knowledge, he declares ironically, "Nothing does he not know of all the things in heaven or on earth, except himself."[33] Because Abelard fails to know himself and especially the limitations upon that self, he fails to know what his reason cannot reveal to him. Citing Saint Paul,

Bernard writes of Abelard, "Nothing does he see through a mirror darkly, but all things he views face to face."[34] Abelard thinks that he can apprehend the truth directly and immediately, as if he were in heaven, and not just indirectly and mediately, as Paul suggests is our fate on earth. Whether a former student of the cathedral schools now enrolled as a Cistercian monk or Abelard himself, all clerics must beware of the pride in their reason which might close them off to God's revelation and doom them to ignorance and error.

Similarly, as Bernard understands it, it is because Catholic clerics are apt to rely excessively upon their own will in their pastoral ministrations that Henry of Lausanne has trusted too much in his voluntary inclinations. As an abbot, Bernard regularly had to deal with monks who decided to flee their monasteries for the open road.[35] In his sermons to his fellow monks, he describes one such hypothetical case. The monk returns to his household, telling himself that by doing so he can persuade others to leave it, Bernard comments, "He goes, and he perishes, this wretch, not so much an exile returning to his fatherland as a dog returning to its vomit. He loses himself, unhappy man, and he acquires no one [for God]."[36] Aspiring to raise the laity up to his level, this monk ends up lowering himself to the level of the laity by losing the virtue specific to his religious calling. The monk takes up the calling of preaching, telling himself that he is "bedewed with supernal grace"[37] and that he should share this grace with others.[38] Bernard remarks that Saint Paul had condemned such self-appointed preachers, for "'How shall they preach, unless they be sent?'"[39] Of that monk who pursues what he sees as the higher good by quitting his monastery or preaching, rather than by doing what his abbot has apportioned him, Bernard writes, "See, now you have . . . your own will for a master, not me."[40] In his letter to Alphonsus Jordan, Bernard indicates that Henry has succumbed to the same temptations to which he had imagined other monks succumbing. He writes, "The man is an apostate who, having abandoned the religious habit (for he was once a monk), has returned to the filth of the flesh and the world, like a dog to its vomit."[41] Having forsaken his monastery, he has broken the rule of stability by which a monk is bound and has become, as Bernard terms him, "a gyrovague and fugitive on the earth."[42] In addition, Bernard reports, "When he began to beg, he set a price on the Gospel (for he is a learned man), and, scattering the Word of God for money, he evangelized so that he might eat."[43] Having preached with no authorization from the local bishop and, worse, with an expectation of financial support for his sermons, Henry has broken the rule of obedience by which a monk is also bound and in doing so has defied Paul's warning, "How shall they preach, unless they be sent?"⁴⁴ With his itinerant lifestyle and his public addresses, Bernard makes clear, he has followed the will he had vowed to relinquish when he became a monk. Whether a monk, now seated before Bernard's pulpit, or Henry, now roaming about the Midi, all clerics must beware of the self-will which, by closing them off to their religious superiors' commands, may lead them astray and may lead others astray with them.

Finally, as Bernard understands it, it is because Catholic clerics and aspiring holy people in general can count excessively upon their capacity for self-mortification that the "Toulousans" in particular have placed too much confidence in their denigration of the flesh. In his sermons on the Song of Songs, Bernard warns his monks that they might be tempted to mistake ascetical endurance for ascetical virtue. A monk may rise out of bed in the morning before his brethren stir but then fall asleep in choir as the others pray. He may prolong his fasts until he is too weak to perform his devotions toward God. He may lengthen his physical labors until he is too exhausted to do those he is assigned.⁴⁵ Such an unwary monk reveals to Bernard the fact that "the cunning Enemy has no more effective stratagem for removing love from the heart than to induce one to exercise it incautiously and without reason."⁴⁶ While what these monks do seems right, the degree to which they do it is wrong. In these same sermons, Bernard recalls that the "Toulousans" avoid meat, eggs, and milk products, not in order to abstain religiously from foods which might cause copulation (for which reason others might fast), but in order to abstain superstitiously from foods which have resulted from copulation. He relates that these heretics condemn sexual intercourse for all members of society not in order to elevate purity but in order to equalize all forms of impurity, so that the adulterer or the sodomite need feel no more guilt than the married man. He reports, finally, that, when consigned to the stake, these heretics go to their deaths joyfully, not because they seek to affirm their faith, like martyrs, but because they seek to destroy themselves, like suicides. He writes, "The constancy of martyrs and their obstinacy have nothing in common because, in the one, contempt of death is at work, on account of their piety, while, in the other, it is hardness at heart."⁴⁷ While what these heretics do seems right, the reason for which they do it is wrong. Whether they are spiritually ambitious monks or heretics, all who aspire to Christian virtue must beware of the singularity that can induce them to follow their own conception of holiness rather than that of their religious superiors.

Bernard reproaches Abelard, Henry, and the "Toulousans" because they too fail to conform to any single, unified model of comportment, be it religious or secular, and instead combine in their selves multiple and contradictory identities. By the time Bernard was writing against him, Abelard had exchanged the life of a master at a cathedral school in Paris for that of a monk and, indeed, that of an abbot (namely, of the Benedictine monastery of Saint Gildas in Brittany). Yet, Bernard affirms, "We have in France Peter Abelard, a monk without a rule, a prelate without responsibility, and an abbot without discipline, who disputes with boys and consorts with women."[48] Though a monk, Abelard is not in residence at his cloister, choosing instead to teach at his school in Paris. Though an abbot, he neglects his monks, catering instead to the young students at this school and to Heloise, once his lover and now an abbess, and her nuns. With all of these contradictions in his person, Abelard is, Bernard states, echoing an Augustinian trope, "a man dissimilar to himself [*homo sibi dissimilis*]: a Herod within, a John [the Baptist] without; a most ambiguous character, having nothing of the monk about him except the name and the habit."[49] As a man who has taken the vows and the habit of a monk but does not act like a monk; as a man who seems holy on the outside, like John, but is wicked on the inside, like Herod; as a man who is unlike his own self, Abelard is not one, self-identical human being but rather a composite of different, contradictory creatures. Henry, too, is a monk who does not act like a monk. As we have seen, Bernard protests, "The man is an apostate who, having abandoned the monastic habit . . . , has returned to the filth of the flesh and the world." He explains, "Frequently, after a day of popular applause, this distinguished preacher is to be found the following night with prostitutes and even with married women."[50] Like Abelard, Henry breaks down the boundary between his religious vocation and the secular world, quitting his monastery, mingling with laymen and, worse, with laywomen; as "a man of God who acts and speaks against God,"[51] he sets into opposition who he is (or at least claims to be) and how he acts. The "Toulousans" are not monks, but they too are people who pretend to a religiosity they do not fulfill. Despite their alleged celibacy, these heretics take women as traveling companions in a manner that arouses Bernard's suspicions. "Every day your side is at the young girl's side at the table, your bed is next to hers in the chamber, your eyes meet hers in conversation, your hands meet hers at work—and you are to be thought continent?"[52] he asks. These heretics profess to imitate the Apostles, yet Bernard jeers, "Where is the apostolic pattern of life of which you boast?"[53] As self-proclaimed celibates who consort with women and as self-proclaimed apostles who lead unapostolic lives, Bernard hypothesizes, these people are not what they allege to be and what they seem to others to be. All of these heretics are too religious, in their monastic or apostolic affiliations, to be considered secular and too secular, in their worldly lives, to be considered religious and thus cannot be understood in either of the two major social categories of their time.

If Bernard's condemnation of those who leave their monasteries, preach to the common people, and undertake extreme ascetical practices seems like a condemnation of himself, he is fully aware of this fact. Like Abelard and Henry, Bernard was a monk and indeed an abbot, who spent a third of his time away from his monastery, occupied with worldly affairs. At times, he defends his journeys by insisting that he travels about only because his superiors order him to do so and because he is obliged to obey them.[54] At other times, he defends them by declaring that circumstances force him to act as he does, by providing no one else who can succor the Church as effectively as himself.[55] Most often, however, Bernard bemoans the discrepancy between the sanctity that is attributed to him, because of his Cistercian habit, and the sinfulness that characterizes him, because of his un-Cistercian lifestyle. After his peers elected him to the archbishopric of Reims (a position he would refuse, along with four other bishoprics), he wrote to the king of France: "If they believe me suitable because of the religious habit I have put on, there is the appearance of holiness in the habit, not holiness itself."[56] He describes his anguish most famously to the Carthusian prior of Portes: "My monstrous life, my bitter conscience, calls out to you. I am the chimera of my age. I conduct myself neither as cleric nor as layman, for I long ago abandoned the lifestyle of a monk, if not the habit."[57] Like the heretics he condemns, Bernard is a monk who has rejected the monastic life through his involvement with the world. Like these heretics, he is a holy man in appearance, venerated by crowds, but he is far from holy in reality and hence far from worthy of such veneration. Like these heretics, finally, Bernard is a monster or, as he puts it, a "chimera,"[58] not because he is part lion, part goat, and part serpent, like this mythical animal, but because he is part cleric and part layman, someone whose contradictory vocation and actions have placed him outside either category. He resembles the sculpted beasts he describes in his *Apologia* on the walls of a monastery cloister, beasts which, in their "ridiculous monstrosity,"[59] have the head of a quadruped and the body of a fish or the front-quarters of a horse and the hind-quarters of a goat. Caroline Walker Bynum has argued that Bernard is fascinated by the "monster" (*monstrum*) or "mixture" (*mixtura*), that is, by the creature which contains within itself different species, not in such a way that these species combine, so that the creature becomes a new entity altogether, but in such a way that these species remain separate, so that the creature remains suspended between two or more different entities and hence unclassifiable and unnamable. Of such monsters, she writes, "the shock of such things, the wonder, appears to lie in the fact that the two . . . approach so closely. But the two-ness remains."[60] The horror Bernard feels in contemplating these heretics, and in contemplating himself, who cannot be understood in any one category, is the horror one feels in contemplating a monster, who likewise cannot be classified.

DRAGONS, WOLVES, AND FOXES

On another, more zealous level of his writings, Bernard depicts heretics, not as particular, temporal individuals who go astray, unconsciously and unintentionally, because they mistake evil for good, but as universal, eternal types who err, consciously and intentionally, because they choose evil over good. As he represents them, Abelard is not just a master of the cathedral schools, perhaps excessively rationalistic in his approach to matters of faith, Henry is not just a preacher of the towns and villages, perhaps excessively vehement in his criticisms of the clergy, and the "Toulousans" are not just partisans of ascetical practices, perhaps wrong-headed in their rationale for this behavior, but these heretics are all the most recent incarnations of beasts depicted in Scripture as allied with Satan and intent upon the destruction of the Church. In accordance with a hermeneutical tradition which extends back to Saint Paul, Augustine, and Gregory the Great,[61] Bernard believes that, when one interprets Scripture, one should consider not just the letter of this text but its spirit and that, by extension, when one interprets history, one should consider not just the literal event, at one time and place, but its spiritual affinity to other events, at other times and places. In his letters, John the Evangelist evokes such mystical correspondences when he warns that there are many "false prophets"[62] and "seducers"[63] who are now going about denying that Christ came in the flesh. Alluding to such a figure, John announces, "This is Antichrist, of whom you have heard that he comes, and he is now already in the world."[64] For medieval (and not just medieval) readers of this passage, Antichrist has appeared in the past, when John was writing these letters; he appears in the present, when heretics reject the Incarnation; and he will appear in the future, when the world is about to come to an end. History takes place, not just as a linear series of discrete, progressive events, but as a circular repetition of the same basic narrative. If Bernard identifies Abelard's errors with those of the late antique Arians, Pelagians, and Nestorians and if he conflates Henry's followers in the Midi with the "Toulousans", it is because he perceives the essential attribute of these heretics, not as what distinguishes one from the other, but as what they have in common. It is only if one transcends the concrete identity of

Abelard, Henry, and the "Toulousans," as human beings, and apprehends their mystical identity, as beasts imperiling the Church, Bernard asserts, that one will respond to them with the appropriate zeal.

In his letters about Abelard, Bernard regularly terms this master a dragon. The Book of Revelation describes a dragon with seven heads and ten horns who fights against Saint Michael and his angels and who is cast down from heaven on account of this insurrection. The author explains, "The great dragon, that ancient serpent, . . . is called the devil and Satan, who seduces the whole globe."[65] At the same time, this book describes a beast with two horns who speaks "like a dragon"[66] and who performs signs with which he seduces human beings. While the first image of the dragon suggests the devil, this second image suggests the "false prophet"[67] who is said to precede the coming of Antichrist. It is this second image that Bernard evokes when he writes, "Peter Abelard has gone before the face of Antichrist to prepare his way."[68] Comparing the Antipope Anacletus, né Peter Leonis, to Abelard, Bernard observes, "We have escaped the roaring of Peter the Lion, who occupied the seat of Simon Peter, but we have run into Peter the Dragon, who attacks the faith of Simon Peter."[69] If Abelard is a dragon, it is, first, because he is infecting people with "his poison"[70] through his books, as dragons were said to infect people. "In writing new doctrines," Bernard states, "[he] has provided for transferring his poison to posterity, by which he harms every generation that is to come."[71] While the antipope, like a lion, caused trouble only while he was alive, in his person, Abelard, like a dragon, Bernard predicts, will continue to disturb the Church after his death, in his writings. If Abelard is a dragon, it is, secondly, because he conceals himself in his lair, as dragons were said to conceal themselves. While the antipope, like a lion, sauntered about openly, Bernard writes, Abelard, "like a dragon, lurks in hidden lairs, so that he may kill the innocent."[72] More dangerous than a raging lion, he states, is "the dragon . . . lurking in his lair."[73] Anacletus openly assailed the Church by denouncing Innocent and by declaring himself pope in his stead, yet, Bernard asserts, Abelard secretly wages such an attack, presenting his errors as truths and befriending members of the curia, including those to whom Bernard is writing. He diffuses his errors as a noxious animal might diffuse a virus, infecting even highly ranked ecclesiastics in such a way that they do not realize that they have been infected. By characterizing Abelard as a dragon, Bernard characterizes him as someone who, as a result of his very bestial and indeed diabolical nature, strives to destroy human beings, but who succeeds in concealing that true nature, so that he does not seem to be as dangerous as he is.

In his letters about Henry, Bernard regularly depicts this preacher as a wolf. As Bernard repeatedly recalls, Christ had warned his disciples, "Beware of false prophets, who come to you in sheep's clothing, but inwardly are ravening wolves."[74] If Henry is a wolf, Bernard makes clear, it is, first, because he causes so much devastation. Bernard informs Alphonsus Jordan, "I have taken off on a journey to those regions that this singular wild animal is especially feeding upon, when there is no one who resists him or who saves people from him. Having been forced to flee all of France for such maliciousness, he found these regions of yours alone open to him, in which, confident under your dominion, he has ravaged the flock of Christ in utter fury."[75] Addressing the people of Toulouse, Bernard refers to having shown them "the wolves [who] . . . devour your people like food of bread, like sheep to be slaughtered."[76] As a wolf, Henry has been hunted from one territory and has fled to another, and he continues to consume the flock in this second land. If Henry is a wolf, Bernard establishes, it is, secondly, because, like the wolves in Christ's admonition, he seems to be a sheep. Bernard informs the count, "He now agitates in your territory, a ravening wolf in sheep's clothing."[77] He advises the people of Toulouse about Henry and other heretics, "Know them to be ravening wolves in sheep's clothing."[78] The problem with a wolf in the guise of a sheep, Bernard makes clear, is that he is not recognized as a wolf and as a result is not considered as dangerous as a wolf. Henry has convinced people, Bernard states, that the Prophets and the Apostles were mistaken and that all human beings who are not his followers will be damned. Bernard wonders how it was that "this man, . . . by some diabolical art, persuaded stupid and foolish people not to believe the manifest facts before their eyes."[79] Like a dragon who can infect innocent people with his poison, without them realizing that they have been infected, this wolf in sheep's clothing can devastate the flock without it or its guardians realizing that it is thus being devastated. In portraying Henry as a wolf, Bernard portrays him as someone, like Abelard, who, by his lupine, even diabolical nature, strives to destroy human beings but who, by his ovine disguise, eludes the defenses that would normally be set up against such predators.

Finally, in his sermons about the "Toulousans," Bernard represents these dualists as foxes. The Song of Songs had bidden its readers, "Catch us the little foxes that demolish the vines,"[80] and, in doing so, according to the traditional exegesis of this passage,[81] had implicitly urged them to catch the heretics who demolish the Church. If the "Toulousans" are foxes, Bernard explains, it is, first, because they destroy the vineyard of the Lord. "This particular heresy is more malign and cunning than other heresies," he writes, "for it feeds upon the destruction of others, neglecting its own glory."[82] While late antique heretics vied overtly with Catholics, in order to achieve victory over them, current heretics contend covertly with them, in order to bring about their fall, without also bringing about their own triumph. "These most malign foxes . . . prefer to harm than to vanquish,"[83] Bernard writes. If the "Toulousans" are foxes, Bernard maintains, it is, secondly, because they achieve the destruction they seek through their guile. He writes about such a heretic, "He is very cunning, his iniquity and impiety having been concealed. He is evidently so paltry and subtle that he can easily frustrate the human gaze."[84] A fox is an animal who lurks in his den and who, when he ventures out, is so small and so tricky that he eludes detection. A heretic, similarly, is a man who conceals his beliefs from strangers, instructing his fellows, "Do not betray our secret,"[85] and who, when he does reveal his beliefs, does so in a way that continues to conceal who he is. This heretic hides who he is not only with this speech but also with his actions. Bernard relates, "He troubles no one, he oppresses no one, he sets himself above no one. His face is pale from fasts; he does not eat, idle, his bread; he works with his hands, from which he sustains his life."[86] Given the gap between who he seems to be and who he is, Bernard asks, "Where is the fox now? We were holding her. How did she slip from our hands?"[87] Like a dragon who infects people with poison or a wolf who disguises himself as a sheep, the "Toulousans" are foxes who cause devastation but without being recognized as doing so and as a result without being prevented from doing so. In depicting the "Toulousans" as foxes, Bernard depicts them as people, like Abelard and Henry, who, by their wily nature, want to destroy the vineyard but also want to cover up their tracks so that they cannot be caught.

As heretics are, for Bernard, not merely Abelard, Henry, and the "Toulousans" living in his own day, but the dragon, the wolf, and the fox mentioned in Scripture, the victims of these heretics' violence are not merely the populace seduced by these heretics' errors, but a bride, a mother, and Christ himself. In the Song of Songs, the bride is imagined as espoused to the Bridegroom as the Church is espoused to Christ, but also as potentially seduced by false teachings. Saint Paul informs her, "I am jealous for you with the jealousy of God, for I betrothed you to one man to present a chaste virgin to Christ."[88] Like the Apostle, Bernard worries that the bride's purity may be sullied by heterodox suitors. He complains of Abelard, "He stains the chastity of the Church."[89] Faced with this assault, the bride, as Bernard envisions her, calls out in tears for assistance from the companions of the Bridegroom, to whom she has disclosed her concerns "more intimately"[90] than to anyone. The image of a lady, dear to oneself but possessed by another, currently pure but in danger of corruption, stirs Bernard's ardor: "How much would I desire to see the friend of the Bridegroom burning with zeal for the bride in the absence of the Bridegroom!"[91] As the bride is a courtly lady, betrothed to their lord, Bernard and his fellow clerics are the chivalric vassals of this lord, beholden to defend his lady in his absence. He reminds his companions, "Because you love the Bridegroom, you will not spurn his bride who is crying out to you in her time of want and tribulation."[92] A bride, the victim of these heretics' violence, is also a mother. In complaining about Abelard, Bernard writes, "Among all the kinds of enemies by which the Church is beset . . . , there is none more dangerous, none more troublesome, than those by whom, when she is holding them to her bosom and nourishing them with her breasts, she is lacerated on the inside."[93] The Church is a mother who feeds her children with her own body but who in doing so finds herself attacked by her wayward, heretical offspring. If Abelard is the Church's wicked son, who harms his mother as he is being nourished by her, the prelates to whom Bernard appeals are her potentially good sons, who would defend the one who cared for them. To one cardinal, Bernard urges, "If you are her son, defend the womb that bore you and the breasts that gave you suck."[94] To another, he insists, "If you are her son, if you recognize the maternal breasts, do not desert the mother in danger, do not withdraw your support from her in time of tribulation."[95] As friends of the Bridegroom, bound to defend the bride against her lecherous seducers, Bernard and his fellow clerics are also sons of this mother, bound to defend her against her ungrateful progeny. The victim of the heretics is, finally, Christ at the time of his Passion. In his sermons on the Song of Songs, Bernard links the sufferings that Christ endured on the Cross with the sufferings the Body of Christ, that is, the Church, has endured at the hands of Roman emperors and barbarian tribes in years gone past and at the hands of schismatics and heretics today. He asks, "If you love the Lord Jesus with all your heart, with all your mind, all your strength, if you see the injuries and the contempt he endures, can you bear this with a calm mind? By no means."[96] The pain one should feel when contemplating the agony of a single man, crucified for our sins, one should also feel, he maintains, when contemplating the sufferings of the Church, persecuted by unbelievers. As Bernard's grief at seeing the Church's doctrines opposed by heretics derives from his grief at imagining a delicate woman, either amorous or maternal, to whom he is affiliated, under attack, it also derives from his sorrow at imagining the Savior of mankind crucified.

According to Bernard, anyone who contemplates the nature of these heretics, as dragon, wolf, and fox of Scripture, and the nature of the Church these heretics assail, as bride, mother, and Savior, will feel sufficient zeal to stand up to them in defense of this Church. In letters both on Abelard and on Henry, Bernard cites the Psalms: "Those who hate you, Lord, have I not hated them? And over your enemies, have I not wasted away? With a perfect hatred I have hated them, and they have become enemies to me."[97] While one might normally associate Christianity more with love than with hatred, Bernard insists, through these citations of Scripture, that the hatred one feels for God's enemies serves as the measure of the love one feels for God himself; it is only if that hatred is present that that love can be reckoned to be present as well. You are to love your neighbor insofar as it remains possible that he will love God as well, yet, Bernard asserts, "When it becomes clear that he will not return to the love of God, it is necessary that you understand him to be, not almost nothing, but entirely nothing, inasmuch as he is in eternity nothing. . . . Not only is he not to be loved, but he is even to be held in hatred."[98] And if you love God and hate his enemies, Bernard continues, you are not merely to feel hatred but you are to act upon it as well. "Those who love," he advises, "burn with zeal."[99] Just as love for God is not genuine unless it is accompanied by hatred for the heretics who oppose him, the desire for justice on God's behalf is not valid unless it is paired with a desire for pursuit of these heretics. "Love justice, you who rule the earth,"[100] Scripture bids us, as Bernard recalls. "The lover of justice seeks after justice and pursues [*prosequitur*] it; indeed, he persecutes [*persequitur*] all injustice,"[101] he explains. As love of the Beloved leads to zeal on his behalf, which puts that love into action, zeal in turn leads to justice, which rectifies the wrongs he has suffered, and justice finally leads to persecution of the wrongdoers.

Insofar as bishops, papal legates, and other prelates have not stood up to Abelard, Henry, and the "Toulousans," though it is their responsibility to do so, Bernard asserts, it is because, as men devoted to action, they have neglected contemplation. Members of the curia might hesitate to condemn Abelard, he worries, because several of them are his former students, whose affection for their onetime master might override their hatred of heresy. The ecclesiastics in the Midi might hesitate to pursue heretics, he fears, because the heretics make it financially advantageous for them not to act. Of these ecclesiastics, he writes disapprovingly, "Princes . . . of the clergy and even from the ranks of bishops, who should rather have been persecuting them, support them on account of their own profit, accepting presents from them."[102] If these authorities evidently do not feel the suffering of the Church afflicted by these heretics, Bernard speculates, it is because they resemble, not Rachel, the beautiful daughter of Laban and the figure of the contemplative life, who earned the love of Jacob and who delighted in his embraces, but Leah, Rachel's blear-eyed but fruitful sister and the figure of the active life, who did not enjoy Jacob's love or rejoice in his embraces but who did bear his children. Like a bride who seeks a secluded chamber in which she can enjoy the intimacy of her beloved, a monk seeks a sheltered environment in which he can enjoy his meditations of God. Bernard states of the bride, "She longs for kisses . . . , she seeks a secret place, she flees the public, she turns away from crowds, and she prefers her own quietude to caring for them."[103] The monk, too, he affirms, longs for "kisses of contemplation,"[104] which intoxicate him with inner sensations. In *De consideratione*, his letter to Eugenius III, once a Cistercian monk, now the pope, Bernard imagines that, like Rachel deprived of Jacob, Eugenius must miss "the sweet delights of a quietude [he] enjoyed not long ago."[105] Ceaselessly badgered with cases he must hear and with problems he must resolve, Eugenius may find his craving for the solitude he has left to be unendurable and as a result may force himself to forget that solitude in order to dull that desire. Shackled to the yoke of his office, he may come not only to accept the hubbub that distracts him from his own soul but even to enjoy it, like the heifer in Hosea 10:11 who came to enjoy threshing. Bernard hypothesizes, "In the midst of your tasks, which are many, you will despair of their end, you will become calloused, and you will eventually repress your sense of a just and useful pain."[106] By inuring himself to this suffering, Bernard writes, Eugenius may develop what he calls a "hard heart,"[107] that is, a heart insensible to piety or entreaty. While the lords of the Church must undertake lives of action in order to fulfill their ecclesiastical roles, Bernard maintains, it is only by continuing to undertake contemplation, at least to some extent, that they will preserve the "sense of a just and useful pain" that will enable them to feel the sufferings of the bride, the mother, and the Savior and to take action in their defense. In order for members of the Church to recall their mission, as promoters of the faith among the people, Bernard suggests that it is necessary for them to remain in touch with a certain contemplative, mystical experience, even as they function within the active, practical world.

Insofar as Bernard stands up to Abelard, Henry, and the "Toulousans," in zealous defense of the Church, though he has no responsibility to do so, it is because, as a monk, he has devoted himself to contemplation. As a monk, he cultivates his love for God. Like Rachel, he can sequester himself in a chamber with his Beloved and can enjoy an encounter with him so intimate that the boundary between self and other is effaced. Under the effects of such amorous or mystical ecstasy, Bernard writes of the soul, "She exceeds and secedes from her bodily senses, so that she, who senses the Word, does not sense herself."[108] While the pope's or the bishop's relentless action threatens to produce in him an apathy toward God that ironically leads him to be less active on his behalf than he should be, the monk's contemplation produces in him an ardor for God that makes him more zealous and hence more active than one would expect. Bernard writes, "It is typical of a true and chaste contemplation that, when the mind is vehemently kindled with the divine fire, it is sometimes so filled with zeal and the desire to acquire for God those who will love him similarly that it willingly interrupts contemplative leisure for the endeavor of preaching."[109] In turning toward God in contemplation, the soul experiences a love so intense that it overflows the boundary of the self, to the point where she feels compelled by this excess of emotion within her to put this love into action by sharing it with others. After going forth into the mystery of God, through her own private communion with the deity, the soul "then returns blazing most vehemently with divine love and surging forth with the zeal of justice, fervent beyond measure in all spiritual endeavors and duties."[110] A desire to experience love of God through solitary meditation naturally leads to a zeal to promote the glory of God through communal encouragement of the pious and correction of the erring. Bernard takes action against heretics—spearheading the campaigns against Abelard and pursuing Henry and the "Toulousans" by letter and in person—where popes, bishops, and legates do not because the contemplation to which he devotes himself in his monastery fosters in him a love of God, which in turn fosters in him a zeal to oppose all those who oppose his beloved.

THE DANGERS OF DISPUTATION

Because heretics are for Bernard incarnations of universal, eternal types, intrinsically drawn toward evil, efforts to persuade them to return to the Church are likely to prove unavailing. On the one hand, like virtually all other Catholic clerics of his time, Bernard acknowledges that clerics should try to bring heretics to repentance. In his sermons on the Song of Songs, he affirms, "If an experienced and learned man of the Church undertakes to dispute with a heretic, he should direct his intention to convincing him where he is erring, so that he may convert."[111] He adds, "Heretics are to be caught, . . . not with arms, but with arguments, by which their errors may be refuted. They themselves, if it can be done, are to be reconciled with the Catholic [Church] and recalled to the true faith."[112] On the other hand, Bernard emphasizes not the importance of such attempts at persuasion but the importance of one's actions once these attempts have proven futile. The question in Bernard's writings, as is always the question in discussions of heretics, is how long one should wait before taking action against them. For some Catholic clerics of Bernard's time, such as Abelard and Gilbert,[113] one can hope to obtain the truth in cases of heresy only after a lengthy process of deliberation, where arguments are considered both for and against the accused. Because the truth is inherently complex, it is best approached with a rational mind that will do justice to its complexity. For Bernard, however, one can expect to obtain the truth in such cases after a brief consideration of the circumstances, ideally outside any adversarial debate. Because the truth is inherently simple, it is best sought with an intuitive insight that will not impute to it a subtlety it does not possess. The same monastic spirituality that allowed Bernard to detect the eternal evil behind the heretics' temporal guise and to respond to that evil with the appropriate zealousness now allows him to rely, not upon human intellect, in its laborious study of the relevant facts, but upon divine grace, in its instantaneous illumination by God, as the final arbiter in cases of heresy.

In his various encounters with heretics (or with people he accuses of heresy), Bernard refused to engage in disputations or even in dialogues with his opponents and instead addressed them in monologues alone. At the Council of Sens, Bernard claimed, he acquiesced only reluctantly and only under pressure from his fellow ecclesiastics to Abelard's demand that he debate with him, and, when the time for the meeting came, he still declined to enter into contention. He recalls, "In the presence of all, one adversary standing facing the other, certain headings excerpted from his books were produced, which ... began to be read aloud."[114] Bernard did not explain his objections to Abelard's teachings on theological topics, such as the Trinity and the Eucharist, and thus did not give him an opportunity to respond to his objections by clarifying those views but on the contrary merely read aloud what Abelard had written, in a way that cut off the possibility of any dialogue between them. Similarly, during his campaign against Henry in the Midi, Bernard did not debate with Henry, which is understandable, given that the preacher fled before his approach, but he also did not debate with any of the other heretics he encountered during his journey either. At Verfeil, for example, the secular priest William of Puylaurens tells us in his chronicle, Bernard preached to the congregation assembled in the church and reproached especially the important families among them for their heterodox affiliations. Offended, these families left the church and returned to their houses, but Bernard followed them into the streets and continued to rail against them while they in turn banged against the inside of their doors and tried to drown out his voice. Not only does Bernard deliver a monologue, but he is so insistent upon delivering it that he pursues his audience when it flees him and attempts to block out what he has to say. In his sermons on the Song of Songs, interestingly enough, Bernard does shift rhetorically from addressing Catholic clerics, who need to be informed about the "Toulousans," to addressing the "Toulousans" themselves. When he is complaining of these heretics' secretiveness, for example, he bids these heretics, "Answer me, . . . that mystery which you hide, is it of God or not?"[115] He contrasts the heretics with Saint Paul, whose Gospel was not hidden, but then, as if anticipating their reaction to this authority, asks, "Perhaps you do not accept Saint Paul? I have heard this said of some of you."[116] Though these sermons show that Bernard could imagine how he might interact verbally with heretics, asking them questions and responding to their answers, there is no evidence that he ever did interact verbally with them in this or in any other manner.

If Bernard refused to enter into disputations or even dialogues with heretics, it seems to have been because he regarded their guilt as easy to discern without such exchanges. While Abelard imagines himself in his *Historia calamitatum* as a knight errant, using his skill at disputation to defeat his opponents, Bernard imagines him as a Philistine warrior, using his human strength to defy God's forces. At Sens, Bernard reports, "Goliath advances, . . . cries out against the ranks of Israel, and upbraids the armies of the saints all the more audaciously, in that he feels David not to be present."[117] If Abelard resembles Goliath, strong and experienced in the warfare of disputation, then Bernard implicitly resembles David, weak in such human conflicts but mighty in the grace of God. He describes himself as heading to meet Abelard "unprepared and unprotected, except by what I turned over in my mind: 'Do not think beforehand about how you will respond. It will be given to you at that hour what you will say.'"[118] Thanks to divine inspiration, Bernard indicates, he knew not to debate with Abelard but rather merely to read aloud the headings from his book. Far from concerned that these headings might not represent the full complexity of Abelard's arguments or that the arguments themselves might be open to multiple interpretations, Bernard expresses confidence that any neutral observer who considered them would immediately understand these views and would immediately apprehend their heretical character. As he explains to one correspondent, he was disinclined to debate with Abelard because "I said that his writings were sufficient to accuse him."[119] As he tells another, "I do not accuse him before the Father. The one who accuses him is his book."[120] Because the book itself accuses him, without need for any gloss, he needs only to read it aloud to bring those accusations into the council. "The headings, having been examined by the judgment of all, were found to be adversarial to the faith and contrary to the truth,"[121] he relates. Truth, as Bernard sees it, is not something that emerges in the course of a contest between two parties but rather something that emerges in the course of one party's reflection upon the matter of hand. Heretics like Abelard, who insist upon challenging their accusers, resemble lawyers who, Bernard writes in *De consideratione*, are also given over to "disputations . . . and fights of words, which tend more to the subversion of the truth than the discovery of it"[122] and who use rhetorical ornaments so that "they may destroy the simplicity of truth."[123] As Bernard saw it, while Abelard sought to obfuscate the truth, with the artificial complexity of his ideas, through a dialogic disputation, he himself succeeded in exposing that truth, in its natural simplicity, through a monologic reading of his book.

In the cases of heresy Bernard recounts in his writings, Catholic clerics typically recognize that the heretic is a heretic, but they cannot persuade him to renounce his errors because of his essentially wicked nature. In the *Vita Sancti Malachiae*, for example, Bernard tells how Malachy, the bishop of Armagh and at times a resident at Clairvaux, once confronted an unnamed cleric from Lismore, in County Waterford, who held heterodox views on the Eucharist. During what appears to have been a disputation before a Church assembly, the cleric of Lismore contended with Malachy about this sacrament but failed to persuade those in attendance of his point of view. Bernard writes of the cleric, "When he attempted to assert and defend his error with all the powers of ingenuity (in which he was practiced to no slight degree), with Malachy disputing against him and convicting him, he was overcome by the judgment of all. He left the assembly, confounded, but not corrected."[124] Though the erroneous nature of his views was made manifest to all, the cleric refused to admit his error. Anathematized, he departed complaining that "he was not vanquished by reasoning but crushed by the bishop's authority"[125] and that all the other clerics were siding with Malachy against him only because they were trying to curry favor with the bishop. Heretics like the cleric of Lismore, Bernard states, resist the sound arguments of their orthodox opponents, not because they find them unconvincing, but because they are incapable of being convinced. When this cleric refused to renounce his errors, he writes, he showed that he could not "come to his senses"[126] and "be made sane."[127] In his unreason the heretic is like a madman, who also mistakes falsehood for truth and who also insists upon this error when he is corrected. As Bernard writes of this cleric, he writes of the "most obstinate"[128] "Toulousans": "These men are not to be convinced by logical reasoning, which they do not understand, nor corrected by authorities, which they do not accept, nor can they be prevailed upon by persuasion, because they are subverted."[129] Through the influence of the devil, who wields "power . . . not only over men's bodies, but also over their hearts,"[130] Bernard relates, "they choose to die rather than to convert. Their end is annihilation, the last thing they await is the fire."[131] Maddened in their reason and hardened in their will, through the effect of the devil, heretics consign themselves to the flames of temporal justice, just as they consign themselves to the flames of eternal damnation. Inaccessible to reason and authority, the two bases of medieval persuasion, these insular and continental heretics lie outside the discursive range of the Catholic authorities who aspire to turn them back from the self-destruction to which they are headed.

Given that Catholic clerics cannot persuade the heretic to return to the Church through either reason or authority, Bernard maintains, they must place hope in grace as the sole means that might save him, by bringing him to recognize his errors. On the rare occasions when the heretic can be converted, it is not through human argumentation but rather through divine intervention. When the cleric of Lismore left the assembly, resistant to all attempts to reason with him, Malachy prayed, "May God . . . have you speak the truth, even out of necessity."[132] As if in fulfillment of the bishop's petition, the cleric collapsed on the road from the council, unable to proceed farther. A madman came by, beheld his plight, and informed him, "This illness is nothing other than death itself,"[133] thus awakening the cleric to the madness of his heresy, which was leading to his spiritual demise. Of the vagabond's words, Bernard comments, "He did not say this of himself, but God corrected him, through a madman, in a beautiful way, who would not gain anything from the sane counsels of sensible men."[134] Returning to the city with the madman's help, the cleric renounced his heresy, was absolved of his sin, and died, presumably to ascend to heaven. Grace alone, and not reason, was capable of penetrating the insanity of the heretic's perceptions and the obstinacy of his will and thus averting the destruction to which he was otherwise destined.

Yet, because grace, though requested, cannot always be counted upon to disperse the darkness of an erring mind, Bernard suggests, Catholic clerics must strive more to rescue the community from the heretic than the heretic from his errors. While, in accordance with Christ's recommendation in Matthew 18:15–19, clerics customarily deliver their first two admonitions to the heretic privately, in order to bring him back to his senses, they deliver their third and final admonition publicly, in order, at least in part, to warn the community about this man, who is now being formally separated from them. When Bernard attended the Council of Sens and confronted Abelard before his fellow ecclesiastics, he did so, he states, primarily because he feared that the faith would be damaged if he acted otherwise. He describes himself as confronting Abelard only because "His error would grow stronger if there were no one to respond and contradict it."[135] Similarly, when Malachy convoked the assembly at Lismore and reprimanded the erring cleric in its presence, Bernard tells us, he did so "sorrowing for so hardened a man, but even more for the injury to the faith."[136] At these councils and assemblies, the primary encounter is not that between the Catholic cleric and the heretic, where the former is attempting to persuade the latter to renounce his heresy, but rather that between the Catholic cleric and a third, listening party, where the former is attempting to convince the latter to distance itself from the heretic. With the popular heresies of Henry and the "Toulousans," as opposed to the academic heresies of Abelard and the cleric of Lismore, Bernard does not stress the importance of trying to persuade these heretics to renounce their heresies. "It is unnecessary and in vain . . . to say so many things against foolish and most obstinate men,"[137] Bernard writes. Instead, he stresses the need to expose these heretics as heretics to their potential converts, so that they will not win adherents to their erroneous faiths. "It is sufficient that they be known, so that people may beware of them,"[138] he states. Even if, at this third and final appeal, the Catholic clerics fail to persuade the heretic to abandon his error, so that he is condemned for heresy and branded, like the cleric of Lismore, or perhaps even condemned for heresy and burned, like heretics elsewhere, they can still feel themselves to have succeeded with him. "For even though the heretic did not arise from his impurity, the Church has been strengthened in faith, and without doubt the Bridegroom expresses joy in the progress of the bride,"[139] he explains. The Church must triumph over heresy, and, when a heretic is publicly recognized as a heretic and rendered harmless through that recognition, that triumph is assured, even if the defeat of an individual is required for that victory.

In accordance with the still relatively lenient ecclesiastical attitudes of his time, Bernard repudiates the violence that the common people occasionally exhibited toward heretics, yet he also expresses admiration for the zeal that led them to that violence. On the one hand, he deplores the people's actions. Echoing his earlier contention that heretics should be "caught . . . , not with arms, but with arguments," he writes, "We do not recommend their action because faith is something that should be recommended, not something that should be imposed."[140] On the other hand, he commends the people's motivations. He states, "We approve their zeal,"[141] and he adds, with a quotation from Saint Paul, "He is a minister of God who is an avenger, in anger, of him who acts badly."[142] Heretics may need to be repressed forcibly, he asserts, if left unharmed, they would persevere in their errors and seduce others into their sect. "It is no doubt better for them to be coerced by the sword of someone who bears not the sword without cause than for them to be permitted to draw many others into error,"[143] he affirms. With these remarks, Bernard makes two statements which, though not contradictory, are in tension with one another: it is better for heretics to be persuaded to renounce their errors than for them to be subjected to force, and it is better for heretics to be subjected to force than for them to convert others. His recognition of the occasional necessity of violence against heretics does not eliminate his reluctance to use it, and his reluctance to use violence does not prevent him from recognizing that it is sometimes unavoidable.

In a similar manner, Bernard's contemporaries criticize the abbot's pursuit of scholastic masters he deemed heretical, but they laud the zeal that stirred him to such campaigns. John of Salisbury states, for example, that "he attacked the two men most famous for their learning—Peter Abelard and . . . Gilbert—and pursued them with such zeal that he secured the condemnation of Peter and only just failed to have the other condemned."[144] As a former student of Abelard's, John gently suggests that Bernard may have been mistaken in thinking these two masters to be heretics, given his ignorance of the philosophy upon which they drew, but he excuses the abbot for pursuing them by adding, "I cannot be persuaded that a man of such holiness did not act out of zeal for God."[145] William of Saint-Thierry likewise writes of Bernard's campaigns against these masters, "Even if the servant of God may have overstepped, in his excessiveness, he left to pious minds an example, not of excessiveness, but of fervor."[146] Though one of Bernard's closest friends and the author of the *Vita prima*, William acknowledges that what the saint did in this case may not have been right, even as he defends why he did it. Troubled by the actions zeal for God sometimes inspired, but still attracted to that zeal, Bernard and his peers express, in different ways, mixed emotions about the prosecutions of heretics which were already happening in their lands and which would happen all the more in coming years.

CHAPTER TWO

Dominic Guzmán: Preacher and Disputant

According to his contemporaries, Dominic Guzmán (1170–1221) was a different man by night and by day.[1] "The night he shared with God,"[2] writes Jordan of Saxony, Dominic's first biographer and his successor as master general of the Order of Preachers. He is said to have kept vigil many a night in churches and chapels and, at those times, to have begged the Virgin Mary to take pity upon human beings, who sinned and who suffered for their sins, and to have done so with such intensity that he sobbed as he prayed. "God had given him a special grace to weep for sinners, for the wretched, and for the afflicted," Jordan explains, "whose distresses he bore in the inmost shrine of his compassion, and his affection, surging inside him, spilled forth, in tears, outside him, through the exit of his eyes."[3] As Dominic's grief for sinners caused him to weep for them, it also spurred him to flagellate himself on their behalf. Three times in a single night, he would whip himself, another biographer, Constantine, the Dominican bishop of Orvieto, reports: once, for himself; a second time, for the sinners of the world; and a third time, for the penitents in Purgatory.[4] Lest one consider Dominic to be only a solitary, morose, and violent soul, however, Jordan adds that, his night having been consecrated to God, "the day he shared with his neighbors."[5] He explains, "During the daytime no one was more sociable with his brethren and companions, no one more happy."[6] He was pleasant when he made conversation with his companions, telling them stories that would incite them to love Christ and to scorn the world. He was pleasant no less when he corrected his brethren, which he was said to have done in a manner so gentle that he never drove them to despair. In general, his inner state was so serene that his outer face shone with cheerfulness, and this cheerfulness lifted up the spirits of his listeners. Despite the apparent conflict between the withdrawn, nocturnal Dominic and his gregarious, diurnal counterpart, the two personas are brought together by a desire to save the souls of others. With his tearful prayers and self-flagellations, Dominic begged God to take mercy upon his fellow men by bestowing his grace upon them, and, with his edifying tales and corrections, he urged his fellow men to take mercy upon themselves by improving their behavior. As Jordan writes, "In his heart was an amazing and almost incredible yearning for the salvation of all."[7]

The desire to save souls which Dominic expressed both at night, during his solitary orisons, and at day, during his social encounters, lay at the heart of the Order of Preachers that he founded. In 1206, Dominic, then a subprior among the canons regular in Osma, in Castile, was traveling in the Midi in the company of Diego of Azevedo, the onetime prior of these canons and the current bishop of Osma, with whose career Dominic was at this point intertwined. Dominic and Diego were troubled by the numbers of heretics they were encountering in this region and were eager to do what they could to curb the growth of their sects. Under the leadership of Pope Innocent III, Arnold Amalric, the abbot of Cîteaux and the head of the Cistercian order, and Peter of Castelnau and Ralph of Fontfroide, monks of the Cistercian abbey of Fontfroide, had resumed the preaching campaign against heretics that Bernard of Clairvaux had launched in this region half a century earlier. They also had been serving as papal legates and, in this capacity, had been attempting to rouse the recalcitrant barons to take action against these heretics.[8] In June of 1206, Dominic and Diego met with these Cistercians at Montpellier and decided to join forces with them in a new preaching campaign, with help from additional white monks from the Midi, including Fulk of Marseilles, the new bishop of Toulouse, and a dozen white abbots from France. By the end of 1207, however, Diego and the other bishops had returned to their sees, the legates had returned to other papal affairs, and the abbots and monks had returned to their monasteries. Only Dominic remained to preach and tend to the *cura animarum* in the Midi, and it was around Dominic that the new Order of Preachers began to develop. In contrast to the Cistercians, who were, in the end, monks, beholden by a vow of stability to remain cloistered in their monasteries, praying and weeping for their sins, the Dominicans would be friars, committed by their very constitutions to wandering about in the world, preaching to the people, and tending to their souls. "It is known that our order was founded, from the beginning, especially for preaching and the salvation of souls," the Primitive Constitutions relate. "Our study should to tend principally, ardently, and with the highest endeavor to the end that we might be useful for the souls of our neighbors."[9] While, as we have seen, Cistercians like Bernard felt torn between the contemplative life in their monasteries, where they were to seek their own salvation, and the active life on the open road, where they would seek the salvation of others, Dominicans combined the contemplative and the active lives, confident that they would save their own souls by saving those of others.

In his desire to save souls, Dominic functioned, some scholars have argued, if not as an inquisitor, then as a kind of proto-inquisitor.[10] As Christine Thouzellier recalls, Dominic received authorization from Innocent, through the intermediary of Arnold Amalric, to proceed against heretics not only pastorally, by preaching to them and disputing with them, but judicially, by judging and reconciling them if they proved repentant, or by abandoning them to the secular arm if they did not.[11] Two surviving letters from Dominic's pen seem to testify to this authority, one, from 1208 or 1209, where he declares a certain Pons Roger, a former Cathar Perfect, reconciled to the Church, and assigns him a penance,[12] and the other, from 1215, where he grants permission for a certain William Hugh, another onetime Cathar Perfect, to be lodged in the house of a resident of Toulouse.[13] On the basis of these two letters, the Dominican friar Peter Calo, writing in the beginning of the fourteenth century, refers to Dominic as "the first inquisitor appointed by the apostolic see."[14] If the two letters show Dominic to have been involved in rehabilitating repentant heretics, Constantine of Orvieto's life of the saint, more disturbingly, shows him to have been involved in releasing obstinate heretics to the secular arm. Addressing Dominic's activities in 1216 or 1217, Constantine relates, "When Dominic, the man of God, was preaching in the district of Toulouse, it happened that some heretics, captured and, by him, convicted [*captos et per eum convictos*] when they did not want to return to the Catholic faith, were handed over to the secular justice."[15] On the basis of this anecdote, Bernard Gui, again writing in the beginning of the fourteenth century, refers to the saint as "exercising the office of Inquisition [*gerente inquisitionis officium*] against the scourge of heresy."[16] Simon Tugwell argues convincingly that Gui would have known full well that Dominic was not an inquisitor in the same sense that he himself was and that, if he represented him as such, it was because he saw him as fulfilling the functions of such a figure. "If, as Constantine implies, Dominic was involved in the conviction of heretics," Tugwell maintains, "then, to all intents and purposes, he was *gerens inquisitionis officium*, as Gui says."[17] In the Midi and later in Italy,[18] Dominic lived in a time and a place where heretics were being arrested, prosecuted, and, on occasion, burned, and he appears in at least few instances to have been implicated in these proceedings.

Yet, however much Dominic seems to have anticipated the inquisitors of later years, it is striking that even in these few episodes he emphasized charity, or the salvation of the heretic's soul, rather than zeal, or the protection of the Church from the heretic. As Marie-Humbert Vicaire has noted, whatever judicial resonance one might decipher in the letters about the two converted Cathar Perfects, Dominic's purpose is to help onetime heretics by certifying that Pons Roger has been reconciled to the Church and by enabling William Hugh to find a place to live. When Constantine of Orvieto refers to the heretics in the region of Toulouse as being "captured and, by him, convicted," he makes clear that Dominic "convicted" these heretics, that is, established them to be heretics, but he leaves unclear who captured them and who handed them over to the temporal powers. Though Constantine depicts Dominic as present when these heretics were about to be burned, he goes on to represent him as rescuing the Cathar Perfect Raymond Gros from the flames, as if he had not been the person who decided that these heretics were to die and as if, at least in Gros's case, he did not agree with that decision. Amid the countless references to Dominic's preaching and disputing with heretics in accounts of his life, Vicaire rightly points out that these passages are the only ones that associate him, however vaguely, with judicial prosecutions and that even they portray him as acting leniently, in the hope that the heretic in question will convert. Tugwell may well be right that Dominic would have perceived no more of a contradiction between "his [own] peaceful methods and the coercive measures being taken by others"[19] than opponents of drunk driving today perceive between advertising campaigns against drinking and driving and prison sentences for those who fail to heed these warnings. Yet, even if, after the onset of the Albigensian Crusade, Dominic lived in an environment where heretics were being pursued with violence and even if he appears to have done nothing to oppose that violence, in his own interactions with heretics, he consistently encouraged them to return to the Church and facilitated their reintegration into its structures.

In the various accounts of his campaigns against heretics, Dominic connects his grief for his own sins and his grief for the sins of the heterodox, and this connection goes a long way toward illuminating his relatively charitable attitude toward this population. Whereas, for Bernard, as we recall, heretics were in large part other than himself, for Dominic, they are the same. When he flagellates himself, he does so for himself, for living sinners, and for dead penitents. With his whip, he identifies his own sins with the sins of others, and he strives to atone for both parties' misdeeds at the same time. As sinners, heretics are thus like Dominic, and their sins are like his own infractions. Whereas for Bernard heretics become heretics in large part because they choose evil over good and, in doing so, ally themselves with the devil over God, for Dominic heretics become heretics because they cannot help doing what they do. When he weeps, he does so "for sinners, for the wretched, and for the afflicted." With his tears, he links those who might seem to be wicked, in actively pursuing evil, and those who might seem to be unfortunate, in passively suffering evil, as if these are not two but one category of people. As sinners, heretics are thus people who, like himself, suffer because of their sins and whose sufferings arouse his compassion. And, whereas for Bernard heretics could be saved only through divine grace, because their problem lies with a perverted will which only God could set aright, for Dominic they can be saved through human arguments because their problem lies with a confused understanding which human beings can rectify. Bernard was pessimistic about the heretics' potential for conversion and as a result strove zealously to assist the Church endangered by their errors, yet Dominic is optimistic about this potential and consequently strives charitably to assist the heretics themselves. Like living sinners and dead penitents, who are linked in the community of souls, for Dominic Catholics and heretics are linked in their universally human bond, sharing a common propensity for sin, a common experience of suffering as a result of this sin, and a common hope of redemption through that suffering.

A GOOD MAN

As we remember, Bernard imagined heretics as savage beasts, intent upon the destruction of the Church. Peter Abelard was "Peter the Dragon, who assails the faith of Simon Peter" and who, "like a dragon, lurks in hidden lairs that he may kill the innocent," Henry of Lausanne was "a ravening wolf in sheep's clothing" who "has successfully ravaged the flock of Christ, in complete fury," and the "Toulousans" were "foxes that destroy the vineyards," "feeding on the destruction of others." By depicting heretics as dragons, wolves, and foxes, allied with the devil, Bernard suggested that they were irrational in their conversion to heresy and malevolent in their attempts to convert others to their creed. Because the possibility that heretics might return to the Church seemed as unlikely as the possibility that wild beasts might become human beings, Bernard expressed concern almost exclusively for the potential victims of these heretics, not for the heretics themselves. Given this Cistercian precedent, it is all the more striking that Dominic perceives heretics not as evil but as unfortunate, that he strives not to guard others against them but to assist them in their misery, and that he expects them to return to the Church, once provided with such aid.

Whereas Bernard believes that people turn to heresy out of a deliberate, spiritual attraction to evil, Dominic thinks that they do so, first, out of an accidental, material need for goods, and he responds to them in kind. Jordan of Saxony tells us, "Once, when he was inducing one of the unbelievers to return to the faithful bosom of the Mother Church with pious exhortations, [the latter] responded that his association with the unbelievers was prompted by the need for worldly things and that the things he needed, which he could not otherwise obtain, were readily provided by the heretics."[20] Similarly, Jordan speaks of Dominic's encounter with "certain noblewomen whose parents, on account of their poverty, had delivered them to the heretics to be educated and brought up,"[21] parents who had done so, Peter Ferrand states more strongly, "compelled by poverty."[22] These women became heretics with the cooperation of their parents not because either generation was drawn to heresy but rather because there were no other options for poor but noble families who sought to have their daughters well raised. Despite the Church's traditional emphasis upon the moral rather than material basis of people's action, Dominic and his biographers seem to have perceived these southerners to become heretics not because they chose to do so of their own will, but because they were forced to do so by circumstances. In response to the man who joined the heretics because of his indigence, Jordan informs us, "[Dominic] was so moved by affection that he immediately decided to sell himself and, in doing so, to redeem the indigence of this endangered soul with his own price. He would have done this, had not the Lord, 'whose riches are for all,' provided for the man otherwise, by which his destitution was relieved."[23] In response to the women who joined the heretics because of their parents' poverty, Dominic (or Diego, depending upon the source) founded Prouille, the first Dominican monastery, between Pamiers and Fanjeaux, in the heart of the "land of the heretics" (*terra hereticorum*), as a refuge for such women. "At a place called Prouille," Jordan writes of Dominic, "he established a monastery to receive certain noblewomen."[24] Far from condemning this man or these women for joining the heretics, Dominic considered the poverty that made them vulnerable to the charitable heretics, and he decided that Catholics must offer such financial support as well. If the heretics' attention to the physical as well as the spiritual lives of their followers has led many people to convert to their sect, as Dominic seems to suspect that it has, he will care for these physical lives as well.

When heretics are not turning to heresy out of an understandable poverty, Dominic believes that they are doing so out of an understandable confusion about the faith. At Toulouse, Jordan of Saxony tells us, Dominic discovered that the innkeeper in whose hostel Diego and he were staying was a heretic. As a result, the biographer recounts, "During the night which they spent in lodgings in [Toulouse], the subprior engaged strongly and fervently with their heretical host, with much disputation and effort at persuasion. At last, when the heretic could no longer resist the wisdom and the spirit which was speaking to him, he returned to the faith, through the medium of the Spirit of God."[25] The heretical innkeeper in this episode is represented not as an irrational and diabolical beast but as a human being, rational enough to argue with Dominic and gracious enough to be open to his wisdom. By the same token, Dominic responds to this innkeeper not as one would respond to such a beast but as one would respond to such a human being. He does not flee from his inn, in horror at his heterodox beliefs, but rather remains in his lodgings, under his hospitality, in conversation with him. He assumes that the reasons that persuade him to remain a Catholic will suffice to persuade this heretic to return to being one. As he connects with the heretical innkeeper of Toulouse, he connects with nine heretical noblewomen of Fanjeaux. According to Constantine of Orvieto, Dominic was one day praying in the church at Fanjeaux when these ladies approached and prostrated themselves at his feet. "Servant of God, help us," they pleaded. "If the things which you preached today are true, the spirit of error has for a long time blinded our minds. For those whom you call 'heretics' and we call 'good men [*bonos homines*],' we believed until this day and we adhered to in all our heart. Now we are wavering in the middle. Servant of God, help us and pray to the Lord your God that he make known to us his faith, in which we live, we will die, and we will be saved."[26] In response to the ladies' request, Dominic bid them, echoing Ezekiel 11:33, "Be patient and wait calmly. I confess in the name of my Lord that he, who 'wants no one to perish,' will show to you to what lord you have adhered thus far."[27] Returning to his prayer, he enabled them to see a large cat with flaming eyes, a long, bloody tongue, and an erect tail circle around them, climb up the rope of the bell-tower, and disappear into the belfry. This beast, he informed the ladies, was the being they have served in following the heretics. Like the heretical innkeeper, the heretical noblewomen are represented as rational enough to recognize the veracity of Dominic's words and gracious enough to seek to resolve any last doubts they have against them. Recognizing their sincerity, Dominic does not stiffen and berate these ladies for their faithlessness but rather accepts the legitimacy of their concerns and provides the proof they need to return to the Catholic Church. As Dominic alleviates the heretics' material needs by providing forms of support appropriate to their circumstances, such as money or a women's convent, he alleviates their spiritual needs by giving them forms of evidence appropriate to their conditions, such as rational arguments or visual proofs of their false deity.

Because Dominic presupposes heretics to be, at heart, good and rational people, he is optimistic that they might return to the Catholic faith. As Constantine of Orvieto tells the story of Raymond Gros, one day Dominic was present as a group of unrepentant heretics were about to be burned. "Catching sight of a certain Raymond, called of *Grossi*," Constantine relates, "he sensed in him something of the beam of divine predestination. 'This one,' he said to the court officials, 'keep back. Let him not be burned with the others.' Turning to him, he said gently, 'I know, my son, I know that you will be a good man [*bonus homo*] and a holy one, although it will take time.'"[28] While Cathar heretics like Raymond Gros were known as "good men" (*boni homines*) to their followers, Dominic predicts that this false, Cathar "good man" will one day become a true, Catholic "good man." Tugwell comments, "He is, in effect, promising that he will find the fulfillment of the very ideals which he thinks he has already found as a Cathar."[29] After having thus been rescued from the flames, Constantine tells, Gros persisted in his heretical blindness for the next twenty years, but in the end he repented of his errors. On April 2, 1236, the Dominican chronicler William Pelhisson reports, Gros appeared at the door of the friar's house in Toulouse, having spontaneously converted to the Catholic faith, and he became a member of their order, as was customary for such high-level converts.[30] While the authenticity of Dominic's prophecy has been disputed,[31] it is notable for its suggestion that Dominic distinguished Gros from Catharism, the heretic from the heresy, and the sinner from the sin, and that he regarded the heretic of today as capable of becoming the saint of tomorrow. Heresy always remained, for Dominic, external to an individual's identity and as a result potentially separable from that identity. Though Gros was resolute enough to be willing to die for his beliefs, though he would persevere in this heresy for another two decades, and though he would win untold numbers of converts to his creed during these years, Dominic sensed that he retained a potential for goodness and even sanctity that would one day come to flower and that it was worth the Church's while to tolerate this wait and these lost souls in order to witness that final virtue. As Dominic himself tells the nine heretical ladies in the church, "The Lord, my God, . . .'wants no one to perish,'" and he appears to place no good, including the rescue of the Church and its flock, above the rescue of individual souls.

Convinced that people become heretics because of good and rational reasons and that they can be brought back to the faith through similarly good and rational means, Dominic feels, not the hatred Bernard experiences for damned and damning souls, but love for those who can be saved. If the Toulousan innkeeper returns to Catholicism, Jordan of Saxony indicates, it is not only because Dominic showed that he understood the faith sufficiently to put forth convincing arguments in favor of orthodoxy, but also because he showed that he cared enough about this man's soul to stay up into the night debating with him and to speak "strongly and fervently" in doing so. Peter Ferrand attributes Dominic's success in converting this man to the fact that he "over[came] him as much by affable persuasion as by logical connections of irrefragable reason."[32] It was not just with this innkeeper that the loving tone of Dominic's speech carried as much weight as his logical arguments. Constantine of Orvieto describes him as converting heretics through "gentle and evangelical persuasion,"[33] and the Dominican priest John of Spain similarly testifies at the canonization proceedings, "He exhorted them charitably to penitence and conversion of the faith."[34] Loving toward heretics in his speech, Dominic was no less loving toward them in his actions. As we recall, Dominic wanted to sell himself into slavery in order to free a poor man from dependency upon the heretics. Jordan of Saxony comments upon this offer that, as with Christ, "Charity, which no one has more than he who lays down his life for his friends, was certainly not lacking in him."[35] By proposing to enslave himself in order to liberate a heretic, Dominic suggests an equivalence between himself and the heretic: the price for which he can be bought is the same as the price for which the heretic may be purchased. Later chroniclers compare Dominic's willingness to redeem a man supported by the heretics by selling himself into slavery to his willingness to redeem a woman's brother captured by the Saracens by taking his place in servitude. Ferrand, for example, introduces his account of both incidents with the declaration, "Not devoid of the perfection of charity, he was ready to lay down his life for the salvation of his neighbors."[36] A man who had joined a heretical sect might normally be held to be guilty of sin in a way that a man who had been seized by a pagan people would not, but, in attempting to liberate these two men in the same way, Dominic treats the apparent sinner no differently than he treats the apparent victim. Whether they were heretics or Catholics, Jordan affirms, "He caught all men in the large embrace of his charity, and, because he loved all, he was loved by all."[37]

WORDS AND EXAMPLES

Before Dominic and Diego arrived in the Midi, Cistercian monks had provided the people in this region with words of good, Christian doctrine but not so much with examples of good, Christian conduct. One day during his preaching campaign in the district of Toulouse, a Cistercian account tells us, Bernard faced an unusually long journey and as a result was provided by his fellow monks with an unusually sturdy horse. When he had finished delivering a sermon against heretics in one town and was mounting this horse to depart, a heretic in the crowd shouted out before everyone, "Lord abbot, know that the horse of our master, who seems to you so wicked, is not as thick-necked and fat as your noisy-footed steed."[38] God inspired Bernard with a quick and appropriate reply, the account tells us. "Know that this horse, about which you insult me, is a brute animal," the abbot observed. "If, because of his appetite, he eats and grows fat, in no way is justice harmed [and] in no way is God offended."[39] Instead of comparing the necks of their beasts, he recommended, the heckler should compare the necks of the religious leaders, in order to determine their respective worth. "Now, therefore, if it please you," he requested, "look at my own neck and see if it is thicker than that of your master, for which you could justly reproach me."[40] Tossing back his cowl, he revealed to the spectators a long, graceful, swan-like neck, whose whiteness competed with its emaciation. Though Bernard is said to have silenced the heretic with this reply, it is nevertheless likely that, in pointing out the plumpness of his mount, the heretic was criticizing not the horse for being greedy enough to become fat but Bernard himself for being wealthy enough to afford such a well-fed steed. While Bernard makes reference to a monastic spirituality, where sanctity is determined by a private practice of asceticism, which may be hidden under a cowl, the heretic may well be alluding to a heretical spirituality, where holiness is determined by a public display of poverty, which may be exhibited by one's gaunt horse. While, for the one, a virtuous life is something pursued on one's own, in isolation from lay society, for the other, a virtuous life is something pursued with other laymen and is therefore subject to their observation. In the years following Bernard's tour in the Midi, heretics continued to decry the magnificence of the Cistercian and other Catholic preachers' equipage and other evidence of their spiritual laxity, but Diego and Dominic responded to this criticism in a new, distinctively Dominican way. They did not reject the validity of the heretics' reproach, as Bernard had done, with a verbal retort designed to win over Catholic spectators to the encounter, but rather they accepted its validity with a behavioral transformation designed to win over the heretics themselves. If Dominic stands out among medieval pursuers of heretics, it is because he is willing to adopt whatever rhetorical technique he sees as necessary, in his actions as well as in his words, to effect a change in the heretics' hearts.

Aware that the common people are more affected by examples of good, Christian conduct, like the choice of a humble mount, than by words of good, Christian doctrine, Dominic and Diego strive to provide them with such examples. According to Jordan of Saxony, when they met with the Cistercians in Montpellier and heard about their difficulties in making headway against the heretics, Diego said to these monks, "It seems to me impossible that men, who are better supported by examples, can be led back to the faith by words alone."[41] The monks then asked the bishop, "What advice do you therefore give us, good father?"[42] and he answered, "Do what you see me doing."[43] According to the Dominican chronicler Stephen of Bourbon, when Diego had first arrived in the Midi, the heretics had asked the common people, "How can you believe this man and his like, who preach to you a Christ humble and poor with such arrogance, with riches, with sumpters and riding-horses?"[44] Because the heretics had criticized Diego and his fellow ecclesiastics for their wealth, Diego now instructs most of his companions to return to Osma with his horses and baggage-train, keeping only Dominic and a few other clerics with him.[45] Because the heretics had rebuked these clerics for their arrogance, Dominic now rejects the title that had set him above his fellow canons. Jordan relates, "From that time forward, he began to be called not 'subprior' but 'Brother Dominic.'"[46] The heretics had accused these clerics of having set into contradiction their words, which praised Christ in his poverty and humility, and their deeds, which denied him in their wealth and pride. Now, under Diego and Dominic's leadership, as Constantine of Orvieto describes the participants in this new campaign, "They began to preach Christ the pauper, themselves on foot and poor,"[47] so that "what the voice of the tongue promised, the merit of the life would confirm."[48] Stripped of their mounts and baggage-trains, trudging through the towns and countryside on foot, the preachers presented themselves to their audiences no longer as powerful and worldly lords but as weak and holy successors to Christ and his Apostles. By adopting the poverty and humility the heretics had already adopted, the preachers sought to furnish the common people with the evidence of the truthfulness of Catholicism through good examples that these people could not grasp through good words.

So far did Dominic go in providing examples of good, Christian conduct that he acted at times in ways that could seem deceptive to those around him. In 1211, the Dominican biographer Peter Ferrand tells us, Dominic and his companion decided to spend Lent in the house of some Cathar women of Toulouse. When the women offered the two clerics ordinary food, Dominic refused to eat it, stating, "We are not used to foods of this type. Show us bread and cold water."[49] When these women then prepared an ordinary bed for the clerics, Dominic refused to sleep in it, explaining, "Not on such soft things but on tables do we take our rest."[50] He requested from these ladies some clothes for himself and his companion, but he insisted that they must be of the right kind. When they asked what sort of clothes those would be, he answered, "hairshirts," adding, "let no one know, let it be attended to in secret."[51] According to his biographers, Dominic often fasted, but not to the point where he lived on bread and water; he often kept vigil, but not to the point where he slept on tables; and he often donned a hairshirt, but not to the point where he wore it continually, even during Lent; yet he gives these women the impression that these are his and his companion's normal habits. Given the discrepancy between the extreme virtue Dominic displayed toward the women and the more moderate virtue he practiced, Ferrand acknowledges, "He offered forth . . . in public a little of the gold with whose shine the hypocrite is furnished,"[52] though he characterizes this gold as "holy hypocrisy."[53] On more than one occasion, he adds, "The holy father admonished his brethren that, when they were among secular people, they must show . . . the appearance of virtue [*virtutis apparenciam*] in themselves, in abstinences, vigils, and the regulation of words and gestures."[54] From the early years of the Church, deception of the kind Dominic practiced had been regarded as a mortal sin. Augustine, for example, had argued that, even if one could induce a heretic to convert by lying, one should not do so, because one would implicitly be converting him not to truth but to a lie and thus not to good morals but to evil ones.[55] In terming Dominic's behavior "hypocrisy," Ferrand acknowledges the negative light in which it could potentially appear.

Yet, it may be, as Dominic's biographers see it, in providing examples of good, Christian conduct, even if remote from their ordinary habits, Dominic and Diego did not deceive but on the contrary revealed the truth. At the meeting in Montpellier, Diego points out to the Cistercian monks, "when the heretics offer up a surface of piety [and] lie through examples of evangelical poverty and austerity, they persuade the simple people of their ways."[56] He does not deny that the heretics pursue poor and austere lives, but he does deny that these lives are anything more than lies, given their disconnection from Catholic truth. In his second letter to the Corinthians, Saint Paul had warned that "to God we are manifest"[57] but that "we use persuasion to men"[58] and that, for that reason, "that which I speak, in this matter of glorying, I speak, not according to the Lord, but, as it were, in foolishness."[59] Given his opponents' false virtues, Diego reminds his fellow clerics, "Paul was compelled to be foolish, listing his true virtues and offering up the austerities and dangers [of his life] in order to burst the conceit of people who were boasting of the meritoriousness of their lives."[60] When the preachers relinquish their horses and entourages to wander about on foot by themselves, as these clerics see it, it is not that they have exchanged a proud and luxurious vice for a humble and simple virtue but rather that they are letting this virtue, which was always present, though hidden, shine forth so that it is visible to all. When the Cistercian monks followed Diego's advice, Peter Ferrand states, "They recalled the souls whom the heretics had deluded with a false image of virtue [*false virtutis imagine*] back to the faith with the true exhibition of holiness and religious life."[61] By the same token, when Dominic ate bread and water, slept on tables, and wore a hairshirt while residing with the heretical women of Toulouse, it was not that he was pretending to a virtue he did not possess but rather that he let the virtue he did possess become apparent (albeit in exaggerated form) to his hostesses, "in order that he might attract them with a display of holiness [*ostensione sanctitatis*]";[62] he recommended that the brethren similarly "show the appearance of virtue [*virtutis apparenciam*] in themselves, . . . for the edification of their neighbors."[63] While Ferrand had condemned the heretics for their "false image of virtue," he now commends Dominic for his "display of holiness" and his "appearance of virtue," which, he suggests, was not false, when it should have been true but merely displayed and apparent, where it had once been under cover. Though Diego and Dominic provide good examples of Christian behavior to counter those of the Cathar heretics, the virtue of which these examples are an expression was always within them.

It is because common people (and, especially, it seems, women) can only grasp concrete examples that Dominic must make his virtue—and the heretics' wickedness—manifest in this manner. The women of Toulouse welcome Dominic and his companion into their house, but it takes the visible display of an extraordinary asceticism to persuade them of the value of their creed. After witnessing the austerities to which Dominic and his companion subject themselves, the women exclaim, "Truly, these are good men [*homines boni*]."[64] Peter Ferrand comments, "Admiring him, they were astounded by such excellence of holiness and began to be more and more attracted to the faith of Catholic truth."[65] In a similar manner, the noblewomen of Fanjeaux are stirred by Dominic's speech, but it takes the visible display of the diabolical cat to persuade them of the error of their heretical faith. Constantine of Orvieto explains, "A terrible vision, exhibited before their eyes, could lead back female minds, so long defrauded by error, more easily than mere persuasion of words, infused through the ears."[66] Both sets of women are impressed not by abstract words, which they can hear, but by concrete examples, such as this vision, which they can see.

Confronted with the common people's imperviousness to rational arguments, Dominic does not regard these people as ravening beasts, as forerunners of Antichrist, or as madmen, as Bernard did. He does not abandon hope of their conversion and forsake them to the secular arm to be burned. Instead, he knows that, as the biographer Conrad of Trent asserts, "The minds of secular people are moved more by examples than by words."[67] If the common people will not respond to logical proofs, like those a learned cleric would find convincing, they might still respond to empirical evidence, like the sight of holy clerics sleeping on tables or unholy cats clinging to ropes. If they will not be persuaded by rational arguments addressed to their intellects, he hypothesizes, they might still be persuaded by virtuous examples addressed to their imaginations. From the biographers' perspective, it is not so much that Dominic is deceiving the people but rather that he is using a particularly effective rhetorical strategy through which to illuminate them.

THE BENEFITS OF DISPUTATION

As we recall, when Bernard traveled about the Midi in the summer of 1145, he attempted to persuade people to renounce heresy in sermons, to which they were given no opportunity to reply. We have seen that, when the abbot censured the heretics at Verfeil, they quit the church where he was speaking, that, when he then followed them out into the streets, they attempted to drown out his voice by banging on the inside doors of their houses, and that, when he preached against the heretics in the district of Toulouse, one of them rebuked him from the audience. Insofar as heretics could make their views known to Bernard, it was only by fleeing the church in which he was preaching, by overpowering his voice, or by heckling him. At the turn of the twelfth and thirteenth centuries, however, Catholic clerics in the Midi began to address heretics not just through sermons, where they alone held the floor, but through disputations, where they shared the floor with heretics in a more or less equitable fashion. In the late 1180s, for example, William, the bishop of Albi, debated with the Cathar heretic Sicard the Cellarer before the knights and burghers of Lombers.[68] In 1190, Bernard Gaucelin, the archbishop of Narbonne, and some fellow ecclesiastics entered into a disputation about the faith with a group of Waldensian heretics in or around his own town.[69] In 1204, King Peter II of Aragon presided over a debate in Carcassonne at which Peter of Castelnau and Ralph of Fontfroide argued, first, with a group of Waldensian heretics and, then, with a group of Cathar heretics.[70] Most importantly for our purposes, for sixteen months, between June of 1206 and September of 1207, Dominic and Diego devoted themselves full-time to traveling about the Midi, to preaching to the people, and to debating with Cathar and Waldensian heretics. At Servian,[71] Béziers,[72] Carcassonne,[73] Verfeil,[74] Lavaur,[75] Montréal,[76] Fanjeaux,[77] and Pamiers,[78] they engaged these heretics in free, equal, and public dialogues. It is not that the Catholic clerics active in the Midi wanted to interact with heretics in this even-handed manner. Since the Gregorian Reform, the Church had been attempting to reserve public addresses about religious matters to the clergy, to the exclusion of the laity, but it had not experienced the same success in implementing such hierarchical distinctions in the Midi as it had elsewhere. Yet, even if these clerics disputed openly with heretics out of tactical necessity rather than out of ethical desire, it is nonetheless significant that they did so and that Dominic in particular sought to accommodate this perceived need.

If Catholic clerics in the Midi, including Dominic and Diego, chose to preach and dispute with heretics instead of prosecuting them for heresy, it is presumably in large part because the temporal rulers through whose lands they were traveling were unwilling or unable to aid them in such prosecutions at this time. Raymond VI, the count of Toulouse and the most powerful southern lord, was rumored to revere Cathar Perfects and to travel about in their company so that he could be hereticated on his deathbed when the time came. The minor lords in whose territories Diego and Dominic preached and disputed were even more clearly affiliated with the heretics who surrounded them. Stephen of Servian is described by the Cistercian chronicler Peter of Les Vaux-de-Cernay as someone "infected with the poison of perfidy"[79] who "had made [the heretics] his familiars and friends."[80] Raymond-Roger Trencavel, the viscount of Béziers and Carcassonne, was the son of Roger Trencavel, probably a Cathar believer and certainly a protector of heretics, and the ward of Bertrand of Saissac, another member of this sect. Girauda, the lady of Lavaur, had a mother and a sister who ran a house for perfected women in Laurac and was herself known to be "a heretic [i.e., a Cathar Perfect] of the worst sort,"[81] as Peter of Les Vaux-de-Cernay puts it. Girauda's brother, Amalric, the lord of Montréal, was said to be a partisan of the Waldensians. Raymond-Roger, the count of Foix, in whose castle at Pamiers the final documented debate was held, was known to visit the Cathar

Perfect and to attend their ceremonies. His wife, Philippa, was probably a Cathar believer, his sister, Esclarmonda, was a Cathar Perfect, and his other sister, Cecilia, was a Waldensian. To the ire of the monks of Saint-Antoninus, who shared the rule of Pamiers with Raymond Roger, Esclarmonda ran a house for heretics in this town, where, Fulk of Marseilles would complain at the Fourth Lateran Council of 1215, "She converted many to her wicked doctrine."[82] Little is know about Izarn "Neblat," the lord of Verfeil, including his religious affiliations, but he is associated in one record with Esclarmonda's late husband. Whatever their personal beliefs, none of these lords or ladies is thought to have made any effort to prosecute heretics and hence to have cultivated a climate in which heretics might fear to express their views.

No doubt because of this tolerant environment, the brief period of interreligious disputation in the Midi in which Dominic and Diego took part stands out in the history of Catholic responses to heresy, first, because the impetus for these debates appears to have been as much on the heterodox as the orthodox side. Because the Catholic clerics were the ones actively campaigning against the heretics' influence in the Midi, it might be presupposed that they were the ones insisting upon the debates, but the accounts of these events indicate that this was not always the case. Among the disputations which took place prior to Dominic's and Diego's arrival in the Midi, that at Narbonne was proposed by Catholic clerics, but that at Lombers was said to have been instigated by heretics. According to William of Puylaurens, the heretical noblemen and burghers of this town approached Bishop William and "insisted before him that he deign have a discussion with their heresiarch."[83] The bishop hesitated to consent to this proposal, given how hardened he saw the heresiarch to be in his error, but the laymen persisted in their demand, "confident that the bishop would be confounded rather than the heretic."[84] Of the disputations in which Dominic and Diego did participate, we are usually not told how they came about,[85] but one debate at Montréal proves an exception to this rule. Peter of Les Vaux-de-Cernay informs us, "One day, all the heresiarchs met at a *castrum* in the diocese of Carcassonne named Montréal in order to dispute together against these men."[86] In both Lombers and Montréal, heresiarchs—presumably Cathar Perfect—are said to have sought to match their wits against Catholic clerics. The Catholic preachers, including Dominic and Diego, appear to have imagined these disputations as an extension of their sermons, where they hoped to demonstrate the superiority of their doctrines to those of the heretics and thus convert the audience to their faith, yet the heretics, from their apparent willingness or even eagerness to argue with the clerics, seem to have understood the debates no less as an opportunity for them to prove the superiority of their creed to that of the Church and in doing so to win those in attendance to their camp.

As both Catholic clerics and heretics organized the disputations, both of them enjoyed equal opportunities to advance their views and to rebut those of their adversaries. At Verfeil, William of Puylaurens tells us, "Many arguments [were] advanced from one side and the other."[87] At Pamiers, Peter of Les Vaux-de-Cernay reports, "The count [Raymond Roger of Foix] himself gave attention one day to the Waldensians and another day to our preachers"[88] in a display of what Peter disparages as "false courtesy."[89] With the floor being given alternately to Catholic clerics and to heretics, both sides were able to present rational arguments and authorities to support their views. It is true that Diego berated the heretics vehemently, to a degree remarkable even given the harsh language common to medieval disputations. At Verfeil, for example, the bishop questioned the heretics about their interpretation of John 3:13, "No one has mounted to the heaven,"[90] and he ridiculed the excessively literal reading of the passage they advanced. The bishop exclaimed, "God curse you, for you are coarse heretics. I thought that you had some subtlety."[91] At Servian, Peter reports, he similarly impugned his opponent Theodoric, telling him, "You have come in the spirit of Antichrist."[92] Yet, even as Diego insults the heretics, declaring them crude in their thinking and inspired by Antichrist, the heretics insult him and his colleagues, affirming that the bishop has come in the spirit of Elijah, whom they regard as demonic, and that his Church is a "harlot."[93] The context within which the two parties speak gives no greater weight to the one set of injuries than to the other. However rough the exchanges between the Catholic and heretical sides may have been, they were grounded in passages from Scripture, about which both parties were able to offer their interpretations. Because both the Catholic preachers, like Dominic and Diego, and the heretics aspired to show the superiority of their faiths during these disputations, both sides accepted that they would encounter each other on a level playing field, out of an apparent sense that this structural equality would reinforce the legitimacy of their ultimate victory in the eyes of their audience.

As Catholic clerics and heretics sought to achieve victory over each other during these disputations, they needed to have a diverse audience present to witness their victory. The chroniclers regularly observe the presence of lay people as well as clerics, of women as well as men, and of commoners as well as noble persons in the audiences of these debates. Jordan of Saxony records in attendance at the disputations, "rulers, knights, women, and the common people, all wanting to be present at discussions of the faith."[94] Peter Ferrand likewise notes, "A multitude of men and women, rich and noble people and common people, convened at the spectacle."[95] Even more remarkably, the authors regularly report the presence of heretics in addition to Catholics, not only among the spectators of the disputations but among the judges as well. At Montréal, Peter of Les Vaux-de-Cernay refers to "judges chosen from the heretical believers."[96] William of Puylaurens identifies these judges as the knight Bernard of Villeneuve, the knight Bernard of Arzens, and the burgher Raymond Gout, all of whom were associated with the Cathar sect, and the burgher Arnold Rivière, who, given Peter's characterization, was presumably no more orthodox than his colleagues. At Pamiers, there appears to have been only one judge, namely, Master Arnold of Crampagna, whom William describes as "a secular cleric, who had been chosen by the two parties"[97] and who, Peter writes, "was favorable toward the Waldensians."[98] The Catholic participants in these events were not always happy with the demographic diversity of these observers and judges. At the disputation in Pamiers, William of Puylaurens quotes a Catholic cleric (and, according to Jean Duvernoy, an early companion of Dominic) as telling the sister of Count Raymond Roger of Foix (presumably Esclarmonda), "Go, lady, spin your distaff. It is not for you to speak in a contention of this kind."[99] As William cited this Catholic cleric deploring the presence—and, apparently, the participation—of a woman at the debate, he himself deplores the selection of laymen as the judges. He exclaims, "How unfortunate that the state of the Church and the Catholic faith had descended to such a degree of baseness among Christians that it had to be placed before the judgment of laymen for such insults!"[100] Yet if the Catholic preachers hoped to use these disputations, like their sermons, as a means to guide the general population back to the Church, it was necessary that the general population be present, even if this openness could disrupt the usual distinction between those who were expected to speak publicly about theological matters and those who were not.

The disputations stand out, finally, because there were no judicial consequences for the heretics who participated in them. Catholic clerics, like Dominic and Diego, attempted "to confound" (*confundere*) and "to convict" (*convincere*) the heretics. At Béziers, Peter of Les Vaux-de-Cernay tells us, the Catholic clerics "confounded [*confundebant*] the heretics."[101] At Pamiers, he states, "A debate was held with Waldensians, who were plainly convicted [*convicti*] and confounded [*confusi*]."[102] By the same token, the heretics aspired "to confound" and "to convict" the Catholic clerics as well. As we recall, the Cathar laymen at Lombers wanted William, the archbishop of Albi, to debate with their heresiarch, "confident that the bishop would be confounded [*confundi*], rather than the heretic," yet, William of Puylaurens tells us, the archbishop proved victorious, leaving the heresiarch "mute and confounded [*confusus*] with his believers."[103] From these conclusions to the disputations, it seems clear that the Catholic clerics sought to "convict" the heretics, not so much in the judicial sense of the word, by proving them guilty of the crime of heresy in the eyes of the law, but in the general sense of the word, by proving them guilty in the eyes of the people.[104] They sought to "confound" them, that is, to refute them, to render them speechless, and thus to convince the large audience not to give them credence. The Church councils at which accused heretics had appeared earlier and the inquisitorial courts at which they would appear later both aimed to evaluate heretics and, if they were found guilty, to condemn them, so that they must either abjure their errors or suffer punishment, but these disputations aimed to evaluate heresy itself and for that reason left its defenders free to depart unmolested.

Over time, Catholic clerics abandoned Dominic and Diego's confidence that truth would win out in a disputation and as a result abandoned disputation itself, at least as these two Castilian clerics had practiced it. Looking back upon the campaign of preaching and disputation, Peter of Les Vaux-de-Cernay recalls, "The holy preachers . . . went about debating with heretics and manifestly convicting them, but, because [the heretics] were obstinate in their malice, they did not succeed in converting them. . . . They could achieve little or nothing by preaching and debate."[105] While Peter blames the heretics' obstinacy for the preachers' lack of success, other Catholic authors suggest that their own inferior learning may have also played a part. We have no evidence that the Catholic clerics ever lost a debate to heretics, but Bernard, the abbot of the Premonstratensian abbey at Fontcaude, was sufficiently troubled by what happened at Narbonne to write a treatise against Waldensians in order to strengthen the position of "some of the clerics involved who, whether because of their inexperience or because of their lack of books, become an offense and a scandal to the faithful under their charge because of their failure to resist the enemies of the truth."[106] When inquisitors began to pursue heretics in the 1230s, they would continue to engage in what they occasionally called "disputations" (*disputationes*),[107] but now they compelled the heretics to come to them, they dominated the exchanges between them, interrogating and even torturing their opponents, and they served as both debater and judge of the debate. Held *in camera*, with only their associates present, the "disputations" were thus aimed at demonstrating to the heretics the folly of their beliefs, and, if the heretics refused to acknowledge this folly, they ended in their death. By the beginning of the fourteenth century, Gui justifies the private nature of inquisitorial "disputation" by citing the wiliness of some heretics, who threaten to get the better of Catholic clerics. He advises, "It is not expedient to dispute in matters of the faith against such astute heretics in the presence of laymen."[108] While these public disputations were short-lived, for the time that they lasted the Catholic clerics who participated in them assumed that, if they made their case for the faith in free, equal, and public exchanges with heretics, the truthfulness of the faith would be evident to all, and all would return to the Church.

Even in the context of these relatively tolerant exchanges between Catholic clerics and heretics, Dominic stands out, in contrast to Diego, for his charitable approach toward his opponents. In one of the most famous episodes of Dominic's legend, at the debate in Montréal,[109] Dominic prepared a collection of "authorities" (*auctoritates*), that is, quotations from biblical and patristic sources, and "rational arguments" (*rationes*) he was using to bolster his points. According to Peter of Les Vaux-de-Cernay, "He handed the paper to a certain heretic so that he could deliberate upon its contents."[110] While Diego, Dominic's religious superior and hence the more dominant figure in their disputations, confronted the heretics as a group before the formal assembly, Dominic approaches one heretic after hours, during an informal encounter. It is as if he suspects that the heretics may be more receptive to Catholic views not during a public battle of words with Catholic clerics but during a private exchange between two individuals. While Diego berated the heretics, cursing them, insulting their intelligence, and identifying them with Antichrist, Dominic merely hands the heretic a written account of the foundations of his Catholic beliefs for him to consider on his own time. Again, it is as if he suspects that the heretic may be more receptive to Catholic views if given time to meditate upon them at his leisure. That night the heretic dealt with this gift as Dominic had intended, taking the paper out among his companions and considering what it said. Peter states, "His companions said that he should throw it into the middle of the fire. If the paper was burned up, it would prove that the faith of the heretics ... was true; if, however, it remained unconsumed, they would admit that the faith preached by our men was good."[111] Like the noblewomen of Fanjeaux, who were attracted to Dominic's sermon, these heretics are intrigued by his authorities and rational arguments. Like these noblewomen, they are unsure whether to persevere in their heresy or to return to Catholicism and ask for a miracle to clarify which of these two faiths is the better one. They end up tossing Dominic's text into the fire not once but three times, only to see it leap out of the flames on each occasion. Unlike the noblewomen, however, these heretics are not persuaded to return to the Church by the miracle they witness. With his private, individual encounter with a heretic, with his gentle appeal to this heretic to consider the Catholic side, and with his miraculous demonstration of the authenticity of this side, Dominic pursues his own ministry to the heretics even in the midst of these debates.

When the disputations failed to bring about the conversions that the Catholic clerics had hoped they would do, Dominic still remains charitable toward the heretics, again in contrast to Diego. According to Jordan of Saxony, Diego at one point grew so frustrated with the heretics that he lifted his arms up to heaven and prayed, "Lord, stretch forth your hand and touch them . . . so that this harassment, at last, will bring them understanding."[112] According to Stephen of Salanhac, Dominic made a similar imprecation. "For many years I sang to you sweetly, preaching, entreating, weeping, but it is commonly said in my land, 'Where a blessing does not work, let a stick work,'"[113] he announced to the heretics. "See, you will arouse against you princes and prelates who, alas [*heu*], will call peoples and kingdoms against this land, kill many with the edge of the sword, demolish towers, topple walls, destroy all of you, unfortunately [*pro dolor*], and lead you into servitude. Thus the *bagols* will work, that is, the strength of the stick, where blessings and sweetness did not."[114] After their many months trudging the roads of the Midi and arguing with those they met, both Diego and Dominic are said to recognize the futility of their gentle efforts to lead the southerners back to the faith and the need for harsher methods to achieve this purpose. With their exclamations, both clerics represent these people as bringing upon themselves the violence of the Albigensian Crusade through their indifference toward the preachers' sermons and their refusal to accept the truth they contain. Yet, while Diego curses these people and hence causes their suffering, Dominic merely foresees that this suffering will occur and regrets its unfortunate necessity. All along, he recalls, he had not only preached to the heretics and entreated them to abandon their errors but had wept for them. Now, with his lengthy description of the death and destruction these people will undergo and with his interjections "unfortunately" and "alas," he continues to express sorrow for their fate in a way that Diego does not. The heretics may need to be punished for refusing to abandon their heresy, but Dominic still pities them for having to suffer such punishment.

When the crusading armies arrived in the Midi in July of 1209, to remain there intermittently for the rest of his life, Dominic played a relatively small role in their activities, in contrast to his Cistercian colleagues from the preaching campaign. Arnold Amalric served as the major recruiter for the crusade, its spiritual leader, and, at certain moments, its military leader as well. When, after the defeat of Béziers, there was concern that heretics might be pretending to be Catholics in order to save their lives, Amalric is famously reported to have ordered, "Kill them. The Lord knows who are his own."[115] Fulk of Marseilles actively propounded the cause of the crusade and even helped to deliver the city of Toulouse into the conquerors' hands. Guy of Les Vaux-de-Cernay helped recruit and support the French armies. It is true that Dominic was known to have become close to Simon of Montfort, the leader of the crusade, and his wife Alice. He baptized their daughter Petronilla in 1211, blessed their son Amalric's wedding in 1214, and received many bequests from them over the years. When Simon and his men were besieging Toulouse in 1211, Dominic could be found outside the gates of the city in their company. Yet, though Dominic's actions reflect a passive collaboration with the crusade, they do not reflect an active engagement in the enterprise. Among the major chroniclers of the crusade, Peter of Les Vaux-de-Cernay mentions him only as the holy author of the book that survived the flames in Montréal, and William of Tudela and his anonymous continuator of the *Canso de la Crozada* say nothing about him at all, again in contrast to Amalric, Fulk, and Guy. Indeed, we know little of what Dominic was doing when he was in the Midi during these years, aside from rescuing some English pilgrims whose boat had capsized near Toulouse. Jordan of Saxony reports, "At the time the crusaders were there, Brother Dominic remained there, an industrious preacher of the word of God, until the death of the count of Montfort."[116] Vicaire makes much of this passage, stressing Jordan's juxtaposition of the military assaults going on around Dominic and the saint's continued pastoral appeals.[117] Though Dominic sided with the conquering force and though he benefited from its victories, he never promoted the crusade among the French barons or regarded the devastation it caused with anything other than sadness. It may be true that Dominic did not stand up against the harsh model of behavior other pursuers of heretics followed at this time, but he himself followed an alternate, gentle model. If Dominic proves more charitable toward heretics than other Catholic clerics, he differs from them not in substance but in emphasis, but again this difference is key.

CHAPTER THREE

Conrad of Marburg: Zealot of the Faith

In letters to German ecclesiastics in 1233, Pope Gregory IX deplored the absence of "zealots of the faith" (*fidei zelatores*) at this moment of history.[1] When the Israelites were intermixing with the idolatrous Moabites, he recalls, Moses brought about the destruction of twenty-four thousand such offenders. When an Israelite visited a Midianite woman in his tent, Phinehas stabbed to death the lovers. When Ahab, the king of Israel, arranged for four hundred and fifty prophets to worship Baal on his lands, Elijah inspired the Israelites to slay these polytheists. "Where is the zeal of Moses?"[2] Gregory asks. "Where is the zeal of Phinehas? . . . Where is the zeal of Elijah?"[3] These Old Testament figures took strong and violent action against fellow Israelites who engaged in illicit religious and sexual contact with their pagan neighbors, but no one in Germany today, Gregory contends, is willing to take similar action against fellow Christians who have likewise corrupted themselves through their heretical activities. So horrific are the deeds of these heretics, he asserts, that "not only men, but the elements themselves should unite in their destruction, wiping them from the face of the earth, without sparing sex or age, and rendering them an eternal opprobrium for the nations."[4] When Gregory proposes that, like the thousands of Israelites who were slain in biblical times, heretics deserve to be "wip[ed] from the face of the earth" today, he makes no mention of the judicial processes which might then have distinguished idolaters from monotheists or which might now distinguish heretics from Catholics. As Gregory sees it, what is important is not so much for ecclesiastical authorities to determine exactly who is and who is not guilty of heresy as for them to take a powerful stance against heresy, which would be weakened by cavils about evidence. A "zealot of the faith" is someone who would recognize the abomination of heresy and who would respond to that abomination with appropriate outrage, putting to death quickly and vigorously large numbers of its adherents.

For many of his contemporaries, including, it appears, Gregory himself, Conrad of Marburg (1180/90–1233) was one such zealot of the faith.[5] Of poor and ignoble background, Conrad was ordained, probably as a secular priest, and he completed a course of study at a university, which allowed him to be called "Master Conrad" and to enjoy a reputation for great learning. He was appointed *scholasticus*, or superintendent of church schools, in Mainz, and penitentiary, or assigner of penances, in this area, but before long the austerity of his morals and the eloquence of his speech brought him to the attention of the papal see. As of 1213, a series of popes assigned Conrad the task of traveling about the country and advocating the repression of heresy, the correction of morals, and the launching of a crusade. In June of 1227, Gregory appointed him to take stronger action against heretics by authorizing him to accuse them before judges, who would then take over the prosecutions. In doing so, he asked him to join forces with two converted heretics, a Dominican lay brother by the name of Conrad Tors and a one-eyed, one-handed layman by the name of John, who were already engaged in such work. According to the *Annales Wormatienses*, Conrad Tors and John claimed a special ability to identify heretics, and they offered no more proof of the guilt of those they accused than their assertion, "They are heretics; we stake our hand against them."[6] To those people, "miserable and fearful,"[7] who asked them, "why do you proceed thus?,"[8] Conrad Tors and John responded, in contravention of a longstanding canonical tradition,[9] "We like to burn one hundred innocent people among whom there is one guilty person."[10] Finally, in October of 1231, Gregory increased Conrad of Marburg's powers over those of his two colleagues by authorizing him to arrest and try heretics himself and to compel secular rulers to assist him in these prosecutions. He instructed him, "If you find guilty and defamed people, . . . you will proceed against them according to our statutes recently promulgated against heretics."[11] With the two functions of investigator and judge united in his person, Conrad became one of the first inquisitors, if not the very first,[12] and, as the *Gesta Treverorum* puts it, "the prince and head of this persecution."[13] In this capacity, between October of 1231 and July of 1233, he had untold numbers of people burned at the stake, if they would not admit their heresy and repudiate this creed, and untold numbers of others tonsured, if they agreed to confess and to abjure these beliefs. At this time, the Cistercian monk Alberic of Trois-Fontaines writes, "So many heretics were burned throughout Germany that their number could not be comprehended."[14] With his enthusiasm for burning countless suspected heretics after what appear to have been only perfunctory trials, Conrad proved himself to be, as the Dominican friar Dietrich of Apolda terms him, "a zealot of the Catholic faith and a most strong exterminator of heretical depravity."[15]

As a zealot of the faith, Conrad aroused mixed reactions among his contemporaries. For most of the nineteen months of his activity as inquisitor, the most powerful members of the German nobility and clergy, including Henry VII, the king of Germany under his father, Emperor Frederick II, and the three great prelates, Siegfried III of Eppenstein, the archbishop of Mainz, Dietrich II of Weid, the archbishop of Trier, and Heinrich I of Müllenark, the archbishop of Cologne, had supported him in his prosecutions. Siegfried, for example, had helped bring about Conrad's appointment as inquisitor by praising him to Gregory, and, for a long time, he defended his prosecutions. As late as March 13, 1233, the archbishop had presided over a provincial council which had declared that, should any nobleman refuse to respond to a summons in matters of heresy, counting upon the strength of his fortresses or the loyalty of his subjects to protect him, his bishop should preach a crusade against him. Conrad's acceptance of accusations from a wide range of witnesses and his refusal of defenses, even from the well born, may have seemed shocking to a population unused to such judicial license, yet, as Alexander Patschovsky has demonstrated,[16] the judicial procedures he was employing already were or would soon become the standard judicial procedures in heresy trials. It was only in the last weeks of Conrad's life that the high nobility and clergy turned against him. With the help of a Dominican penitentiary by the name of Bernard, Siegfried wrote a letter to Gregory, complaining of the unrestrained nature of Conrad's prosecutions of heretics, and numerous annalists seconded the archbishop's objections in their accounts of the events of this time. However determined Conrad may have been to eradicate heresy, these ecclesiastics make clear, he should not have listened to every person who was accusing someone of this crime, especially if that person was disreputable, and he should not have refused to listen to any person who wished to defend himself against this charge, especially if that person was distinguished. With everyone accusing everyone else, up and down the social ladder and within the same households, Siegfried and Bernard protest, "A confusion unheard-of for centuries resulted."[17] The zealotry the German authorities originally perceived as appropriate, given its potential to cleanse the nation of sin, they eventually perceived as excessive, given the social disruption it ended up producing.

If one is to understand how Conrad could be so embraced by the German authorities and then so abandoned by them, one needs to understand the conflation of judicial and penitential tribunals that the inquisitors in general and Conrad in particular brought about. Within a judicial framework, such as that of both traditional secular and ecclesiastical law, people may be innocent or guilty. In order to pass an appropriate judgment on their cases, the judge needs to consider the validity of both the accusations that have been made against them and the defenses that can be made on their behalf. Weighing the evidence both pro and con, the judge deliberates before giving his verdict. In contrast, within a penitential framework, people are always guilty. Though the confessor would not assume that the penitents before him to be guilty of a particular sin, such as heresy, he would assume them to be guilty of *some* sin, be it mortal or venial, because all human beings are guilty of some sin, and he would urge them to do penance for it. The confessor aims, not to act justly, punishing the guilty and setting free the innocent, but to bring all people to an appreciation of their sinfulness and the necessity of atoning for that sinfulness through suffering. While scholars such as Ernst Ludwig Theodore Henke, Balthasar Kaltner, Paul Braun,[18] and Patschovsky have focused upon the historical background to Conrad's prosecutions of heretics, we will be focusing instead upon the textual representations of these prosecutions, including their use of simultaneously judicial and penitential language. One might presuppose there to be a difference between an accused party who has been charged by a neighbor with a crime and who unwillingly undergoes arrest, punishment, and execution and a penitent who charges himself with a sin and who willingly embraces obedience, patience, and martyrdom, but, as we shall see, this is a difference that Conrad, in his zealousness, does not acknowledge.

ELIZABETH OF HUNGARY

When Conrad began to serve as an inquisitor against heretics, it was only after he had served as confessor to Elizabeth of Hungary (1207–31) for six years.[19] The daughter of the king of Hungary, Elizabeth had been brought up together with Ludwig IV, the young heir of Thuringia and her betrothed, at his magnificent court at the castle of Wartburg, near Eisenach. The two are said to have loved each other tenderly, first as siblings and then as spouses, and their marital happiness was soon increased by the arrival of two children, Hermann and Sophia. In 1227, however, Elizabeth's life took a turn for the worse. With her encouragement, Ludwig left her, pregnant with their third child, Gertrude, to accompany the emperor on the Sixth Crusade, and he succumbed to the plague en route. When the news of his death reached Elizabeth, she is said to have gone almost out of her mind with despair, hurling herself against the walls of her chamber and crying out, "He is dead, and the world is dead to me, and all things which are pleasing in the world."[20] On Good Friday of 1228, in the church of the Friars Minor in Eisenach, she turned away from her previous life and became a Franciscan tertiary, that is, someone who cultivates a Franciscan spirituality in the secular world.[21] Moving to Marburg, where Conrad was then living, she inhabited a small house outside the town, separate from her children, her kinsmen, and the maids she had known all her life, and supported herself through her spinning. As she had done previously in Wartburg, she constructed a hospital for the poor and nursed its invalids, tending especially to lepers and others with disfiguring diseases. A relative who visited her at this time expressed amazement that the daughter of a king should be living in such wretchedness. It was presumably, at least in part, because of this harsh life that Elizabeth survived for only four years after her husband's death, passing away on November 17, 1231 at the age of twenty-four. While Elizabeth was generally regarded as a saint and heretics were generally regarded as sinners, it is striking how similarly Conrad treated these two objects of his pastoral attention. From a judicial perspective, he appears unjust and cruel to both Elizabeth and accused heretics. He assumes both of these parties to be guilty of serious infractions, despite evidence of their innocence, and he imposes upon them harsh punishments, out of all proportion to their alleged misdeeds. From a penitential perspective, however, he seems not so much unjust or cruel as rigorous with these two parties.[22] Like an athletic coach, he causes his charges pain, but he does so in the expectation that, if they can respond to that pain, not as a passive victim of its physical and emotional torment, but as an active collaborator in its spiritual discipline, they will become stronger and better as a result of it. While Elizabeth received Conrad's ministrations in the spirit he seems to have intended, even inflicting similar ministrations upon those subject to her, the accused heretics did not prove equally appreciative.

As Elizabeth's confessor, Conrad may have seemed unjust in his efforts, not so much to eradicate the sinful inclinations of her will (for she seems to have had no such inclinations), but to eradicate her will altogether. Once, when Ludwig was still living, Elizabeth's maid Isentrude relates in a statement for her canonization, Elizabeth had been prevented from attending a service at which Conrad was to preach because her sister-in-law, the margravine of Misnia, had paid an unexpected visit. "Offended"[23] by her disobedience to him, Conrad sent Elizabeth the message that he no longer wished to be her spiritual advisor. It was only after Elizabeth prostrated herself at his feet and humbly begged his pardon that he changed his mind, and he still had her and her maids stripped to their chemises and flogged for her infraction. It is telling that, like later commentators who address the maids' testimony,[24] Isentrude emphasizes, not the justice with which Conrad had Elizabeth and her maids beaten—there is no indication that she believed his actions to be just—but rather the harshness with which he treated her. On another occasion, after her husband's death, the maid Irmengard testifies, Elizabeth traveled to the convent of Altenberg, near Wetzlar, where her daughter Gertrude was already placed. The nuns asked Conrad if he would give Elizabeth leave to visit the enclosure, and he answered, "Let her enter, if she wishes."[25] When Conrad heard that Elizabeth had gone inside, however, he chastised her for having entered and Irmengard for having opened the door for her. Ordering the lady and her maid to prostrate themselves, he had his companion, the Franciscan friar Gerard Lutzelkob, flagellate them with a long, thick rod while he chanted *Miserere mei Deus*. Irmengard later remarked, "After three weeks, she still had the traces of the blows, and even more did the Blessed Elizabeth, who was beaten more harshly."[26] It is telling that, again like later commentators,[27] Irmengard stresses not the injustice with which Conrad had her mistress and herself beaten but rather the severity of the beating and its long-lasting scars. By giving Elizabeth absolute and ambiguous commands and by punishing her severely when she failed to obey them, Isentrude relates, "Many times Master Conrad tempted her constancy, breaking her will in all things."[28]

If one considers his actions toward Elizabeth from a penitential perspective, as Elizabeth herself appears to have done, however, Conrad can be seen to have broken her will not capriciously but purposefully, so that she might develop the virtue of obedience.[29] In 1225, even before Ludwig's death, in the church of Saint Catherine in Eisenach, Elizabeth made a vow to obey Conrad, insofar as such obedience would not interfere with marital duties. Unlike an oath of obedience, which would have united her and her confessor in a binary tie, a vow of obedience united her and God, designating Conrad as its guarantor. By submitting to Conrad, she submitted to God because the very act of submission to a spiritual authority is a holy act, irrespective of who that spiritual authority is or how appropriately he is acting. By obeying Conrad, however much it pained her to do so, Elizabeth felt herself to resemble Jesus Christ, who obeyed his Father, however much it caused him suffering. She did not her own will but the will of Conrad, Caesarius of Heisterbach explains, "knowing Christ, . . . who is the strength of God, to have said, 'I have come to do not my own will, but the will of him who sent me,' that is, of the Father, without murmur of the heart and contradiction of response."[30] Insofar as Conrad sought to thwart Elizabeth's will, Conrad himself makes clear in a letter he wrote to Gregory in support of her canonization, it was because Elizabeth wanted him to do so. He relates that, when she was living in Marburg, she arranged for poor, humble people to eat at her table because she had spent so much of her life dining with wealthy, proud people. He cites her as having told him, "It was necessary for her thus to correct contrary things with their contraries [*contraria contrariis*]."[31] Caesarius of Heisterbach confirms Conrad's testimony. He writes that "Master Conrad . . . proved constancy in the blessed Elizabeth in many things, breaking her will in all things, so that from this the merit of her obedience to him would increase. For this reason, so that he might afflict her more, he ordered things contrary to her heart [*contraria cordi*]."[32] The more arbitrary the demands Conrad made upon Elizabeth, the more contrary they were to her own inclinations, the more he was testing and hence developing her capacity for obedience.

Conrad sought to cultivate Elizabeth's capacity for obedience, the sources suggest, because he knew, and she knew, that in obedience can be found freedom. After Elizabeth and her women had been beaten for visiting the convent, she stated, according to Irmengard, "It is appropriate for us to support such things willingly because it is with us as it is with the sedge grass which rises up in the flood. The grass, having been inundated by the rising water, is bent down and depressed when the flooding water passes over it. The inundation ceasing, the sedge grass rises up and grows in strength, merrily and delightedly. Thus, it is appropriate for us to be bent and humbled and afterwards to rise up, cheerfully and delightedly."[33] At another time, when Conrad called Elizabeth back from a trip she was making to an anchoress, she told the messenger he had sent to her, "We are like turtles, which, when it is raining, withdraw into their houses. Let us thus withdraw from the journey on which we began to go, so that we may obey."[34] In both of these analogies, Elizabeth compares Conrad to a force of nature. Just as one does not question the violence of a flood or a downpour, Elizabeth suggests, she does not question the violence of Conrad's verbal or physical abuse. In both of these analogies, Elizabeth compares herself to a creature which, while submitting to the force of nature, retains its selfhood under this onslaught. In the flood, the sedge grass does not break, but bends, only to rise up again, "merrily and delightedly," after the water has receded. Under the downpour, the turtle retires into its shell, only to reemerge when the storm has cleared. However violent Conrad's ragings may be, Elizabeth indicates, they can be borne because they are temporary and, though oppressive, not ultimately destructive. If Elizabeth was resigned to Conrad's violence, it was because, like Job, she was resigned to God's violence. When Ludwig's body was returned to their castle, she is said to have told God how much she would rejoice to have her husband back alive. Still, she informed him, "Against your will, I would not want to buy him back with one hair of my head. I now commend him and myself to your grace. With us, let your will be done."[35] It was Elizabeth's tendency to respond to the misfortunes that happened to her, whether they be a beating from her confessor or the death of her husband, not by focusing upon the external cause of so much pain, which she cannot (or, in Conrad's case, will not) control, but by focusing upon her internal response to that pain, which she can control. By obeying Conrad, she showed that nothing Conrad could do would have any effect upon her, let alone force her to break the vow of obedience she had made to him, and that she was thus strangely free of the man who exercised so much power over her.

As Elizabeth's confessor, Conrad may have seemed cruel in his efforts to separate her from all those dear to her. A young mother, Elizabeth loved her children, who were all under five at the time of Ludwig's death. She is cited as referring to "how much I love to have them nearby"[36] and as expressing concern that "she loved [her son] excessively."[37] The French chronicler John of Joinville relates that when Blanche of Castile, the queen of France, met Elizabeth's son, then eighteen years old, she kissed him on his forehead "because she had heard that his mother had kissed him many times."[38] Nevertheless, Isentrude states, "because Master Conrad persuaded her to have contempt of all things,"[39] Elizabeth sent away her children to be brought up by others. In addition to her children, she loved her maids, especially Guda, whom she had known since she was five years old, and Isentrude, whom she had long held in her closest confidence. According to the maids' testimony, she called them "beloveds or friends"[40] and insisted that they call her "Elizabeth" and use the familiar voice in addressing her. Yet, just as Conrad had brought about Elizabeth's separation from her children, so did he bring about her separation from her maids. Isentrude relates, "He sent away those beloved to her from her family and from her servants, so that he might afflict her more, and he sent them away one by one, so that she might grieve for each of them separately."[41] Forced to dismiss these women, Elizabeth did so, Isentrude comments, "with much distress of mind and with infinite tears,"[42] as they too wept to leave her. In the place of these kind and gently-born maids, Conrad obliged Elizabeth to live with a widow, deaf and bad-tempered, and a religious virgin, coarse and low-born, who demanded that she prepare the potherbs for their household's meals and wash the dishes afterwards and who complained when, not having been trained in these tasks, she performed them badly. When Guda and Isentrude came to visit her, Elizabeth did not dare greet them, let alone give them anything to eat, in the absence of Conrad's permission. Jealous of any bond she enjoyed, whether with her family members or with her companions, Conrad strove to isolate her entirely, so she would be subject to him alone, despite—or even because of—whatever pain this isolation might cause her.

Again, however, if one considers his actions toward Elizabeth from a penitential perspective, as Elizabeth herself seems to have done, Conrad can be seen to have separated her from those she held dear not capriciously but purposefully, so that she might develop the virtue of patience. Of Elizabeth's children, Isentrude states, "And because Master Conrad persuaded her to have contempt for all things, she begged God . . . that he take away from her love of her children."[43] After having made this request of God, Elizabeth told her maids, Isentrude continues, "The Lord has heard my prayer. . . . As God is my witness, I do not care for my children. However much I love having them nearby, I commit them to God. Let him do with them what is pleasing to him."[44] At the same time as she announced the end of her love for her children, she announced, "I consider all worldly possessions, which I once loved, to be dung. . . . I love nothing except God alone."[45] While Conrad instructed Elizabeth to cultivate contempt for all things, it was Elizabeth who accepted this instruction into her heart and who prayed for God's help in fulfilling it. It was Elizabeth, moreover, who not only applied Conrad's general encouragement of contempt to her specific feelings for her children but decided to apply it in such a manner as to send the children away. Irmengard relates, "The Blessed Elizabeth ordered that her son—being a year and a half old—be removed from her, lest she love him excessively and lest she be impeded by him in the service of God."[46] Of Elizabeth's maids, Isentrude states, "He feared that we would speak with her about her past greatness and thus perhaps tempt her or cause her to grieve,"[47] explaining, "He took from her any human comfort she might have in us, wanting her to cling to God alone."[48] Conrad isolated her from her family and friends, it seems, because he saw them as members of the secular world, who threatened to drag her down with them into carnal depths instead of letting her ascend, with his help, to spiritual heights. The more Elizabeth loved her children and her maids, Conrad brings her to understand, the more her separation from them was necessary in order to release her from worldly attachments.

As Conrad sought to cultivate Elizabeth's capacity for obedience because he knew, and she knew, that in obedience can be found freedom, he sought to cultivate her capacity for patience because they both knew that in patience can be found joy. Elizabeth supported the pain Conrad put her through, the Dominican hagiographer James of Voragine asserts, "in order to possess her own soul by patience."[49] By the very fact that she was able to support her separation from her children and her maids, she was able to become a person no longer dependent upon other human beings. She existed, no longer in relation to other people, but unto herself or, as James puts it, in possession of herself. However much pain Elizabeth underwent through these separations from her loved ones and through the other trials imposed upon her, she is represented not as passively suffering these travails, with the misery one might expect of a victim, but as actively supporting them, with the cheerfulness one might expect of an athlete of God. Isentrude states, for example, "She supported all things most patiently and joyfully."[50] Caesarius of Heisterbach states, as well, "The Blessed Elizabeth . . . supported the tribulations thrown upon herself . . . with much happiness of heart."[51] Elizabeth herself referred to having supported them "cheerfully and delightedly," as we have seen. As fire purifies gold, Caesarius writes, "Tribulation with patience gladdens the just, in that it proves them, purges them, and glorifies them."[52] However much Elizabeth may have been capable of an ordinary, happy life as a wife, mother, and landgravine, what is most terrible about her story is that, from what we are told, she did not want this ordinary, happy life, but an extraordinary, even "unhappy" one, which, with its emotional self-sufficiency before God, she experienced as joyful beyond all bounds.

As Conrad could seem unjust and cruel toward Elizabeth, it is also true that she in turn could seem unjust and cruel toward those around her. Once, she noticed in the entourage of a visiting noblewoman a young man by the name of Berthold who was "dressed in a worldly manner."[53] She began to pray for him, and, as she prayed, the young man felt his body become so hot it seemed to him to be aflame. He cried out, "O my lady, cease from praying, because I am dying,"[54] but we are told, "She insisted upon praying all the more intently."[55] The maid Elizabeth recounts that Berthold was sweating from the heat, emitting smoke from his body, and flailing his arms about like a madman. She and Irmengard grabbed a hold of him, but his limbs were so hot they could barely stand touching him. It was only when he cried out a third time, "In the name of the Lord, I pray that you cease from praying because I am consumed by fire,"[56] that Elizabeth finally halted her orison and that Berthold's pain was eased. On another occasion, Elizabeth encountered in her hospital in Marburg a young girl by the name of Hildegund, who was endowed with exceptionally lovely, ornate hair. As she deduced from Berthold's fashionable clothes that he was of dissipated mores, she deduced from Hildegund's beautiful and carefully arranged locks that she too devoted her time to frivolous pursuits. And, as Elizabeth had Berthold's body become hot, she had Hildegund's hair shorn, despite the girl's wails and bystanders' protests, justifying her actions by stating, "At least she will not frequent dances with this hair any more."[57] In a final incident, Elizabeth was attempting to persuade a poor, old woman to confess her sins and receive communion. When the old woman defied Elizabeth's demand, Isentrude relates, "She beat her with rods because she was lying about, like a lazy, drowsy woman, and she was not paying attention to the admonition to confess."[58] In attending, perhaps excessively, to their costume or their coiffure or in neglecting to receive the sacraments when they were available, these people may show themselves to be worldly, by the standards of their time, but they do not commit a sin, at least to the degree to warrant such punishments. When Elizabeth's maids reach out to Berthold or when the bystanders at the hospital speak up in Hildegard's defense, they seem to sympathize with the sufferings these young people are undergoing at Elizabeth's hands. The disproportion between these people's infractions—if they can be deemed infractions at all—and Elizabeth's punishments recalls the similar disproportion between Elizabeth's alleged misdeeds and Conrad's correction of them.

Yet, if one considers Elizabeth's actions toward Berthold, Hildegard, and the old woman from a penitential perspective, as they themselves appear to have done, she can be seem to have harmed them physically only in order to help them spiritually. Elizabeth prayed for Berthold with her incendiary prayers only after she had said to him, "You seem little modest. Why do you not serve your Creator?"[59] and only after he had replied, "Oh my lady, I entreat you to pray for me, so that the Lord give me his grace to serve him."[60] After feeling the flames of her prayers, we are told, Berthold experienced a change of heart sufficient enough for him, years later, to become a Franciscan friar. Dietrich of Apolda praises "with what ardor of charity [Elizabeth] burned and with what heat she dried the flood of secular concupiscence and inflamed someone with love of eternity."[61] Likewise, Elizabeth cut off Hildegund's hair only after she had asked the girl if she had ever considered a better life and only after the girl had answered that she would long ago have become a nun if she had not been distracted by the beauty of her hair. The locks were shorn, a religious habit was provided, and the hospital in Marburg received a new worker. Perhaps, implicitly, because of her lower birth, the old woman did not meet Elizabeth halfway toward her conversion, as Berthold and Hildegund had done, but Elizabeth beat her because she knew that only such violence could overcome her hardness of heart and bring her to admit her sins. In his account of this incident, Dietrich of Apolda writes, "Though [Elizabeth] was gentle, the zealot of souls [*animarum zelatrix*] beat her with rods. Having awakened her with blows from the sleep of negligence, she led her to confession."[62] In each case, Elizabeth assumes that a good will exists within these individuals that could potentially turn them from a secular to a sacred life and that it is her mission to call forth this good will, even forcibly, if need be. Dietrich comments, "With these and other exercises of piety, . . . [Elizabeth] was displeasing to lovers of the world, among whom, even the pious, she appeared reprehensible; now, however, she shines forth among saints like the sun."[63] What might seem to start as an antagonistic relationship between Elizabeth and Berthold, Hildegund, and the old woman, where the imperious landgravine vanquishes these lesser-ranked subjects, ends as an antagonistic relationship between these three individuals and themselves, where, with this lady's help, they vanquish their own sinful inclinations.

If Conrad's approach toward Elizabeth suggests that he believed even the holiest of human beings inclined toward evil, his approach toward heretics indicates all the more that he held a dark view of human nature. During the time Conrad was pursuing heretics in the archdioceses of Mainz, Trier, and Cologne, there were Cathars and Waldensians in these regions,[64] yet both Conrad and other Catholic clerics appear to have perceived these sectaries, not as Cathars or Waldensians, but, to quote Alberic of Trois-Fontaines, as members of "the pestiferous sect of Luciferians."[65] While Catholic clerics of the Midi and Italy viewed heretics as misguided Christians, albeit unconsciously and unintentionally allied with the devil, their counterparts in Germany viewed them as anti-Christians, consciously and purposefully allied with the prince of evil.[66] We possess no writings by or even about Conrad which represent his perception of heretics, but we do possess a letter by Gregory from June of 1233 which, based, as it is thought to be, upon a lost missive from Conrad, supplements that lack and which portrays heretics in this Luciferian guise.[67] In this letter, Gregory reports of heresy, "The initiations of this plague are carried out in this way."[68] When a novice is to be inducted into a sect, the heretics gather in an assembly where they are visited by a series of nefarious creatures, including a toad, "occasionally"[69] the size of a duck or goose and "more often"[70] the size of an oven, and a large cat (not unlike the cat who appears in response to Dominic's prayers in Fanjeaux), who descends a statue "which was accustomed to be in assemblies of this sort."[71] The heretics worship these creatures in various ways, kissing the toad on its lips, so that its tongue enters into their mouth, and kissing the cat on its posterior, if they feel worthy of such an act. A pale, thin man, with black eyes and ice-cold skin, appears; as the novice kisses him, he loses all memory of his Catholic faith. At a certain point in the ceremony, the lights are extinguished, and the guests engage in indiscriminate carnal intercourse, including with members of their own families and their own sex. When the candles are relit and each person has returned to his or her place, a final creature emerges from a dark corner, a man brighter than the sun above his loins, "as they say,"[72] and as hairy as a cat below, to whom the novice is consigned. Siegfried and Bernard confirm that Conrad shared this diabolical vision of heretics. When the master was interrogating an accused heretic, they write, "It was necessary that the accused person confess to being a heretic and to having greeted a toad, a cat, a pale man, and such monsters of unbelief with the kiss of peace."[73] If Conrad pursued heretics as vehemently as he did, it may have been because he saw them, not merely as mistaking a good for an evil, as Bernard of Clairvaux sometimes did and as Dominic Guzmán consistently did, but rather as worshiping evil itself.

As an inquisitor, Conrad may have seemed unjust in his efforts not only to oppose the sinful inclinations of accused heretics, who, he believed, participated in diabolical ceremonies, but to oppose their will altogether. His critics charge that he accepted all accusations of heresy as credible, without any consideration of the circumstances which produced them and hence without any consideration of their veracity. According to Siegfried and Bernard, "A certain vagrant woman of twenty years of age by the name of Alice . . . fashioned herself to be a heretic and her husband to have been a member of this sect."[74] Alice brought Conrad's assistants to Clavelt, her native region, and there she proceeded to accuse of heresy "many people acquainted with her and related to her by birth and marriage, who seem to have disinherited her."[75] Encouraging accusations from malicious witnesses like Alice, who wanted to harm those whom they believed had done them wrong, Conrad also encouraged accusations from compromised witnesses like accused heretics, who wanted to save themselves from prosecution by naming others. When Conrad asked an accused heretic about his companions in error, Siegfried and Bernard relate, the latter would reply, "I do not know whom to accuse. Give me the names of those whom you suspect,"[76] and then, when hearing the names of possible heretics, would confirm their guilt. Having accepted all accusations of heresy as credible, his critics contend, Conrad then refused to consider any self-defense on the part of the accused party which might draw into question that credibility. The *Gesta Treverorum* states, "So great was the zeal of all that no excuse or counterplea would be accepted from anyone, even though they were merely under suspicion, nor would any exception or testimony be admitted, [nor] would an opportunity for defense be granted."[77] For Conrad's critics, truth can be determined only a posteriori, that is, only through the careful consideration of empirical evidence both for and against the accused party and only through the critical analysis of that evidence, to establish its trustworthiness. Yet, just as Conrad is seen as taking for granted that Elizabeth is guilty, whatever arguments she or her maids could put forth to the contrary, he is seen as taking for granted that the accused heretics are guilty, whatever defenses they or their supporters could mount. Just as Conrad is seen as imposing his will upon Elizabeth, not brooking the slightest resistance from her, so is he seen as imposing his will upon the heretics, not brooking the slightest challenge from them. After Conrad joined forces with Conrad Tors and John, the *Annales breves Wormatienses* relates, he wanted to burn heretics "with no contradiction,"[78] and, the *Annales Wormatienses* adds, together, "Their will prevailed everywhere."[79]

If one considers his actions toward accused heretics from a penitential perspective, however, Conrad can be seen to have opposed their will, again, not capriciously but purposefully, so that they might learn to distance themselves from the worst evil. When Siegfried and Bernard allege that "It was necessary that the accused person confess . . . to having greeted a toad, a cat, a pale man, and such monsters of unbelief with the kiss of peace," they suggest that the accused person had not greeted such creatures with such a kiss but that Conrad forced them to admit having done so. From internal evidence, it is clear that Gregory's narrative of these greetings did not originate in any confession a heretic made to Conrad, though it might have been confirmed by such a confession, in the manner in which Siegfried and Bernard indicate. The narrative provides no specific details about where the diabolical ceremony took place, when it happened, and who was present at it, as one might expect from a confession; instead, it refers to how large the toad "occasionally" is and how the statue is "accustomed" to be there, as if these gatherings have occurred in many places, at many times, and with many different participants. The narrative recounts the initiation from the point of view of the novice, but it does not identify this individual or suggest that he provided this information; instead, it notes only that the initiation occurs "as they say," as if multiple, though still unnamed people had attested to these events. As this narrative did not derive from a judicial confession, it seems to have derived instead from a literary tradition, which had been developed by late antique authors such as Justin Martyr, Minucius Felix, and Tertullian,[80] and which had been revived by medieval authors such as Paul of Saint-Père de Chartres, Guibert of Nogent, and Walter Map.[81] All of these authors recount how heretics meet in secret conventicles where the devil appears in the form of a toad, a cat, or a thin man, how they then worship this being, in this guise, with foul forms of reverence, and how they give themselves up to incestuous and sodomitical intercourse. For Conrad, truth can be determined a priori, that is, through the study of the literary tradition about heretics, across time and place, and through the application of that reading to a particular case. If he encourages accusations and discourages defenses of heretics, it is because he already knows, from these extensive and authoritative sources, what it is that heretics do. Accounts of Conrad's dealings with accused heretics do not insist upon the spiritual benefits of his seemingly unjust actions, as accounts of his dealings with Elizabeth do, yet the numbers of such people he is said to have not burned but tonsured suggest that he sought not just to cleanse Germany of sin but to correct the sinner as well, by breaking his will and bringing him to acknowledge his error.

As an inquisitor, Conrad may have seemed cruel in his efforts to put to death accused heretics who did not submit their will to his. As we have seen, the historical records typically represent these parties as unfairly accused, unfairly prevented from defending themselves, and as a result unfairly abandoned to the secular arm. The *Annales Wormatienses* reports of Conrad and his colleagues, "They condemned many who in the hour of death invoked Our Lord Jesus Christ with their whole heart and implored the help of the holy Mother of God and all of the saints in the fire with a powerful clamor. Hear how great was this misery!"[82] While the annalist bemoans the fate of these accused heretics, who died with the names of Christ, the Virgin Mary, and other saints on their lips and who were, presumably, good Catholics, he makes clear that Conrad, "a judge without mercy,"[83] felt no such compassion for them. Ecclesiastical authorities are typically said to have burned heretics because they were forced to do so by the heretics, who obstinately refused to return to the Church, yet Conrad is said to have burned heretics because he *wanted* to do so: the *Annales breves Wormatienses* relates, "Brother Conrad of Marburg . . . wanted [*volebat*] to burn heretics throughout all of Germany."[84] It was because he wanted to kill accused parties, it seems, that he was so eager to believe accusers. Siegfried and Bernard state, "Master Conrad . . . believed [Alice] excessively"[85] and he believed another informant, "fulminating in his judgment."[86] It was because he wanted to kill, it seems, that he was so quick to condemn. The *Annales Colonienses Maximi* reports that "Conrad doomed many to the torment of fire through different German locales (if it may be said) with excessively rushed sentences. For on the same day on which someone was accused, whether justly or unjustly, . . . he would be condemned and thrown into the cruel flames."[87] Just as Conrad is seen as seeking to cause Elizabeth sorrow, by separating her from those dear to her, so is he seen as seeking to cause accused heretics sorrow, by consigning them to death as rapidly as he could.

Yet, if one considers Conrad's actions as an inquisitor from a penitential perspective, as Conrad appears to have done, he can be seen to have harmed people physically—and even to have put them to death—in order to help them spiritually, again, as he was seen to have done to Elizabeth. According to Siegfried and Bernard, when accused parties refused to lie and confess to heresy, for which they would have been saved in body but damned in soul, and instead told the truth about their innocence and were burned, "to these people the master promised martyrdom."[88] With this language of martyrdom, Conrad implicitly recalls that Christ himself was unfairly accused and unfairly put to death. To take the example of one thirteenth-century saint (whom we will be considering in the next chapter), the Dominican Peter of Verona was once wrongly charged with a crime. When he complained to Christ of the injustice he suffered, the Savior is said to have responded, "And I, Peter, what evil did I do, that, with such opprobrium and contempt, I would be condemned to a cross? Learn therefore from my example to bear all things with equanimity."[89] By willingly submitting to the Crucifixion, despite his innocence, Christ modeled to humanity the virtue of patience, which he expects us to follow. In the end, Peter did not attempt to clear himself of the charge, reasoning instead, "Who is able to say, 'I am so free of sin that I am not in need of pardon?'"[90] While Peter may not have been guilty of this particular sin, he was guilty of some sin, as we all are, and for that reason deserves to suffer. To take the example of another thirteenth-century saint, with whose legend Conrad would have been especially familiar, Francis of Assisi is said to have "burn[ed] with a desire for holy martyrdom"[91] and to have traveled to Saracen lands in the hopes of receiving its crown; though refused this wish, he was granted the stigmata, which thus identified him with the Crucified. Francis himself writes, "Our friends . . . are all those who unjustly bring us distress and anguish, shame and injury, sorrow and punishment, martyrdom and death; we must love them greatly for we will possess eternal life because of what they bring us."[92] As Elizabeth experienced her subjection to Conrad as an occasion of obedience and her suffering at his hands as an occasion of patience, Conrad's logic suggests, accused but innocent heretics might experience their executions as an occasion of martyrdom, which will earn them the highest rank in heaven. Instead of passively and unwillingly suffering the flames, they might actively and willingly support them as a test in which they can prove their virtue. While the condemned heretics might have lamented on the pyre and their supporters might have reviled the "judge without mercy" who had consigned them to such a fate, Conrad seems to have expected that these suffering people might act like Elizabeth: "In all the aforementioned injuries and afflictions," Isentrude tells us, "she thanked God, rejoicing that he thus deigned to flagellate her many times because she whom the Lord castigates, he loves."[93]

THE COUNT OF SAYN

After almost two years of pursuing heretics, the tide turned against Conrad in the summer of 1233. He had accused Henry II, the count of Sayn, in the northern Rhineland-Palatinate, of adhering to heresy, and he was said to be preparing to accuse some other noble persons at this time. Instead of submitting to Conrad, however, the count prevailed upon Siegfried to convoke a synod, where all the bishops and clerics of the province could consider his case, and not just this single inquisitor. On July 25 of this year, the synod met in Mainz, in the presence of King Henry and many other secular lords. Conrad attempted to prove his case against the count, but he failed to do so. According to the *Gesta Treverorum*, "The accusers and witnesses withdrew. Some claimed that they had been forced or goaded into saying wicked things about the count, and others were branded with presumptive hatred of him."[94] Seeing the collapse of the case, Dietrich, the archbishop of Trier, declared to the assembly, "I announce to you that the count of Sayn goes from here unconvicted and a good Catholic man,"[95] in response to which, it is recorded, "Master Conrad said, muttering, 'If he had been convicted, it would have been a different matter.'"[96] Now that these ecclesiastical and secular authorities perceived Conrad's accusation of the count as unjustified, they began to perceive his accusations of other people as suspect as well. First alone and then with the archbishops of Trier and Cologne, Siegfried chastised Conrad for his manner of pursing heresy, bidding him "that he conduct himself with more moderation and discretion in this business."[97] Together with King Henry, these archbishops sent another Conrad, the *scholasticus* of Speyer, to Gregory, with letters in which they complained about Conrad's methods. Yet Conrad's downfall would not end with these prelates' reprimands. On July 30, he was returning from Mainz to Marburg with Gerard Lutzelkob and an entourage of other clerics when, on the banks of the Lahn River, at Hof Kapelle, a band of knights and their attendants approached and raised their swords against him. It is said that the assassins wanted to spare Gerard, but the faithful companion embraced Conrad so tightly that it was impossible to kill one cleric without the other. In the discussion of Conrad's assassination which were held over the next two years, his contemporaries debated whether "the Church" might be identified with the concrete community of Christians, including the nobility and clergy of Germany, whom Conrad was seen as persecuting, or with the papacy in Rome and the more abstract *Ecclesia* this see represents, which he was seen as protecting. Scorning the judicial ethos, which demanded that he act justly toward Christians, Conrad was seen as championing, again, the penitential ethos, which demanded that he act faithfully toward the Church.

According to his critics, Conrad was killed because he had harmed or had threatened to harm certain individuals, who sought to defend themselves against him. The *Annales Colonienses Maximi* reports, after relating how Conrad would condemn people without any consideration of their possible innocence, "For this reason, Friar Conrad, the minister of this persecution of heretics, was killed near Marburg by some noblemen who had found no occasion of pardon or grace in him."[98] The *Annales Wormatienses* likewise describes Conrad's assassins as "some people whom [Conrad and his assistants] had defamed and condemned, as much in their relatives as in their own persons."[99] Both annalists connect Conrad's harshness in accusing, prosecuting, and condemning people for heresy with his death at the hands of his victims. Apparently because of this view that the assassins' violence toward Conrad was justified by his violence toward them, neither ecclesiastical nor secular lords appear to have taken any action against these men for half a year. On February 2, 1234, six men who had been present at Conrad's death appeared spontaneously at the Diet of Frankfurt to be judged for heresy and for murder. Whatever sympathy those present might have felt for Conrad, who had been put to death by these men, was soon displaced by an outpouring of sympathy for his victims. A procession of tonsured penitents marched into the meeting, carrying a large cross before them and declaring that they had confessed to heresy only out of fear for their lives. The *Annales Erphordenses* relates, "Their loud, complaining voices having risen up pitifully against the late Conrad, so suddenly did a tumult and turbulation begin to rise up that those who had been on Master Conrad's side despaired of escaping the hands of their adversaries."[100] At the Council of Mainz two months later, the clerics in attendance excommunicated the murderers and sent them to Gregory for their penance, yet they seem to have done so only out of respect of the pope's already evident anger at their inaction. As Conrad's prosecutions increasingly came to be perceived as unwarranted, based, as they were, upon false accusations and false confessions, his assassins' actions increasingly came to be perceived as justified, based, as they were, upon legitimate defense of themselves and their fellows.

Though the German sources represent Conrad as the perpetrator of a crime against the individuals who killed him, Gregory represents him as the victim of a crime by these individuals. When Conrad the *scholasticus* arrived at the papal court with the letters protesting Conrad's persecutions, the pontiff acknowledged some justice in the German authorities' complaints and composed responses in which he recognized "the procedures of Master Conrad of Marburg [to be] invalid."[101] When Conrad Tors appeared not long thereafter with news that his master had been struck down, however, Gregory tore up those drafts and wrote a series of letters expressing outrage at Conrad's murder and insisting that his assassins be pursued. In these epistles, Gregory makes no mention of the fact that Conrad welcomed accusations against innocent Catholics, that he allowed these Catholics no chance to defend themselves against these accusations, and that he quickly had these Catholics tonsured as penitents or burned at the stake as hardened heretics. For Gregory, the central action is not what Conrad may have done in pursuing accused heretics immoderately and indiscreetly—and he never refers to this immoderation and indiscretion as anything more than alleged—but what the armed knights did do in attacking an unarmed cleric and committing what he terms "a most shameful and criminal homicide."[102] Putting aside Conrad's purported wickedness as a judge, Gregory stresses his personal holiness as "a man of consummate virtue,"[103] and the assassins' personal wickedness as "sons of perdition."[104] In a quasi-Manichaean series of contrasts, Gregory represents Conrad as good, passive, and innocent and the assassins as wicked, active, and guilty. While Conrad was a "minister of light,"[105] the assassins are "sons of darkness."[106] He complains, "The sons of perdition . . . shed the innocent blood of the master"[107] and "those blood-thirsty men . . . presumed to seize with sacrilegious hands the said Master Conrad . . . and to slay him with a savage mind."[108] Identifying the assassins with all that is evil, Gregory goes so far as to identify them with the devil himself. He states, "The Enemy of the human species . . . extinguished Master Conrad of Marburg . . . by the hands of his ministers."[109] By allying themselves with the forces of evil against the forces of good, with darkness against light, and with the devil against God, the assassins performed a crime of cosmic consequences, he alleges: "They provoked heaven and earth against them."[110] When these assassins finally appeared before Gregory, imploring penance for this murder, he ordered them to prepare to travel the following March to the Holy Land as crusaders. In the meantime, he commanded them to appear, barefoot and naked, with a halter around their necks and a rod in their hands, at all the larger churches in the vicinity of their crime, to chant the penitential psalms and confess their guilt publicly, and to have themselves scourged by priests. The act of violence here, as Gregory understands it, is not that which Conrad possibly committed against the assassins and their relatives, by prosecuting them for heresy, but that which the assassins definitely committed, by slaying him in cold blood, and for which they must now atone.

As his critics see it, Conrad had been killed not only because he set himself against certain individuals but because he set himself against the noble class to which these individuals belonged. It is true that King Henry and the other feudal lords had initially supported Conrad Tors' and John's prosecutions, allegedly because they allowed them to confiscate the goods of condemned heretics. When these two men began to accuse people of heresy, the *Annales Wormatienses* relates, "The lords attending them rejoiced greatly, leading them into their cities and towns, digging pits and [making people] fall into them."[111] Yet, when Conrad of Marburg began to accuse not only peasants but noblemen like themselves, this king and these lords became troubled. While Philip Augustus, the king of France, and his barons had turned against Raymond VI, the count of Toulouse, in response to Innocent III's declaration of the Albigensian Crusade, neither King Henry nor the other German lords would turn against the count of Sayn, whom the chronicles characterize as an exemplary Christian knight. The *Annales Wormatienses*, for example, describes him as "Lord Henry, the illustrious count of Sayn, . . . a very powerful and wealthy Christian man, living a most honorable life,"[112] and as "a most Christian man, wanting to defend his Catholic faith as much as he could."[113] The *Gesta Treverorum* depicts him as "a wall for the mansion of the Lord."[114] Rich, honorable, and indisputably orthodox, the count of Sayn is portrayed as the archetypal nobleman, with all the virtues of his class. And as the count is seen as representing the nobility, the nobility in turn is seen as representing Germany. The *Annales Wormatienses* cites the clerics at the Synod of Worms in 1233 as promising "to go to the Roman curia for the defense of the count, the lords, and all Germany,"[115] with a telling association of these three categories. In defending the count, the annals make clear, the clerics defend the noble class to which the count belongs and the German nation which this noble class helps constitute.

While the German sources depict Conrad as the perpetrator of abuse against the noble class, Gregory represents him as the victim of this class, whose members think that they can commit murder with impunity. He describes noblemen not as "illustrious" or "honorable," as the German sources tend to do, but as "people whom the Lord enables to obtain a place of magnitude among the preeminent shoots of the Church."[116] Their exalted position derives, as he sees it, not from their own intrinsically noble qualities but from God's gift to them, which they can use well or badly. Gregory depicts the noblemen not as embodying the German nation to which they belong but as setting an example for this nation, for good or for evil. When those inferior in rank "observe the perpetrators of such a crime . . . to have escaped immune from their due reward,"[117] he worries that "a powerful example is granted, contrary to presumed devotion, to those inferior in rank."[118] Nobility is not a status which should render its bearers freer than those of low birth by enabling them to escape prosecution for their crimes; on the contrary, Gregory contends, it is a status which should render its bearers more constrained by obliging them to submit to those laws to which they expect their subordinates to adhere. The Church must ensure that Conrad's assassins are punished, Gregory argues, "so that the immensity of the penalty, made known through the world, will terrorize similarly pestilential people, so that these people will not only hold back their hand but even avert their thoughts from such deeds."[119] As Gregory understands the situation, it is not that Conrad has infringed upon the prerogatives of the noble class but rather that this class has flouted the law that all are bound to obey.

Finally, as his critics understand the situation, Conrad was killed because he set himself against the clergy, with whom the nobility was intertwined. He offended Siegfried, who had long counted among his strongest supporters. At the Synod of Mainz, the archbishop claims to have spoken gently to Conrad, not challenging his authority to prosecute heretics but only recommending that he do so more prudently. Yet, in response to this request, he relates, "He did not acquiesce, but preached a crusade publicly against our admonition in Mainz. This having been seen, some people murdered him among his people near Marburg."[120] By linking Conrad's defiance of his authority and his vulnerability to attack, Siegfried seems to explain and even to justify his murder. Offending Siegfried, Conrad offended the German clergy as a whole. At the Diet of Frankfurt, when Conrad's murder was brought up, twenty-five bishops and archbishops united in condemning the master, with only Conrad II of Riesenberg, the bishop of Hildesheim, and a Dominican by the name of Otto coming to his defense. The *Annales Erphordenses* reports, "When many things were being alleged for and against the late Conrad, one among the prelates burst forth in these words, saying that Master Conrad of Marburg was worthy of being unearthed and burned as a heretic."¹²¹ Having once accused others of heresy and burned them at the stake, Conrad is now accused of this crime and threatened with the flames himself. The *Gesta Treverorum* affirms that, with Conrad dead, "Thus ceased this stormy persecution, the most dangerous since the days of Emperor Constantius the Heretic. There had been none like this since Julian the Apostate."¹²² Having once enjoyed Roman authority to pursue heretics, Conrad is now seen to resemble two fourth-century Roman emperors, the one an Arian heretic and the other a pagan apostate, who were remembered as persecuting Catholics. Whereas Conrad had perceived himself as inside the Church and the people he accused as heretics as outside it, now his contemporaries represent these people as inside the Church and, indeed, as constituting the Church, and Conrad as outside this body.

While the German sources portray Conrad as a persecutor of the Church, Gregory represents him as its protector. He does not identify the Church with the German prelates Conrad has offended, with the German people he has persecuted, or indeed with people at all. When Gregory thinks of Conrad, he thinks of him not in terms of his actions toward Christians, which may have been harsh, but in terms of his actions toward Christianity itself, which were always gentle. He recalls how effectively Conrad preached God's Word, as "a crier of the Christian faith" ¹²³ and "a special crier of the Highest King."¹²⁴ He asks, "Did the tongue of this dog of the Lord not terrorize grave wolves with his great barking?"¹²⁵ With his words in defense of the Church and in opposition to its enemies, Gregory states, Conrad was "advantageous for the development of the Catholic faith of many."¹²⁶ While the *Gesta Treverorum* had described the count of Sayn as "a wall for the mansion of the Lord," Gregory describes Conrad as "a wall of Christian sanctification," which, through the knights' violence, has now "broken down."¹²⁷ Because Conrad represented the Church, as Gregory sees it, an attack upon this master constituted an attack upon the Church itself. If the German authorities have not taken stronger action against Conrad's assassins, he concludes, it is because they have evidently not been stirred to defend that Church. When Gregory considers the indifference the German authorities showed toward Conrad's murder at the Diet of Frankfurt, he concludes, "In this the zeal of Catholic faith was middling and the papal see was revered with meager attention."¹²⁸ He asks, "Why is it then, O prelates, if you care even a little for the sufferings of your flocks, that you do not weep for Master Conrad of Marburg, the paranymph of the Church?"¹²⁹ While German sources express pity for the Church as a concrete community undermined by Conrad's reckless prosecutions, Gregory expresses pity for the Church as an abstract principle, undermined by the unavenged murder of its chief defender.

Though the German nobility and clergy and the Roman papacy disagreed as to whether Conrad's zealousness made him a persecutor or a defender of the Church, history tended to take the side of the Germans. Shortly after Conrad's death, some of his contemporaries recognized in Conrad, as well as in Elizabeth, a saint. His body was brought to Marburg and buried beside Elizabeth's remains, first, in the Spitalkirche and then in the Elisabethkirche, in recognition of their spiritual bond. A chapel was erected on the site where he had been assassinated. At the hearings for Elizabeth's canonization, two men testified that, after their prayers for Elizabeth's intervention on their behalf had gone unanswered, they had prayed to Conrad and their wishes had been granted.[130] Two other men, hoping for cures, disagreed as to which of these two figures would be a more powerful intercessor. Yet, while Conrad could be perceived as holy or even saintly (though only in conjunction with Elizabeth, interestingly enough), no significant cult ever developed around him. He had been killed in retaliation for his prosecutions of heretics, but he would never be recognized as a martyr, in contrast to Peter of Verona, as we will see. As public feeling turned against Conrad, it turned against his associates as well. In Strasbourg, when Conrad Tors attempted to resume his prosecution of heretics by pursuing the Junker Heinz of Müllenheim, he ended up being killed by his intended victim. In Freiburg, John was recognized and hanged. Of their deaths, the *Annales Wormatienses* relates, "And thus with the help of God, Germany was freed from this enormous and unheard-of judgment."[131] So great was the reaction against Conrad's and his companions' prosecutorial abuses that inquisitors would not resume functioning in Germany until the fourteenth century, and, even then, their investigations would be relatively restrained.[132]

In the end, it was precisely the zealotry that Gregory and, for a time, other secular and ecclesiastical rulers had admired in Conrad that proved his undoing. Conrad insisted upon treating people not as members of society but as individual souls before God. As Conrad had disregarded Elizabeth's status as a landgravine, he disregarded the ranks of the accused heretics. Siegfried and Bernard relate, "His accusations began to ascend gradually from peasants to honorable burghers and their wives, and then to knights and their wives, and from there to castellans and noblemen, and in the end to the counts set near and far."[133] Whomever he suspected of heresy, he expected that person to submit, humbly, to his judgment, as Elizabeth had done. For twenty months, the *Gesta Treverorum* affirms, "Supported by [papal] authority and endowed with firmness of purpose, [Conrad] became so bold that he feared no one—not even a king or a bishop, who rated no higher with him than a poor layman."[134] And as Conrad had showed himself to be indifferent to Elizabeth's sanctity, he proved indifferent to accused heretics' reputations for orthodoxy. The *Gesta Treverorum* affirms of his prosecutions, "There was no one so pure of conscience as not to fear meeting a calamity of this sort."[135] For Conrad, there was neither nobleman nor peasant, there was neither illustrious person nor rascal, there was neither Catholic nor Cathar, for they were all one, by sin, in his judgment. At a certain point, the German authorities made clear to Conrad that, although they had appreciated his firmness of purpose when it was directed against base and disreputable people, they no longer appreciated it when it was directed against their respectable peers, yet, even then, he did not cease his campaign. However much opposition he encountered at the Synod of Mainz, the *Annales Wormatienses* conveys, "It was not enough for the most hard judge Brother Conrad, nor did he, with his people, desist from their activity, though all the bishops and clerics were crying out against him."[136] As someone, in his zealousness, utterly without social inhibitions, Conrad would not, or could not, restrain himself when his society called upon him to do so, even in order to save his own life. As Conrad saw it, all people should be considered as pure, autonomous beings, separate from social or familial ties, as Elizabeth had wanted to be considered on earth and as all of us will have to be considered in heaven, and all people should be made to do penance for their sins, as Elizabeth had wanted to do penance and as all of us have to do penance, should we wish to merit Paradise.

CHAPTER FOUR

Peter of Verona: Martyr of the Faith

The Portinari Chapel in the Basilica of Saint Eustorgius in Milan contains, in its center, a magnificent marble tomb, which represents on one of its bas-reliefs a scene of murder.[1] On the left-hand side, a man has grabbed a Dominican friar and is striking his head with a crude blade, as his victim cries out and struggles to free himself. On the right-hand side, three men have seized this assassin in order to lead him to justice. In the center, another friar is kneeling on the ground with his head bent down and his eyes closed in prayer.[2] The gash on this second friar's skull shows that he has already suffered a mortal blow, and the two angels directly above him reveal that they are leading his soul to Paradise. Before this scene of violence took place, the viewer of this bas-relief would know, the friars depicted here had lived in the Dominican convent attached to this basilica, and it was from this base that the one who prayed as he died had pursued heretics. Now, the body of this friar, felled by an assassin in the pay of those heretics, lies in this sepulcher.

At first glance, the friar honored in the Portinari Chapel—Peter of Verona or "Saint Peter Martyr" (1203/05–1252)—may seem to recall Conrad of Marburg in his adversarial approach toward heretics. Like Conrad, Peter stood out, first, as a preacher. He attended the University of Bologna, and it was in that town that he joined the Friars Preachers. He spent much of the 1230s and 1240s traveling throughout Lombardy, Tuscany, Romagna, and the Marches of Ancona, as well as other regions of Italy, speaking out against heresy and other vices with great success. Enthusiastic crowds are said to have sallied forth with trumpets blaring and banners fluttering to meet him as he approached and to have assembled in the churches or piazzas where he was to speak well before he arrived. In Milan, Peter's followers constructed a movable podium, which could protect the preacher from the press of the crowds. In Florence, they enlarged the space before the Dominican church of Santa Maria Novella in order to accommodate the throngs he attracted.[3] Like Conrad, in addition, Peter stood out as an inquisitor. By 1244–45 he was associated with Roger Calcagni, the inquisitor of Florence, and with two confraternities of lay Catholics which sought to provide a bulwark against heresy.[4] In recognition of his longstanding efforts against heretics, Pope Innocent IV appointed Peter and his companion, Vivian of Bergamo, inquisitors in Cremona in June of 1251, and he appointed Peter inquisitor in Milan and Como that September. Like Conrad, finally, Peter was assassinated, in April of 1252, by heretics whom James of Voragine describes as "judging that they would be able to live peacefully if this strong pursuer [*persecutor*] were taken from their midst."[5] Given Peter's efforts to oppose heretics, as a preacher and as an inquisitor, it is no surprise that his biographers in general depict him, as James does, as "a fighter for the faith"[6] who waged "a continual contest against fell opponents with an intrepid mind and a fervent spirit."[7]

Yet, in the end, Peter differs from Conrad because he comes from a heretical family and as such perceives the heresy he is opposing as internal rather than external to his self. From its inception, the Dominican order had welcomed those fleeing the Cathar sect, whether they be the noble girls it embraced at Prouille, who would otherwise have been educated by heretics, or the converts from this heresy it accepted in other convents. Once Cathar Perfects repented of their errors, they typically joined the Dominican order, which waived for them the one year's novitiate required for all other candidates, in recognition of their training in the ascetical life. And once these Perfects had joined the order, they typically atoned for their heresy by assisting in the prosecution of the heretics among whom they had so recently been numbered. By the mid-thirteenth century, numerous inquisitors were former Cathars, including Robert *le Bougre* of France, Conrad Tors of Germany, and Raynier Sacconi of Italy, as were numerous assistants to inquisitors, such as Raymond Gros, Sicart of Figuerias, and Peter Raols. It is not true that these friars' previous heretical allegiances necessarily made them more gentle toward their onetime confederates than their consistently Catholic brethren. Robert *le Bougre* and Conrad Tors were no less vehement in their persecutions of heretics than was Conrad of Marburg. Yet it is true that the product of a Cathar household, like Peter, knew the dualist heresy from the inside, not just from the outside, as other friars did. Because of Peter's origins, Thomas Agni of Lentini, the author of his official *vita*, writes, "He had been familiar with heretics since he was a boy, with how they perverted the meaning of Scripture and with what words they shielded their stricken consciences."[8] Whether or not because of his heretical origins and his consequent inside view of the heretical faith, Peter seems to others and even, at one point, to himself, as we shall see, someone in danger of becoming a heretic, as other members of his family were heretics, in a way that would be unimaginable for Conrad or other inquisitors. If the inquisitor experiences the struggle against heresy not only as a struggle against another human being but also as a struggle within himself, as Peter seems to have done, who is the true champion of Christianity, who its true enemy? To triumph over a wily heresiarch is, for Peter, to triumph over a tendency within himself as well.

Peter differs from Conrad not only because he comes from a heretical family but also because, from all accounts, he willingly submits to the murder the heretics deal him and in doing so treats this act as an internal rather than external challenge.[9] By the mid-thirteenth century, numerous inquisitors had been severely assaulted by associates of those whom they accused of heresy, including Arnold Catalan, Roland of Cremona, and Roger Calcagni, and several of them had been killed, including not only Conrad of Marburg, Conrad Tors, and John, as we have seen, but also William Arnold, Stephen of Saint-Thibéry,[10] Pons of Blans, Peter of Arcagnano, and Peter of Bracciano.[11] Even amid this group, Peter stands out for the equanimity with which he walked into a heretical ambush and accepted the assailant's blows. Through his martyrdom, as through his penitence, Peter transformed the antagonistic relationship between the Dominican friar and the heretic, otherwise evident in his *vita*, into a collaborative relationship. If, as we see with Peter, the victim of an assault does not experience blows as blows but as a mortification of the flesh, and the victim of an assassination does not experience death as death but as an entry into a new, better life, as Peter seems to have done, who is the true victor, who the true victim? With a dialectical sublation of his opponent, Peter recasts their contest so that the victory of the one will constitute no longer a defeat of the other but rather his victory as well. While Conrad's penitential impulses made him more zealous toward heretics, given that he perceived himself as the instrument through which God chose to cleanse his Church, Peter's penitential impulses make him more charitable toward them, given that, like Dominic Guzmán, he perceives himself as their partner in repentance and their partner in pain.

Any effort to identify Peter with the willing suffering of penance and martyrdom, it may be objected, is necessarily complicated by the obscurity of his personality. Of all of the inquisitors we will be considering, he was the most celebrated, both during his own time and for centuries thereafter.

In 1253, less than a year after he had died, Innocent IV deemed this friar a saint, in a process that remains to this day the fastest official canonization in Church history. So great was his sanctity, Innocent declared, that his feast day would be featured in the Church calendar, his name would be included in litanies of the saints and lists of martyrs, and his tomb would serve as a site of pilgrimage. In 1254, the General Chapter of the Friars Preachers ordered that his picture be mounted in ecclesiastical buildings alongside those of the order's founder; over the years, his image appeared in virtually every Dominican church in virtually every town in Western Europe, painted by artists as celebrated as Cimabue, Simone Martini, Fra Angelico, Filippo Lippi, Sandro Botticelli, Giovanni Bellini, Titian, and El Greco. As his cult was promulgated in numerous artworks, it was promulgated in numerous saints' lives, including, in the thirteenth century, those of the Dominicans Thomas Agni of Lentini, Gerard of Frachet, and James of Voragine, and, in the fourteenth century, those of the Dominicans Berengar of Landorra and Peter Calo. As celebrated as Peter was as a saint, however, he is less well known as a person. The records of his canonization proceedings have disappeared, so we have no sworn testimony about him from his closest associates. In contrast to Bernard of Clairvaux, Dominic Guzmán, and Elizabeth of Hungary, his *vitae* are dominated not by descriptions of his day-to-day activities, provided by those who know him well, but by legends of miraculous feats, contributed by distant devotees. As a result, the inquisitor we will be considering is necessarily even less a historical individual, represented by his intimates, and even more a legendary figure, constructed by a certain medieval and early modern *imaginaire*, than the pursuers of heretics we have considered thus far. Despite these qualifications, as we shall see, this legendary figure possesses a distinct and consistent character which extends across the various accounts we have of him, a character which is embodied in the solitude and suffering of that sculpted friar, praying as he died.

THE SOLITUDE OF THE PENITENT

Even in a century marked by its penitential fervor, Peter stands out in the ascetical practices to which he subjected himself. Thomas Agni of Lentini writes, "During his novitiate, he was aroused with an excessive zeal against the flesh."[12] So harsh were the fasts and the vigils he imposed upon himself early in his career, Thomas tells us, that he became too weak to open his mouth to receive nourishment, and, "exceeding the measure of his own fragility, he nearly lost his life."[13] Thomas reassures us that Peter learned his lesson from this near-death experience and moderated his behavior, yet Peter Calo attests that, many years later, when Peter was prior of the convent of Piacenza, he again submitted himself to such harsh mortifications of the flesh that his friars again feared that he might die. In 1887, Henry Charles Lea linked what he saw as Peter's unhealthy attitude toward himself with what he saw as his unhealthy attitude toward others. He writes, "Without assuming that a man such as Saint Peter Martyr was mad, it is impossible to read the extremity of ascetic macerations which he habitually practiced—fasts, vigils, scourgings, and every device which perverse ingenuity could suggest—without recognizing morbid mental conditions."[14] Starved, exhausted, and depleted by self-flagellations, Peter lived in a state of "nervous exaltation"[15] which, Lea alleges, fed his desire to rid the lands in which he lived of heresy, first as a preacher and then as an inquisitor, and which made him, in the eyes of heretics, "such an object of terror that, in despair, a plot was laid for his assassination."[16] In 1953, Antoine Dondaine effectively disproved Lea's characterization of Peter as a bloodthirsty inquisitor by pointing out that this stage of his career lasted a mere ten months and that he accomplished so little in this role that his earliest biographers say nothing at all about it.[17] Yet, even if there is no evidence that Peter's penitential practices led him to terrorize the heretics of northern Italy, as Lea contends, there is much evidence that these practices led him to pursue heretics, to a more moderate extent, as a threat both external and internal to himself. In the texts we have about him, the militaristic paradigm of struggle between the friar and the heretic, embodied in James of Voragine's reference to Peter as "a fighter for the faith," consistently gives way to the penitential paradigm of the struggle between Peter and himself.

In accordance with the tendency of a certain kind of historical scholarship to emphasize general changes over time as opposed to individual cases in time, recent research into Peter has emphasized the development of his cult as opposed to the distinctive quality of his persona. In the first decades after his death, Donald S. Prudlo has argued, Peter was venerated as a saint, one of whose virtues was his opposition toward heretics. Because, at this time, the role of inquisitor was not yet perceived as essentially separate from that of preacher or disputant, the antagonistic potential of the inquisitor, with his authority to release heretics to the secular arm, was not yet being accentuated. It was only at the turn of the thirteenth and fourteenth centuries that Peter came to be venerated as an inquisitor. Prudlo writes, "'Peter the Inquisitor' was not an initial theme of cultic construction. Only gradually did that title become important, especially when, between the fourteenth and sixteenth centuries, it came to dominate the cult entirely."[18]

As Peter's authority to burn heretics—never apparently used—emerged as central to his cult, the saint became a marker of the divisions between Catholic and heretic and more generally between supporters of the Church and the Dominican order and their critics. So much did Peter become identified with the Catholic Church, in its opposition to heretics, that, in the sixteenth century, he came to be recognized as "Prince of the Holy Inquisition"[19] and patron saint of its Spanish office. Despite its lack of justification in the original documents about this figure, Prudlo observes, "His image became fixed as a rigid and unyielding inquisitor, because that was what the Counter-Reformation idealized in an anti-heretical figure."[20] Whatever Peter's own spiritual, let alone penitential practices may have been, it was the changing nature of the Church that affected the changing perception of his inquisitorial practices.

Yet, if one returns to the medieval texts about Peter, one finds that they insist, not upon general changes over time, but upon the individual case in time of Peter's life and in particular upon his renunciation of his heretical family. Thomas Agni of Lentini writes, for example, "The Blessed Peter Martyr . . . took his origin from heretical parents, like a light from darkness, a rose from thorns, or a flower from brambles."[21] With an almost baroque play of contrasts, Thomas imagines Peter as a singular entity, luminous or floral, defined by its beauty, its clarity, and its fragility, emerging out of dark and dangerous surrounding and, even as it comes forth, threatened by that environment. One day in Verona, when "Little Peter [*Petrinus*]"[22] was seven years of age, his biographers tell us, he was returning home from school in the company of his paternal uncle, who was of heretical beliefs, like most of his family. The uncle asked Peter what he was learning in school, and the boy replied that he was studying the Creed.[23] According to Gerard of Frachet, he then proceeded to recite "I believe [*Credo*] in God Almighty, the Creator of heaven and earth."[24] Alarmed by the orthodox lessons his nephew was receiving, the uncle protested, "Do not say 'Creator,' for God is not the creator of visible things, but the devil is,"[25] and he cited a number of "authorities, in the manner of heretics,"[26] to bolster his opinion. Despite the advantage the uncle held over Peter, as an educated adult, Gerard continues, "Strange to say, [Peter] turned all of his authorities against him, so that [the uncle] could not resist him in any manner."[27] Thomas explains Peter's resistance to his uncle by writing, "The celestial anointing of good character instructed the boy that he flee, triumphant, venomous serpents and ravening wolves, [and that] he recognize his enemies, covered over with the skins of sheep, and avoid their company."[28] Even as a small child, Gerard suggests, Peter was able to see his uncle, not just as his uncle, but as a poisonous snake and a rabid wolf and to interpret any affection the uncle might have for him as the sheepskin concealing his wolfish identity. In rejecting his family, Peter resembles other Italian saints of this time, including most famously Francis of Assisi, who also rejected their families, though typically because of their worldliness rather than their heresy. As Donald Weinstein and Rudolph M. Bell write, between the twelfth and the thirteenth centuries, "The story of the saint who had been a dutiful adolescent gave way to the drama of conversion crisis, family conflict, and sexual temptation,"[29] and "conflict between parents and teenagers over religious vocations was frequent and intense." Even as a small child in the bosom of his family, Peter rejects that family so thoroughly that its members never again feature in accounts of his life.

As Peter flees his family members in Verona, out of concern for the threat they represent to his orthodoxy, so does he flee his fellow students in Bologna, out of concern for the threat they represent to his chastity. In describing Peter's encounter with these students, Thomas Agni of Lentini recalls "the assaults of heretics"[30] he had already shown Peter to have endured at home, adding, "when it happened that he was separated from the pressure of heretics, new kinds of assaults were not lacking."[31] Now that Peter joined the crowds of students in Bologna and was exposed to the distractions available to them, Thomas asks, "who guards sufficiently the integrity of the mind and body among the enticements of the flesh, the fallacies of the world, the traps of the Enemy, and the dangerous company of friends?"[32] As the attacks of heretics are mapped onto the attacks of friends, the temptations of the mind, that is, of heretical arguments, are mapped onto the temptations of the flesh, that is, of lecherous allurements. If Peter, among his heretical family, resembled a flower among brambles, now, among his young companions, he risked having, as Thomas puts it, "the flower of his modesty plucked by the struggles common to his adolescent state."[33] Thomas imagines Peter as being (or as possessing) a delicate, vulnerable flower, whether that of virginity or that of orthodoxy, which he attempts to protect from the environment, whether heretical or lascivious, which threatens to harm it. In depicting Peter's flight from his spiritual and carnal temptations, he writes, with a conventional play on words, "Apprehending that it was not safe to dwell with scorpions, like another Joseph, he left his cloak in the hands of the Egyptian lying in wait for his modesty. Fleeing to the refuge of religion, leaving the world [*mundum*] with its flower cut off and his relatives with their error extinguished, he, pure [*mundus*], entered the Order of the Preachers."[34] The world the young friar fled was at once that of heterodoxy and that of lubricity, and the clutches from which he freed himself were at once those of his family and Potiphar's wife. In mind and in body, Peter will remain pure, immune, closed off from the world, his flower protected.

Spurning the community of both family and friends, Peter spurns community altogether. When he rejects his uncle's heretical arguments in favor of the Catholic Creed, he informs him "that he would rather say what he had read and that he would rather believe what was written."[35] As Peter affirms, the oral assertion, like that which one might hear at home, is to be believed less than a written statement, like that which one might read at school. The rote quality of the Creed, to which Peter was even then and would continue to be so attached, preserves its "written" or fixed, unchangeable quality, even when it is recited aloud. Walter Ong has compared the education of medieval boys in grammar schools to a tribal rite, where the acquisition of Latin served as a marker separating the domestic, mixed-sex realm of the family, from which the child emerges, and the institutional, exclusively male arena of this clerical world, into which he enters.[36] For Peter, the transition from the personal, vernacular setting of his home and family to this impersonal, Latin setting of his school and schoolmasters is particularly charged as it is mapped onto the transition from heresy to orthodoxy. Yet, by rejecting the spoken in favor of the written, Peter rejects not just the heretical community but the orthodox community as well. He refuses to situate himself synchronically, with contemporary speakers, whether they be his uncle or his classmates, who share the time and place he inhabits, and instead insists upon situating himself diachronically, with the past authors who composed the Creed and with all the Christians who have adhered to it, past, present, and future, wherever they may live. Having affirmed the Creed, when confronted by his uncle as a boy, Peter would continue to affirm these words, as we shall see, when confronted by an assassin as an adult. Thomas Agni of Lentini states, "As a herald of the faith, [Peter] never abandoned the Creed, which the boy did not want to forsake on account of the blandishments of his uncle, nor did he give up confessing it on account of the pains of his death."[37] Having rejected his affiliation with all local, immanent communities, domestic or academic, Peter declares his affiliation with the universal, transcendent Church, symbolized by the affirmation "I believe [*credo*]."

As Peter flees his family and his fellow students, he escapes to a religious order which will allow him to preserve his solitude, even as a member of its society. In entering the Friars Preachers, he seems to feel himself to be exchanging, not one community for another, but all community for a solitude before God. Peter had the honor of entering the order under the supervision of Dominic Guzmán himself, who, Prudlo speculates, may have visited the young man in his rooms, as he is said to have done with other potential converts, but there is no indication of any special bond between the two men. Gerard of Frachet, who records the connection between the two friars, states simply that Peter "entered the Order of Preachers under Blessed Dominic."[38] Thomas Agni of Lentini cites Gerard and then writes, "Following the footsteps of poverty and humility [of] the Blessed leader Father Dominic, the virgin following the virgin, he attained the great apex of perfection, always advancing from virtue to virtue and proceeding like the light shining until the full day."[39] Peter does not so much join Dominic as follow him, placing his feet in his footsteps, imitating his poverty, humility, and virginity, and, by pursuing the path the founder marked out, ascending to great and even saintly virtue. In contrast to the close companions who accompany Bernard of Clairvaux and Dominic in their own conversions to the religious life, Dominic, the sole individual named in the account of Peter's conversion, functions not as a friend or mentor but rather as a model, distant even if attractive. And, in contrast to William of Saint-Thierry and Diego of Osma, whose friendships with Bernard and Dominic softened the severity of these earlier saints' lives, or even Elizabeth of Hungary and Gerard Luzelkob, who played a similar role in Conrad of Marburg's life, no other human beings interrupt Peter's solitude. Like all religious, Peter had companions who accompanied him in his travels and in his labors, including Vivian of Bergamo and a certain Dominic, who died with him, yet there is no indication of any affection between them. If the path from heresy to orthodoxy and from the secular world to religious life which Peter takes seems to bring about a new conception of the self, it is one defined by inner relationship with God, in the privacy of one's conscience, instead of an outer relationship with one's fellow men.

It is before others, in the world, that heretics attempt to deceive Peter's senses. One day, Berengar of Landorra tells us, a nobleman with whom Peter had been accustomed to reside when traveling in his region refused him hospitality.[40] The nobleman explained his change of heart by recounting how the heretics of his *castrum* had brought him to their church, how they had shown him a shining and lovely lady with her a child in her arms, like the Virgin Mary with her Child, and how this lady had hovered above their altar and reprimanded him for having listened to Peter. Hearing the story, Peter seems to become uncertain as to whether the Catholic or the heretical faith is the true one. Berengar relates, "With the use of prudent counsel, he pretended to waver a little, on account of the things he heard from him, which seemed, in part, reasonable. He said to the nobleman that he should willingly listen to [the heretics] in their church and that, if they showed him reasonable words or signs, he should faithfully adhere to them."[41] When one receives (in this case) empirical evidence that something is true, Peter suggests to his interlocutor, it is right to believe that it is true, whether it favors the Catholic or the heretical cause. Berengar accounts for Peter's apparent hesitation between the two faiths by writing, "Although he wanted to rise up, he had to bend down in order to approach [the nobleman], imitating the Apostle, who said, 'I became a Jew to the Jews in order that I might win Jews.'"[42] So convincing was this apparent hesitation that this author reports, "The heretics rejoiced, reputing themselves blessed if they could have him favorable whom they had had as a most strong opponent."[43] They agreed to let Peter behold the apparition as well, so that he could be fully convinced, like his former host. It is members of the nobleman's community who succeed in drawing the nobleman astray, and it is the nobleman himself, Peter's former host, who attempts to draw Peter astray as well by inducing him to rely upon what he sees or hears as a guide to the truth.

Tested through his senses, Peter withdraws into solitude and prayer, in accordance with his penitential habits. In order to prepare himself for the encounter with the alleged Virgin and Child, Berengar of Landorra reports, "The Blessed Peter remained sleepless that night, emptying himself with devotion and entreaties that the piety of Christ unveil the machinations of the devil to the honor of the Catholic truth."[44] Having fortified himself with prayer, Peter then fortifies himself all the more with the Eucharist. Berengar continues, "Rising up in the early morning, around matins, he left the house and, celebrating mass at the church of the Catholics, consecrated two hosts, one of which he consumed and the other of which he bore, hidden underneath his mantle in a pyx."[45] When Peter leaves his house and celebrates mass, there would presumably have been other Catholics present, but Berengar represents him as alone. When he arrives at the heretical conventicle, where "all the heretics had assembled,"[46] there are many people present, but our author depicts him, once more, by himself. Among all of these heretics, who hope to welcome him into their fold, Peter is a Catholic and indeed a secret Catholic, having concealed his intentions under his apparent open-mindedness as he now conceals the pyx under his mantle. Beholding the false Virgin, he brandishes the consecrated host and declares, "If you are truly the Mother of God, adore this, your Son."[47] With a crash and a stench, the false Virgin disappears, thus exposing herself to have been an illusion produced by a heretical necromancer. While the nobleman was deceived as a result of his attendance at an assembly of human beings, Peter discerns the truth as the result of his retreat into a solitary communion with God. And while the nobleman had been deceived through his reliance upon his human faculties of sight and hearing, he discerns the truth through his reliance upon divine aid. He succeeds in grasping the reality of the situation by resisting others and even by resisting himself, insofar as his own senses might indicate to him what this reality is, and by depending instead upon God alone.

It is before others in the world, again, that heretics attempt to deceive Peter's reason. One day, multiple sources tell us, a heretic engaged Peter in a public disputation about their faiths and proved to be so persuasive that the friar asked to suspend the exchange until he could collect brethren skilled in debate to assist him. At the rescheduled disputation, Gerard of Frachet tells us, "The heretic came with a multitude of heretics,"[48] so that, as Thomas Agni of Lentini puts it, "What they could not [overcome] with reason, they could overcome through talkativeness,"[49] while Peter, having failed to recruit other religious, appeared with only his companion. Once again, the heretic proved to be a formidable opponent. Gerard describes him as "a heretic of the most acute intelligence and singular eloquence, tending to tricks."[50] Thomas depicts him as "a noisy and garrulous man, learned in malicious tricks of words."[51] While these biographers attribute the heretic's success to rhetorical flourishes and logical sophistries rather than to theological insights, they do acknowledge that, during a debate like that with this heretic, Peter not only seemed to become uncertain as to whether the Catholic or the heretical faith was the true one but in fact did become uncertain. Though Gerard is not addressing this disputation per se, he writes of other such debates, "Applying himself to disputations and grave conflicts with heretics, he afterwards found his mind beginning to be driven back by some points."[52] Because of the similarity between Gerard's accounts of the private crisis of faith and the public disputation, Antoninus of Florence, in the fifteenth century, represents Peter as suffering the crisis of faith during the disputation. As he argued with the eloquent heretic, he writes, "Some movement of wavering arose in him."[53] In both authors' texts, when one receives (in this case) rational evidence that something is true, Peter thinks, for this moment, it is right to believe that it is true, whether it favors the Catholic or the heretical side. The heretical orator succeeds in raising doubts about the Catholic faith in Peter's mind by inducing him to rely upon what he understands as a guide to the truth.

Tested through his reason, Peter withdraws again into solitude and prayer. In his account of the public disputation where Peter was failing to rebut heretical doctrines, Gerard of Frachet reports that he requested an intermission and retreated to a nearby oratory. There, he relates, "Prostrating himself before the altar, with many tears, he asked the Lord to defend his cause and either to infuse the light of faith [in the heretic] or to deprive him of the speech which he abused by turning it against God."[54] When Peter returned from the oratory to face the heretic, he asked him to restate his argument, but, due to the grace of God, the heretic had been struck mute and was obliged to retreat confounded. In his account of the private crisis of faith where Peter was failing to rebut heretical doctrines, Gerard relates, similarly, "Because he understood the suggestion to be from the Malign One, he ran to an oratory, and prostrating himself before the altar of the Blessed Virgin Mary, began to pray to her most devoutly that, by her Son, she lift this temptation to his piety from him."[55] Finally, the image of the Virgin above the altar spoke, echoing the words that Christ said to another Peter: "I have asked for you, Peter, that your faith not be lacking."[56] Once Peter had heard the Virgin's words, he is said to have told others, "He immediately felt all scruple of doubt to have receded, nor afterwards . . . did he ever again feel this movement."[57] As Gerard cites Peter as asking the Lord, "with many tears," "to defend his cause" by silencing the heretic, Antoninus cites him as asking the Virgin, "with tears,"[58] "to provide a defense of her true faith"[59] by silencing his own doubts. As a result of prayer, he writes, "He felt himself becoming firm in the faith, all doubt having been withdrawn. From this he was strengthened."[60] While the eloquent heretic has been deceived through his reliance upon his human faculty of reason, Peter succeeds in ascertaining the truth by resisting others and even by resisting himself, insofar as his own reason might inform him what the truth is, and depends instead upon God alone.

As Peter experiences his sense of reality as weakened when he is consorting with others, the same is the case with heretics, the biographers report. One day, Peter Calo tells us, a heretic arrived at a heretical assembly, "many heretics having been convoked,"[61] and declared that he had a plan that would expose the seemingly saintly Peter as a fraud: he would persuade Peter to cure him of an illness and then, he announced, "When the people tell of the miracle, I, on the contrary, will announce myself to have been in no way sick, you will support this by your sworn testimony, and in this manner no one will attribute any more faith to his miracles."[62] The heretic develops his plan to debunk Peter during a gathering of heretics, and it is with their assistance that he expects to triumph. Another day, after Peter's death, Gerard of Frachet tells us, a young Florentine heretic entered Santa Maria Novella with some of his friends. When they came upon a painting of Peter's assassination, which showed a soldier brandishing his sword, he bragged, "If I had been there, I would have struck him more strongly."⁶³ Like his predecessor, this heretic develops his desire to have assaulted Peter during an exchange with his heretical companions, and it is with the expectation of these companions' approbation that he boasts. When these tales begin, the heretics are functioning as members of a group, delighting in their malevolence and strengthening each other in their evil intent.

And, as Peter recoups his sense of reality when he withdraws into solitude and prayer, the same is the case with the heretics. When the first heretic approaches Peter with his feigned illness, he is seized with a fever so severe that he has to be carried home to bed, where physicians called to see him despair of his life. Instead of giving him the blessing he expected, Peter had prayed, "If you are ill, I ask my Lord Jesus Christ that he restore your health to you. If, however, you are fraudulently feigning your illness, let him grant your body an illness for the salvation of your soul."⁶⁴ Realizing his error on his sickbed, the heretic asks, now "with a devotion that was not feigned,"⁶⁵ that Peter come to him so that he may confess his wicked plot and abjure his heresy. Thus, Peter Calo writes, "He was freed from his illness of mind and body."⁶⁶ Similarly, when the young Florentine claims that he would have stabbed Peter more strongly than his assassin, he is struck mute, to the perplexity of those with him. Though his companions attempt to drag him home, the young man breaks free from their grasp, rushes to the nearby church of Saint Michael, throws himself before the altar, and begs Peter's pardon, promising to abandon his heresy if he is cured. In answer to his prayers, the youth's tongue is loosened, and he returns to Santa Maria Novella, where he recounts his experience to one of the friars. In the isolation of their own afflicted bodies, the heretics experience the presence of Peter's spirit as they had never experienced it in the community of their associates. It is alone, on the border between life and death, that the first heretic confesses his sins to Peter, and it is alone, wrenched physically and mentally from his companions, that the second heretic prays to him. Apprehending Peter, not through the gaze of a group or spectators, but through their own, unmediated gaze, the heretics focus, not upon the shame that one of them must suffer in being confounded by the other in public, but upon the guilt that they themselves feel in the privacy of their conscience. As heretics, they had functioned as members of a group, defined at least in part by their heretical beliefs, yet, now, as Catholics, they function as individuals, defined by their remorseful consciences. Though these heretics had failed to triumph over Peter by disproving his sanctity or by stabbing him, Peter in return does not so much triumph over them as bring them to triumph over themselves, so that, rejecting their companions and even their previous selves, they become new, Catholic subjects, solitary, inward-looking, and stricken with regret.

Peter was a penitent, the medieval texts about him make clear, not only insofar as he strove to overcome weaknesses of his flesh, such as lust or gluttony, through fasts and vigils, but also insofar as he strove to overcome weaknesses of his mind, such as heresy, through solitary reflection. Though tempted by his senses, he realizes that what appears to be the Virgin is not the Virgin but a phantasm. Though tempted by his reason, he realizes that what appear to be intellectual qualms to be worked through are spiritual temptations to be overcome. He realizes that what might seem to be external crises—of a Virgin professing Cathar beliefs and a heretic professing irrefutable arguments—are in the end internal crises and that he will achieve victory over them only if he achieves victory over himself, with the help of God or the Virgin Mary. Peter has come to possess an interiority absent from his heretical family and community, though an interiority of a particularly anguished variety.

THE SUFFERING OF THE MARTYR

During Easter Week of 1252, a group of heretics plotted to bring about Peter's death, and they hired a certain Carino of Balsamo to perform this deed. As Peter was spending the week in the Dominican convent of Como, where he was serving as prior, instead of the convent of Milan, where he normally resided, Carino traveled to this lakeside town. After frequenting the convent for three days, he learned that Peter would be returning to Milan on Saturday, April 6. He ran to find Albertino Porro, who had agreed to assist him with the murder, and together they lay in wait for their victim in a grove by the name of Barlassina, in between Meda and Seveso, about halfway to Milan, where they expected him to pass by. At midday, the group in which Peter was traveling arrived in Meda and divided into two pairs so as not to overwhelm their lunchtime hosts. While a certain Friar Conrad and his unnamed companion went farther down the road to find their meal, Peter and his companion Dominic ate quickly at a nearby Benedictine monastery and then, sending notice to their fellow voyagers for them to catch up with them, continued on their journey. As Peter and Dominic were approaching the ambush, Albertino suddenly had reservations about the plot and returned to Meda. On his way back, he encountered Conrad and his companion and informed them, "in tears,"[67] of the trap into which their brethren were heading. The two friars raced off to assist their brothers, but when they arrived on the scene, they saw that they had come too late.

Peter lay on the ground, felled by five blows from Carino's *falcastrum* or bill-hook, a tool used by peasants to cut hedges, and stabbed once in the chest by his knife. Nearby lay Dominic, still alive but mortally wounded. The perpetrator of these crimes could also be found there, seized and bound by a courageous peasant who had presumably responded to Dominic's cries. Soon, many other people gathered at the scene. Some bore Dominic back to Meda, where he would survive for another six days; others carried Peter's body the rest of the way to Milan, though they were so hindered in their progress by crowds that they were obliged to spend the night at the convent of Saint Simplicianus, outside the city walls, before entering; and still others dragged Carino back to the Lombard capital, where he was cast into prison. From what we are told, one and all condemned the vicious act of the heretics and praised the virtuous life of the friar who had succumbed to their brutality. As Innocent would soon claim, in the assassin's encounter with Peter, one could witness "the wolf against the lamb, the savage against the meek, the impious against the pious, the frenzied against the mild, the unbridled against the restrained, the profane against the saintly."[68] Despite this easy opposition of predator and prey, however, the accounts of Peter's death suggest that, in passively falling beneath Carino's blows, the friar actively rose above his assailant and that, in being vanquished by Carino, he became his victor. However much the heretics may set up an antagonistic relationship with the friar, Peter deconstructed the supposed antinomy of their roles through the logic of his martyrdom.

In accordance with the tendency of a certain kind of historical scholarship to emphasize historical circumstances over individual cases, recent research has emphasized the Church's and the Dominican order's agency, in using Peter's martyrdom for their own purposes, as opposed to Peter's agency, in submitting to this death. Both Grado Giovanni Merlo and Christine Caldwell Ames recall that, on Peter's feast day, in 1291, the Dominican friar (and inquisitor) Thomas of Aversa gave a public sermon in Naples in which he compared Francis of Assisi's stigmata unfavorably with Peter's wounds of martyrdom. While Francis's stigmata were the signs of "a dead and not living God,"[69] Thomas claimed, Peter's wounds were the signs "of a resurrected and living God."[70] When Thomas's sermon came to his attention, the Franciscan pope Nicholas IV, irked, banned him from preaching for seven years. Merlo and Ames agree that Thomas's sermon reflects the way in which, by dying as he did, Peter provided the model of a distinctive Dominican spirituality to juxtapose with the model of a distinctive Franciscan spirituality promulgated by the charismatic *Poverello*. While Francis had impressed his contemporaries as a "new Christ" through his dramatic poverty, humiliation, and willing stigmatization, Peter could now be presented as a "new Christ" as well through his no less dramatic martyrdom. For Merlo, the important aspect of Peter's *imitatio Christi* was the way in which it presented an inquisitor not as a persecutor, as one might expect, but as a victim of persecution. The Cathar heretic cited in Salvo Burci's *Liber super Stella*, written in Piacenza in 1235, exclaims, "O Roman Church, you have your hands filled with the blood of martyrs!"[71] Now, with the image of Peter being struck down by an assassin in the pay of heretics, Merlo suggests, it is the Cathar church which has its hands filled with the blood of martyrs. "The evident intent of the papacy and of the hagiographic tradition to present a defenseless saint, victim of another's violence, may be a response to the accusations turned against the Church by the heretics' party,"[72] he writes. For Ames, however, the important part of Peter's imitation of Christ was the way in which it presented an inquisitor not as a mere officer of the Church but as the representative of God on earth. She states, "Such a death stressed that the conflict between heresy and orthodoxy, in which inquisition played a part, was fundamentally an earthly microcosm of the conflict between Satan and God that stretched far beyond."[73] Whether one interprets the Church's and the Dominican order's promotion of Peter's cult as a cynical, political ploy, as Merlo suggests it may have been, or as "a natural expression of Dominican conceptions of heresy, orthodoxy, good, evil, and violence,"[74] as Ames sees it, these scholars agree that, with Peter's death, the role of the Catholic cleric who enters into contention with heretical (and, later, Protestant) forces, who suffers and dies as a result of this contention, and who, like Christ, emerges triumphant from this death, became central to a certain Catholic self-perception. As Ames notes, "Inquisition changed what it meant to be a martyr, to be holy, and to be an imitator of Christ."[75]

If one returns to the medieval texts about Peter, however, one finds that they insist not upon the Church's or the Dominican order's use of Peter's martyrdom but upon his own use of Christ's active passivity as a model for his behavior. Before the attack took place, we are told, Peter was well aware of the conspiracy which was being mounted against him, but he took no action to thwart the murderous intentions of the conspirators. Two weeks or even a month before his death, he announced during a sermon before thousands of people in Milan, "I know for certain that the heretics are dealing for my death and that the money for my death has already been deposited."[76] In retrospect, Peter's words and deeds on the day of his murder would seem to reflect his foreknowledge of what was just about to befall them. Before leaving Como, he made his confession with special assiduousness, as if conscious that it would be his last. While the friars proceeded along their route, Peter helped them pass the time by recounting the lives of martyrs, as if aware that he would soon be joining their ranks, and by singing hymns with Dominic, most notably *Victimae paschali laudes*, as if recognizant that they too were about to become "victims of Easter." When Conrad attempted to join his voice to that of the other two friars, Peter turned to him and said gently, "I ask that you permit Friar Dominic and me to sing alone, because you are not in harmony with us,"[77] as if indicating that only he and Dominic were to enjoy this sacrifice. Peter's fellow travelers expressed concern that they might not arrive in Milan before the gates were closed, given that Peter was still weak from a recent quartan fever, but Peter reassured them that "if we cannot get as far as the friars' house, we can be lodged at Saint Simplicianus,"[78] with an apparent presentiment that his body would be obliged to rest in this convent that night before entering the city. Even though Peter knew who was arranging for his death, what progress they had made in their plans, and around what time they were intending to strike, he did not make any effort to prevent the murder from taking place. Far from halting the prosecutions that had provoked the heretics' anger, Roderick of Atencia writes of Peter and his colleagues, "They did not desist from the vigor of justice, either much or little, on account of this."[79] Peter's refusal to curtail his prosecutions in the face of the heretics' threat may reflect his courage, but his refusal to take other precautions against their potential violence is not so easily explained. While returning to Milan, he did not travel in the company of armed guards or even in a large party, which might have deterred or fended off an assault. Even more tellingly, after taking his midday meal, he did not wait for Conrad and his companion to rejoin them before setting forth from Meda but rather went on without these friars, though the presence of two additional travelers may well have protected Peter against what was ultimately only one assailant. If Peter showed himself to be aware of the heretics' plot and yet unwilling to take any action to forestall it, his biographers suggest, it was because he longed for this assassination no less than the heretics did. Gerard of Frachet cites Peter as praying to the Lord "that he may never permit me to die otherwise than for the faith of Christ."[80] James of Voragine remembers him as having prayed to God, "with numerous, intent appeals . . . , that he not suffer him to migrate from this light except having taken up for him the chalice of his Passion."[81] By willingly dying in defense of the faith, Peter hopes to bring his actions into conformity with those of his Savior, who also died for the Christian faith.

As Peter did not seek to prevent Carino's attack before it took place, neither did he attempt to defend himself against it during its commission.

When the assassin leapt out of the bushes with his weapon, Roderick of Atencia depicts Peter as "not defending himself [and] not fleeing,"[82] while Innocent portrays him as "not turning away from his enemy."[83] Instead of resisting the attack physically or verbally, Roderick reports, Peter stretched out his hands toward heaven and called out in a clear voice, "Into thy hands, Lord, I commend my spirit,"[84] thus identifying the Passion of Jesus Christ with his own martyrdom. In addition to commending his spirit to God, Innocent adds, Peter began to recite the Creed before he was struck down, while Thomas Agni of Lentini suggests that he not only began but completed this recital. It was only gradually that the most famous story about Peter's behavior as he was dying emerged. John of Colonna was probably speaking metaphorically when he asserted that "he wrote the Creed . . . in the effusion of his innocent blood,"[85] but, by the end of the century, Guy of Evreux was speaking literally when he claimed that Peter wrote the first words of the Creed in his blood on the ground. Whether in consigning himself to God or in reiterating the Catholic Creed for which he was dying, Peter is said to have displayed the equanimity of the true martyr at the moment of his death. From the heretics' point of view, in seeking Peter's demise, they hope to defeat their orthodox opponent. Given that there is nothing people normally want so much than to preserve their lives, those who succeed in depriving others of their lives, as the heretics do with Peter, succeed in triumphing over them. From Peter's point of view, as it is reflected in his behavior, however, he defeats those who would defeat him. Thomas Agni of Lentini imagines Peter's inner state when he exclaims, "O blessed man, to whom from this present life the future had already begun, whose feet were already standing in the atrium of the celestial Jerusalem, and who was already tasting, placed in corruptible flesh, the first fruits of incorruptible glory and perpetual praise!"[86] As Thomas suggests, Peter seems to have imagined himself not en route to the earthly Milan but at the portal of the heavenly Jerusalem and not in the company of Dominic (for whom he exhibits little concern) but in the presence of the saved souls. If Peter had called for help or had striven to fend off Carino's blows, he would have admitted his preference for temporal life over eternal life, in accordance with the heretics' assumptions, and the loss of his temporal life would have constituted a true defeat. As it is, by welcoming his death, Peter transformed what might have been an external, physical struggle between Carino and himself into an internal, spiritual struggle between his latent affection for this world and his actual desire for the next, and in doing so he transformed his defeat by another into a victory over himself. Through his comportment during his death, Peter redefined his weakness as strength, his victimhood as sanctity, and his murder as martyrdom.

Presiding over his assassination before and during the event, Peter presided over it afterwards as well. He had prophesied of the heretics, "Let them do what they wish because I will do them more harm dead than alive."[87] When news of Peter's assassination spread through Milan, the entire populace, it was said, descended upon Saint Eustorgius, where Peter's body soon lay, to express their grief. As people learned of Peter's heroic comportment during the assassination, reports began to spread of visions of Peter ascending to heaven and miracles caused by his relics. Interrogated in this atmosphere, Carino was subjected to "the gravest tortures"[88] and made to confess his crime. Probably as a result of his confession, Stephen Confalonieri, one of the heretical conspirators, was condemned to exile within a week of the murder, and James of Chiusa, another conspirator, left the region voluntarily for an unknown fate. Carino escaped his prison, allegedly because of the influence the heretics brought to bear upon Peter the Advocate, the *podestà* of the city, but a mob, outraged by this official's complicity in this crime, broke into one of his houses and pillaged his property. As a result of popular admiration for Peter and anger at his heretical assassins, we are told, many heretics returned to the Catholic faith for which Peter had sacrificed his life. James of Voragine states, "So many relinquished their error and flew back to the bosom of the Holy Church that the town and county of Milan, where so many conventicles of heretics had resided, were so purged that, between the heretics expelled and the heretics converted to the faith, none dared to show themselves there any longer."[89] A Cathar bishop by the name of Daniel of Giussano,[90] who was said to have been apprized of the plot against Peter, became not only a Catholic but also, like other Cathar Perfects, a Dominican inquisitor in the region of Brescia and, strangely enough, the apparent assistant of that other heresiarch-turned-inquisitor, Raynier Sacconi, in his investigation of this plot.[91] It is apparently with figures like Daniel in mind that Thomas Agni of Lentini writes that, after Peter's death, "Many of the worst and most famous heresiarchs, having entered the Order of Preachers, pursued heretics and their favorers with a miraculous fervor."[92] In killing an inquisitor, it was clear, the heretics had succeeded only in creating a martyr who would harm them far more through his cult than he had ever done through his inquests. Like grapes giving forth sweet juice in the winepress, like spices exuding sweet perfume in the mortar, like Samson crushing the Philistines around himself as he brought down the temple, James suggests, Peter destroyed the heretics at the moment of his death, exposing them to be, not heroes relieving the people from a persecutor, but persecutors themselves dispatching a saint.

While thirteenth-century documents tell us nothing about Carino's fate after his flight from Milan, sixteenth- and seventeenth-century sources fill in this gap in this story. Prudlo, the only recent scholar who has studied Carino, accepts the reliability of these sources, yet, given the three-century gap between Peter's assassination and the first accounts of this assassin's later adventures, it may be best to regard these adventures as an early modern contribution to Peter's legend.[93] According to numerous authors from this time period,[94] Carino fled Lombardy for Rome, perhaps, as Paolo Bonoli suggests, out of hope for absolution for his infamous crime. In the city of Forlì, south of Bologna, he fell ill, and he soon found himself in the hospital of the Battuti Bianchi.[95] Next to the hospital was a Dominican complex with a church dedicated to Saint James the Apostle and a convent of friars.[96] As Pier-Tommaso Campagna would later write, "It was there that his victim awaited him, to exercise upon him the vengeance of saints."[97] Perhaps spontaneously or perhaps, as Giovanni Michele Piò proposes, at Carino's request, one of the friars from the convent arrived at his bedside to console him in his illness, unaware of who this invalid was, and Carino confessed his full sins to him, including his role in Peter's murder. The prior of the convent, who was quickly brought in on this case, informed Carino that, if he survived his illness, he would need to enter the Dominican order in order to atone for his sin, and Carino agreed to accept this penance. Recuperating, Carino became a *converso*, or a Dominican lay brother, one of the lower-class and illiterate men who performed manual labor in Dominican convents in order to free the upper-class and learned choir religious for preaching and the care of souls.[98] For the rest of his life, we are told, Carino labored in the kitchen and the garden of the convent, striving to atone for his great sin.

The sixteenth- and seventeenth-century authors who inform us about Carino's later years affirm that he meditated continually upon Peter's death, and this meditation produced in him an anguish that separated him from his brethren, as the dead are separated from the living. Every year since his arrival in Forlì, the convent would have celebrated the feast day of the Dominican martyr whom he had put to death. When the General Chapter of the Dominican Order decreed that images of Peter be set up in all of their churches, an altar at the convent church was dedicated to the new saint, almost certainly decorated with a picture of Peter with Carino's billhook wedged in his skull and possibly with his knife inserted in his chest.[99] Exposed to constant verbal and visual reminders of the man he had killed,

Carino is said to have continually reminded himself of this crime as well. During the day, we are informed, he labored with a bill-hook which recalled to him the death he had caused with it. He performed numerous acts of penance—fasting, wearing a hairshirt, and flagellating himself—all in apparent recollection of the great crime he had committed. He wore a lay brother's black scapular, Francesco Maria Merenda relates, "to contemplate always the atrocity of the misdeed he had performed."[100] During the night, we are instructed, he kept vigil in the church, praying and lamenting. So much time did he spend kneeling in front of the major altar of this church, "with his head in his hand, sighing and weeping for his sin,"[101] as Piò describes him, that the marble stones underneath his knees became concave from his weight. Merenda writes, "He seemed to be always in the act of lamenting, to have always before his eyes such a horrible sacrilege that, in thinking of it, he almost went out of his mind."[102] Not infrequently, Merenda adds, Carino's reflections upon his guilt led him to collapse. He writes, "O, how many times, considering the atrocity of the fault he had committed, . . . not being able to stand on his feet, he fell flat on the ground."[103] Alone in his nocturnal lamentation in the church, Carino feels affinity not with the other friars peacefully asleep in their cells but with the dead rightfully executed for their crimes. According to Merenda, he believed "that only among the dead did he deserve a place, not among the living."[104] In 1293, after forty-one years of penance, he was lying on his deathbed when he made one last request of the prior: that he be buried, not among the other brothers, but in the cemetery of the criminals adjacent to the convent.[105] On account of these many decades of repentance, Carino was regarded as a *beatus* and developed a cult which survived into the twentieth century.[106]

As his assassin, Carino was not only the disgraced perpetrator of Peter's murder but also, according to these sixteenth- and seventeenth-century authors, the honored witness to his martyrdom, transformed by what he saw. Serafino Razzi comments of Carino's conversion, "These are the vengeances which holy martyrs seek, that is, not only the conversions of their killers, but even their sanctity and beatitude."[107] Peter Ribadenyra writes similarly, "This is another victory of Saint Peter Martyr, and a most excellent and glorious revenge which he took of his enemy."[108] In terming Carino's conversion and eventual blessedness an act of "vengeance," Razzi and Ribadenyra acknowledge the violence implicit in the act of conversion. To abandon the world, to enter a convent, and to pursue a life of self-mortification is to die, in a sense, no less than to expire on the road to Milan. As Carino sought to assert his power over Peter by killing him, so does Peter assert his power over Carino by, in his own way, taking his life. At the same time, in terming

Carino's conversion an act of vengeance, these authors make clear that such an act takes an altogether novel form when performed by a saint like Peter. As Merenda states, Peter's blood did not cry out for vengeance, like the blood of Abel, "but concede[d] pardon to the converted heart."[109] When Peter responded to Carino's blows not by shielding himself against them but by offering his soul to God, he avenged himself on Carino by teaching him to value, not heresy, which produces murderers, but orthodoxy, which produces martyrs, and not this life, with which heretics are concerned, but the life to come, toward which Catholics are oriented. His "vengeance" takes the form of the assassin's painful realization that, as Peter gave up his life through dying, he must also give up his life through a living death. Having killed a Dominican, Razzi, Bonoli, Piò, Merenda, and the Bollandists all make clear, Carino realized that he must become a Dominican, in order to replace the friar he had taken from this order. With their lives having become equivalent to each other, Peter and Carino enter into a curious intimacy. Merenda cites Peter as one of the saints to whom Carino was most devoted and hence from whose intercession he most expected assistance. Brought together by the assassination in which they were both involved and by the conversion which that assassination sparked, Peter and Carino were also brought together by the daily prayers which the murderer directed toward his victim and by the daily sustenance which the victim offered to his sacrificer. In reflection of this spiritual affinity between saint and assassin, just as Peter is traditionally depicted with Carino's bill-hook in his skull, Carino, in the Church of Saint James the Apostle, was portrayed with Peter's cracked skull in his hands. Iconographically, the two function as paired saints, like Peter and Paul, Catherine and Margaret, and Sergius and Bacchus. In 1505, in a choir stall in the basilica of Saint Eustorgius, an anonymous artist painted a group portrait of Dominican saints and *beati* with names appended to their images,[110] in which he placed, next to Peter of Verona, "Blessed Acerinus of Balsamo, Petricide [*Beatus Acerimus de Balsamo, Petricida*]."[111] As Alfredo Ildefonso Schuster, the archbishop of Milan, wrote in 1934, building upon this Counter Reformation logic, Carino became "appointed companion in heaven of him of whom, on earth, he had been the proud murderer."[112]

THE LETTER AND THE SUMMA

It is through others' representation of him—in his written *vitae* or in the visual images that emerged out of those lives—that Peter helped shape the developing notion of the inquisitor in Western Europe, but it is also through his own representation of himself, at least implicitly, in two texts attributed to his pen, that he can be known today. Around 1235, Peter appears to have composed a summa against heretics which refutes the errors of the Cathars, the Waldensians, and three minor heretical sects.[113] Though it may be surprising that a summa by a figure as famous as Peter was not better known at this time, Thomas Kaepelli has demonstrated convincingly this work was written by a Dominican friar active in the campaigns against heretics in northern Italy, especially in towns like Bergamo, Milan, and Piacenza that Peter knew well, and one of its two surviving manuscript was inscribed, at some point, the *Contra Patarinos Petri martiris*. In addition, in 1248 or 1249, Peter wrote a letter to the unnamed prioress of the Convent of Saint Peter in Campo Sancto, in Milan, in which he mentions a visit he expects to pay her in the near future and offers her spiritual counsel in the meantime.[114] While these texts present a less clear and vivid personality than that we have encountered in other works, they do confirm the impression of a friar divided in his attitude toward heretics.

In these two writings, Peter expresses a zeal toward heretics not unlike that we observed in Conrad of Marburg. He devotes an entire section of his summa against heretics to championing the authority of the Church to take action against heretical sects. If the Church corrects and punishes heretics, he affirms, it is because "God allows us to correct and punish delinquents,"[115] whether these delinquents be thieves or brigands, who prey upon merchants and pilgrims traveling through the woods, or heretics, who prey upon the common people living among them. As criminals who must be restrained because of their wickedness, heretics are also madmen who must be refrained because of their insanity. The author refers to them as people who suffer from "insanity,"[116] who "rave,"[117] and who are lead "by ... diabolical fantasies."[118] Though Peter does not mention heretics in his letter to the prioress, he devotes a section of this epistle to urging her to take action against wayward nuns. He writes, "Imitate John to the incestuous, Phinehas to the apostate fornicators, Peter to the liars, Paul to the blasphemers, and Christ to the sellers of holy things."[119] As John the Baptist reprimanded Herod for his marriage with his brother's sister, as Phinehas stabbed the Israelite for his liaison with the Midianite woman, as Peter cursed Ananias and Sapphira for deceiving the Apostles about money they had received from the sale of some property, and as Paul abandoned Hymenaeus and Alexander to the power of Satan for their blasphemy, he suggests, the prioress must act firmly with her nuns who go astray. Reflecting upon his own life, Peter regrets that it has been so devoted to action at the expense of contemplation. "I remain, thus far, in the valley of solicitude, and I have spent almost my whole life for others,"[120] he complains. Still, whether in the world or in a convent, Peter insists that Church authorities must correct heretics and other sinners, and he justifies such corrections with precisely those Old and New Testament figures who were most often cited as prototypes of the inquisitor.

Yet, even as the Peter of these texts seems ready to crush heretics violently, he also seems ready to converse with them peaceably in a way that Conrad never did. The author of the summa makes no reference to having come from a heretical family, as one might expect in Peter's case, yet he displays familiarity both with Cathar teachings, in the way in which they were expounded in northern Italy at this time, and with Cathar teachers from this region, including John the Jew, John the Judge, and Garatus. At one point, he appeals to the Cathar heretic Peter Gallus (who appears to have fallen into disfavor among his heretical peers), urging him to exchange his false, heterodox church for the true, orthodox one. Referring to the Cathar belief that anyone who has lost the gift of the Holy Spirit cannot regain it, he states, "Come out, Peter Gallus, from the middle of Babylon because, according to the doctrine you teach, you are damned without any hope of redemption, and come to the Church of God."[121] Not only does this author show himself to be familiar with this heretic's teachings and with his circumstances in his sect, but he uses this knowledge to argue, from the heretic's own perspective, that it would be in his best interest to abandon this sect for the Catholic Church. As in this passage the author directly addresses a heretic, elsewhere he sets up a disputation between a "Catholic" (*Catholicus*) and a "Patarine" (*Patarinus*), or Cathar heretic, in which both sides have the opportunity to argue for their religious beliefs and to rebut the arguments of their opponents. Though the Catholic is consistently allowed the last word in his exchanges with the Patarine, it is striking how fairly the author moderates the interaction between the orthodox and the heretical parties. Heretics, as Peter represents them in this work, are at once criminals and madmen, who must be restrained with force, and learned and thoughtful people, who can be reasoned with and persuaded to return to the Church, on their own terms. While we do not see in the texts attributed to Peter the same connection between his inner, penitential life and his outer, inquisitorial life evident in the texts written about him, we do see a complex and even conflicted approach to the heretics he encountered.

If the story of Peter of Verona proved as resonant as it did, both among members of the Dominican order and among the population at large, it seems to have been so not so much because his life was so laudable as because his death, recalled by every image of him, gazing serenely at the viewer with a blade embedded in his skull, expressed an essential truth about the nature of Catholic suffering. For years before Peter's death, Catholic clerics had perceived heretics as the aggressors and the Church (and themselves) as the victims of their aggression. Thomas Agni of Lentini, for example, speaks of "the assaults of heretics"[122] which were opposed by Peter, "the defender of the faith."[123] As heretics are by definition aggressive, insofar as they twist and deform Christian truth, a preacher or an inquisitor like Peter is by definition defensive, insofar as he attempts to protect this truth against their attacks. Whether one wishes to read this interpretation as cynical or sincere on the part of the Church or the order that promoted it, when Peter submitted himself, passively and graciously, to Carino's attack, he illustrated the fact that the Catholic Church, in its representatives as well as in its doctrines, is an innocent victim of heretical sects. The single, historical incident of Peter's assassination exemplifies what was seen to be a general, structural pattern. The inquisitor, as Catholic clerics saw him, is someone who seeks not to kill heretics but to save their souls, and who, after his death, avenges himself upon this heretic not by having him imprisoned and executed but by having him brought to repentance and saved. The blood of the martyr is the seed of the Church, not only in Late Antiquity, when Christians were killed by pagans, but in the Middle Ages, when inquisitors were killed by heretics.

CHAPTER FIVE

Bernard Gui: The Inquisitor as Performer

For many observers, both medieval and modern, Bernard Gui (1261/ 62–1331)[1] was important not so much as an inquisitor but as an administrator and a historian. A native of the hamlet of Royère, near the village of Roche-l'Abeille in the Limousin, Gui received his primary education at a school in Limoges run by the Dominicans, whose order he then entered when he was around nineteen years old.[2] Though he was not destined to travel to Paris to become a theologian, as the most brilliant members of his order were doing at this time, he spent many years learning philosophy and theology in his order's "houses of study" (*studia*) in the Midi. Between his early thirties and his mid-forties, he served as sublector, lector, and then prior in the Dominican convents of Albi, Carcassonne, Castres, and Limoges.[3] In 1316, when he was forty-five years old, he moved to Avignon, where he represented the Dominicans' interests before the papacy and where on two occasions he served the pope on diplomatic missions. During these years of administrative service, Gui also established himself as an important and prolific chronicler of his country, his Church, and his order. For learned clerics in general, he wrote histories of the Roman emperors, the French kings, the Church councils, the popes, and the saints, and for members of his own order he prepared catalogues of the general masters, the provincial masters, and the acts of the general and provincial chapters. As we have seen, he completed Stephen of Salanhac's history of the Friars Preachers,[4] and he provided an account of the convents in the provinces of Toulouse and Provence.[5] When his fellow Dominican Thomas Aquinas was being considered for canonization, he contributed to these proceedings.[6] The nominal bishop of Tuy, in Galicia, Gui became the actual bishop of Lodève in 1324, when he was sixty-three years old, and he once again proved himself to be an energetic and effective manager.[7] After he died in 1331, at the age of seventy, he was buried in the Dominican church in Limoges and received some degree of veneration for his sanctity. A biography written shortly after his death, presumably by his nephew and fellow Dominican Peter Gui, stresses Gui's accomplishments as a bishop, a diplomat, and a historian,[8] while an epithet set over his tomb in the sixteenth century recalled his service as a prelate and a papal legate.[9] Modern scholars have followed these medieval and early modern precedents in their appreciations of this figure. The most extensive biography of Gui today devotes sixty of its sixty-five paragraphs to his work in the service of his order, his diocese, and his pontiff and to his work as a historian,[10] while a recent collection of articles about him consecrates twelve of its fifteen entries to his accomplishments in these areas.[11] To the extent that Gui stands out in the history of the Dominican order, it is, for many both past and present, because of the practical intelligence he exhibited in his administrative service and in his historical writings.

When scholars do recall Gui's seventeen years of work, between 1307 and 1323, as an inquisitor in the Toulousain and the Albigeois, they tend to stress the moderateness of his prosecutions.[12] We know much about his inquisitorial activity, in part because he compiled a register of the sentences he delivered during his long career, the *Liber sententiarum*,[13] and, in part because he composed an inquisitors' manual, the *Practica inquisitionis heretice pravitatis*,[14] filled with lessons he had learned over the course of this career as well as lessons his fellow inquisitors had acquired in the course of their own investigations. While the *Practica*'s instructions on how to proceed against heretics rely heavily upon quotations from the writings of these fellow inquisitors, especially those attributed to the Franciscan David of Augsburg[15] and the Dominican Stephen of Bourbon,[16] it is Gui who selects these passages and who incorporates them into a vast and comprehensive treatise, whose influence would extend far beyond that of its predecessors.[17] As an inquisitor, Gui was a key figure in prosecuting the Cathars, who had experienced a resurgence in the Sarbatès, a region south and west of Foix, during the early fourteenth century under the leadership of the heresiarch Peter Autier,[18] and, to a lesser extent, the Waldensians, who had also seen their numbers increase in the diocese of Auch.[19] In addition, he seems to have pursued Pseudo-Apostles, or adherents of an apocalyptic, penitential cult which flourished in central Italy between 1260 and 1307 before going underground,[20] and Beguins, or followers of the Spiritual Franciscan Peter John Olivi, who were active in Provence in the 1310s and 1320s. In the course of eleven large "general sermons" which Gui held between 1308 and 1323 in the cathedral of Saint Stephen in Toulouse and later in the cemetery of Saint John the Martyr in Pamiers, he judged 627 individuals to be guilty of heresy, while in eight smaller such events, devoted to the cases of one or two notorious heretics, he judged nine additional persons to be guilty of this crime.[21] Of the 636 individuals he convicted all together, Gui reconciled the vast majority to the Church, though he often assigned them harsh penances, including years of imprisonment or the obligatory wearing of crosses to signify their penitential status. He released to the secular arm forty-two people (or 7 percent of those he convicted), in addition to another three who were to meet a similar fate if they could be found. Given that Gui reconciled so many more people to the Church than he condemned to the stake, he has typically been perceived not only as a reasonable administrator and a reasonable historian but as a reasonable inquisitor as well.[22]

Despite Gui's relatively positive reception by scholars today, he ranks among the more zealous of inquisitors, I would like to argue, not so much because of the number of people he had killed (which remains not inconsiderable) but rather because of the performative aspects of his prosecutions.[23] In his bestselling 1980 novel *The Name of the Rose*, Umberto Eco provides a portrait of Gui which, though criticized as influenced more by the myth of the inquisitor than by historical fact,[24] remains solidly grounded in Gui's own writings. In this novel, Gui stops at a Benedictine monastery in northern Italy during one of his diplomatic missions and ends up prosecuting two of the lay brothers for their previous adherence to the Pseudo-Apostles and a local peasant girl for witchcraft. Eco may be using his imagination when he describes Gui's gray eyes as "capable of staring without any expression ... , shrewd both in concealing thoughts and passions and in deliberately conveying them,"[25] but the suggestion, implicit in this description, that Gui consciously crafted a persona in order to produce certain effects is rooted in the inquisitor's own writings. As the *Practica* indicates, identity is, for Gui, not something one is, as a result of one's inherent nature, but rather something one adopts, as a result of one's conscious choice and effort. Gui sees heretics as performing when they preach their errors to the people and later when they respond to their interrogators. He sees the inquisitor in turn as performing when he questions heretics *in camera* and when he pronounces his judgment upon them at the general sermon. Gui emphasizes the performative aspects of the inquisitor's behavior because what matters most to him is not the heretic himself, whose soul has been endangered by his errors, but the common people who are watching his encounter with the heretic, whether from a distance, when they hear of its outcome, or from nearby, when they attend the general sermon. Even as Gui's inquisitor interacts with the heretic before him, it is toward this audience that he orients himself, in the hope of convincing its members to remain loyal to the Catholic Church. Though both Dominicans of his own time and scholars of recent years have downplayed the importance of Gui's activity as an inquisitor and the harshness of his inquests, in his writings Gui expresses little concern for the individual heretics he pursues and much concern for the communities from which they come.

IN THE TOWNS AND VILLAGES

The heretic, whether Cathar, Waldensian, Pseudo-Apostle, or Beguin, preaches his creed in the towns and villages through which he travels. For his believers, Gui suggests in his *Practica*, this heretic incarnates a certain Christian ideal. While the parish priests the believers encountered would have known little theology, the heretic could argue persuasively about the faith and illustrate his points with quotations from Scripture. While parish priests were notoriously lustful, friars gluttonous, and bishops covetous, the heretic lived from all appearances in chastity, abstinence, and poverty. For Gui, however, the heretic does not so much incarnate the Christian ideal of learning and virtue as imitate this ideal and, in imitating it, counterfeit, falsify, and debase it. Like the coiners to whom Aquinas compares them, heretics pretend to reproduce a value they do not have the authority to reproduce and, through this pretense, corrupt that value. To be a heretic, as Gui sees it, is, not to have a natural identity, which one happens to express to others, but to construct an artificial identity for the purpose of performing it to the public. Gui disdains heretics because he sees them, not as learned and virtuous, but as "learned" and "virtuous," that is, as self-consciously displaying the qualities they know their audiences will find admirable in order to gain their allegiance.

According to Gui, heretics may appear to be learned, but it is only because they contrive to give this impression. At a time when Catholic clerics possessed a quasi-monopoly on the knowledge of Scripture, the writings of the Church Fathers, and medieval theological works, heretics distinguished themselves from Catholic laymen through their study of these texts.[26] When heretics read or hear read theological books, however, Gui insists that they do so, not spontaneously, in order to discover the truths they contain, but instrumentally, in order to justify the errors that members of their sects already hold.[27] He writes of the Cathars, "They read the Gospels and the Epistles in the vernacular, interpreting and expounding them for themselves and against the establishments of the Roman Church."[28] While Catholic clerics presumably interpret and expound Scripture as it is naturally to be interpreted and expounded, these heretics, he contends, twist it to serve their own purposes. Similarly, he writes of the Waldensians that when they preach, they quote Scripture to support their contentions, claiming, "This is found in the Gospel, or in the Epistles of Saint Peter, Saint Paul, or Saint James."[29] While Catholic clerics presumably deliver sermons genuinely founded in Scripture and quote from its books in order to reference that foundation, these heretics, he asserts, deliver sermons with no such basis and cite these texts "in order that their words be more accepted by their listeners."[30] Heretics, he suggests, approach Scripture and other theological texts not as the ends of their study, by which they will learn what they will then know, but as the means by which they can justify what they are already thinking. The problem with heretics is not just that they are "stupid people [*ydiote*],"[31] as Gui claims that they are, that is, people incapable of understanding complex issues, or that they are "unlearned people [*illiterati*],"[32] as he also claims that they are, that is, people unprepared to read a text, or to read a text in Latin, or to understand what they have read. The problem with heretics is that, insisting upon reading Scripture themselves, they treat its pages not as the source of truth but as the source of quotations, which may be plucked to support whatever beliefs they a priori hold. Incapable of being genuinely learned or wise, the heretics, consciously and intentionally, perform learning and wisdom in order to gain influence over others and lead them astray.

Similarly, Gui argues, heretics may appear to be virtuous, but it is only because they contrive to give this impression. The Cathars may emphasize the superiority of the spirit to the flesh, the Waldensians the excellence of preaching, the Pseudo-Apostles the necessity of penitence, and the Beguins the example of Francis of Assisi, yet all of these sects agree, Gui reports, that the true Christian, like Jesus Christ, the Apostles, and their own holy men and women, should live poor and itinerant lives tending to the spiritual needs of the common people. If heretics pursue apostolic lives and encourage their believers to do so as well, however, Gui insists that they do so again, not spontaneously, in order to inculcate virtue and eradicate vice, but only instrumentally, in order to make themselves seem virtuous when they are not. The Pseudo-Apostles, for example, Gui reports, wander about towns and villages with their long hair and white tunics, chanting *Salve regina* and calling out, "Do penance, for the kingdom of heaven is at hand."[33] In addressing the people, Gui admits, "They make certain remarks which, on the surface, seem praiseworthy."[34] Despite these holy garments and utterances, Gui warns, the Pseudo-Apostles do not inwardly cultivate devotion but rather "outwardly adopt signs of devotion to God, all of which, at first glance, seem good and pious to their listeners."[35] These heretics are not authentically good or pious, but rather they merely give "some similitude of goodness or piety, in order that their words may be rendered more credible."[36] However laudable their remarks may seem, Gui makes clear, they utter them only "in order that they may attract and win over listeners."[37] Juxtaposing primary clauses, which convey the surface of these heretics' words, with subordinate clauses, introduced by "in order that [ut]," which convey their hidden purpose, Gui juxtaposes the heretics' apparently selfless intention to save the souls of their audiences with their actually selfish desire to gain converts for their sect. Like their learning, the heretics' virtue is manufactured to produce an effect upon their audience, to earn the confidence of those for whom it is performed, and, in doing so, to gain influence over them.

With their virtuous lives, the heretics perceive themselves as the true successors of Christ and the Apostles, yet, Gui affirms, they are only their false imitators. As the heretics portray themselves, they are the true heirs of the founders of the Christian faith because they alone imitate their poor, itinerant, and predicatory lifestyle. Gui writes of the Cathars, "They commonly say that they occupy the place of the Apostles,"[38] and he describes the Waldensians as "saying that they are the successors of the Apostles and boasting that they maintain and observe evangelical and apostolic poverty."[39] Of the Pseudo-Apostles, he relates that they chose the name of "the Apostles or the Order of the Apostles"[40] because they believed themselves to follow their path, and, of the Beguins, he claims that they believed themselves to comprise "the spiritual Church, composed of people . . . who follow the life of Christ and the Apostles."[41] For these heretics, if one acts like the Apostles, one is like the Apostles, while, if one diverges from these models' behavior, as Catholic clerics are alleged to do, one cannot count oneself among their heirs. If these heretics go wrong, as Gui asserts that they do, it is because, similar to Pelagians, they assume that one becomes a successor of the Apostles through the active pursuit of human merit alone and not through the passive reception of divine grace, like that which the Catholic priest receives during his ordination. The Waldensians in particular, Gui states, allege "those to be successors of the Apostles who imitate and uphold their way of life,"[42] forgetting that the Apostolic Succession is determined not by the imitation of the Apostles' behavior but by the inheritance of Saint Peter's keys. Audacious in believing themselves to be heirs of the Apostles, the Waldensians are audacious, all the more, in announcing this affiliation to others. Gui describes them as "boldly declaring that they were imitators and successors of these Apostles."[43] He restates this protest: "Comparing apostolic life and perfection with their own and considering their merits to be on an equal level, they vaunt themselves vainly, saying they are successors to the Apostles and boasting that they maintain and observe evangelical and apostolic poverty."[44] Whereas the Waldensians attest that they resemble the Apostles, Gui attests that *they say* that they resemble the Apostles; what was, for the Waldensians, the mere communication of a fact becomes, for Gui, an astonishing act of self-praise. Instead of admiring these sectaries for the degree to which they take after the Apostles, he chastises them for thinking that they could ever approach their purported prototypes.

Though Gui contrasts the heretics' false learning and virtue with Catholic clerics' genuine possession of these qualities, he makes clear that the heretics deceive not only laymen but clerics as well. On the surface, he states, Waldensians might seem to be the ideal Catholics. He writes, "They attend churches and sermons, in all other ways comport themselves in a religious and seemly manner, and strive to use vocabulary that seems unctuous and discreet."[45] Both in public religious gatherings and in private encounters with clerics, they show themselves as supporters of the Catholic Church, just as in their overall demeanor they seem to exemplify its values. At a time when anticlerical attitudes were commonplace, Gui observes, "They sometimes push themselves into feigned familiarity with members of religious orders and the clergy, lavish favors or gifts upon them, or adopt a fawning or servile attitude toward them."[46] Yet, Gui warns, the apparent esteem and affection in which Waldensians hold clerics is merely a pretense through which they hope to escape prosecution for their heresy. If they attend masses and sermons, if they behave piously and appropriately, if they offer clerics flattery or presents, these are all just external actions which may impress observers favorably and which, indeed, are designed to impress them favorably but which do not reflect any genuine internal sentiment. With the clergy as well as with the laity, the Waldensians, as Gui depicts them, are performers who may seem likeable but who are conspiring, consciously and intentionally, to endear themselves to those they meet, "so that they may acquire for themselves and theirs a freer opportunity to remain undiscovered, to live, and to injure souls."[47] Whatever human feeling an inquisitor may have sensed in a heretic who might have attended his sermons, expressed an interest in him, or even befriended him, Gui cautions, this was only a ruse on the heretic's part, designed to deflect the inquisitor from his prosecution, and should be responded to as such.

Gui pursues heretics as zealously as he does, he makes clear, because he regards their seemingly positive qualities so skeptically. Gui's inquisitor may encounter a heretic who is able to justify his heresy by pointing to passages in Scripture which support his beliefs, but he will not be impressed by this heretic's intelligence or knowledge, let alone consider the possibility that this man may be in the right. He may encounter a heretic who lives in poverty and chastity and propounds Christian ideals to his fellow men, but he will not be impressed by this heretic's virtue, let alone consider the possibility that he may be a good or even a holy man. He may encounter a heretic who attends his Catholic services, who praises his sermons, and who gives alms to his order, but he will not feel any reciprocal affection toward him. Between heretics and himself, Gui's inquisitor imposes a barrier of suspicion, inclined, as he is, to interpret their apparently good qualities as pretenses of good qualities, calculated to deceive and manipulate him.

IN THE INQUISITOR'S CHAMBER

As one moves from the towns and villages where the heretic preaches his creed to the hall where the inquisitor interrogates this heretic or his believers about their errors, we might seem to move from a performance before an audience to an interaction between two parties, but, surprisingly enough, this latter interaction proves no less dramatic. Earlier, during the public disputations Catholic clerics like Diego of Osma, Dominic Guzmán, and Peter of Verona used to hold with heretics, the Catholic cleric and the heretic vied with each other as two relatively equal contestants before an audience who determined which side had won. Now, during the private interrogation, the inquisitor seems to dominate as both prosecutor and judge of these proceedings. Despite this shift, however, Gui consistently represents the inquisitor and the accused party as two relatively equal contestants vying with each other before an audience who will still determine which side has triumphed. If the inquisitor succeeds in establishing the guilt of the accused heretic, so that the latter must either confess and abjure his errors or be abandoned to the secular arm, he will have defeated the heretic and by extension his heresy, as the audience must then recognize. If, however, the accused heretic succeeds in thwarting the inquisitor's efforts to establish his guilt, so that he must be released back into his community, he will have defeated the inquisitor and by extension the Catholic faith, as the audience, again, will perceive. Despite the massive shift in power relations between the Catholic cleric and the heretic as one shifts from disputation to inquisition, the encounter remains, in Gui's mind, a trial by battle where both camps are attempting to overcome the other and, in doing so, to earn the confidence of the audience distantly monitoring their combat.

When heretics are brought before inquisitors, they present themselves, Gui reports, not as the "stupid and unlearned people" he depicts them as being, but as "simple people" (*simplices*). From the time of Saint Paul, "simple people" had been understood to be those who grasp the letter of Scripture and not its spirit, its milk and not its meat, its surface and not its depths. Given Christianity's traditional valorization of simplicity over subtlety, simple people were never portrayed as inferior to intelligent and learned people, as "stupid and unlearned people" were, but they were portrayed as necessarily dependent upon these people for the correct understanding of their faith. Aquinas, for example, maintains that "divine revelation reaches those of lower degree through those who are over them, in a certain order.... The unfolding of faith must needs reach men of lower degree through those of higher degree."[48] Given this tradition, when they are being interrogated, the Waldensians protest that they should not be required to answer difficult questions because "they are simple people and do not know how to answer wisely,"[49] and the Beguins claim that they should be granted a similar dispensation "because, they say, they are laymen and simple folk."[50] If the inquisitor inquires of a Waldensian if he believes in the Crucifixion, the Resurrection, and the Ascension, for example, the latter will ask, "And you, sir, do you so believe?"[51] The inquisitor will affirm, "'I believe it unreservedly.'"[52] The Waldensian will then state, "And I believe likewise." He promises broadly, "I believe anything you and the other good doctors command me to believe."[53] Far from asserting his own theological views, based upon his own interpretation of Scripture, as a heretic might be expected to do, he seems to defer to the inquisitor's judgment, as a simple person should. While heretics were seen as active and predatory, using the literal level of Scripture to justify their heretical doctrines, simple people were seen as passive and innocent, perhaps in danger of being misled by these heretics, but never in danger of misleading others in turn. Gui, for example, refers to the Cathars as speaking "in order thus to deceive simple persons"[54] and to the Pseudo-Apostles as urging people to do penance "to seduce the hearts of the simple."[55] Given the traditional semantic opposition of simple people, in their ovine guilelessness, to heretics, in their vulpine cunning, the heretics, by identifying themselves with the simple, implicitly deny that they are heretics.

Yet, Gui argues, the heretic's apparent simplicity during the interrogations is only a guise designed to enable him to escape discovery and condemnation. The heretics may not be learned, but neither are they simple, he asserts. Contradicting the Beguins' assertion that they are merely "laymen and simple folk," Gui affirms, "As a matter of fact, they are astute, cunning, and crafty."⁵⁶ When asked questions about theological matters, the heretic does not so much flounder, terrified of saying the wrong thing, as elude his interrogator through what Gui calls "duplicities of words,"⁵⁷ "flights of words,"⁵⁸ "sophistries,"⁵⁹ "tricks,"⁶⁰ and "tergiversations."⁶¹ The Waldensian who, interrogated about an article of faith, turns the question back on the inquisitor and, upon hearing his answer, claims, "I believe likewise" is not actually claiming that he believes what the inquisitor believes, Gui asserts, but rather, "meaning [only] that he believes that [the inquisitor] so believe[s]."⁶² Similarly, the Waldensian who affirms that he will believe anything that the inquisitor "and the other good doctors" command him to believe is not alluding to good Catholic doctors. "Those good doctors whom you are willing to believe are members of your sect," Gui's inquisitor retorts. "If I agree with them, you believe me, but otherwise you do not."⁶³ Far from adhering to the inquisitor's views in theological matters, the heretic merely pretends to do so, while preserving secretly his own religious opinions. As Gui understands him, the heretic is not a learned or wise person who can see through one, superficial level of meaning, such as the letter of Scripture, and detect another, deeper level, such as the spirit of this text, but he is nevertheless an "astute" and "cunning" person who can manipulate the superficial and the deeper levels of his own speech to deceive his listeners. Gui's inquisitor demands of the Waldensian, "If you are a simple man without learning, answer and act simply, without a screen of words,"⁶⁴ yet it is precisely upon such a screen that the Waldensian depends, in order to avoid seeming to be a Waldensian. Far from being a simple sheep, the heretic proves to be a wolf in sheep's clothing.

When heretics are brought before inquisitors, Gui asserts, they present themselves not only as simple people but as simple people being tormented by their interrogators. At various moments of the session, the Waldensian seems "perturbed,"⁶⁵ "trembling,"⁶⁶ and "in anguish."⁶⁷ He is troubled, first, by the implications of the inquisitor's questions, which seem designed to raise doubts in his mind about accepted tenets of the faith. Gui relates, "Upon being asked if he believes so and so, the suspect replies in surprise, as if indignant, 'What else should I believe? It this not what I ought to believe?'"⁶⁸ By questioning him about such topics, the heretic implies, the inquisitor seems to be admitting, himself, that they are questionable. He warns, "I am a simple and unlearned man. I am ignorant of these matters, these subtleties. You could easily trip me up and lead me into error."⁶⁹ By encouraging him to ponder articles of faith, whose nuances are beyond his comprehension, the heretic suggests, the inquisitor is encouraging him to make rash statements for which he could then be penalized. The Waldensian is disturbed, in addition, by the manner in which the inquisitor responds to his answers. When the inquisitor points to a hidden level of meaning in his responses, the heretic protests, "If you wish to interpret everything I say otherwise than sensibly and simply, then I do not know how I may answer you. I am a simple man, without learning; pray do not trap me in my words."[70] As a simple man, he expresses himself on one level. If the inquisitor finds another level of meaning in his speech, he suggests, it is because this learned cleric, with his multivalent mind, perceives a multivalence in his words that was not originally there. If the dexterous inquisitor cannot induce him to make heterodox statements he does not want to make, the Waldensian worries, he will interpret his orthodox statements as possessing a heterodox meaning he had not intended to express. As the heretic presents the situation, if he seems to be a heretic, it is only because the inquisitor creates the heretics he seems to find, by obliging them to address theological matters beyond their depth and by construing in every Catholic utterance they make a heretical subtext.

Yet, Gui maintains, the heretic's apparent suffering during the interrogations is again only a guise designed to make the spectators in the courtroom sympathetic toward him and hostile toward the inquisitor. Gui states explicitly that the Waldensians pander to the notary or the clerical assistants in attendance in order to have themselves better thought of. "When they see that those present are inclined to sympathize with them as simple people who are being mistreated and in whom no evil is found," he writes, "they gain confidence, pretend to weep, [and] appear miserable."[71] Pretending to be shaken and confused and claiming repeatedly, "I am a simple and unlearned man," the Waldensian categorizes himself in the way that a subtle and learned person, watching these proceedings, might be likely to categorize him and in a way that, for such an observer, might excuse his failure to respond to the inquisitor's questions. At the same time, Gui also makes clear, these heretics pander to these spectators in order to have the inquisitor less well regarded. He adds, "It is their design . . . to bring the inquisitor into ill repute among laymen for seeming to molest simple folk without cause and for appearing to seek an excuse for ruining them by tricky examination."[72] As the observer is meant to understand the situation, the heretic is simple and innocent of heresy, suffering as a result of the inquisitor's abuse. As Gui understands the situation, however, the heretic is crafty and guilty of heresy, and, if he "weep[s] and appear[s] miserable" in response to the inquisitor's justified sternness, it is only because he is feigning to suffer. If an observer has the impression that the inquisitor is treating the heretic overly harshly, Gui proposes, it can only be because the heretic has manipulated the situation to give a third party that impression.

Because the heretic pretends to be innocent when he is guilty, the inquisitor, as Gui envisions him, must pretend to know the heretic to be guilty when he has no judicial reason to do so. At this time, in order to convict an accused heretic, the inquisitor needed to obtain either the confession of this individual or the testimony of two respectable eyewitnesses against him. Gui acknowledges, "It is exceedingly difficult to catch heretics when they themselves do not frankly avow error but conceal it, or when sure and sufficient evidence against them is lacking."[73] Insofar as an inquisitor is interrogating an accused heretic, it is because he does not yet have the "sure and sufficient evidence" that eyewitness testimony would constitute and hopes to supplement that lack by eliciting a confession. If he fails to obtain that avowal, Gui repeatedly recognizes with consternation, the inquisitor will be obliged to set the accused heretic free. Though, judicially speaking, the inquisitor may not yet possess the proof necessary to establish the accused heretic's guilt, Gui nevertheless encourages him, practically speaking, to presume that guilt because he has so often seen such a presumption justified. Once heretics are persuaded that their guilt is so well established that they are destined to be burned no matter what they say, he asserts, they acknowledge that which they had been denying thus far. He describes Pseudo-Apostles who, despairing of their fates, begin "openly to profess and to defend their doctrine in every way and under all circumstances."[74] He recounts one exemplary case: "I have seen and had experience with one [heretic] who, after being held in prison and examined frequently for almost two years, was still quibbling with the truth and would not confess. Finally, he spoke out and revealed it."[75] Because some accused persons have made such confessions after extensive protestations of innocence, Gui argues that all accused persons can be brought to make similar avowals. Although he remarks at several points in the *Practica* that some accused persons know less about their heretical sect and doctrines than others, at no point does he refer to the possibility that an accused person might be entirely ignorant, let alone innocent, of heresy. Although he encountered cases, documented in the *Liber sententiarum*, where people had brought false witness against their neighbors and although he dealt with those perjurers harshly, nowhere in the *Practica* does he refer to the possibility that those brought before the inquisitors might have been maliciously, mendaciously, or simply mistakenly accused. Rejecting every protestation of innocence as a lie, Gui's inquisitor makes clear that he will accept only an acknowledgement of guilt as the truth.

In one passage of the *Practica*, Gui admits the possibility that an individual accused of heresy may be, if not innocent of this crime, then incapable of being proven guilty, yet here too, he advises, the inquisitor should continue to act as if he knows this person to be guilty. On the one hand, Gui states, the inquisitor has no desire to condemn someone to the flames who has not been established to be a heretic. He writes, "His conscience torments him if an individual is punished who has neither confessed nor been proven guilty."[76] On the other hand, he adds, the inquisitor has even less desire to release someone who, though he has not confessed to heresy or been proven guilty of this crime, is indeed a heretic. He continues, "It causes even more anguish to the mind of the inquisitor, familiar through much experience with the falsity, cunning, and malice of such persons, if by their wily astuteness they escape punishment, to the detriment of the faith, since thereby they are strengthened, multiplied, and rendered more crafty."[77] Should the inquisitor release a heretic, Gui warns, he would be strengthening him in his heresy and he would be weakening the community to which he returns in its Catholicism by allowing its members to think that a heretic has outwitted an inquisitor. Disillusioned by the inquisitor's failure to see through the heretic's ruses and to expose him for what he is, Gui reports, "The faithful laity see occasion for scandal in the fact that the proceedings of the Inquisition, once started against someone, are abandoned, as it were, in confusion, and they are thus mocked by low and uncouth persons."[78] With this passage, Gui suggests that the inquisitor err on the side of condemning an innocent Catholic (or, as he puts it, someone who has not yet been proven to be other than an innocent Catholic), rather than on the side of releasing a guilty heretic. Though the inquisitor does not know this accused person to be guilty, he must presume that he does know this for the benefit, if not of the accused person himself, then of the community from which he comes, which must be strengthened in its faith.

Gui pursues heretics as zealously as he does, he makes clear, because he regards not only their seeming virtues but their seeming suffering so skeptically. He may encounter an accused heretic who, when asked complex theological questions, professes ignorance, but he will refuse to accept that this person has no views on these matters. He may encounter an accused heretic who protests that he is a good Christian, that he believes all that one should believe, and that he will believe all that the inquisitor will teach him, but he will interpret all of these remarks as possessing a secret, heretical meaning. He may encounter an accused heretic who weeps under his relentless interrogation and who pleads with him or with others present in the room for mercy, but he will remain unmoved by his visible distress. Given that Gui assumes that all accused heretics are guilty, he never makes clear how an accused heretic who is innocent could protest his innocence with words that could not be suspected of having double meanings or how he could bewail his situation with expressions of distress that could not be suspected of being feigned. Just as the heretic's appearance of learning and virtue when he was preaching to his followers was false, so too, Gui insists, is his appearance of simplicity and suffering when he is responding to the inquisitor's questions.

AT THE CATHEDRAL

On Thursday, October 23, 1309, Gui delivered a general sermon in the Cathedral of Saint Stephen in Toulouse before what he tells us was an immense crowd of clerics and laymen. About two dozen distinguished personages were in attendance, including the consuls of Toulouse, the two canons representing the bishop of this town, judges from this town and nearby regions, and a representative of the king. Numerous Dominicans were present, as well as Franciscans, Augustinians, Carmelites, and Cistercians. Many of these dignitaries would have been seated on a platform, so as to be visible to the audience that had gathered in this building. Among all of these authorities, however, it was "Friar Bernard Gui, of the Order of Preachers, inquisitor of heretical depravity delegated to the kingdom of France by the apostolic authority,"[79] as he styled himself before the crowd, who delivered the sermon and presided over the event. It was Gui who said of the single condemned man, chained and guarded before him, "We declare and pronounce him to be a heretic, by definitive sentence in these acts, and we release him as such to the secular court."[80] Even more than the private interrogation in the inquisitor's chamber, the public sermon in the cathedral was a performance in which Gui directed his attention, not to the condemned man who was about to be consigned to the flames, but to the audience of the sermon who might be tempted to sympathize with him.[81] Here he would establish, once and for all, not only that the heretic is a heretic who has willfully separated himself from the Church, but that he and his colleagues have made every effort to bring him back within this institution's fold. A contrast between what Gui says to this crowd, in the sentencing of this heretic, and what he says to his fellow inquisitors, in the *Practica*, however, suggests that he is less concerned with the salvation of this heretic's soul than with the impression this audience might have of his handling of his case.

The Cathar heretic who was being condemned that day was Amiel of Perles, the companion of Peter Autier, the dominant figure in the resurgence of Catharism.[82] Around ten years before, Amiel had joined Peter Autier, then a notary in Ax, Peter's son James, Peter's brother William, and their fellow southerners Prades Tavernier and Peter Raymond of Saint-Papoul in traveling to Lombardy, where a Cathar hierarchy was still in residence, and in becoming perfected at these officials' hands. Having returned to the Sarbatès, Amiel spent most of the following decade wandering the region with Peter Autier, preaching the Cathar faith and tending to the spiritual needs of its believers. So that they would not be seen by Catholics who might betray them to the inquisitors, these heretics would conceal themselves by day in the houses of their followers, descending periodically from the attics to preach to their believers and to receive their adoration. At one point when a safe house was not available, Amiel is said to have lodged and preached in a cave. In the fall of 1309, Peter Autier was seized while he was taking refuge in a shepherd's hut, and Amiel seems to have been taken shortly thereafter. In the *Practica*, Gui states that Cathar Perfects, like Peter Autier and Amiel, should be imprisoned for a long period of time "in order more frequently to urge them to conversion, for their conversion is especially helpful."[83] He explains, "The conversion of Manichaean heretics [i.e., Cathar Perfects] is usually genuine and seldom feigned; when they are converted, they tell everything, reveal the truth, and betray their confederates, whence results a great harvest."[84] Given the disclosures such Perfects might make, Gui adds, their believers were terrified so long as they were imprisoned, lest they be implicated in their testimony. It was in the hope of obtaining such testimony and of spreading such fear, it seems, that Peter Autier was kept alive until April of 1310.[85] In contrast, Amiel was being released to the secular arm not long after his capture because he had ceased to eat and drink from the time he was taken into custody and was thus threatening to take his own life before the authorities could take it from him. By bringing Amiel in chains before the crowd, Gui was exposing to the public a notorious heretic central to the revival of Catharism in the surrounding lands and hence worthy of the special attention he was receiving.

In the course of his sermon in the cathedral, Gui establishes that Amiel is guilty of heresy. He refers to "Amiel of Perles, also called 'of Auterive,' from the diocese of Pamiers, having been arrested and apprehended for the crime of heresy in the diocese of Toulouse, where he committed numerous infractions in matters of heresy, in hereticating people, and also in corrupting the faith by his false doctrine."[86] After citing the grounds upon which Amiel was seized, Gui explains how these grounds were established. Many witnesses have testified against Amiel, he asserts. His heresy, Gui states, "is established by us, regularly and clearly, after several testimonies received regularly over the course of the investigation."[87] Indeed, in Gui's register, well over a hundred witnesses identify Amiel as a heretic, citing the sermons all of them heard him or his companion deliver and the heretications several of them saw him perform. Proven guilty by witnesses' testimony, Amiel has also been proven guilty, Gui asserts, by his own confession. His guilt, he states, "is established by us, regularly and clearly, . . . after the confession or, rather, the profession, as execrable as it was profane, of Amiel of Perles."[88] Unlike Waldensians and members of other heretical sects, Gui states in the *Practica*, Cathar Perfects like Amiel would not attempt to persuade inquisitors that they were not heretics, for such mendacity was contrary to their moral code, but rather they would openly avow their heterodox faith, as Amiel appears to have done. It was not only with his words but also with his deeds that Amiel affirmed his membership in the forbidden sect. When Amiel and Peter Autier were at one point brought together in the courtroom, Gui recalls, the former companions performed the *melioramentum*, the ritual greeting Cathars were accustomed to enact before their Perfect: "Before us, the two of them adored each other reciprocally, the one and the other bowing down to the ground, in accordance with their rite."[89] That Amiel would not only confess his faith but, as Gui puts it, would profess it; that he would not only profess his faith but would enact it in the inquisitor's very presence; that, through these words and deeds, he would demonstrate himself to be a "manifest heretic," strikes Gui as a brazen defiance of the orthodox norms under which his courtroom and, now, the cathedral were operating. Gui condemns Amiel for heresy, he makes clear, only because this man has made so unambiguous his adherence to the heretical faith.

By making such a point of Amiel's guilt in his sermon at the cathedral, Gui is demonstrating to the audience that he does not convict innocent men. Sometime after 1244, the Dominican friar William Pelhisson had written a chronicle of his order's travails as they prosecuted heretics in Toulouse between 1230 and 1238. According to Pelhisson, whenever the inquisitor and his fellow friars pursued a heretic, such as Bernard of Soler, John Textor, or Arnold Sans, the burghers of Toulouse would rise up against them and declare the accused party a good Catholic. During these years, Pelhisson relates, "The town was . . . very much stirred up against the friars. . . . Their cry was, they were unjustly accusing decent married men of heresy."[90] So outraged did the burghers become that they ultimately expelled the friars from the town in November of 1235, permitting them to return only after four months. If the friars were able to escape these burghers' vituperations, it was only because God exposed the guilt of these accused heretics. When Bernard of Soler, despite his protests of orthodoxy, fled to Lombardy, the refuge for heretics, Pelhisson relates, "His partisans stayed behind in confusion. Blessed be the Lord, and blessed be Dominic, his servant, who thus defends his own."[91] When John Textor finally acknowledged himself publicly to be a heretic and thus vindicated the friars' charges against him, he writes, "In all things, blessed be God, who delivered the friars who were in grave danger and magnified his faith in the face of his enemies. Hence, Catholics rejoiced greatly, and heretical sympathizers were confused and refuted."[92] As Pelhisson sees it, God silences the friars' critics because, in doing so, he promotes the Catholic faith. Himself a historian of Toulouse, Gui was well aware of Pelhisson's chronicle and had even made a copy of it for his own use. He was also well aware of other revolts against inquisitors, such as those in Albi and Carcassonne, which were also waged on the pretext (as he saw it) that these friars were prosecuting good Catholics. Though, by his time, the inquisitors had grown more adept at soliciting testimony against heretics and thus at building up stronger cases against those they accused, Gui too expresses satisfaction at the exposure of heretics' guilt. Writing of the testimony repentant heretics were required to provide as evidence of their conversion, he observes, "Accomplices and errors are uncovered by such confession. From this, truth and falsity are uncovered, and the Office [of the Inquisition] is made to prosper."[93] When Gui devotes such a large ceremony at the cathedral to Amiel's condemnation and when he informs the audience of the evidence against this heresiarch provided by witnesses and by the accused party himself, he is establishing to this audience, as his predecessors struggled to do, that the condemned man is in fact guilty as charged.

In the course of his sermon, Gui establishes not only that Amiel is guilty of heresy but also that he and his colleagues have made every effort to persuade him to abjure his errors. He states, "We and many other people often exhorted and requested him to confess, to believe [the Catholic faith], to adhere to it, and to recoil from his errors."[94] With this admonition to Amiel, Gui recalls his insistence in the *Practica* upon the pastoral aims of the Inquisition. Instead of intending the condemnation of heretics' bodies to the stake, he asserts, "It intends principally the salvation of souls and the purity of the faith."[95] In *Omnis utriusque sexus*, the canon which had required all Christians to confess their sins at least once a year, the Fourth Lateran Council of 1215 had announced, "Let the priest be discreet and cautious that he may pour wine and oil into the wounds of the one injured after the manner of a skilful physician, carefully inquiring into the circumstances of the sinner and the sin, from the nature of which he may understand what kind of advice to give and what remedy to apply, making use of different experiments to heal the sick one."[96] At this time, confessors regularly described themselves as "physicians of souls" who sought to diagnose sinners' maladies by questioning them and who developed plans of treatment based upon these sinners' answers.[97] Gui describes the inquisitor, like such a confessor, as a "physician of souls"[98] when he writes, "Just as no one medicine is for all diseases, but rather different and specific medicines exist for particular diseases, so neither is the same method of questioning, investigation, and examination to be employed for all heretics of the various sects, but for each, whether there be one or many, a particular and suitable method ought to be utilized."[99] Like the physician, who proceeds differently with different invalids, and the confessor, who proceeds differently with different sinners, the inquisitor proceeds differently with different heretics, in order to cure them most effectively. So salutary are the inquisitor's aims, Gui asserts, that even now, should Amiel show signs of repentance, the inquisitor will welcome him back into the Church and allowed to live. Even after the heretic has been condemned, even after he has been fastened to the stake, even after he has begun to suffer from the heat and the smoke of the flames, he affirms in the *Practica*, should he cry out that he wishes to abjure, the inquisitor will have him released from the pyre by the secular officers. Gui states, "He is to be kept back, to be returned to the inquisitors, and to be received by them."[100] However skeptical one might be of the sincerity of such a delayed conversion, he indicates, the slight chance that it might be genuine requires the inquisitor to receive the heretic back into the Church, albeit as a penitent consigned to spend the rest of his life in prison, because "equity is to be preferred to rigor."[101] No less than a parish priest faced with a parishioner, Gui asserts, an inquisitor faced with a heretic like Amiel seeks to encourage his repentance for his sin and his reconciliation to the Church.

Though, by making such a point of his and his colleagues' efforts to persuade Amiel to abjure his errors, Gui is demonstrating to his audience that he wants to save condemned heretics' souls, in general he gives little indication of such a desire. The considerable confessional literature that was produced in the twelfth and thirteenth centuries instructs confessors not only on how they might diagnose and treat sinners but also on how they might bring them to contrition for their sins and, in doing so, save their souls.[102] In his influential *Summa de casibus poenitentiae* of 1234, the Dominican friar Raymond of Peñafort explains how such a confessor should comport himself in order to produce such a response in the sinner. He writes, "He must with pious, sweet, and soft address induce [the sinner] to compunction and confession, propounding to him the benefits which God offers him."[103] Should the sinner appear ashamed to confess, the confessor should remind him that he confesses not to a man but to God; that God loves people, like Saint Peter, Saint Paul, and the good thief, who repent of their sins; and that, if he repents of his sins, he will be absolved of them. "If, however, [the sinner] does not want to confess," Raymond adds, "let [the confessor] propound to him the terrors of judgment, the punishments of hell."[104] The confessor might cite, for example, the Book of Zephaniah's description of the Last Judgment, rendered famous in Thomas of Celano's thirteenth-century hymn *Dies irae*: "That day is a day of wrath, a day of calamity and misery, a day of tribulation and distress, of darkness and obscurity, a day of clouds and whirlwinds, a day of the trumpet and alarm."[105] Given that Gui would have been familiar with confessional literature, including Raymond's treatise, and given that he employs, in Amiel's sentence and in the *Practica*, a confessional language drawn from this tradition, it is all the more striking that he never addresses how the inquisitor might bring heretics to repentance. When he discusses the conversions of Cathar Perfect, he celebrates not the salvation of their souls but the testimony they provide about their former confederates. When he discusses the conversions of heretics in general, he affirms, with approval, as we have seen, not that they have been rescued, body and soul, but that, "From this, truth and falsity are uncovered, and the Office [of the Inquisition] is made to prosper." His interest lies not in the inward, spiritual salvation of heretics but in the outward, judicial triumph of the Inquisition. When he explains why the heretic who repents at the last moment is to be released from the pyre, he states, not just that equity is to be preferred to rigor, but that "The scandalizing of weak people, if the Church refuses the sacrament of penance to penitents, is to be avoided."[106] What is important, he indicates, is not so much that the Church refrain from undue harshness but rather that it refrain from giving the impression of undue harshness to "weak people," who might be appalled by such evident callousness. What is important is not so much that the Church have concern for that damned soul, still capable of redemption, but that it seem to its audience to have such concern for him.

In the course of his sermon, Gui establishes, finally, that, if Amiel will now be burned at the stake, it is because, despite the inquisitor's efforts and those of his colleagues, the heretic chose his own destruction. Though these Catholic clerics urged Amiel to abandon the Cathar sect and to return to the Catholic Church, Gui relates, "He did not want [*nec voluit*] to separate himself from this sect, nor to believe the faith of the Roman Church, nor to speak it with his mouth."[107] He describes him, again, as "the said Amiel, here present, not wanting [*nolentem*] to convert to the Catholic faith."[108] That Amiel seeks death is evident, according to Gui, from his refusal, not just to convert, but to eat and drink since his capture. "Like a son of perdition and Gehenna, rushing to his death and hastening toward eternity," Gui announces, "since the time of his capture, he did not want [*noluit*] to eat or to drink, and he revealed himself to be his own murderer."[109] Whether Amiel's death be from burning or from starving, it is here imagined as the result of his own suicidal impulses and not as the result of the actions of the inquisitors. Amiel thus resembles the Cathar heretics Gui discusses in the *Practica* who, on account of "either their faith or, rather, their perfidy choose rather to die than to convert."[110] In his insistence upon Amiel's agency, drawn out by his repeated references to what he wanted (*voluit*) and did not want (*noluit*) to do, Gui recalls the traditional definition of the heretic, not just as someone who errs in matters of the faith, but as someone who, even after being corrected, obstinately perseveres in his error. Gui refers to Cathars who, "after their conversion has been repeatedly urged and invited, . . . do not want [*noluerint*] to return to the faith and seem to be obdurate."[111] He refers to Waldensians who show themselves to be "stubborn [*pertinaces*],"[112] Pseudo-Apostles who show themselves to be "obstinate [*obstinati*],"[113] and Beguins who show themselves to be "obdurate [*indurati*]"[114] in their similar disinclination to return to the faith. Like these heretics, Gui reports of Amiel, "He still persists in his perfidy with an obdurate spirit [*animo indurato*], despising all these counsels."[115] If the trial proceeds inexorably in the direction of his condemnation and excommunication, he states, it is because this heretic willfully chooses for this to happen.

In his condemnation of Amiel, Gui denies that inquisitors exercise moral agency and hence bear moral responsibility in bringing about the deaths of such heretics, but in the *Practica*, he is ambiguous about this point. In his description of the ideal inquisitor, Gui declares, "Let the inquisitor be even as a just judge. Thus, let him not only serve the rigor of justice inwardly, in his mind, but also show compassion outwardly, in his face [*in facie . . . exterius*], in order that he may avoid the appearance of indignation and wrath which leads to a charge of cruelty."[116] In this passage, Gui acknowledges that the inquisitor may feel indignation and wrath, yet he argues, not that he should strive to overcome these passions in himself, but that he should strive to hide them from others, lest he be accused of cruelty. When the inquisitor is confiscating property from condemned heretics, in particular, Gui states, it is crucial that he not only "serve the severity of judgment inwardly, but that he display the truth of justice outwardly, on his face [*in facie exterius*], because he is compelled to do so by the necessity of justice, not attracted by the attraction of cupidity."[117] He acknowledges that the inquisitor may feel covetousness, yet, he argues, again, not that he should strive to overcome this passion in himself, but that he should strive to conceal it from others, lest he be charged with this sin. He concludes, "Let mercy and truth, which should never be absent from the mind of a judge, shine forth from his face."[118] Affirming that mercy should be present internally, in the inquisitor's mind, he stresses that it should be evident, externally, in his countenance. In his demeanor, Gui argues, the inquisitor should demonstrate to observers that he is driven by an impersonal law and not by a personal desire, yet, by the very fact that he is making this argument, he indicates that the inquisitor's lack of personal desire is something performed rather than expressed. Juxtaposing primary clauses which convey the surface action of the inquisitor with subordinate clauses, introduced by "in order that [*ut*]" or "because [*quia*]," which convey his hidden purpose, Gui juxtaposes the inquisitor's apparently clear intention to enforce this law with his actual, unclear motivation. Gui does not admit that the inquisitor may exercise moral agency, let alone bear moral responsibility, in condemning Amiel and other heretics to the stake, but he does set forth that his impersonal enforcement of the law is a conscious act, for the benefit of those watching him.

In Eco's *The Name of the Rose*, the protagonist William of Baskerville, an English Franciscan friar, asserts of Gui, "Bernard is interested not in discovering the guilty but in burning the accused."[119] On one level, William's assessment of Gui's character seems clearly wrong. In contrast to a Conrad of Marburg, for example, Gui is aware of the numerous regulations regarding the prosecution of heretics that have been passed by popes and councils, and he functions within the confines of those regulations. If he does not possess sufficient eyewitness testimony against an accused heretic and if he cannot obtain a confession to supplement this lack of testimony, it seems, he feels obliged to let this individual go. One could never imagine Gui declaring, as Conrad Tors and John were said to have declared, that he is happy to burn a hundred Catholics in order to burn one heretic, if only because he seems to be constitutionally averse to contravening regulations, as he would have to do in order to act in this manner. On another level, however, William's estimation of Gui's character seems right. Nowhere in the *Practica* does Gui address seriously the possibility that the testimony the inquisitor has received about the accused heretic may be false, let alone the possibility that the confession he has obtained from the accused heretic may be untrue. Nowhere in his work does he address seriously the manner in which a heretic might be brought back to the Church. Everywhere, instead, he shows himself to be concerned, not so much with the well-being of the accused heretic, who might be proved to be a good Catholic, or with the well-being of the condemned heretic, who might be reconciled with the Church, as with the well-being of the Office of the Inquisition, which needs to maintain its prestige before the common people by ensuring that that no heretics elude its grasp. If Gui is interested in burning the accused—or at least in assigning them penances—it is because he believes that, in doing so, the inquisitor most effectively demonstrates the inexorable justice of the Inquisition and in doing so persuades the common people to remain faithful to the Church.

CHAPTER SIX

Bernard Délicieux: The Scourge of Inquisitors

The life of Bernard Délicieux (1260–1319/20) followed the path of many inquisitors.[1] Délicieux was born into a noble family in the traditionally Catholic stronghold of Montpellier, which was then encompassed within the kingdom of Majorca. Around the age of twenty-four, he entered the Franciscan order, whose members had been serving as inquisitors alongside Dominicans for many years.[2] At times, representatives of both mendicant orders were asked to pursue heretics together in the same region. In the 1230s, for example, Friars Minor and Friars Preachers were named co-inquisitors in Toulouse, Aragon, and Navarre, and in later decades they worked together in Burgundy, Lorraine, and the region of Ravenna. More often, given the continual quarrels between the two orders, they were assigned to different districts.[3] In what is now France, the north and southwest, including the regions of Toulouse, Foix, and Carcassonne, were given to the Dominicans and the southeast, including Provence, to the Franciscans.[4] In what is now Italy, the north was accorded to the Dominicans and the center to the Franciscans. Having entered an order invested in the prosecution of heretics,[5] Délicieux appears to have received the education typical for those selected to become inquisitors.[6] He was presumably trained in theology, given that he was appointed lector of the convents in Narbonne and Carcassonne, and he was presumably familiar with the law as well, given that he was repeatedly entrusted with important administrative duties. Well-educated, Délicieux was, finally, well spoken, again, as an inquisitor would have been expected to be. He delivered sermons so spellbinding that he was said to have repeatedly aroused his audiences to action. Yet, instead of emerging as a leader of the Inquisition, as his exact contemporary and acquaintance Bernard Gui had done, Délicieux emerged as the scourge of this institution and, indeed, as Gui represents him, as "the commander-in-chief and standard-bearer of the iniquitous army against the Friars [Preachers] and the Office of the Inquisition."[7] The action to which Délicieux stirred his audiences was not against heretics but against inquisitors, who, he alleged, were pursuing innocent Catholics for heresy and thereby trying to destroy the towns in which those Catholics resided.

The uprising Délicieux led against the Dominican inquisitors in Carcassonne was preceded by a similar movement against these friars twenty years earlier. In the 1280s, the Dominican inquisitors John Galand and William of Saint-Seine solicited (or, some said, coerced) testimony,[8] collected in two folio volumes known as Registers X and XI, which had implicated over four hundred people in the Carcassès and Albigeois regions in the Cathar heresy.[9] Significant numbers of these people were arrested and imprisoned in the inquisitorial prison (or "Wall") adjacent to the City of Carcassonne,[10] where some were condemned to perpetual incarceration and others were kept languishing for years, unconvicted and unsentenced.[11] One account from the time relates that the prisoners were kept shackled, lying on the cold earth in their urine and excrement, in dark, airless cells reverberating with cries of lamentation.[12] Troubled by the situation of the prisoners in the Wall, the people of Carcassonne agitated on their behalf, boycotting the Dominicans' masses and sermons and subjecting these friars to physical and verbal abuse. In response, in 1295, the Dominican inquisitor Nicholas of Abbeville excommunicated the entire population of Carcassonne for their "favoring" (fautoria) of heretics and their resistance to the work of the Inquisition. The consuls of the town, who were elected every year from the most prominent families of the Bourg (or the area outside the walled City) were anxious to mend the rift between its population and the Church. On October 8, 1299, they signed the Accord of 1299, a document in which, on the people's behalf, they confessed their guilt of these crimes and expressed repentance for their deeds.[13] Despite the apparent calm that followed the signing of this accord, between December of 1299 and March of 1300 the Wall received thirty-five new prisoners, the vast majority of them members of important families from Albi who had fallen afoul of Bernard of Castenet, the bishop of that town and an ally of the Dominican inquisitors.[14] The suspect registers which were used to justify the imprisonment of so many possibly innocent people, the dire conditions of these people's incarceration, and the implication of the entire population of Carcassonne in these people's alleged heresy, after they had risen up in their defense, all provided the seeds from which Délicieux's rebellion against the inquisitors would grow.

Between 1300 and 1303, Délicieux built upon the Carcassonnais' grievances to lead the major uprising against the inquisitors during the Middle Ages.[15] In the first months of 1300, Nicholas of Abbeville sent his deputy Fulk of Saint-Georges and thirty sergeants to arrest some suspects of heresy who had taken refuge in the Franciscan convent, yet Délicieux and his fellow friars defended their premises, forcing these officials to retreat. Not long thereafter, Nicholas charged the friars with protecting Castel Fabre, a wealthy merchant of Carcassonne who had recently died in their convent and who, Nicholas alleged, had been hereticated shortly before his death, yet Délicieux and two other friars succeeded in appealing this case to the pope. In the spring of 1301, John of Picquigny, the vidame of Amiens, and Richard Leneveu, the archdeacon of Auge, agents appointed by King Philip the Fair to investigate and correct governmental abuses, arrived in Carcassonne and allied themselves with Délicieux against Nicholas and his brethren.[16] With their help, Délicieux and his associates secured an audience with Philip in Senlis that October, and there they persuaded the king that the Dominicans were producing such discontent among the people of Carcassonne as to threaten royal authority. While Délicieux succeeded in persuading Philip to prevent the inquisitors from initiating new cases against suspected heretics, he remained troubled by the Dominicans' continued position as inquisitors and by the prisoners' continued confinement in the Wall. Returning to Carcassonne, he delivered a series of sermons between August 4 and 10, 1303 in which he decried the activities of Geoffrey of Ablis, the new Dominican inquisitor,[17] and his fellow friars. When Geoffrey attempted to respond to Délicieux's criticisms from the pulpit of the Dominican church, a mob chased him from his podium to the bishop's mansion. With the inquisitor out of its reach, the crowd returned to the church, smashing its windows and vandalizing its altar, and then marched to the houses of the former consuls who had signed the Accord of 1299 and other citizens deemed friendly to the Dominican friars, ransacking and looting their interiors. About two weeks later, probably on August 23, the vidame led a motley force against the Wall and transferred the prisoners being held there to a royal fortress, with Délicieux reportedly directing the actions from the side. In addition to Carcassonne, Délicieux preached at this time in Albi, Cordes, Castres, and Limoux, inciting the people of these neighboring towns against the Inquisition as well. While there had been revolts against the inquisitors before, Délicieux's success at uniting the king, his deputies, and the people of the Midi against them was unprecedented.

In retrospect, the transferal of the prisoners from the Wall would prove to be Délicieux's finest hour. During the months that followed this triumph, Délicieux urged Philip to take further action against the inquisitors, yet, from Philip's point of view, the Franciscan friar now seemed to be not so much protecting the crown's interests against insurrection as instigating this insurrection himself. Frustrated by French king's new indifference to his demands, Délicieux turned to Ferrand, the third son of James II, the king of Majorca, in the spring of 1304 and urged him to usurp Philip's power in the Midi. Though nothing came of their conspiracy, fifty-five burghers from Carcassonne and Limoux who had supported it were hanged. Philip was not Délicieux's only antagonist at this time. In October of 1303, the Dominican Benedict XI had been elected pope, and this new leader of the Church did not hesitate to use his position to strengthen the hand of his order's inquisitors. Alarmed by Benedict's efforts to undo his work, Délicieux was said to have plotted with the Catalan Arnold of Villanova, the pope's physician, to bring about his patient's death through poison and necromancy.[18] On July 7, 1304, shortly after Benedict had excommunicated Délicieux and ordered his arrest, the pontiff did, in fact, pass away, so that the Franciscan friar once again eluded punishment. As the years passed, the ongoing review of the prisoners' cases and the relative inaction of the inquisitors in Carcassonne helped to abate what Gui would call "the *Carcassonais* raving."[19] During this lull, Délicieux was residing in the Franciscan convent of Béziers, where he fell in with the Spiritual Franciscans, whose criticisms of papal power accorded with his own views; as he had once been head of the opponents to the inquisitors, he now emerged, as the Dominican Raymond Barreau puts it in a letter to Pope John XXII, as "the diabolical leader and head of the Beguins and the Spiritual Friars Minor."[20] Despite his efforts to impede the inquisitors, to betray the king, and to kill the pope, Délicieux had for years escaped prosecution, thanks to the protection of members of the Franciscan order, the bishops of Narbonne and Béziers, the cardinals of the curia, and Pope Clement V. It was only in May of 1318 that he was finally arrested and only between September and December of the following year that he was finally tried for these crimes.[21] Brought to confess and abjure his sins, he was degraded from clerical status and condemned to live out his days in the Wall, though, given his advanced age and his physical weakness, he was granted a decent diet and freedom from fetters.[22] He appears to have died within a few months of his condemnation, at the age of fifty-nine. It is a testament to Délicieux's centrality to the Church that, even as he worked from its margins, attempting to thwart its inquisitors, he remained free for so long and that, even when he was prosecuted, he received what both the pope and the king perceived to be a lenient sentence.

What enables Délicieux to become such an effective opponent of the inquisitors is, ironically, the fact that he thinks like the most zealous of these friars. Bernard Gui serves as a particularly interesting point of comparison to Délicieux, given that he observed first-hand the uprising in which Délicieux participated, as prior of the Dominican convents of Carcassonne between 1297 and 1301 and Castres between 1301 and 1305; produced a brief, exclusively critical account of this uprising in his *De fundatione et prioribus conventum provinciarum Tolosanae et Provinciae Ordinis Praedicatorum*;[23] and contributed to Délicieux's trial, drawing up the sixty articles which served as the basis for his interrogation and sentence.[24] Insofar as Délicieux resembles an inquisitor like Gui, it is because he focuses on the outer world of groups struggling with each other (namely, inquisitors and heretics), as opposed to the inner world of individuals struggling with their own souls. It is because he is concerned with the here and now instead of the hereafter or, in other words, with political rather than spiritual ends. Insofar as Délicieux differs from someone like Gui, it is because he inverts the values Gui attributes to those groups, championing accused heretics over inquisitors and, in doing so, championing a local, civic power structure over a universal, ecclesiastical organization. While inquisitors like Gui claim that the prisoners of the Wall are guilty of heresy, Délicieux claims that they are innocent. While inquisitors insist that the defenders of these prisoners committed acts of violence against them, Délicieux insists that they were only responding to the inquisitors' earlier acts of violence. While inquisitors allege that Délicieux has betrayed his ecclesiastical superiors in leading the people of Carcassonne against them, he alleges that these superiors had already betrayed these people by oppressing them. Délicieux employs the same basic vocabulary as the inquisitors—guilt and innocence, persecution and long-suffering, treason and loyalty—but he places these words in a different syntax so that what had been subjects become objects, what had been causes become effects, and what had been means become ends. The mirror image of an inquisitor, Délicieux finds the structures he needs to defend accused heretics in the structures that had been set up to prosecute them.

HERESY

To this day, it is not clear if the prisoners of the Wall in Carcassonne were heretics or Catholics. In his writings about these prisoners, Gui expresses confidence in their guilt because he trusts the procedures used by the inquisitors who found them to be guilty. As he sees it, the truth in such cases is discovered directly, through the inquisitors' investigation into the accused party's case. If many of the traditional protections for the accused party in Roman law are to be disregarded in prosecutions for heresy, as he asserts that they are, it is because these protections impede investigations of this crime. Those who object to the removal of these protections for accused parties, he suggests, are merely objecting to the prosecution of heretics and are thus themselves guilty of abetting their heresy. In contrast, in his statements about the prisoners, Délicieux expresses skepticism about their guilt because he distrusts the procedures used to establish that guilt. As he sees it, the truth is discovered dialectically, through the struggle between the accuser and the defendant. If the protections for the accused party should not be lifted, as he argues that they should not, it is because only when the accused party has an opportunity to rebut false allegations against himself that the truth can be ascertained. Those who want to remove protections for accused heretics, he insists, merely want to convict people, whether they are Catholic or heretical. The difference between Gui's and Délicieux's perspectives on the prisoners of the Wall reflects the difference between those who care most about convicting the guilty, even if some of the innocent are swept along with them, and those who care most about protecting the innocent, even if some of the guilty thus escape punishment.

From Gui's perspective, the prisoners of the Wall are guilty of heresy because they have been proven guilty by established judicial procedures. In a departure from Roman law, Gui observes in the *Practica*, the pope has allowed the names of eyewitnesses and by extension the nature of their testimony to be kept concealed from accused heretics because so many of these witnesses have ended up slain by the heretics' associates. Gui writes, "If it seems to the inquisitors that the witnesses giving testimony would be threatened with danger from the publication of their names, they can, in the presence of some people, utter the names of the witnesses not publicly but secretly."[25] In order for the inquisitors to obtain the testimony they need, Gui argues, they must be able to offer witnesses protection against reprisals for this testimony. In another departure from Roman law, Gui notes in the same work, the pope has permitted the use of torture to facilitate confessions in cases of heresy. Citing Innocent IV's *Ad extirpanda* of 1252, he writes of the Cathar Perfect that "Such heretics may be tormented by torture 'without the maiming of limbs and the danger of death, as brigands and murderers of souls and as thieves of the sacraments of God and the Christian faith.'"[26] Given that torture was regularly being used by this time against common felons like murderers and thieves to obtain their confessions and as a result their convictions, Gui reasons, with Innocent, all the more should it be used against the spiritual counterpart of these criminals, whose crimes are even more harmful to society. While both of these shifts in Roman judicial proceedings might seem to strengthen the hand of the inquisitor against the accused party, Gui expresses confidence that the inquisitor will be able to take advantage of this license without abusing it. The names of the witnesses may not be made public, but they are still shared among the judges and his associates. Torture may be used, but only, Gui clarifies, "on the recommendation of qualified persons, as the nature of the case and the status of the individual involved may require."[27] If Gui approves of the condemnation of the prisoners of the Wall, it is because these prisoners have been proven guilty through the testimony of eyewitnesses or through their own confessions. In *De fundatione et prioribus*, he affirms that the inquisitors and the bishop of Albi "condemned people . . . for the crime of heresy, which they had confessed and of which they had been convicted."[28] Once popular resistance prevented the inquisitors from prosecuting heretics in the dioceses of Albi, Pamiers, Carcassonne, and Toulouse as they wished, he declares, in an allegation he echoes in his sixty articles against Délicieux, heretics arrived in these regions and converted people to their errors, "as became evident later thanks to a legitimate inquisition [*per inquisitionem legitimam*] and the arrest of these heretics and their believers."[29] Heretics are identified as heretics not through the caprice of their judges but only through eyewitness testimony and confession, Gui believes, and they are thus convicted only through "legitimate inquisition."

From Délicieux's perspective, however, the prisoners of the Wall have not been proven guilty because the judicial procedures used to convict them were not appropriate. While accepting that the testimony of eyewitnesses can establish an accused party's guilt, Délicieux takes issue with the concealment of these witnesses' identities. In a remarkable address to Philip in Toulouse in January of 1304, he asserts not only that the prisoners could not have defended themselves in such circumstances but that no one could have defended himself in their place. "If Saint Peter and Saint Paul lived today, if they were accused of having adored heretics, and if they were tried for this adoration, as many people have been tried by some inquisitors," he asserts, "they would have no way of defending themselves."[30] Accused of having "adored" heretics (that is, of having performed the ritual *melioramentum*), Peter and Paul would ask who had made this accusation, but they would be refused this information. "If they asked the names of the witnesses . . . ," Délicieux states, "they would not be given to them."[31] These saints would then inquire as to the names, the ages, and the conditions of the heretics they were said to have adored and of the time when they were said to have adored them, but they would be denied these facts as well. In sum, Délicieux states, "They would not be told anything which would permit them to know who these heretics were whom they were accused of having adored."[32] Given the difficulty of rebutting such vague charges, Délicieux asserts, "No one can say ... that these Apostles, who are so holy, could defend themselves of such a stain before men."[33] Dismissing the value of the witnesses' testimony, Délicieux dismisses as well the value of the prisoners' confessions. He is said to have claimed that, "If Saint Peter and Saint Paul were before the inquisitors, despite what good Christians they were and are, the inquisitors would treat them so badly that they would make them confess heresy."[34] These saints would suffer the same fate as the people of Albi, who, he contends, "had confessed to having adored the heretics because of the force of torture."[35] While Gui cites the inquisitors' use of "legitimate inquisition" to justify the validity of their convictions, Délicieux asserts that this inquisition produced false testimony and false confessions and as a result invalid convictions.

As the prisoners of the Wall have been proven guilty of heresy by established judicial procedures, Gui alleges, those who deny this guilt, like Délicieux and his associates, do so not because they truly believe them to be innocent but because they are complicit in their crime. He attests, "At this time and during these years, there rose up many partisans of the heretics [hereticales] or members of heretical families [de genere hereticorum] from Albi and Cordes, allied in evil with those of Carcassonne."[36] He describes these insurgents as "alleging the iniquity of the inquisitors and the bishop and their proceedings [and] declaring the condemned parties to be justified and Catholic."[37] In terming the defenders of the prisoners "partisans of the heretics" and "members of heretical families," Gui indicates that these people take up their cause not out of any impersonal concern for justice but rather out of a very personal concern for the heretical sects or the heretical kin groups with which they are affiliated. These defenders object to the process of the trials only because they object to the results of these trials, he alleges, but they know that, if they protest the results instead of the process, they will themselves be subject to prosecution. After the arrival of the vidame and the archdeacon in Carcassonne—the period when Délicieux was most active—Gui states, "The partisans of the heretics began to raise their horns, to rage more gravely, and to rave even more."[38] He perceives these defenders as offering not rational objections to possibly flawed procedures but a taurine raging and raving against entirely legitimate methods. Any protest against the manner in which the inquisitors prosecute is necessarily, Gui attests, a protest against the fact that they prosecute at all.

Though there is no evidence to suggest that Délicieux was sympathetic with the Cathar heresy or with particular prisoners in the Wall, he does assume that, because the inquisitors' procedures can lead to false convictions, they have necessarily done so. He asserts that "he believed that these procedures were wicked and unjust, that the condemned people [of Albi] had been condemned unjustly, and that they were true and faithful Catholics."[39] Even if the procedures were wicked and unjust and even if the prisoners were condemned unjustly, it would not necessarily follow that the prisoners were "true and faithful Catholics." However coercive these procedures may have been, the people accused may still have been guilty and hence rightfully condemned. At another point, Délicieux backs away from this series of deductions, as if recognizing this logical problem: "He never said that [the prisoners of the Wall] were good and Catholic, for he never knew them. . . . He sometimes said, referring to what he had heard, that it was by torments that they had been forced to confess that for which they were condemned."[40] In general, however, Délicieux rejects not only the possibility that there are heretics among the prisoners but the possibility that there are heretics in the region. The transcripts report, "He said that he was certain that no heretic or heretical person had been found for forty years in this country, that is, in the Carcassès, the Albigeois, and the Toulousain."[41] Elsewhere, he acknowledges that there may be heretics in this area, but only a small number. He cites the Dominican William Peyre-Godin who, he claims, attested before the king "that in all of Languedoc there were only forty or fifty heretics and that they were around Albi, Cordes, or Carcassonne, or two leagues from there."[42] Denying or minimizing the existence of heretics in this region, Délicieux never expresses concern about the heretics who may still reside in their midst—and who, as the registers of Jacques Fournier reflect, would continue to circulate in the Midi until at least 1321. Though he purportedly opposes the inquisitors only for the procedures they use in pursuing heretics, he never gives any indication that he would support them if they used other procedures and hence never disproves Gui's complaint that he secretly opposes their pursuit of heretics altogether.

If Délicieux is so categorical in denying the existence of heretics in his region, it may be, as he claims, because he genuinely regards those accused of heresy as innocent. In a sermon in Carcassonne in August of 1303, Délicieux compared the prisoners of the Wall to innocent sheep: "One reads that there were once many rams in a beautiful green field irrigated with different streams and fountains. Every day two butchers went out of the city and seized the rams, sometimes one, sometimes two a day."[43] These butchers cut the throats of the rams, then sold their pelts and ate their flesh.

He asked his audience, "Lords, who are these fat rams except the men of the field, that is of the *Bourg* of Carcassonne, green because of the Roman Catholic faith, which is irrigated by temporal and spiritual riches? Who are these rams except the rich men of Carcassonne, rich and fat, who have their throats cut by the butchers, that is, by the inquisitors, who seize the rich men, sometimes one, sometimes two, on account of their wealth?"[44] In another sermon in Carcassonne during the same month, Délicieux compared the prisoners to innocent birds. He affirmed, "Lords, know that many doves were one day eating grain in a field. A sparrow-hawk, a raptor, came suddenly, lifted up a dove, took it away, and ate it. The next day he took another, and another even the third day."[45] Through the Christian iconography of sheep and doves, Délicieux represents the prisoners as meek, passive victims of violent, active predators. The prisoners apprehended by the inquisitors are no more deserving of their fate, he implies, than is a ram seized by a butcher or a dove seized by a sparrow-hawk. If the prisoners seem to be heretics, he argues, it is only because the inquisitors "make" them heretics. When Délicieux was preaching at the Franciscan convent in Albi, he was said to have warned the audience of the possibility that "someone wanted to make heretics [*facere hereticos*] out of you, and you were not heretics."[46] When he was preaching at the Franciscan convent in Limoux, he was similarly said to have affirmed "that the inquisitors had made a heretic [*faciebat hereticum*] out of Sir Arnold Embry of Limoux and that there would not remain a rich man in all this town of Limoux or in all the land whom the inquisitors would not make a heretic [*facerent . . . hereticum*], unless people strongly resist this."[47] "Heretics," as Délicieux uses this word, are not people who adhere to an erroneous faith but rather people who happen to be charged with doing so by inquisitors.

Yet, if Délicieux denies the existence of heretics, it may also be, he suggests—though never explicitly maintains—because he does not in fact believe that heresy should be prosecuted as a crime. In one of few times he acknowledges the possibility that there may be heretics around him, we are told, "He said sometimes to several different people that, if they felt themselves [*si sentiebant*] to be guilty of the crime of heresy, even if it cannot be proved, they should confess to the inquisitor."[48] At another point, when collecting money from his supporters, he advises, "If anyone feels himself [*sentiat se*] to be a heretic, even if it cannot be proved, let him abstain from contributing."[49] With these words, he admits that there may be heretics in this area and indeed even among the audience he is addressing. By assigning the responsibility of uncovering and eliminating this heresy, not to the inquisitor, but to the heretic himself (who may "feel himself [*sentiat se*]" to be a heretic), however, Délicieux suggests that this problem can best be handled, not within a judicial framework, but within an exclusively pastoral context. Heretics may be sinners for Délicieux, but they are sinners no different from lechers or gluttons. Just as a lecher or a glutton is allowed to confess his sins to his confessor without being summoned or prosecuted for this fault, he may be indicating, the heretic should be allowed to repent of his sin as he wishes. Délicieux's reluctance to pursue heretics judicially may be due to his reluctance to pursue thought crimes in general. Questioned about the conspiracy against Philip the Fair, he concedes that the plot was an evil idea, but he adds, "An evil idea which was never put into action should be punished not by man but only by God."[50] Similarly, asked about a book of necromancy found in his personal possessions, he avers that "To know or to see evil is not evil, but only to practice it. As he never used [the book] nor put faith in it, . . . he had no guilt in seeing and reading it."[51] In these passages, Délicieux distinguishes between evil thoughts and evil deeds, identifying only the latter as deserving of condemnation and leaving the former free from such prosecution. An erroneous religious belief was considered heretical not so much when it was entertained as when, having been corrected, it was pertinaciously defended; it became subject to prosecution, especially, when it was propounded to others or acted upon in some such way. Still, given that heresy is at its core an evil thought and not an evil action, Délicieux appears to consider it something which should be dealt with in an internal, penitential tribunal, and not in an external, judicial one.

DEFAMATION

As Gui and Délicieux disagree about the prisoners' guilt of heresy, they disagree as well about the inquisitors' guilt of persecution. Both friars acknowledge that the inquisitors condemned the prisoners to the Wall; that Délicieux preached, in often fiery language, to the people against these condemnations; and that the common people then liberated the prisoners from the Wall and ransacked the properties of the Dominicans and their supporters, but the order they impose upon this series of actions differs. As Gui sees it, Délicieux has defamed the inquisitors and the bishop and in doing so has aroused the population against them. As Délicieux sees it, the inquisitors and the bishop have defamed this population and have thus provoked the violence from which they now suffer. While, for Gui, Délicieux and his allies constitute the subject of this violence and the inquisitors and the bishop the object, for Délicieux, the inquisitors and the bishop serve as the subject of the disturbance and the people of this area the object. Though both sides agree as to the sequence of the events that took place in Carcassonne in August of 1303, they disagree as to the causality behind that sequence.

According to Gui, Délicieux defamed the inquisitors and the bishop by spreading false rumors about them. In *De fundatione et prioribus*, he describes the friar and his cohorts as "calumnying and impugning in many ways their sentences and judgments."[52] In the sixty charges, he alleges that "Brother Bernard Délicieux publicly and privately defamed the inquisitors and their trials and the sentences given by them and by the lord bishop of Albi against people guilty of heresy."[53] In particular, Gui objects to the misrepresentations he sees Délicieux as having made of Registers X and XI. Though the testimony contained in these registers was generally regarded as unreliable, to the point that, over the years, three popes authorized inquiries into it, Gui attributes the problem with this testimony to corrupted versions of these registers publicized by Délicieux and his associates, which, he alleges, included the names of people more numerous and more orthodox than the original copies: "They spread throughout towns and castles certain false scrolls fabricated in the name of the inquisitors and the bishop, in which were said to be contained, to an incredible number, the names of many living and dead people who were innocent and blameless."[54] In addition to misrepresenting Registers X and XI, Délicieux also misrepresented the Accord of 1299, Gui maintains. "He exposed many things as being contained in this instrument . . . which do not contain the truth,"[55] he writes. He "much exaggerat[ed] the words of the abjuration."[56] It was not only the documents of the Dominican inquisitors but also their characters that Délicieux is said to have maligned. Gui attests that the Friar Minor attempted to persuade a Jewish servant of his to claim that Fulk of Saint-Georges had extorted money from Jews. In all of these allegations, Gui echoes the author of the first set of charges, who asserts that Délicieux told his audiences that, "With truth or with falsity, they should do all they can to ensure that, at the least, the Friars Preachers lose the Office of the Inquisition of Heretical Depravity."[57] As Gui sees it, Délicieux spoke falsely about the Dominican inquisitors and the bishop, making them appear to be persecutors of large numbers of innocent Catholics (and innocent Jews), when they knew full well they were not such persecutors, in order to make them lose their good reputations.

According to Délicieux, however, it is not that he has defamed the inquisitors and the bishop but rather that the inquisitors and the bishop have defamed the people of Carcassonne and nearby towns by charging them, falsely, with heresy. While Gui depicts Délicieux and the others as "calumnying" the inquisitors and the bishop, Délicieux depicts these ecclesiastics as having "calumnied" this populace. When the Dominicans insisted that the consuls of Carcassonne sign the Accord of 1299, implicating the entire population of this town in heresy, for example, Délicieux claims, "These Preachers . . . committed a great calumny and falsity against a large community."[58] Similarly, while Gui represents Délicieux and his fellows as "defaming" the inquisitors and the bishop, Délicieux represents these ecclesiastics as having "defamed" the people of this area. He describes their region as "a land which was to such an extent defamed [*diffamata*] by the testimony of these inquisitors."[59] He warns the residents of this region, "Your dishonor [*infamia*] has stretched to different parts of the world, to the point where no one going outside the diocese dares to admit himself to be from the Albigeois."[60] Given Délicieux's concern for the sufferings the people have endured as a result of the inquisitors' defamation of their orthodoxy, he shows little concern for the sufferings the inquisitors are said to have endured as a result of the people's complaints about this defamation. "As for the inquisitors, they had been defamed by many people for many years before Brother Bernard had anything to do with it,"[61] the records paraphrase him as having affirmed. Insofar as he speaks out against the inquisitors, he suggests, he is only repeating what many people had already been saying about them, for a long time, as a result of the inquisitors' own misdeeds. It is the defamation of innocent citizens by the inquisitors and bishop that deserves sympathy, he maintains, and not the so-called "defamation" of the inquisitors and bishop by those citizens' defenders, who merely point out their crimes.

In objecting to Délicieux's and his associates' "defamations" of the inquisitors and the bishop, however, Gui objects not only to the fact that they spoke out falsely against these ecclesiastics but also to the fact that they spoke out against them at all and that, in doing so, they aroused the populace against them. Through their "false suggestions and defamations,"[62] he alleges, "They aroused [*concitarunt*] . . . all the land against the inquisitors and the bishop."[63] In the sixty charges, Gui claims not only that Délicieux aroused the people against the inquisitors and the bishop but that he sought to do so: he preached to the people "to arouse [*ad concitandum*] their hearts under the appearance of good,"[64] "to arouse [*ad concitandum*] them against the Office of the Inquisition, the bishop of Albi, and the inquisitors,"[65] and "so that [*ut*] they would take action against the bishop and inquisitors."[66] It is not just the content of Délicieux's and his allies' complaints but the purpose ["*ad* . . ." or "*ut* . . ."] to which these complaints are being put that is troubling to him. Whatever may be the truthfulness of Délicieux's objections to certain inquisitors or bishops, Gui argues that he should not have acted in such a way as to harm the effectiveness of the Inquisition. If Délicieux speaks in order to arouse the people against the inquisitors and the bishop, as Gui asserts that he does, it is because he seeks ultimately to impede the work of the Inquisition through this popular unrest. In his *Practica*, Gui defines favorers of heresy as those "who impede [*impediunt*] the Office of the Inquisition and oppose its operations."[67] In *De fundatione et prioribus*, Gui cites "the impediments [*impedimenta*] Brother Bernard Délicieux brought and raised up against the Office of the Inquisition and the inquisitors of heretical depravity, arousing towns and peoples against them."[68] He claims that Délicieux became "the principal adversary, impeder [*impeditor*], and detractor of the inquisitors."[69] Even if the illocutionary value of Délicieux's and his allies' words may be true, Gui seems to be saying, their perlocutionary effect—in impeding the proper functioning of the Inquisition—remains undesirable.

In contrast to Gui, Délicieux claims that it is not himself and his associates who have aroused the people against the inquisitors and the bishop but rather the inquisitors and the bishop who have aroused the people against themselves. Délicieux developed this point most fully in an *exemplum* at the end of a sermon he made in the Franciscan convent in Carcassonne: "It happened that, in a certain town, there was a worthy man [*probus homo*], who, from what was commonly said, hardly ever or never could become angry or could be aroused to anger. And then some scoffers or mockers said, 'Let us do something so that this worthy man will be aroused [*concitabatur*] to anger.'"[70] At first, these troublemakers told him, "You are a murderer,"[71] but the worthy man only replied, "God spare you."[72] Then they said, "You are a thief, you are an adulterer, you are a murderer,"[73] but still he answered, "May God pardon you."[74] Finally, one of the taunters accused him of being a heretic. Délicieux recounts of the worthy man that now, "Moved to anger, he said that he lied by the throat, and he struck forcefully with his fist him who said this."[75] With this *exemplum*, Délicieux suggests that it was not he who aroused the people of the region against the inquisitors and the bishop but rather the inquisitors and the bishop who aroused these people with their verbal attacks upon them and, in particular, with their accusation of heresy. He acknowledges that the people did strike out against the inquisitor and the bishop—the worthy man does punch his interlocutor—but he maintains that this violence was not an aggressive act upon an innocent victim, as Gui would have it, but a defensive act against a guilty tormentor. As we have seen, Gui compares Délicieux's allies to horned animals who rage and rave: "The partisans of the heretics began to raise their horns, to rage more gravely, and to rave even more." As we have also seen, Délicieux compares these people to horned animals as well, namely, to rams being taken away, one by one, for the slaughter, yet he represents their eventual use of these horns quite differently. He quotes the rams as saying to each other, "But we have horns. Let us rise up all together against the butchers, let us hit them with our horns, let us chase them from the field, and we will thus save our lives and the lives of those close to us."[76] As Délicieux depicts these beasts, they use their horns, not because their inner nature has prompted them to do so, but rather because an outer threat has pushed them in this direction. Both the worthy man and the rams are inherently gentle, placid creatures who turn to violence only when another's attack gives them no other option. As Délicieux explains, "He did not arouse [*concitavit*] the people of Carcassonne against the inquisitors, but it was the false instrument that the inquisitors had made against the whole of the *Bourg* of Carcassonne . . . which aroused [*concitavit*] this whole."[77]

As Délicieux's statements about heretics make one wonder if he believes the prisoners of the Wall to be innocent of heresy, as he claims, or if he believes that no one, whether innocent or guilty, should be prosecuted for heresy, his statements about the Inquisition make one wonder if he simply wants the inquisitors who convicted these prisoners to be corrected, as he maintains, or if he actually wants all inquisitors to cease from functioning effectively. On the one hand, the text of Délicieux's condemnation states, echoing Gui's words, "Though, until the time of [Délicieux's] speeches, the inquisitor of Carcassonne was able to exercise his Office freely and peacefully, since then . . . the community was too aroused and scandalized [*concitata . . . et scandalisata*] for the Office of the Inquisition to function as before and was, on the contrary, impeded in many ways."[78] If the Inquisition ceased to be able to pursue heretics during the time of Délicieux's campaign and for years thereafter, this text suggests that this inactivity was the objective and the result of this campaign. On the other hand, Délicieux insists, "It was never his intention to do anything against the Office of the Inquisition. Rather, it was always his will to promote the honor of this Office.'"[79] While, according to his opponents' hypotactic logic, it was because Délicieux spoke out against the Inquisition that the Inquisition ceased to be able to function, according to Délicieux's paratactic logic, he may have spoken out against the Inquisition and the Inquisition may have ceased to be able to function, but there is no causal connection between these two events. For Délicieux's opponents, the "scandal" of the Inquisition was the allegation that innocent people had been falsely convicted of heresy and imprisoned and the weakening of this Office that followed upon this allegation, yet, for Délicieux, the scandal is that these people had been thus convicted and imprisoned.

TREASON

As Gui and Délicieux disagree about the guilt of the prisoners in the Wall and hence about the legitimacy of the movement to release them from confinement, they disagree about the responsibility of the inquisitors, the bishop, and Délicieux in this controversy. Both friars acknowledge that one should remain faithful to the civic or ecclesiastical organizations to which one belongs, both see themselves and their associates as having remained faithful to these organizations, but both see the other side as having proven treacherous toward these groups. According to Gui, the community of Carcassonne is to be identified with the ecclesiastical authorities who preside over it, so that anyone who rebels against these authorities' power and thus causes "sedition" is to be considered a traitor. According to Délicieux, however, the community of this town is to be identified with the people over whom these authorities preside, so that anyone who opposes the best interest of these people is to be regarded as the traitor instead. Insofar as Délicieux differs from Gui and his fellow judges, it is not only because he resists prosecuting heretics and seeks to prevent the Inquisition from doing so, but because he conceives of the community to which he belongs, not as the universal community of the Church, with which these Catholic clerics identify, but as the local community of Carcassonne, to which his fellow citizens of this town, clerical or lay, adhere.

For Gui, Délicieux is a traitor because he revolted against the legitimate authorities of his region and led others to do so as well. In *De fundatione et prioribus*, as we recall, Gui writes that, at this time, "There rose up [*insurrexerunt*] many partisans of the heretics or members of heretical families ... against the Office of the Inquisition, the inquisitors of heretical depravity, and also Lord Bernard of Castenet, the bishop of Albi."[80] He observes that they pillaged and destroyed fifteen of the inquisitors' allies' houses in the *Bourg* of Carcassonne and thus "fomented in the people the greatest sedition."[81] In the sixty articles against Délicieux, Gui charges that this friar, in particular, made "seditions and arousals of the people against the bishop and many people,"[82] that he brought "a seditious multitude"[83] of people from Albi to Carcassonne, and that he addressed to the people "venomous and seditious words."[84] In using the language of "uprising" (*insurrectio*) and "sedition" (*seditio*) to describe the events in Carcassonne, Gui makes clear that he regards the inquisitors and the bishop as the legitimate authorities in this town and Délicieux and his cohorts, who rise up against them, as illegitimate insurgents. To rebel against one's lawful rulers is, for Gui, shameful. He writes of this band, "I reckon it better to refrain from speaking, let alone writing, one by one, about the evils they committed and inflicted upon the Inquisition, the friars, and their friends, on account of the honor of the multitude, which cannot be entirely excused. . . . It would be shameful to say more about it."[85] While Délicieux and his followers rose up against the Dominicans and their allies, the "multitude" of the population of Carcassonne also bears some responsibility for their actions, which they tacitly supported. The community of Carcassonne is, for Gui, defined by the inquisitors and the bishop, who exercise lawful authority over the people, and to revolt against these ecclesiastics is to revolt against that community in a disgraceful manner.

While Gui regards him as a traitor, Délicieux regards the inquisitors, the bishop, and their allies as traitors in turn. In a sermon in the Franciscan convent of Carcassonne on the theme of "Seeing the city, Jesus wept over it,"[86] Délicieux is said to have expressed regret to his congregation about "your faith and your reputation, which had been taken from you by others, namely, by two traitors who wear the habit of the Preachers, that is, Brother Fulk and Brother Nicholas."[87] Nicholas of Abbeville and Fulk of Saint-Georges are traitors because they have accused the inhabitants of their town of favoring heretics and have excommunicated them as a result, but they are not, for Délicieux, the only traitors here. He added, in reference to the Accord of 1299, "Know that I found a treacherous instrument in which some traitors of the town confessed on their behalf and on the behalf of all the town that they are heretics, and they had themselves and all the town absolved of heresy by Brother Fulk in this instrument."[88] The consuls who signed the Accord of 1299 are traitors because they accepted the validity of the inquisitors' accusation and excommunication of their neighbors. Later in the sermon, he referred again to "the traitor inquisitors and the traitor consuls."[89] According to Bernard Trèves, he even called out in a loud voice in the church, "I see here some traitors!"[90] and pointed his finger at various individuals in the audience. As Délicieux represents the situation, the traitors are not himself and his company, who have spoken out against the inquisitors and the bishop, but rather the inquisitors, the bishop, and their allies, who have acted against the best interest of the people. While, for Gui, the dishonor of Carcassonne lies in that which its citizens have done to deserve excommunication, for Délicieux this dishonor lies in the excommunication itself. According to witnesses at the trial, his concern was not with the citizens whose houses had been ransacked by this population but with the people of Carcassonne who had been defamed by those citizens. Philip Perry recalls Délicieux commenting upon those citizens: "See, those whose houses have been damaged request an indemnity for four broken tiles. They should not request an indemnity but should ask mercy from the community of the town and unite with her."[91] While, for Gui, it was the rioters who did wrong in raiding these houses, for Délicieux, it was the homeowners who did wrong in breaking ranks with the community and in allying themselves with its enemies. While, for Gui, the community of Carcassonne is defined by the inquisitors and the bishop, for Délicieux, it is defined by the people, and those who betray this people by impugning their orthodoxy betray the community as a whole.

For Gui, Délicieux is "seditious" because this Friar Minor is ultimately concerned not with the well-being of the community in Carcassonne but with his own well-being and in particular with his own financial and social prosperity. It is true that Délicieux did receive a salary from the town of Carcassonne for his labors on its behalf and that, in 1307, he sued the consuls for failing to pay him, as their predecessors had done. It is true as well that he urged the citizens of this town to contribute liberally to his campaign against the inquisitors and the bishop, to the point off selling their houses, their gardens, and their vineyards. Even if these citizens were left with a quarter of what they now possessed, he maintained, in the end this quarter would be worth more than all of their current property because all they now own is vulnerable to ecclesiastical confiscation. In the sixty articles against Délicieux, Gui attests, "For many years, Brother Bernard pursued the business assumed by the people of Carcassonne, Albi, Cordes, and some other towns against the bishop and the inquisitors . . . , and he received stipends, great fees, and much money from these towns for the pursuit of this business."[92] Presenting Délicieux's fundraising in this matter-of-fact manner, Gui suggests that the friar sought money not as a means toward succeeding in his campaign against the inquisitors and the bishop but as an end in and of itself. Elsewhere, he couples Délicieux's defense of the heretics with the fact that he was "remunerated to this effect by the people of Carcassonne, Albi, and Cordes,"[93] as if this defense were motivated, at least in part, by this remuneration. While Gui stresses the desire for financial gain as Délicieux's motivation, the author of the earlier set of articles against him stresses his desire for power: "He had himself named procurer, defender, and plaintiff of these people against the bishop and inquisitors by the inhabitants of these people."[94] Again, presenting Délicieux's appointment to these offices so forthrightly, the author indicates that he sought these positions not as a means toward relieving the injustice caused by the inquisitors and the bishop but as an end in itself. Délicieux may present himself as concerned with others' well-being, yet Gui warns, he is actually concerned with his own wealth and prestige.

While Gui considers Délicieux to be a traitor because he is more concerned with his own financial and social well-being than with the well-being of the community, Délicieux considers the inquisitors and the bishop to be traitors because they are similarly covetous and ambitious. It is true that the inquisitors reserved the right to confiscate the property of condemned heretics for the benefit of the royal crown. In his *Practica*, Gui writes, "The power of inquisitors in punishing is strong and excellent. They can punish . . . in the substance of goods and things,"[95] and he quotes Innocent IV as ordering secular leaders to confiscate the goods of such heretics in order to prevent them from supporting their sect. Just as the judges claimed that he sought financial gain, Délicieux claims that the inquisitors and the bishop undertook these confiscations in order to obtain riches. In his parable of the rams, we recall, Délicieux asserts that the inquisitors pursue the wealthy citizens of Carcassonne not because they are heretical but because they are wealthy. He asks, "Who are these rams except the rich men of Carcassonne, rich and fat, who have their throats cut by the butchers, that is, by the inquisitors, who seize the rich men . . . on account of their wealth?" A witness cites him as having alleged that the inquisitors and the bishop forced innocent people to confess to heresy "in order to extort money from them."[96] Just as his judges claimed that he sought power, Délicieux claims that the inquisitors and the bishop sought political importance. He reports having heard that, at the General Chapter of the Dominicans, it was resolved that "The order would retain the procedures and acts of the inquisitors, whatever they were, . . . so that it would retain power in those parts where there was the Inquisition."[97] In addition, he relates having heard that the inquisitor at Carcassonne at one point wanted to return to France because he could not find anyone in the town worth accusing of heresy but that two other friars warned him, "If the inquisitor goes away, we will no longer be esteemed and feared in these parts. We must thus find a way to have ourselves feared in these parts and, as a consequence, esteemed."[98] It was in order to be thus "feared and esteemed," Délicieux asserts, that the inquisitors made the charges they made. Peter Prous reports that he once asked Délicieux how the inquisitors could be so wicked as to condemn good Christians for heresy and that Délicieux replied that "The inquisitors did it because they wanted to dominate the land."[99] Just as Gui and the other judges perceived him as seeking money and power not as a means but as an end, Délicieux perceives the inquisitors and the bishop as using the pursuit of heretics as a pretext through which they can enrich and strengthen themselves.

The same model of thought that inquisitors used to condemn heretics, Délicieux uses to condemn the citizens of Carcassonne who, he believes, have betrayed the town. As we have seen, inquisitors justified the prosecution of heretics by quoting Christ's parable of the wheat and the cockle and by comparing the angels' labor at the Last Judgment in uprooting the weeds from the good grain to their labor now in uprooting heretics from the good Catholics. During his trial, Délicieux acknowledges having quoted this parable during the troubles of Carcassonne, and he claims to have interpreted the cockle, as inquisitors did at this time, as heretics: "By 'weeds,' I understood the heretics, exhorting that they be expelled if they be found."[100] Several witnesses testify, however, that, when Délicieux cited the parable to them, he glossed this passage very differently. Bernard Trèves recalls, for example, "He called 'weeds' the men of the *Bourg* of Carcassonne who were commonly reputed as favorable to the Inquisition and others who consented to the [the Accord of 1299]."[101] William Rabaud likewise attests that Délicieux meant by "weeds" those in the *Bourg* who favored the inquisitors and who had signed this Accord. Like an inquisitor, Délicieux uses this parable to illustrate the problem of wicked people living among good people and the necessity of these wicked people being separated from their good neighbors and punished. Unlike an inquisitor, however, he identifies these evildoers not as heretics but as supporters of those who pursued heretics. As we have seen, in addition, inquisitors made clear that, should heretics wish to repent of their errors and return to the Church, they would be welcomed for doing so,[102] but that, should they not wish to do so, they would be abandoned to the secular arm and their descendents prohibited from occupying public office. In his addresses to the people of Carcassonne, Délicieux echoed this language of repentance and punishment. According to Philip Perry, he stated that those whose houses were damaged during the riots "should ask mercy from the community of the town and unite with her, for, if they did this, I would do what I could to have them received with mercy."[103] Should these citizens not repent of their treachery, however, he warns, "We should proceed to seize them, kill them, and destroy them and all their lineage, so that none of their brood remains in the *Bourg*."[104] In distinguishing sinners from good people, in offering these sinners a chance to repent, and in threatening them with destruction if they do not choose to do so, Délicieux follows the judicio-penitential model of the inquisitors of his time, yet he applies this model not to heretics but to the inquisitors' allies.

The same model of thought that inquisitors had used to extol their fellow inquisitors Délicieux uses to extol himself, for opposing the inquisitors and their allies. When he was giving the sermon on "Seeing the city, Jesus wept over it," he is said to have stopped to weep for as long as it would take to say *Miserere mei Deus*, wiping his eyes with the sleeve of his habit. After having wept, we are told, he said, "Thus I am Jesus Christ, on the mission of Jesus, that is, as your savior. Christ was anointed by the grace of the Holy Spirit, which incited me many years ago to the defense of your faith and your reputation."[105] However much Délicieux asks his followers to sacrifice, he claims to be ready to forsake far more himself. One article condemning him reports, "In Toulouse, in the presence of the lord king with his counselors, noblemen, and prelates, he said that he had labored for many years so that the business and the actions of the Inquisition would come to light, and that he had shouted so much that his throat was made hoarse because of it."[106] Another article cites him as stating, "If I spend your money, it is not surprising because all things I have, whether they are books or other things, I have spent in pursuing this business, and I have become someone who has nothing. But it does not matter to me, for I am ready to expose my body itself."[107] He exhorts the people not to fear death, it is reported, "because Brother Bernard wanted to be the first martyr."[108] He has exhausted himself laboring for the benefit of the people of Carcassonne and the neighboring region, he has preached to them until he lost his voice, he has given up all that he owns, and he is ready to give up his life itself. Like the inquisitors before him, Délicieux affirms his zeal for the cause for which he is fighting and his willingness to die for that cause, as Christ himself did. Unlike these inquisitors, however, the good for which he is willing to die is not that of the Church but rather that of the town.

If one wants to understand why it was that Délicieux, though inhabiting the same clerical culture as Gui, became not an inquisitor but the scourge of inquisitors, it is tempting to attribute his difference to his being a Franciscan.[109] While Franciscans often served as inquisitors themselves, in everything Délicieux did in support of accused heretics, whether it be sheltering them, when living, in the convent, burying them, when dead, within its walls, or opposing the Dominicans who sought them out, he received the full support of his brethren.[110] As Gui notes, sadly, "Out of honor for this order, I will be silent about the names of several other members of his order, who caused harm in many a way, who behaved themselves badly, and who aroused many people against the Office of the Inquisition."[111] In later years, when Délicieux resurfaces as the defender of another group of people accused of heresy, it is as the defender of the Spiritual Franciscans. In 1317, after the Spirituals of Narbonne and Béziers had risen up against their Conventual superiors, John XXII released the bull *Quorumdam exigit*, which declared that, while poverty, which the Spirituals so espoused, may be a virtue, obedience is an even greater one.¹¹² Though most of these Spirituals bowed to John's will, four stood firm and in 1318 were burned for their beliefs in Marseilles.¹¹³ Yet, while Délicieux might understandably sympathize with yet another popularly supported movement persecuted by ecclesiastical authorities, it is difficult to see in his defense of the Spirituals or of other accused heretics any specifically Franciscan, or even Christian, ethos. Spurning the logic of Christian patience, by which one humbly submits to one's persecutors, Délicieux affirms instead the logic of civic justice, by which one proudly stands up to them. Gerald of Meaux quotes Délicieux as advising his audience, "If someone calls you a heretic, defend yourself if you wish, for you have the good right to defend yourself,"¹¹⁴ and others cite him as expressing contempt for those who did not exercise this right. When the consuls of Limoux declared that they would not join with the people of Carcassonne in opposing the inquisitors, for example, John Laures reports, "Brother Bernard told these consuls that they always wanted to remain in the mud like pigs."¹¹⁵ Someone who has been attacked has a right to defend himself against this attack and, indeed, should defend himself, if he is going to act as a man and not as a pig. In general, in his efforts on the accused heretics' behalf, Délicieux distinguishes himself, not in his meekness, humility, and gentleness, but in his audacity, conviction, and courage. With his horses, his servants, and (according to William of Villanova) his mistress, Délicieux shows little inclination toward an ascetical life. His concerns are judicial, perhaps political, but not, at least in any ordinary sense, spiritual.

If the context of Délicieux's hostility toward inquisitors is not to be found in the Franciscan order to which he belongs, it may be found instead in his Catalan friends and the Mediterranean port towns from which they came. During his trial, Délicieux refers to having obtained a book "from Master Raymond Lull, a Catalan of Majorca."¹¹⁶ He describes this book (probably Lull's *Ars brevis* or *Arbor scientiae*) as "a book which bears in it a general table for all fields of knowledge and certain propositions related to the principles of those fields, and a book in which the articles of the Catholic faith are proven by necessary reasons."¹¹⁷ He may have met the Illuminated Doctor in Montpellier between 1285 and 1298, when Lull's patron James II was living there in exile, and may have seen him again in Majorca itself in 1304, when Délicieux was conspiring with James's son Ferrand. As a native of Majorca, Lull hailed from a country which had been ruled by Muslims until 1229, three years before his birth, and which continued to possess a significant Arabic-speaking community.[118] Fluent in Arabic himself, he founded schools in Majorca and in Sicily to encourage the learning of Arabic and other oriental languages. Though he became a Franciscan missionary and traveled three times to Tunis to convert Muslims to the Christian faith, he clearly enjoyed engaging in dialogue with unbelievers. In his *Liber de gentili et tribus sapientibus*, he portrays a Christian, a Muslim, and a Jew as debating the relative merits of their faiths, with such emphasis upon the common principles behind the three creeds that a stranger, listening to them, is surprised to learn that they are not of the same religion.[119] In his *Libre de contemplació*, he depicts heretics as possessing human nature, like that which Jesus Christ assumed, and he argues that they should not be put to death.[120] The reason shared by all human beings, the rational principles shared by all fields of human knowledge, and the common ground created by these fields of knowledge were, for Lull, more significant than the differences of doctrine separating them. Friends with Lull, Délicieux was also friends, as we have seen, with Arnold of Villanova, whom he also refers to during his trial as "a friend, Arnold of Villanova, alias the Catalan."[121] Like Lull, Arnold knew Arabic (as well as Hebrew), was familiar with Arabic learning, especially medicine, natural science, and philosophy, and promoted such studies among Christians. Like Lull, as well, Arnold had a reputation as an alchemist, though, unlike his fellow Catalan, this reputation was in fact warranted.[122] While Christians of the Middle Ages tolerated Muslims and Jews in a way in which they did not tolerate heretics, the fact that both Lull and Arnold evidently delighted in their contacts with Muslim and Jewish thinkers, the fact that they seemed to value intellectual over confessional connections, and the fact that they too made statements that brought charges of heresy down upon themselves or their followers suggest that they inhabited a small, philosophical world with Délicieux where the prosecution of deviants in the faith did not rank among the highest priorities.

CHAPTER SEVEN

Nicholas Eymerich: Toward the Spanish Inquisition

In June of 1758, the abbé André Morellet was browsing the library of the house where he was staying in Rome. As his host was an auditor of the Rota, one of the Church's highest courts, there were on his shelves various works of theology and canon law, including a large, folio volume entitled *Directorium inquisitorum*,[1] which had been composed by the Aragonese inquisitor Nicholas Eymerich (c. 1320–99)[2] in Avignon in 1376 and then amplified by the Spanish canonist Francis Peña (1540–1612) in 1578.[3] Opening up this book, Morellet was appalled by the account of inquisitorial procedures he found in its final section. In 1762, he published a selection of what he deemed to be "the most revolting"[4] passages from the third section of the book, translated into French and organized in the form of an actual trial. In editing this work, he reports, "I forbade myself all reflection because the text alone would suggest that which I could have made."[5] His contemporaneous *philosophes* had already developed a negative opinion of the Inquisition from its recent victims' published accounts, yet now, for the first time, in reading this volume, they felt their view to be confirmed from an inquisitor's own perspective. Jean Le Rond d'Alembert referred to the *Directorium inquisitorum* edited by Morellet as "this monument of atrocity and ridiculousness, which renders humanity at once so odious and so pitiful."[6] Voltaire informed a correspondent, "I am reading with edification the manual of the Inquisition, and I am very angry that Candide killed only one inquisitor."[7] It was presumably Morellet's abridgement and not Eymerich's original text (which survives only in folio or quarto sizes) that Edgar Allen Poe had in mind when his narrator discovers "a small octavo volume of the *Directorium inquisitorum*, by the Dominican Eymeric de Gironne"[8] in the library of the sinister House of Usher. From the perspective of its eighteenth- and nineteenth-century readers, Eymerich's *Directorium inquisitorum* constituted not only the most representative work of the Inquisition but the most explicit account of its terrible practices.

Despite the forbidding aspect of the inquisitor in his manual, Eymerich himself did not experience much success in this role. When he was fourteen years old, he entered the Dominican convent in his hometown of Gerona, in Catalonia, where he proved sufficiently promising to be sent to the University of Paris for his doctorate in theology. In 1357, at the age of thirty-seven, he was appointed inquisitor general of Aragon, with a jurisdiction that included the kingdom of Valencia and the county of Barcelona. In the early fourteenth century, Cathars, Waldensians, Fraticelli, Spiritual Franciscans, and a few Pseudo-Apostles had all found safety from persecution by traveling across the Pyrenees, yet, by Eymerich's time, only a few Waldensians and Fraticelli remained. An active inquisitor like himself had to turn his attention instead to the apparent errors of the Dominicans Vincent Ferrer and Raymond of Tarraga, the Franciscans Nicholas of Calabria and Peter Bonageta, and the followers of the late Raymond Lull, who were then sponsoring chairs in the Illuminated Doctor's name at the universities of Barcelona and Valencia.[9] Presumably because he was pursuing members of the clerical elite instead of the lay masses, Eymerich often found his prosecutions blocked by these individuals' supporters, whether in the papacy, the curia, or the royal house of Aragon. Partial to the Lullists himself, King Peter IV of Aragon for a time prevented Eymerich from serving as inquisitor and finally in 1376 compelled him to flee to the papal court in Avignon. Returning to Aragon five years later, Eymerich renewed his campaign against the Lullists and eluded Peter's attempts to have him banished only with the help of Peter's son John. After John succeeded Peter in 1386, however, the new king decided that his father had been right about this fractious Dominican after all and forced him to withdraw once more to the papal court. It was only in 1397, after John had died, that Eymerich was able to return to Aragon, to his old convent in Gerona, where he passed away two years later. Whether because of Eymerich's unwarranted attacks upon Lullists and other respected Catholics or because of secular and ecclesiastical authorities' unwarranted protection of those heretics, Eymerich was unable to eradicate the errors he saw around him as he would have liked.[10] It would not be until the ascent of Ferdinand of Aragon and Isabella of Castile as *los reyes católicos* and the appointment of Thomas of Torquemada as Grand Inquisitor in the 1470s that the Spanish Inquisition would become the feared Holy Office of legend.

However ineffective Eymerich may have been as an inquisitor, his *Directorium inquisitorum* would provide the judicial foundation of the Inquisitions of the early modern era, especially once it had been edited by Peña. The later cleric hailed from the same Aragonese region as Eymerich—from Villarroya de los Pinares, near Saragossa—and he too obtained a doctorate in theology as well as one in canon and civil law. Yet, instead of serving as an inquisitor in Spain, as Eymerich had done, with all the controversy that position brought with it, Peña served as an advisor in inquisitorial and other canonical matters in Rome, with the relatively tranquil life that position could afford. As a jurist, he occupied himself preparing new editions of the most important texts in canon law, such as the *Corpus iuris canonici* and Gratian's *Concordia discordantium canonum*. It appears to have been at the request of Pope Gregory XIII and the Inquisition that he undertook a new edition of the *Directorium inquisitorum*, copies of which he found in the papal and inquisitorial libraries.[11] On the one hand, the objects of inquisitorial prosecution had changed significantly since the fourteenth century, when Eymerich had written this manual. While the old, high medieval heresies had died off, new, late medieval and early modern heresies, including Lollardy, Hussitism, and, most importantly, Protestantism, had replaced them. Witchcraft, which had been a marginal issue for medieval inquisitors, now assumed a central status. On the other hand, the procedures inquisitors used in prosecuting deviants in the faith and the justifications they cited in using these procedures had not changed markedly over the years. While Peña added commentaries to the sections of Eymerich's book, addressing recent heresies and recent papal and conciliar statements about them, he retained the basic structure of his predecessor's book and used this new information primarily to bolster his points. As Edward Peters observes, "He sometimes seems to write in a timeless world of institutional regularity in which he and Eymerich . . . are not separated by periods of time or changing relations with the Church and between the Church and other powers."[12] Whatever differences one might find between the medieval inquisitors, who included Eymerich in their number, and the early modern Roman and Spanish Inquisitions, which Peña's version of Eymerich's manual helped shape in seven editions between 1578 and 1607, it was the continuity in the prosecution of heretics between these two eras that Peña and these later Inquisitions most sought to emphasize.

If Eymerich's *Directorium inquisitorum*, with Peña's commentaries, stands out for us today, as it did for the Enlightenment *philosophes*, it is, in its explicit defense of the harsh treatment of accused parties. Eymerich was far from the first inquisitor to deceive and torture accused parties or to burn them at the stake once they had been proven guilty, but he was the first we have considered to address and justify these practices at length. The accused party represents, for Eymerich, not a passive, powerless object of the inquisitor's violence but rather an active, powerful subject of his own deeds, because Eymerich conceives of him principally not in terms of his body, which may admittedly undergo suffering, but in terms of his soul, which remains free. Will the accused party repent of his heresy and return to the Church or will he remain obstinate in his error? Will he remain closed off from God and from the inquisitor who stands in for him or will he open himself up to the mercy of these eternal and temporal judges? What is occurring during the trial, as Eymerich imagines it, is not so much an encounter between an inquisitor and an accused party as an encounter between God and the accused party, where the inquisitor serves as the intercessor through whose intervention this connection takes place. While, for most modern readers, an accused party who is imprisoned, tortured, and then burned possesses no agency worth speaking of, for Eymerich this individual remains dangerous, threatening to elude the inquisitor's interrogations, to withstand his tortures, and to disrupt his general sermon. In his additions to the text, Peña supports Eymerich's vision of what is happening during the trial and, indeed, exchanges Eymerich's medieval reticence in speaking about the possibly questionable aspects of the inquisitor's behavior for a new, early modern candor. The spectacle of the accused party in judgment is, ultimately, for Eymerich and for his commentator, not the spectacle of a body consigned by an other to be imprisoned in perpetuity or charred on a pyre, but that of a soul deciding for itself whether it is to be reunited with God or forever alienated from him.

DECEPTION

As Eymerich represents him, the accused party is brought into the inquisitor's chamber. He may have been apprehended and imprisoned a few days beforehand, so that he is now being dragged forth in irons and shackles from his cell to this room. He may have been merely summoned from his house to appear here at this time, under the threat of excommunication should he fail to do so, so that he arrives on his own. In either case, he is ordered to sit down on a low stool, "so that his soul will be more pacified and quiet,"[13] and to swear on the Gospels to speak the truth about all that he will be asked. Facing the accused party, on a high armchair, is the inquisitor, who now begins his interrogation. Where was he born? Where was he brought up? Has he moved from this place of origin and, if so, why? In the places he has lived, has he ever heard talk about theological questions—perhaps about the poverty of Christ or about the Beatific Vision? Has he ever expressed an opinion about such matters himself, and, if so, what has he said? What is, in fact, his opinion about these issues? Like Gui and other inquisitorial authors before him, Eymerich represents the accused party as responding to the inquisitor's questions with "cunning" (*astutia*), "guile" (*dolus*), "wiles" (*versutiae*), "cavils" (*cavillationes*), and "ruses" (*cautelae*), insofar as he chooses words that at once express the guilty truth and veil that truth from his listener. Unlike his predecessors, however, Eymerich (with Peña's concurrence) advises inquisitors to respond to such duplicities by becoming duplicitous themselves. "When the inquisitor sees a cavilling, wily, and cunning heretic who does not want to uncover his error but rather circumvents the issue with cavilling responses and tergiversations," Eymerich suggests, "then, in order that 'a nail be driven out by a nail,' the inquisitor must use ruses so that he can catch the heretic in his error."[14] Once the inquisitor has caught the heretic in his own trap, he states, he can proclaim with Saint Paul, "As I was cunning, I have caught you with guile."[15] By encouraging the inquisitor not merely to expose the accused parties' deception, as Gui did, but also to engage in deception in his own right, Eymerich recognizes that the inquisitor who deceives a heretic may be imitating a heretic, precisely in one of the traits he finds most wicked in him, yet he insists that, so long as the inquisitor speaks truthfully to God and to a good purpose in uttering these false words, he need not be regarded as wicked himself.

It is because the accused party is already speaking with equivocations to the inquisitor, Eymerich suggests, that the inquisitor may in turn use equivocations with him. The accused party may claim, "I believe in one holy Church," yet, Eymerich states, he means by this phrase "his and his accomplices' congregation, which he calls a 'church,' and not our Church."[16] The inquisitor will use a similarly ambiguous vocabulary in speaking with the accused party. "When the accused person requests a reprieve [*gratia*]," he writes, "it is said to him that more will be done for him than he requests, and such general words of this sort."[17] The inquisitor should encourage the accused party to confess to being a heretic, telling him that, if he does so, "I can release you more quickly or even immediately and grant you a reprieve, so that you may go on your way to your house."[18] It is clear that the accused party identifies the "reprieve" of which the inquisitor speaks with the imminent release from prison and return to his house, to which this judge has alluded. However the accused party may understand these words, Eymerich establishes that the inquisitor understands them differently. He states, "The inquisitor . . . will promise to grant a reprieve, and he will do it, for all is a reprieve [*gratiosum*] which is done for the conversion of heretics, and penances are reprieves and remedies."[19] Insofar as the inquisitor has already brought the accused party to confession and seemingly to repentance, Eymerich suggests, he has already granted him a reprieve in the sense that he has already brought him to "grace" (*gratia*). As a result of this confession and repentance, the inquisitor has ensured that the accused party will escape the stake and be allowed to live, albeit in prison, perhaps for the rest of his life. Peña justifies the equivocation that allows the inquisitor to promise the accused party a reprieve and then to keep him imprisoned: "When inquisitors promise a reprieve to accused parties, they are referring only to those penalties which are placed under their control, which are many penitential penalties."[20] Even if the inquisitor relaxes those penalties by a very slight degree, Peña claims, he will have kept his word. By speaking with "general words" of a reprieve, Eymerich proposes, the inquisitor can purposefully suggest one meaning to the accused party, even as he retains another meaning for himself.

It is because the accused party is already making ambiguous intimations to the inquisitor, Eymerich continues, that the inquisitor may in turn hint at something to him without actually saying it. Asked if he believes marriage to be a sacrament, the accused party may assert, "If it please God, I believe it well,"[21] "meaning," Eymerich observes, "that it does not please God that he believe this."[22] Similarly, during the interrogation, the inquisitor should seize the accused person's file, leaf through its pages, and declare on the basis of what he appears to have found, "It is clear that you are not speaking the truth and that I am speaking the truth. Therefore, speak the truth clearly about this business!"[23] At another point during the interrogation, when the accused is rejecting a particular allegation, the inquisitor should hold aloft a piece of paper from this file, "as if astonished."[24] "How can you deny it?" he will ask, brandishing the document. "Is it not clear enough?"[25] Eymerich adds, "He will then read from the document, and he will pervert it."[26] In general, Eymerich writes of his model inquisitor, "He speaks to him gently and mildly, intimating to him [*dando sibi innuere*] that he knows what he has done."[27] About such exchanges, Peña comments, "It is to be observed that Eymerich does not say that, when the inquisitor uses this ruse, he says [*diceret*] to the accused person that he already knows what he has done, for if he did not know this and he said that he did, he would sin, which he should in no manner do, even if the truth could be hoped to be uncovered through this. Rather, the inquisitor intimates [*det . . . innuere*] to him that he knows what he has done."[28] It is one thing to say something false and quite another to give the impression of something false. The inquisitor may not speak brazenly, asserting that he knows all things already, yet, Peña states, "The inquisitor can speak cautiously, so that the accused person believes him to know all things already, and this is allowed and greatly to be accommodated."[29] If the accused party misunderstands what the inquisitor is saying, the fault lies not in the inquisitor who uttered these words, but in the accused party who interpreted them falsely, however much he may have been encouraged to do so.

It is because the accused party is already dissimulating to the inquisitor, Eymerich indicates, that the inquisitor may dissimulate in turn to him. The accused party exclaims, as he had exclaimed in Gui's manual, "Oh, lord, I am a simple and unlearned man who serve God in my simplicity. I know nothing about these questions, nor about these subtleties. You could easily catch me and lead me into error."[30] While Gui's inquisitor exposed the accused party's pretense to simplicity as a ruse, Eymerich's inquisitor plays along with his act, seeming to pity him for his lack of sophistication. He declares, "You see, I have compassion for you because you have been duped in your simplicity, and you will lose your soul because of the beastliness of someone else. Certainly, you are somewhat guilty, but he who instructed you in such things is much more so. Do not make the sin of another your own. Do not make yourself a master when you were a disciple.... Who is he, who taught you these errors—you who knew nothing of evil?"[31] With this speech, the inquisitor accepts the accused party's claim that someone has been attempting to take advantage of his simplicity and to lead him into error by speaking to him of complex theological matters, but he identifies this seducer, not as himself, but as the accused party's heretical master, whose identity he would be wise to reveal. Similarly, the heretic attempts to deflect questioning by alleging to be ill, announcing, "Pain afflicts me excessively. Spare me, for the love of God. I am going to bed."[32] While Gui's inquisitor would have confronted the accused party, insisting that his claims to sickness are a ruse, Eymerich's inquisitor appears to accept these claims. He announces that he must leave on a journey, from which he does not know when he will return. During this potentially long absence, he reports, with apparent regret, the accused party must remain in prison, in irons. He states, "You see, I have compassion for you, and I want you to tell me the truth, so that I can send you forth and expedite your case and so that you will no longer remain captive because you are delicate and could easily incur an illness."[33] Just as the accused party's purported mental weakness becomes all the more reason for him to name the heresiarch whose subtlety has led him astray (and hence to admit his own error), so does his purported physical weakness become all the more reason for him to confess and thus conclude his trial. As the accused party pretends to be frail so as to inspire the inquisitor's compassion, the inquisitor pretends to have compassion for this frailty so as to inspire the accused party's trust. The accused party does not lie when he pretends to be simple, humble, and vulnerable, even though he is none of these things, and neither does the inquisitor lie when he pretends to sympathize with the accused party, to diminish his guilt of heresy, and to wish him to be free of irons, though both purposefully give misleading impressions.

Eymerich's defense of the inquisitor's use of ambiguities of speech may derive at least in part from the influence of his fellow Dominican Raymond of Peñafort from the late thirteenth century, whose cause he promoted for canonization.[34] Augustine had condemned lying across the board in his treatises *De mendacio* and *Contra mendacium*, but he had also maintained that a lie is defined, not objectively, in terms of the accuracy of the speaker's words, but subjectively, in terms of the sincerity of the speaker's intentions. "Not every person who utters a falsehood lies, if he believes or assumes what he says to be true,"[35] he writes. Because a speaker lies only if he means to deceive his listener, Augustine maintains, someone who speaks metaphorically, with "the transfer of a word [*verbi . . . translatio*] from its own object to an object not its own,"[36] does not lie, even if his listener does not understand this metaphor. For Raymond, however, it is not only the individual who, while intending to speak the truth, uses an ambiguity of phrase that happens to be misinterpreted who cannot be said to lie, but also the individual who, while intending to deceive, uses an ambiguity of phrase that he ensures is misinterpreted who cannot be thus charged. If a man being pursued by assassins takes refuge in someone's house, he proposes, using an example from Augustine, the host may speak elliptically to the assassins who come to his door and inquire about their intended victim. "He should respond with equivocal speech, such as 'He is [*est*] not here,' in the sense that 'He does not eat here,' or something similar,"[37] he suggests, thus playing on the double meaning of *est* as "he is" (from *sum, esse*) and "he eats" (from *edo, esse*). In such a manner, he asserts, "He will speak the truth, but equivocally."[38] Alternatively, the host might respond to the assassin's question with another question, thus deflecting his inquiry. "One should transfer [*transferat*] to another topic, if one can, interrogating him about some fact or another,"[39] he recommends. As Raymond reformulates Catholic teaching, one may be held innocent of intending to lie and hence of lying if one is speaking equivocally or digressively, as, indeed, heretics are reputed to do, with the expectation that the audience will not be able to see through these equivocations and digressions. If Eymerich recommends that the inquisitor use equivocations, promising the accused party that he will be "merciful," that he will grant "more . . . than he requests," and that he will bestow upon him a "reprieve," even as he knows full well that the accused party will see in these words a meaning that he does not intend to fulfill, it is Raymond whose teachings he appears to be following.

While Eymerich appears to have been influenced by Raymond in his defense of the inquisitor's use of ambiguities of speech, Peña appears to have been influenced by the theologians and canonists who developed Raymond's line of thought in the sixteenth century, especially in Spain.[40] In the 1550s, Martin of Azpilcueta, commonly known as "Doctor Navarrus," built upon the work of the Dominicans Dominic Sota and Silvester of Prierio to argue in his courses at the University of Salamanca that, however purposefully a speaker may mislead someone, he cannot be accused of lying if he can claim to be speaking in accordance with his own intention. In *Humanae aures*, Gregory the Great had developed Augustine's theory of the subjectivity of the lie by contrasting the words heard by other people and the words heard by God. "The ears of men judge our words as they sound outwardly, but the divine judgment hears them as they are uttered from within," he writes. "Among men the heart is weighed by the words; with God the words are weighed by the heart."[41] In a commentary on Gregory's work, Navarrus asserts that a man who tells a woman "I take you as my wife" makes a verbal utterance to the woman, which gives her the impression that he regards her as his wife, yet he may also make a mental utterance to God, which clarifies that he regards another woman as his spouse. As the woman grasps only the man's spoken words and not the silent thought which accompanies it, she later deems his speech to have been false, yet, Navarrus states, "As our most blessed and omniscient God knew [the speech] to be mixed and composed of two parts, he knew all to be true before him and in the forum of conscience."[42] With this example, Navarrus championed what would become known as "strict mental reservations," that is, statements which, though superficially false, become true with the addition of an unspoken qualification. With strict mental reservations, as Peter Zagorin writes, "the communicative relationship existed only between the speaker and himself and the speaker and God, who of course knew the reserved mental part and therefore understood the true meaning of the utterance."[43] Because strict mental reservations seemed to justify lying to one's fellow man, under the pretext that one is speaking the truth to God, they were vigorously criticized, most notably by Blaise Pascal in his ninth *Provincial Letter* of 1656, and they were ultimately condemned by Pope Innocent XI in his *Sanctissimus Dominus* of 1679.[44] If Eymerich's and Peña's inquisitor speaks not to the accused party but to himself and to God, if he attends to the words themselves of his utterance and not to their communications to other human beings, if he cultivates an inner virtue, directed toward his conscience and toward God, and not an outer virtue, directed toward his fellow man, it is because of such theologians' casuistry.

When Eymerich and Peña are not defending equivocations, intimations, and dissimulations as truthful, with the support of thinkers like Doctor Navarrus, they are defending them as useful. If the inquisitor deceives, these authors make clear, it is for the benefit of the accused party. As we recall, Eymerich writes, "All is a reprieve which is done for the conversion of heretics, and penances are reprieves and remedies."[45] He recommends that the inquisitor promise such a "reprieve" not only so that the heretic confess his sin but also "so that . . . the heretic convert."[46] Of such sort of ruses, Peña affirms, "It is very praiseworthy to employ them . . . for the converting of sinners."[47] Though the accused party may believe that his best interest lies in denying that he is a heretic and avoiding the penances to which heretics are subject, the inquisitor, as Eymerich envisages him, knows that his best interest lies in confessing his heresy and welcoming such penances. Though the accused party may seek his temporal well-being by returning to his house and resuming his earlier life, the inquisitor knows that he should seek his spiritual well-being by remaining in prison and undertaking penance. If the inquisitor deceives, Eymerich and Peña also make clear, it is also for the benefit of the community from which the accused party comes. The guile of the accused person is wicked and pertains to his own private purposes, so that he might escape detection, condemnation, and punishment, but, Peña states, "The guile [*dolus*] [of the inquisitor] is good and pertains to public utility, so that, with the truth of the accused person having been understood, [he can] be condemned and his crimes not go unpunished."[48] While it may be blameworthy to use "fraud [*fraudes*]" for committing offences and perpetrating vices, Peña affirms, "It is very praiseworthy to employ them for the uncovering of fraud, for the avoidance of vices, and for the converting of sinners."[49] Though the inquisitor's use of deceit may seem in itself to be wrong, it can help the accused party by compelling him to confess his heresy and thus to accept his penance, and it can also help the community in which the accused party resides by protecting it from undetected and unrepentant heretics, who might lead more of its members astray.

Eymerich and Peña's defense of the inquisitor's use of ambiguities of speech as useful may derive at least in part from the influence of earlier theologians and jurists. Aquinas, like Augustine, categorically rejects not only lying but also the kindred sins of "craftiness" (*astutia*), whereby one contrives "to adopt ways that are not true but counterfeit and apparently true, in order to attain some end either good or evil";[50] of "guile" (*dolus*) and "fraud" (*fraus*), whereby one puts into practice these feints and pretenses through false deeds and words; and of "dissimulation" (*simulatio*), whereby one expresses, not the contrary of what is in one's mind, but "the contrary of what is in oneself."[51] Yet, though Aquinas condemns not only lying but deception across the board, he also maintains, unlike Augustine, that the sinfulness of a lie is defined not just in itself but also in the end to which it is put. He writes, "If the end intended be not contrary to charity, neither will the lie, considered under this aspect, be a mortal sin, as in the case of ... an useful lie (*mendacio officioso*), where the good also of one's neighbor is intended."[52] Though Aquinas criticizes the person who lies in order to help another person, he concedes that his sin is a venial one. "It is evident that the greater the good intended, the more the sin of lying is diminished in gravity,"[53] he acknowledges. As theologians like Aquinas could see some good, not in the harmful lie, but in the "useful lie" (*mendacium officiosum*), jurists could see some good, not in "wicked guile" (*dolus malus*), but in what they called "good guile" (*dolus bonus*).[54] Ulpian writes that, while some persons deceive their neighbors so that they may cheat and harm them, other persons do so in order that "they may serve and protect either their own interests or those of others."[55] He defines this type of "good guile [*dolum ... bonum*]"[56] as "adroitness, ... especially if anyone uses it against an enemy or a thief."[57] Doctor Navarrus had recalled this classical distinction in his commentary on Gregory.[58] Echoing these classical and contemporary jurists, Peña writes, "There are two types of ruses: There are those which are deceptive, directed to a wicked end and designed to deceive, which must never be employed and which are detested by the law. And there are others which are praiseworthy and appropriate to the courts in the investigation of the truth and in which not iniquity but reason, judgment, and utility are engaged to a good end."[59] However much Eymerich's and Peña's predecessors may have disliked lies and deception, some of them believed that these practices could occasionally be justified for a good purpose, such as the conversion of an accused party and the safeguarding of a Catholic community.

The inquisitor, as Eymerich and Peña depicts him, is in a complex position. On the one hand, these authors recognize that lying is an intrinsic evil, undermining the confidence that one man should be able to feel in another man's speech and by extension the trust that one man should be able to feel in another man's character. On the other hand, they recognize that giving the accused party a mistaken impression of what is known about him and what is going to happen to him can be useful for their purposes. "It is a very different thing to feign or to dissimulate [*fingere seu simulare*] something . . . and to lie and deceive,"[60] Peña asserts. In accordance with the scholastic or casuistic thought of their day, they recommend that the inquisitor use not so much lies as equivocations, intimations, and dissimulations to produce this mistaken impression, with the rationale that the accused party is already employing such verbal tricks against him and that the ends the inquisitor seeks to attain will be to the accused party's benefit. Ultimately, Eymerich and Peña feel that it is not a sin for the inquisitor to speak in this manner because they imagine the inquisitor to be addressing, not just the accused party before him in his *camera*, but God above them as well. Speech functions not just as a communication from one person to the other, which the listener may or may not find accurate, but as an expression of the soul before God, whose veracity only this deity can appreciate. If the Enlightenment *philosophes* felt, in contrast, that it was a crime for the inquisitor to speak in so duplicitous a manner, it was because they did not perceive anyone to be present in the chamber aside from the inquisitor and the accused party and hence did not esteem the purely expressive value of the inquisitor's utterances.

THE THEOLOGY OF TORTURE

If the accused party refuses to confess after many days of interrogation, the inquisitor sentences him to be tortured, to encourage him, as Eymerich puts it, to "speak the truth."[61] While Eymerich is silent about exactly which tortures the accused party will undergo, Peña notes, "We are accustomed to enumerate five stages of torture, from the order in which they are inflicted,"[62] and he refers his readers to the manuals of Paul Grilland and Julius Clarus for more details about these ordeals.[63] According to Grilland, in the first stage of torture the accused party is stripped and his wrists are fastened behind his back to the strappado, or pulley: "Although the body truly is not tortured, the soul is tortured, and it suffers the excoriation of fear, which, in a broader sense, can be called torture,"[64] he writes. In the second stage the accused party is again stripped and his wrists again tied to the strappado, but now he is hoisted slightly above the ground and held dangling for the length of time it would take to say a prayer, perhaps the brief *Ave Maria*, the longer *Pater Noster*, or the still more time-consuming *Miserere*. In the third stage, the accused party is kept elevated for the length of time it would take to say one or two *Misereres*, or even more. In the fourth stage, the accused party is held suspended for between a quarter of an hour and a full hour, the time being determined by the gravity of the crime and the strength of the "pieces of evidence" (*indicia*) against him. Whereas in the earlier phases the accused person was merely raised up, kept aloft for a certain period, and then gently set down, now in the fourth stage he is raised up, dropped precipitously, and then jerked to a stop. In the fifth and final stage the accused party is again suspended and subjected to the sudden release and catch of the pulley, but now heavy weights are attached to his feet so as to increase the pressure upon his joints and limbs. Grilland warns, "This final stage and means of torturing should be used very rarely, and the judge should never come to it easily, except in certain cases and for the most atrocious crimes, such as heresy, treason, and the overthrowing of the state, . . . where the safety of the country and the salvation of many people are concerned."[65] It is only once the accused party has been subjected to these five stages of torture that he can be said to have been "decently" (*decenter*) or "sufficiently" (*sufficienter*) tortured. In using torture, Eymerich does not differ from earlier inquisitors, who appear to have been employing this practice as early as 1243 or 1244 and, as we have seen, who were officially authorized to employ it after 1252. In writing explicitly about torture in his manual, however, he does differ from his predecessors, who remained silent about this aspect of the trial, perhaps because clerics were forbidden to supervise it until 1256[66] and perhaps because, even after this date, there remained a sense that it was unseemly for a cleric to involve himself in such acts of violence.[67] If Eymerich and Peña champion the use of torture, as they do, it is, again, because they regard the accused party as an active, powerful subject, even in circumstances where he might appear to be entirely passive and powerless, and because they perceive the inquisitor as needing to use violence to overcome this agency and obtain the cooperation he is due. The purposeful infliction of pain upon another human being's body, so horrifying to Enlightenment readers, does not appall these authors because they have inherited a penitential tradition which regards the sensation of pain, not as a necessarily negative, world-shattering ordeal, but as a possibly positive, redemptive experience.[68]

Eymerich and Peña perceive, not the inquisitor, but the accused party as determining whether or not he will be tortured. In a passage quoted by Peña, Aquinas had established that, because human beings in general must obey their superiors in those areas over which these superiors' authority extends, the accused party is duty-bound to respond satisfactorily to his judge's questions, and that, "If he refuse to tell the truth, which he is under obligation to tell, or if he mendaciously deny it, he sins mortally."[69] The accused party errs, Eymerich makes clear, not only insofar as he is a heretic but also insofar as he refuses to admit that he is a heretic, though the context of the trial is such that he is required to make such an admission. He is tortured the first time, Eymerich writes, "If he remains firmly in denial and does not at all . . . want to speak the truth."[70] He is tortured the second time, he relates, if, "having been tortured decently, he does not want to speak the truth."[71] He is shown other instruments of torture, Eymerich adds, "having been told that it is appropriate [*oportet*] for him to undergo all of them, unless he makes known the truth."[72] Here, and in similar passages throughout the text, Eymerich depicts the accused party as someone who decides not to reveal the truth and who therefore compels the inquisitor to resort to torture as the only means by which the truth, to which he is entitled, might be obtained. Highlighting the accused party's agency in determining his fate, Eymerich obscures the inquisitor's agency in this matter. If the accused party decides not to speak the truth, it is not that the inquisitor then decides that he will undergo torments, but that "it is appropriate" for him to undergo such pain. Once the accused party makes his decision to conceal his guilt, he sets into motion an automatic judicial process that will end in causing him suffering.

As it is the accused party and not the inquisitor who determines whether he will be tortured, it is the accused party and not the inquisitor, again, who determines whether he will break under torture. There are some accused parties who remain silent under torment, Eymerich reports, because they have hardened themselves to bear the pain. He writes of some persons, already familiar with torture, that "They support the tortures better than others because they immediately flex and clench their arms."[73] Such people, he indicates, "are so obstinate that, however much they are distressed, truth cannot be obtained from them."[74] Peña similarly refers to certain accused parties as "most criminal and robust men,"[75] "criminal men who are familiar with the use of fraud and hiding the truth,"[76] and men who "harden [themselves] through strength of body."[77] He recalls Aristotle, Quintilian, the author of the *Rhetorica ad Herrenium*, and Ulpian,[78] all of whom had long ago made the obduracy of the "thick-witted, tough-skinned, or stout of heart"[79] under torture a commonplace in legal writing. While some accused parties remain silent under torment because they have strengthened themselves physically, others keep quiet under such circumstances because they have fortified themselves magically. Eymerich observes, "Some are bewitched and use witchcraft under torture, because they will die before they say anything. They have been made almost insensible."[80] Peña, too, refers to those who are "bewitched . . . so that they do not feel the ferocity of the torments."[81] He explains that such people write passages from the Psalms or from other books of Scripture or the names of unknown angels on scraps of paper and hide them "in some secret part of the body"[82] so that they will be magically protected against torture. Only last year, Peña recalls, he discovered on the body of a low-born man who was being led to prison one such piece of paper, "on which were curious circles, characters, and wonderful figures, much related to superstition."[83] As Eymerich and Peña portray him, the accused party has prepared for this torture, perhaps physically, by hardening his body, flexing and clenching his muscles, like a wrestler bracing himself against his opponent, or perhaps magically, by concealing superstitious words on his self, like a sorcerer fortifying himself against his enemy. The torture session takes the form not so much of a one-way act of violence, where an active, energetic inquisitor abuses a passive, inert accused party, but of a two-way athletic competition, where an active, energetic inquisitor, applying tortures, contends with an active, energetic accused party, resisting them.

Finally, as it is the accused party and not the inquisitor who determines whether he will be tortured and whether he will remain silent under torture, it is the accused party and not the inquisitor who determines whether he will be released after the torture is completed. If the accused party confesses to heresy under torture and then, two or three days later, confirms that confession, he will have been established to be a heretic. If, however, having been subjected to a full cycle of torments, the accused party does not confess, he will be set free from prison. As Eymerich writes, "When the accused person, having been decently exposed to the tortures and torments, still does not want to uncover the truth, he is harmed no more, and he is released to depart freely."[84] When Peña states that "The *indicia* are purged [*purgata*] through torture,"[85] he uses the language of a traditional trial by God, where an accused party "purged" himself of the guilt imputed to him through an oath, ordeal, or combat. Yet, whereas a queen who defended herself against a charge of adultery by walking safely over burning plowshares was thought to perform this miracle through the assistance of God, who wants to reveal her innocence, the accused party who defends himself against a charge of heresy by refusing to confess this crime, even under torture, is deemed to enact this marvel through his own strength or cunning and thus to conceal his guilt. For that reason, when the accused party is released, Eymerich asserts, his sentence should state, not that he is innocent of the heresy of which he was charged, but merely that "Nothing was found which could legitimately prove . . . the crime of which he was accused,"[86] in order to leave open the possibility that one day some evidence will be found which will retrospectively prove the crime of which he was accused. Not only does the accused party bring torture upon himself through his refusal to answer the inquisitor's questions and not only does he brace himself to withstand it through his physical and magical preparations, but, if he succeeds in withstanding the torture, he can defeat his interrogator and thus thwart the judicial procedures which are supposed to establish his guilt.

During Eymerich's and Peña's times, there was no conception of "human rights" which would condemn torture as an infringement upon an essential human dignity, but there was a conception of "cruelty" (*crudelitas*), inherited from both the classical and the Christian ethical traditions,[87] which, though not used to prohibit torture in general, was used to prohibit a certain application of torture. In his essay *De clementia*, Seneca imagines "the cruel" (*crudeles*), first, as people who hurt others because they take pleasure in doing so. They rejoice in causing pain to others and even in killing them, and in doing so they abandon their humanity, their rationality, and their minds, so that they resemble animals rather than human beings and madmen rather than sane people. Later in the essay, however, he refers to people who harm others because of the inhuman, irrational pleasure they take in such acts not as "cruel," but as "savage" (*feroces*). He imagines "the cruel," now, as authorities who hurt, not others in general, but others who have committed crimes for which they deserve to be punished, though not as excessively as these authorities punish them. "Cruelty is nothing else than harshness of mind [*atrocitas animi*] in exacting punishment,"[88] he writes. He recalls Phalaris, the Sicilian tyrant, who was said to have punished malefactors by enclosing them in a brazen bull and then having the sculpture heated from below, so that their cries seemed like the bellows of the animal, and he writes, "Those, then, that I call cruel are those who have a reason for punishing, but do not have moderation in it, like Phalaris, who, they say, [tortured] men, even though they were not innocent, in a manner that was inhuman and incredible."[89] In the *Summa theologica*, Aquinas provides the first major Christian commentary on Seneca, in which he follows the classical philosopher's second definition of cruelty but narrows its scope: only the inner intention, namely, "the hardness of heart, which makes one ready to increase punishment,"[90] constitutes "cruelty,"[91] while the outer action that results from that intention constitutes "injustice." If one follows Seneca's and Aquinas's logic, the inquisitor is cruel, not insofar as he tortures accused parties (which, under the Roman law both authors recognized, could be seen as an aspect of justice), but rather insofar as he tortures them sadistically, with pleasure in their screams, or vindictively, with satisfaction at the disproportionate retribution for their crimes.[92]

That it was not so much torture as the cruel application of torture which medieval thinkers found troubling is demonstrated in a rare medieval account of an inquisitorial torture session from the point of view of the accused party.[93] In his *Liber chronicarum, sive tribulationem Ordinis Minorum*, Angelo Clareno, a Spiritual Franciscan and an associate of Bernard Délicieux, relates how in 1304 his fellow Spirituals in the province of Ancona were subjected to such abuses by the Dominican inquisitor Thomas of Aversa. In an excessive employment of the fifth phase of Grilland's tortures, Thomas had one friar dangled from the strappado for an hour, then had him raised and suddenly dropped thirteen times, with a stone attached to his feet. During the thirteenth elevation, the rope of the pulley broke, and the friar fell from a great height onto the hard floor. The inquisitor then had his servants throw the half-dead body into a cesspool. Turning to another friar, Thomas had his head bound so tightly that the bones of his skull could be heard to crack. Throughout this account, Clareno blames not the judicial procedures which allow an inquisitor to torture accused parties but the angry temperament of this inquisitor which inspires him to torture them excessively. At the beginning of the account, Clareno explains that, having been irked by a local lord, "The inquisitor, filled with an insane furor, . . . turned all the indignation and wrath of his soul on the poor brothers he had arrested."[94] If Thomas tortures the friars as he does, and if he devotes "all the authority and power of his office to cruelty,"[95] it is not because he rationally feels the torments to be necessary for the investigation but rather, Clareno explains, because he is "angry,"[96] "driven out of his mind by insane furor,"[97] and "vexed by an insane furor."[98] Elsewhere, Clareno suggests that "He seemed to be agitated by a malign spirit rather than governed by human sense or will."[99] Clareno blames, not the standard judicial procedures which allow Thomas to have accused parties' bodies hoisted up to the ceiling or their heads crushed, but the senselessness, at once vicious, insane, and diabolic, with which Thomas applies these procedures. The inquisitor was cruel, it appears, not because of *what* he did, that is, because he tortured, but because of *how* he did it, that is, excessively, and *why* he did it, that is, because of the depravity of his will.

Familiar with this classical and medieval discussion of cruelty, Eymerich and, even more, Peña, acknowledge that the inquisitor can on occasion be cruel in his use of torture, and they seek to curb this tendency in him. Before the torture session has commenced, the inquisitor can reveal himself as cruel by proceeding too eagerly in this direction. Peña writes, "One can characterize as bloodthirsty those judges of today who proceed easily and straightforwardly to torture, without any other proofs having been sought."[100] As the inquisitor orders his servants to strip the accused party of his clothing, Eymerich recommends, he should ensure that they do so "not with rejoicing, but as if troubled,"[101] and he thus recognizes and reproaches the pleasure that some can take in causing suffering. Peña and Eymerich object to the inquisitor who turns quickly to torture and whose servants delight in preparing the accused party for these ordeals because they seem to torture, not out of judicial necessity, but out of personal delectation. When the torture session has begun, the inquisitor can, again, reveal himself as cruel by inventing new torments.[102] Eymerich criticizes the inquisitor who tortures in "a new or exquisite [*exquistus*] manner."[103] Peña writes, even more disapprovingly, "There have not lacked judges who thought up [*excogitaverint*] many kinds of torment,"[104] recalling one commentator who mentioned fourteen different varieties. "If I am to say frankly what I feel," he states, "this treatment of new, thought-out [*excogitandis*] torments is more the work of cruel executioners than that of jurists and theologians."[105] Eymerich and, even more, Peña object to the inquisitor who spends his time developing "exquisite" (*exquisitus*) and "thought-out" (*excogitatis*) tortures, again, not only because such a judge is more likely to maim or even to kill the accused party than if he had adhered to more conventional procedures, but because he seems to torture as a result of his own desire to cause pain. Finally, when the torture session is completed, the inquisitor can reveal himself as cruel by beginning it again. While some jurists are of the opinion that the accused party may be subjected to three or more cycles of torture, Peña condemns torturing the accused party a third time, "for that beyond which is said to be stipulated by no certain law seems excessively cruel and inhumane."[106] If the inquisitor tortures the accused party eagerly, inventively, or repeatedly, Eymerich and Peña agree, he is showing that he tortures, not because he needs to do so as a result of the circumstances of the case, but because he wants to do so as a result of his own "cruel," "savage," and "bloodthirsty" appetites.

As Eymerich and Peña acknowledge that the inquisitor can at times be cruel, they admit as well that he can extort a confession of guilt from an innocent party. Thanks to the writings of Aristotle, Cicero, the author of the *Rhetorica ad Herrenium*, Ulpian, Augustine, Jerome, and Pope Nicholas I,[107] among others, it was generally recognized that the same physical pressure which compels the guilty to admit their crimes can compel the innocent to invent such misdeeds. At the turn of the thirteenth and fourteenth centuries, not long before Eymerich was writing, accused heretics in two famous cases were alleged to have made false confessions in order to escape the tortures to which they were being subjected. As we saw in the last chapter, in the 1280s large numbers of accused parties from Carcassonne and Albi were said to have been forced to make such avowals. Bernard Délicieux asserted of these citizens "that it was by torture that they had been forced to confess that for which they were condemned."[108] Both the papacy and the royal crown recognized, to some extent, the legitimacy of Délicieux's complaints, as did the mob that liberated the prisoners from the inquisitor's prison in Carcassonne. In an even more notorious case in 1307, Philip the Fair had the Knights Templar of France arrested on charges of heresy, diabolism, and sorcery. Subjected to torture as well as to other forms of pressure, large numbers of Templars confessed to these crimes, yet many of them later claimed to have made these confessions only because of the pain they were suffering. Ponsard of Gizy, a Templar serving brother, asserted, for example, "Whatever he and other brothers of the Order had confessed to . . . was false, and their previous statements had been made under duress and on account of danger and fear, because they were being tortured . . . by their enemies."[109] In light of both the ancient authorities and these recent examples, Eymerich recognizes, "Some are so soft and faint-hearted that they concede all things under light torture, even if they are false."[110] Peña concurs: "It often happens that, from the savagery of the torments, many say that they have done things that they have not committed."[111]

Though Eymerich and Peña acknowledge that the inquisitor can sometimes torture accused parties cruelly and can sometimes extort false confessions, they insist that, if he follows the proper procedures, he can avoid these temptations. Before the accused party is put to the question, the inquisitor should establish that he is probably guilty of heresy and hence that the confession he makes under torture will probably be true. An individual who was suspected because of the existence of only one *indicium* against him, such as the testimony of one eyewitness, could not normally be tortured, given the possibility that this *indicium* is false and that any confession torture produced would be false as well. Instead, Peña states, "Torture is applied not so much in order to investigate the facts as in order to possess the truth from the mouth of the delinquent himself, when he disavows the deeds or words he is said to have committed."[112] In other words, he suggests, torture should serve not so much to establish truth as to confirm a truth already established. Even when the inquisitor is sure that the accused party is a heretic, Eymerich states, he should see if he cannot procure a confession through means other than torture, such as "frequent meditation, the inconveniences of prison, and repeated exhortation by worthy men."[113] He explains, "The inquisitor should not be very eager to torture someone, for tortures and torments are not to be introduced except in the absence of other proofs, and he is to seek out these other proofs."[114] As the inquisitor should show restraint before turning to the torture session, by ascertaining that the accused party is guilty of heresy and by attempting to persuade him to confess through other methods, he should show restraint during the torture session as well, by using only customary tortures, to customary degrees. Eymerich writes of the accused party, "Let [the inquisitor and the bishop] torture him moderately and without effusion of blood"[115] and "Let him be tortured in the accustomed manner, and not in any new or exquisite manner."[116] Apportioning the pain in accordance with the crime with which the accused party is charged, the degree of suspicion in which he is held, and the sturdiness of his physique, the inquisitor should take care to apply sufficient force as to break the will of a strong heretic, but not so much as to drive a weak Catholic to confess. Not only before and during the torture session but afterwards as well, the inquisitor should show restraint. If the accused party retracts the confession he has made under torture, as he has the right to do, and thus leaves uncertain whether he is or is not a heretic, the inquisitor may require him to complete the cycle of tortures he interrupted with his confession, but, according to Eymerich (but not Peña) he may not require him to undergo a new cycle. As Eymerich writes, "If he has not yet been decently tortured, one can subject him again to tortures and torments, not repeating them, but continuing them."[117] While he acknowledges that abuses have happened, even that abuses tend to happen, in the use of torture, he expresses confidence that, if the inquisitor turn to torture only reluctantly, if he apply it only moderately, and if he refrain from repeating it unnecessarily,[118] he can avoid these abuses. As Peña states, "Where these preceeding rules are observed, one may go on to torture, according to the order and usage that Eymerich prescribes most accurately."[119]

Yet even if the inquisitor should torture an innocent person to the point where he makes a false confession and should then condemn him on the basis of that confession, the Catholic ethical tradition Eymerich and Peña inherited excuses this judge because he did not intend to produce this result. In *De civitate dei*, Augustine addresses the case of a magistrate who unwittingly tortures and executes an innocent individual. Of the infliction of such undeserved suffering and death, he states: "He does not reckon such evils to be sins. The wise judge does not act thus out of a will to do harm, but out of an unavoidable ignorance."[120] Once again, for Augustine, the moral worth of what the magistrate does can be found, not in how he behaves toward the accused party, that is, in his external action, but in how he behaves toward God, that is, in his internal intention. Aquinas makes a similar point in the *Expositio in librum beati Iob*, where he compares the judge who tortures an innocent accused party to God, who strips the virtuous Job of his health, his family, and his property. Like Augustine, Aquinas refuses to blame the judge for harming an innocent man and instead cites the defects in human knowledge. Knowing only the outer testimony of the false witnesses and the outer confession of the accused party, Aquinas writes, "The judge cannot know the inner conscience of the accused."[121] Paulette L'Hermite-LeClercq is struck by "this spontaneous assimilation . . . of the *adversitas* of existence, these *tormenta*, these *flagella* suffered by Job, on the one hand, and the tortures anticipated in the strict framework of judicial procedure, on the other hand."[122] She concludes, "If torture is only one misery among many others, its judicial specificity disappears; in the end, the ulcers of Job or the rack are one and the same."[123] While both Augustine and Aquinas recognize the injustice suffered by this innocent man, tortured and perhaps executed, their interest lies not in the body which undergoes these travails but rather in the soul, which, if truly innocent, has nothing to fear from them. And, just as these authors insisted that someone who speaks an untruth out of ignorance cannot be considered a liar, so do they insist that someone who tortures and even executes out of ignorance cannot be considered a sinner. The inner soul of the magistrate, in its communion with God, defines him in a way that his outer acts toward his fellow man do not.

If the magistrate who tortures an innocent person should not be condemned, it is not only because he does not want to torture an innocent person but also because, again according to this Catholic ethical tradition, the pain he inflicts upon him may be not entirely to his detriment.[124] When Eymerich recommends the language the judges should use when sentencing the accused party to a continuation of the torture, he proposes, "And we, the said bishop and inquisitor N., assign you to the continuation of torture on such a day, so that the truth may be wrested [*eruatur*] from your own mouth."[125] Not only here but throughout the text, Eymerich uses the language of "wresting" in describing the process by which the accused party is questioned or "put to the question"; he imagines the truth as an entity hidden within the accused party's body which can only be forced out, through his mouth, by a verbal or physical violence.[126] If truth is imagined as an entity lodged within the body, which the self willfully resists disclosing, then that self and that will must be broken to wrest truth into the light. As, through the processes of judicial confession, the judge convinced the accused party to articulate his criminality in an avowal whose authenticity was established by the sufferings with which it was accompanied, so also, through the processes of pastoral confession, the confessor persuaded the penitent to articulate this sinfulness in an avowal whose authenticity was measured by the tears and expressions of anguish with which it was uttered. Comparing the sufferings of the penitent and those of the accused party, Lisa Silverman writes, "Much as chosen suffering sought to crush the rebellious will and thereby to make spiritual space for the indwelling truth of God, so too did judicial torture, by inflicting pain on an accused, seek to destroy the willfulness that diminished the truth of testimony."[127] Like Jesus Christ, who underwent judicial torments and in doing so atoned for the sins of the world, accused parties who undergo similar suffering might also experience this suffering as redemptive.

THE MYSTICISM OF THE STAKE

As the trial comes to a conclusion, it is announced throughout the town that a general sermon will take place at a certain time, on a certain day, in a certain public square, so that the people will attend and witness its events.[128] On a platform raised above the crowd, surrounded by ecclesiastical and civil authorities, the inquisitor delivers a sermon, informing the people before him of the danger of heresy and especially of the heresy to which the accused party has adhered. He then bids the notary to read aloud the *culpae*, or the grounds on which the accused party has been condemned, and asks the accused party, "Are not all these things in truth as they have been read?"[129] Once the accused party has confirmed the *culpae*, the inquisitor then inquires how he would like to proceed with these heresies: "Do you want . . . to reject and abjure them, so that you can save your soul and preserve your corporeal life?"[130] The accused party, "inspired by God,"[131] may agree to reject these errors and to return to the Church, in which case the inquisitor orders him to kneel down, place his hands upon the Gospels, and read aloud a statement of abjuration in which he swears to do all that is necessary to bring about this reconciliation. Alternatively, the accused party, "in his stubbornness and impenitence,"[132] may refuse to abjure his errors, whether because he denies having been a heretic or because he has decided to affirm his heresies until the end, in which case he is delivered to the secular court and, as Peña states, "burned in the sight of the people."[133] On the one hand, these authors represent the general sermon, like the torture session, as a demonstration of the power of an active, aggressive inquisitor over a passive, suffering accused party. As Peña asserts, the trial and the punishment is "not primarily for the correction [of the accused person] and for his own good, but for the public good, namely, that others be terrorized [*terreantur*] and be called back from committing evil deeds."[134] The sight of the repentant heretic kneeling before the inquisitor or alternatively of the impenitent, rebellious heretic burning alive "terrorizes" the spectators, who see illustrated before them the benefits of such submission and the dangers of such defiance.[135] On the other hand, these authors represent the general sermon, like the torture session, as a contest between these two figures, from which either side could emerge triumphant. Should the accused party refuse to play the role of the virtuous penitent, deserving of the Church's mercy, or the role of the wicked heretic, deserving of its justice, Eymerich and Peña fear, he could impress the audiences not with the Church's power but with its tyranny and, in doing so, could achieve a victory over this institution in this conflict.[136]

The inquisitor will succeed, Eymerich and Peña make clear, if he brings about the accused party's conversion. During his trial, the inquisitor encourages the accused party to renounce his errors. He tries to weaken his heretical will through harshness. He keeps him in "a horrible, dark prison,"[137] with irons on his ankles, chained to the wall, in solitary confinement, not because these unpleasant conditions satisfy his personal taste for cruelty but, Eymerich explains, because "The calamities of prison and its constant vexations frequently open understanding."[138] If the inquisitor cannot weaken his heretical will through harshness, he tries to do so through sweetness. He has him transferred to a sunnier prison. He has his wife and his children brought before him, especially if the children are small, in the hope that they will persuade him to repent. In addition to these family members, he arranges for ten to twelve learned men, whether friars or parish priests, clerics or laymen, to visit him frequently and to strive to demonstrate to him the error of his beliefs. If the accused party remains obdurate, the inquisitor continues to encourage him to abjure his heretical faith during the general sermon. The spiritual counselors who had pleaded with him in prison plead with him as he is being led to the stake, as he is being fastened to it, and even as he is burning, withdrawing only, Eymerich notes, after he has died. In sum, he observes, "The bishop and the inquisitor must do all that they can, either by themselves or by others, so that the relapsed repent and return to the Catholic faith."[139] Even if the inquisitor is able to save the soul of the accused party through these unceasing ministrations, Peña suggests, he may still act "for the public good" by displaying to the people the Church's mercifulness toward sinners.

Yet, while the inquisitor will triumph if he brings about the accused party's conversion, Eymerich and Peña make clear, the accused party will triumph if he feigns conversion. Eymerich warns the inquisitor of the accused party, "Be shrewdly on the lookout, lest he abjure with a simulated conversion and act the wolf under the appearance of a lamb."[140] He recounts how a heretical priest in Barcelona was already attached to the stake and his side already in flames when he began to cry out that he wanted to abjure. Fourteen years later, Eymerich observes, it came to light that this priest had remained a heretic and had led others astray for all of that time. Condemned anew, he no longer pretended to repent of his errors, presumably because he knew that as a relapsed heretic he could not be saved by such feigned repentance again, and he died at the stake. As the accused party possesses the power to repent of his sins at the general sermon and thus save his life, he also possesses the power to pretend to repent of his sins, in order to save his life. In doing so, he threatens to get the better of the inquisitor, eluding the punishment he deserves and even, in the priest's case, continuing to lead others astray under the cover of his penitential status. As a result, Eymerich advises that inquisitors imprison for life penitents of the last hour "because this conversion and abjuration are presumed to have been made more out of fear of death than out of love of truth."[141] While the accused party who sincerely confesses and renounces his heresy, who willingly accepts the penance he is assigned, and who gratefully receives the absolution he is granted demonstrates to the audience the mercifulness of the Inquisition, which is always ready to forgive those who have erred, the accused party who feigns a repentance he does not feel and assumes a penance he will not complete makes a mockery of the Inquisition's mercifulness, showing this Office to forgive where it should condemn.

While the inquisitor will succeed if he manages to demonstrate to the audience the accused party's guilt, Eymerich and Peña continue, the accused party will succeed if he persuades the spectators of his innocence. When the inquisitor has the notary read aloud the *culpae* and when he asks the accused party to confirm their accuracy, the accused party may deny that they are true, with the result, Eymerich worries, that "The people would be scandalized."[142] Peña adds: "The greatest inconvenience could arise if the accused party, agitated by an evil spirit, denies those things which he has done in the presence of the people, and if those things which have been discovered and investigated with great labor are cast into doubt."[143] All the inquisitor can do to avoid such embarrassing moments, Eymerich reasons, is to attempt to determine whether the accused party seems to be "well-converted [*bene conversus*]"[144] and, if he does not, to refrain from asking him to confirm the *culpae*. Even worse, when the inquisitor gives the accused party the opportunity to speak, this person may acknowledge that he believes the doctrines he is said to believe, but he may proclaim that these doctrines are not in fact heretical but rather orthodox and that he is therefore not a heretic but rather a martyr of the faith. Eymerich warns that "there are many fervent right from the start to be burned,"[145] "believing themselves to suffer for the sake of justice and to be martyrs, [and] believing themselves thus to fly up to heaven."[146] Peña, more cynically, warns of accused parties who are happy to be burned not so much because they believe themselves about to become martyrs as because they believe themselves about to be recognized and venerated as martyrs by their followers. Given the danger of these would-be martyrs witnessing to what they see as the truth, Peña suggests, "When they are being burned alive, it is altogether to be arranged beforehand that their tongues be bound and their impious mouths be gagged, lest they be able to speak freely and offend the listeners . . . with impious blasphemies."[147] While the accused party who acknowledges his errors, refuses to abandon them, and is thus released to the secular arm demonstrates to the audience the justice of the Inquisition, which is compelled to condemn impenitent heretics, the accused party who denies that he adheres to these errors or that they are errors at all makes a mockery of its justice, showing this Office to condemn those it should acquit or even (in the case of a martyr) those it should canonize.

The heretic exercises agency either in accepting the Church's mercy, with a genuine conversion, or in exploiting it, with a feigned change of heart, and either in accepting the Church's justice, with a silent acknowledgment of his guilt, or in protesting against it, with noisy denials of his guilt, yet, Peña affirms most remarkably, the Catholic who has been falsely accused and unjustly condemned of heresy exercises agency no less. This innocent party has the option of confessing falsely that he is a heretic and that he repents of his errors. In doing so, he will save his body, but, Peña warns, he will damn his soul. Given the magnitude of the crime with which he is charged, he reasons, "Just as he who defames another about such a crime sins gravely, he who defames himself also sins."[148] The false witnesses who testified against the accused party have sinned in lying, yet the accused party should not repeat that sin by lying as well and thus collaborate in the injustice from which he suffers. Alternatively, the innocent party has the option of declaring truthfully that he is a Catholic and has always been a Catholic. In doing so, he will lose his body, but, Peña promises, he will save his soul. He recommends, "Let him do this with a tranquil soul, and let him rejoice that he suffers death for the truth,"[149] and "Let him remember that if he patiently endures wrongdoing and capital punishment, he will be crowned as a martyr."[150] In dying at the stake, the accused party may suffer "for the truth" and hence, in some sense, for the Truth.[151] He may lose his temporal life, but he will gain in recompense eternal glory as a member of the highest rank of blessed souls in heaven. In refusing to sin in order to escape death for another's sin, the accused party, like the early Church martyrs, asserts his power over circumstances that might seem to have power over him and in doing so affirms truth over lies, virtue over sin, and eternal glory over temporal existence. In giving him the opportunity to prove himself to resemble these martyrs, the death of an innocent man is not an outrage or even a misfortune but rather a privilege.

In representing of the burning of an innocent Catholic positively, Peña is again following a Catholic ethical tradition. For Augustine in *De civitate dei*, the accused party who is being put to death for a crime he has not committed might be encouraged to perceive what he is undergoing not as a gross act of injustice but rather as an occasion for patience. While God causes the wicked to suffer in order to punish them for their sins and to drive them to penance, he causes the good to suffer as well in order to remind them that the things of this world are not to be valued. While the wicked respond to suffering by execrating God and blaspheming, to their own damnation, Augustine writes, "The good offer up prayers and praises,"[152] knowing that what they undergo is designed to "test, purify, and strain"[153] them. He concludes, "What makes a difference is not what someone suffers but who it is who suffers."[154] If Augustine expresses indifference toward the sufferings even the best of people undergo, it is because he perceives the external world only as a test to measure the nature of the internal world. For Aquinas, who expands upon Augustine's ideas, the same execution which a guilty man might experience as vindictive punishment for his crimes, the innocent man experiences as a satisfactory penance for his sins. He explains, "If the scourges, which are inflicted by God on account of sin, become in some way the act of the sufferer, they acquire a satisfactory character. Now, they become the act of the sufferer insofar as he accepts them for the cleansing of his sins, by taking advantage of them patiently."[155] To those who might retort that such scourges are not under man's power, he counters, "In some respect they are, insofar as we use them patiently. In this way man makes a virtue of necessity, so that such things can become both meritorious and satisfactory."[156] Even in a situation where a human being experiences what might seem to be the least possible degree of control over his external circumstances—when he is being put to death—these authors insist that he can still exercise a high degree of control over his internal circumstances, so that this death, though inflicted by another, becomes an act against himself.

Not only medieval theologians but modern historians of the Middle Ages have stressed that, at this time, death, and especially the death of the condemned man, could be perceived as a positive experience. While Philippe Ariès's study of death in the Western world has been criticized for its tendency to rely upon written and perhaps idealized accounts of dying which may be at odds with lived, realistic experiences of this process, his interpretation of these written texts concurs with what we see in Eymerich and Peña's manual. For centuries, Ariès argues, people commonly believed that their comportment at the time of death would determine whether they would be saved or damned. Will the dying man repent of his sins, or will he despair of them? Will he place hope in his good deeds, or will he take pride in them? Will he turn toward God, or will he cling to his mortal envelope? As Ariès writes, "God and his court are there to observe how the dying man conducts himself during this trial—a trial he must endure before he breathes his last and which will determine his fate in eternity."[157] While the death of any human being was fascinating for its spectators, at least from the accounts that have survived of public executions, it seems that the death of a criminal, like a heretic, was particularly gripping. Here was a person who had been a sinner, who had refused so far to repent of these sins, and who seemed destined to be damned to Hell, unless he took advantage of these last few minutes of his life to open himself to grace. When he is being asked, one final time, if he will return to the Church, when he is being dragged up onto the platform above the firewood and tied to the stake, when he is beginning to feel the heat and to smell the smoke of the fire beneath him, will he now, at last, ask pardon of God? Though the spectators of his death remain within the temporal world, they catch a glimpse of the eternal world, into which the accused party is entering, through his last words and gestures. As Mitchell B. Merback has written, spectators at such executions are commonly portrayed as feeling compassion for the accused party in his final suffering, but this compassion had little to do with modern humanitarianism. These spectators would hope and pray that the accused party would give signs of penitence because, if he did so, he would justify the priest's lesson that no one, no matter how hardened in sin, is incapable of redemption. "'If such an unfortunate wretch can thus be saved,' so the reasoning goes, 'so can a sinner like me,'"[158] Merback represents them as thinking. In the inquisitorial writings of Eymerich and Peña, as in the scholarly writings of Ariès and Merback, the individual condemned during a general sermon is not just a passive object of the Church's violence but the active subject of his own potential redemption or damnation.

If one's perspective upon the Inquisition is shaped by Voltaire's *Candide*, one will find little to admire in Eymerich's and Peña's description of the encounter between the inquisitor and the accused party. Master Pangloss and his pupil, the young Candide, having arrived in Lisbon, are arrested by the officers of the Inquisition, "the one for speaking his mind and the other for seeming to approve what he had said."[159] The two are cast into dark dungeons, and then, a week later, are attired in san-benitos and mitres, both decorated with devils and flames; while Pangloss's devils have claws and tails and the flames are upright, Candide's devils have no claws or tails, and the flames point downwards. Voltaire writes, "Thus attired, they marched in a procession and heard a very moving sermon, followed by a beautiful recital of plainchant. Candide was flogged in cadence to the singing...., and Pangloss was hanged, though this was not the custom."[160] If Voltaire is appalled by the Inquisition, it is because he stresses the external facts of its operations, including its arrests, its imprisonments, and its executions. The killing of a human being during a religious ritual, complete with a procession, a sermon, and liturgical music, reminds him, as it did other *philosophes*, of a human sacrifice to propitiate the gods. Yet if Voltaire is appalled by the Inquisition, it is also because he disregards the internal processes the inquisitors believed underlay those operations. Though Pangloss and Candide would have been interrogated and repeatedly urged to repent of their errors, the author makes no mention of the examination of conscience these verbal encounters were meant to bring about. Though he observes the upward-pointing flames on Pangloss's garments and the downward-pointing flames on Candide's attire, he does not explain that the direction of these flames indicates that Pangloss has proved unrepentant and for that reason has been destined to be executed and that Candide has proved repentant and has thus saved himself from the fire. Even when Candide ends up killing the Grand Inquisitor, he is depicted, not as deciding to do so as a result of any moral deliberation, but as being compelled to do so by circumstances in order to save his life and that of his beloved Cunégonde. The victims of the Inquisition, as Voltaire represents them, have no inner lives in which they struggle to determine whether the heretical or the Catholic faith is better and how they should act, in the theater of the interrogation hall, the torture chamber, or the *auto-da-fé*, based upon this determination, but only outer lives in which they find themselves treated capriciously, absurdly, and violently by alleged men of God. Were the Grand Inquisitor to respond to Voltaire's depiction of him, he might well assert that, because accused heretics do indeed possess inner lives, they are not purely passive bodies, with no control over the actions that happen to them and thus no responsibility for these actions, but rather active souls with such control and such responsibility.

CONCLUSION

Our people are under attack. According to our informant, the prisoner we are holding has participated in the assaults against us, though he denies that this is the case. In these exceptional circumstances, some of our advisors are insisting that our first responsibility is to protect our people against threats like this prisoner. If we tell the prisoner the name of his accuser and the nature of his accusations, he may use that information to have our informant killed and, in doing so, may imperil our investigations into these acts of violence. If we allow him access to a lawyer, he may discover how to use loopholes in the law to get himself released from prison and, having done so, may renew his offenses against us. Unless we put pressure upon him to speak, he may continue to conceal what he knows about his confederates' upcoming assaults upon our people and prevent us from intercepting those assaults. Hardened fighters like this prisoner, we are told, are trained to take advantage of our softness as they pursue their destructive agendas. Given the danger in which our people are living, anything we do to break this prisoner and compel him to give us the information we need can be excused. At the same time, other advisors are insisting, our first responsibility is to determine whether this prisoner may be innocent, as he claims to be. Without the opportunity to challenge his accuser and without the assistance of an attorney, he may be unable to demonstrate the charges against him are false. It is possible that, if subjected to sufficient pressure, he will give us the confession we seek, but it is also possible that this confession will reflect only that pressure and not the truth of his case. However the prisoner may have been trained, we must adhere to our own society's principles, including the rights we accord a defendant. Even if the prisoner is, to some degree, guilty, it is worth remembering that he is a young man, under the influence of others, and may well be capable of rehabilitation.

While the first set of advisors, in their zeal for the people we are beholden to protect, emphasize the need to interrogate vigorously someone who may be endangering this people, perhaps at the expense of a just consideration of this individual's case, the second set of advisors, in their charity for the prisoner we are holding, emphasize the need to judge this individual justly, perhaps at the expense of the people's safety. In the days when such prisoners were accused heretics, Catholic clerics, like those we have examined, developed three models of how to weigh these competing arguments.

According to the more zealous Catholic clerics of the Middle Ages, in order to defend our people against the enemy, we must become like this enemy. These clerics stressed the violence of the heretic against the Church. For Bernard of Clairvaux, the heretic was not just a particular, temporal individual who happened to mistake evil for good, but the embodiment of a universal, eternal principle of evil, whose error was predetermined by his innate malice. In every heretic living here and now, Bernard perceived Heresy, as it has been since Late Antiquity and as it will be until the end of time. For Conrad of Marburg, the heretic was not just a well-known member of society but a secret practitioner of diabolical rites, gathering together with fellow devotees to worship the devil and engage in indiscriminate carnal intercourse. In every heretic who had been accused, Conrad perceived a sinfulness that needed to be purged by the penitential flames of his pyre. For Bernard Gui and Nicholas Eymerich, the heretic was not the object but rather the subject of their prosecutions, constantly threatening to wrest the interrogation, the torture session, and the general sermon from the inquisitor's control and to turn these events to his own advantage. Though Gui and Eymerich did not dehumanize and demonize the heretic, as Bernard and Conrad did, they still depicted him as the possessor of an extraordinary and maleficent agency. Because the heretic is so violent toward the Church, in his assault upon its fundamental doctrines and structure, these clerics alleged, it is necessary for the defenders of the Church to be violent toward him. As the heretic is the minister of the devil, who is an attacker, in anger, of him who acts well, Bernard states, quoting Saint Paul, "He is a minister of God who is an avenger, in anger, of him who acts badly." As the heretic committed appalling crimes, Conrad's colleagues asserted, with their master's presumed concurrence, the pursuer of heretics must also commit what might seem to be appalling crimes, sacrificing one hundred innocent people in order to eliminate one guilty person. And as the heretic strove to vanquish the inquisitor, Gui and Eymerich claim, so must the inquisitor strive to vanquish the heretic; it is only with a nail, they argue, that one can dislodge a nail. While the pursuer of heretics and the heretic act similarly, these clerics maintain that the violence of the one differs from the violence of the other insofar as it is the response of an essentially good party to an attack by an essentially evil party.

According to the more charitable Catholic clerics of the Middle Ages, in order to defend our people against the enemy, we must not become like the enemy but rather must induce the enemy to become like us. These clerics stressed their submission to the heretic's violence. One day, Jordan of Saxony reports, when Dominic Guzmán and his companions were traveling, they passed by some heretics who were lying in wait to ambush them, though they refrained from doing so. Later, the heretics asked Dominic, "Do you not fear death? What would you have done if we had seized you?"[1] He replied that he would have requested that they not kill him immediately but rather mutilate his limbs, then gouge out his eyes, and then either end his life or leave him wallowing in his blood, as "by such a protracted death I would merit the greater crown of martyrdom."[2] When Peter of Verona and his companion were journeying to Milan, they were ambushed by Carino of Balsamo. Instead of trying to flee or defend himself, Peter lifted his arms to heaven, commended his spirit to God, and, according to some accounts, wrote the first words of the Creed on the ground with his blood before he expired. Because these clerics submitted to the heretics' violence, their chroniclers alleged, the heretics in turn submitted to them. Of the heretics who had plotted to kill Dominic, Jordan states that they abandoned their conspiracy, "inasmuch as, by bringing about his death, they would be complying with his wishes rather than harming him."[3] Of the heretics who had plotted to kill Peter, the saint had declared, "Let them do what they wish because I will do them more harm dead than alive." Destroyed by the heretics of his region, Peter destroyed the heretics in turn, we are told, by displaying such fortitude at his death that all were drawn to the Catholic faith he died affirming. Peter avenged himself upon Carino by inspiring his assassin to convert and to become his companion, not only in his order but in his sanctity. While the pursuer of heretics may act differently than the heretic, responding submissively to the other's assertion of dominance, these clerics' chroniclers assert, it is by submitting to the heretic that he overcomes him, in an overcoming that, by dissolving this opposition, constitutes his triumph as well.

For one, final figure we have considered, Bernard Délicieux, we must neither become like the enemy nor induce him to become like us, but rather we must realize that we ourselves are the enemy. While the zealous and the charitable pursuer of heretics both perceived the heretics as violent and differed only in how they chose to respond to that violence, Délicieux claimed that it is the inquisitor himself who is violent. It is he, Délicieux argues, who "makes heretics," extorting false testimony from witnesses and false confessions from accused parties and condemning good Catholics to years in the Wall. What we perceive as our defense of our people, he asserts, is actually an attack upon an innocent party. What we perceive as the heretic's aggression toward us, he maintains, is actually a Catholic's entirely justified defense against our aggression. What we perceive as our virtuous zeal against error is actually our vicious desire for the accused party's possessions and for power over him. If the pursuer of heretics is in fact a persecutor of Catholics and if the accused heretic is in fact the victim of this persecution, it is incumbent upon us neither to attempt to dominate the heretic nor to submit to him but instead to recognize that he is not a heretic after all and that it is only we who have made him seem to be such a threat.

In deciding whether to act toward our prisoner like the zealous cleric, the charitable cleric, or the skeptical cleric, we need to consider the situation in which we find ourselves. Insofar as our people are under attack, are we ready to resist this assault? There have been situations where people needed to be defended against an aggressor by actions that seemed similar to those of the aggressor, but there have also been situations where the alleged defense of a people either was not provoked by an attack or was not proportionate to that attack. If the zealous pursuer of heretics seems to us now to have been misguided, it is because, though he used physical metaphors to describe the attack he experienced, this attack was not physical but metaphysical and therefore, for many readers nowadays, nonexistent. Insofar as we are under attack, are we ready to submit to this assault, even to the point of martyrdom? There have been circumstances where the willing death of an individual has helped to diffuse the violent tendencies that had brought about this individual's death, but there have also been circumstances where such a death was unreported, uncelebrated, and as a result ineffective. If the charitable pursuer of heretics seems less misguided to us than his zealous counterpart, it is because, whatever we may think of the cause for which he died, he witnessed to it with a remarkable courage and perseverance. Finally, are we really sure that our people and ourselves are in fact under attack? There have been circumstances where the enemy was more the product of our imaginations than reality, but there have also been circumstances where he was very much real. If Délicieux seems most admirable of all these clerics to us, it is because today we too regard the inquisitor as the aggressor and the accused heretic as the victim. While we may feel personally attracted to zeal, charity, or skepticism, as a general, philosophical principle, this may be because we are thinking of particular historical examples where this principle either was applied appropriately or should have been applied. Given the diversity of historical (and current) examples, however, and the diversity of approaches these examples require, the lesson of the Inquisition may be not to embrace across the board any one general principle, as appealing as it may seem, but to exercise our judgment to determine, as best we can, given these different models, which principle is best applied to which case.

NOTES

ABBREVIATIONS

AD	L'Année dominicaine, ou vies des saints, des bienheureux, des martyrs, et des autres personnes illustres ou recommandables par leur piété de l'un et de l'autre sexe de l'Ordre des Frères-Prêcheurs distribuées suivant les jours de l'année. 12 vols. Rev. ed. Lyon: X. Jevain, 1883–1909.
AFP	Archivum Fratrum Praedicatorum
Bouquet	Martin Bouquet et al., eds. Recueil des historiens des Gaules et de la France. 24 vols. Paris: Aux dépens des librairies, 1739–1904.
CC	Corpus Christianorum
CF	Cahiers de Fanjeaux
CCCM	Corpus Christianorum, Continuatio Mediaevalis
Fearns	James Fearns, ed. Ketzer und Ketzerbekämpfung in Hochmittelalter. Göttingen: Vandenhoeck & Ruprecht, 1968.
MD	Memorie Domenicane
MGH SS	Monumenta Germaniae historica ab anno Christi quingentesimo usque ad annum millesimum et quingentesimum . . . Scriptores. 32 vols. Stuttgart and Hanover: Hannsche Buchhandlung, 1823–96.
MOPH	Monumenta Ordinis Praedicatorum Historica
Mansi	Giovan Domenico Mansi, ed. Sacrorum conciliorum nova et amplissima collectio. 53 vols. Florentiae: Expensis Antonii Zatta Veneti. Paris: H. Welter, 1759–1927.
PL	Jacques Paul Migne, ed. Patrologiae cursus completus . . . ab aevo apostolico ad tempora Innocentii III, anno 1216 . . . series latina. 221 vols. Paris: Garnier Frères, 1844–64.
Ripoll	Thomas Ripoll and Antonin Brémond, eds. Bullarium ordinis Fratrum Praedicatorum sub auspiciis SS. D. N. D. Benedicti XIII, pontificis maximi, ejusdem ordinis. 8 vols. Rome: Ex typographia Hieronymi Mainardi, 1729–40.

ST	Thomas Aquinas. *Summa theologica*. Translated by the Fathers of the English Dominican Province, 2d ed. 22 vols. London: Burns, Oates & Washbourne, 1928; *Summa theologiae*. Edited by Enrique Alarcón Pampilona: ad Universitatis Studiorum Navarrensis, 2000.
Wakefield and Evans	Walter L. Wakefield and Austin P. Evans, eds. *Heresies of the High Middle Ages: Selected Sources, Translated and Annotated*. New York: Columbia University Press, 1969. Rpt. 1991.

All quotations from the Bible are from the Vulgate: *Biblia sacra iuxta vulgatam versionem*, edited by Robert Weber and Roger Gryson. 4th ed. Stuttgart: Deutsche Bibelgesellschaft, 1994.

INTRODUCTION

1. The word "charity" derives from the Latin *caritas*, which translates the Greek *agape* in the New Testament. The most famous description of charity is that provided by Paul (1 Cor 13:1–13), where it is said to constitute one of the three Christian virtues, alongside faith and hope, and to be the greatest among these virtues. Charity is traditionally contrasted to the Latin *amor* and, even more, the Greek *eros*, insofar as it designates, not the erotic love of one individual for another, but the brotherly love that unites all human beings in Christ. It is often rooted in Christ's injunction that we love (*agapao*) God and love our neighbor as ourselves (Mt 22:37–41), with the suggestion that there exists a connection between these two types of love. According to Christ, whoever feeds, shelters, or clothes another human being feeds, shelters, and clothes him: "as long as you did it to one of these my least brethren, you did it to me [*quamdiu fecistis uni ex his fratribus meis minimis, mihi fecistis*]" (Mt 25:40). Translations are my own, unless otherwise indicated.

2. The word "zeal" derives from the Latin *zelus* and by extension from the Greek *zelos*, which signifies "enthusiasm," though an enthusiasm which is expressed negatively, whether as righteous indignation or as jealousy. In the Old Testament, several figures are characterized as "zealous" (*kanna* in the Hebrew original and *zelos* in the Septuagint), including Moses (Num 25:2), Phinehas (Num 25:13), and Mathathias (1 Macc 2:27). In these passages, "Zealots" (*kanna'im*) are those Israelites who insist upon adhering to the law, especially in its prohibition of the worship of any god but "the jealous God" (*el kanna*), and who commit acts of violence against fellow Israelites who do not adhere to this law as faithfully as they should. By the first century AD, the "Zealots" had become not just a religious sect but a political party, defined by its refusal to compromise with polytheistic nations. In the New Testament, Saint Paul speaks warily about zeal, expressing concern that it can lead to self-deception (Rom 10:2) and to contention (1 Cor 3:3). While Gregory the Great commends zeal for its power to banish lukewarmness of heart, he also criticizes it for its tendency to slide into immoderate censure of others and even into cruelty. See Gregory the Great, *Register epistolarum* 1.25 and *Regula pastoralis* 2.6–10. See also "Zèle pour le salut du prochain," in *La Bibliothèque des prédicateurs*, ed. R. P. Vincent Houdry, rev. ed. V. Postel (Paris: Adolphe Jossé, 1867), 18 vols., at 8:624–71.

3. "Diliges Dominum Deum tuum ex toto corde tuo, et in tota anima tua, et in tota mente tua," Mt 22:37. Cf. Mk 12:30–31 and Lk 10:27.

4. "Diliges proximum tuum, sicut te ipsum," Mt 22:39.

5. "nolo mortem impii, sed ut revertatur impius a via sua et vivat," Ez 33:11.

6. "clericalem . . . mollitiem," Guibert of Nogent, *Autobiographie*, ed. and trans. Edmond-René Labande (Paris: Société d'Édition "Les Belles Lettres," 1981), 434.

7. On this shift, see Raoul Manselli, "De la *persuasio* à la *coercitio*," *Cahiers de Fanjeaux* 6, *Le Crédo, la morale et l'Inquisition* (Toulouse: Privat, 1971), 175–97. Of the reason behind this shift, Manselli speculates, "Si les indications que nous avons recueillies chemin faisant sont exactes, il faut chercher [la raison] dans l'angoissante conviction que l'hérésie ne pouvait être vaincue en un libre débat et par force de la vérité, mais qu'elle devait à la fin être écrasée par la force" (195). See also Grado Giovanni Merlo, "Coercition et orthodoxie: Modalités de communication et d'imposition d'un message religieux hégémonique," in *Faire croire: Modalités de la diffusion et de la réception des messages religieux du XIIe au XVe siècle* (Rome: École Française de Rome, 1979), 101–18.

8. See Yves Dossat, "La Repression de l'hérésie par les évêques," *CF*, vol. 6, *Le Crédo, la morale et l'Inquisition*, 217–51.

9. On the shift toward inquisitio, see Adhémar Esmein, *Histoire de la procédure criminelle en France et spécialement de la procédure inquisitoriale depuis le XIIIe siècle jusqu'à nos jours* (Paris: L. Larose & Forcel, 1882), esp. 66–134; Louis Tanon, *Histoire des tribunaux de l'inquisition en France* (Paris: L. Larose & Forcel, 1893); and *La Preuve*, part 2: *Moyen Âge et Temps Modernes*, Recueils de la Société Jean Bodin pour l'histoire comparative des institutions, vol. 17 (Brussels: Éditions de la Librairie Encyclopédique, 1965).

10. The recent series of conferences at the Dominican Historical Institute on the Dominicans' role in the Inquisition have done much to shed light upon this topic. See *Praedicatores, Inquisitores*, vol. 1: *The Dominicans and the Medieval Inquisition*, Acts of the 1st International Seminar on the Dominicans and the Inquisition (23–25 February 2002), ed. Wolfram Hoyer (Rome: Istituto Storico Domenicano, 2004). See also Laurent Albaret, "Les Prêcheurs et l'inquisition," in *L'Ordre des Prêcheurs et son histoire en France méridionale*, *CF*, vol. 36 (Toulouse: Privat, 2001), 319–41.

11. In "*Crimen exceptum*: The History of an Idea," *Proceedings of the Tenth International Congress on Medieval Canon Law*, Syracuse, New York (13–18 August 1996), ed. Kenneth Pennington, Stanley Chodorow, and Keith H. Kendall (Vatican City: Biblioteca Apostolica Vaticana, 2001), 137–94, Edward Peters describes heresy as a *crimen exceptum*, that is, an "offense so serious and, in some instances, so difficult to prove that it requires virtually its own criminal procedure, rules of evidence, and forms of punishment [and] that permits and even invites what are later called cruel and unusual punishments and extraordinary and irregular investigative and judicial procedures" (137–38).

12. Around 1244, the bishops of the provinces of Narbonne, Arles, and Aix, at the Council of Narbonne, referred to papal approval of such secrecy, as did the *Processus inquisitionis* of 1244. In 1254, Innocent IV approved of names being kept secret, "if it happens that you see a danger to threaten accusers, witnesses, yourselves, or other people who have been received regarding the crime of heresy, from the publication of their names [*Sane si accusatoribus, aut testibus, quos a vobis, vel aliis vice vestra super crimine hereseos recipi contigerit, ex publicatione nominum eorundem, videritis periculum*

imminere]," Ripoll, 1:250. This exception was confirmed by Urban IV, Clement IV, and Nicholas IV. The ordinance of 1276 allows not only the names but the depositions of the witnesses to be withheld from the accused party. On the secrecy of these trials, see Albert C. Shannon, "The Secrecy of Witnesses in Inquisitorial Tribunals and in Contemporary Secular Criminal Trials," in *Essays in Medieval Life and Thought Presented in Honor of Austin Patterson Evans*, ed. John H. Mundy, Richard W. Emery, and Benjamin N. Nelson (New York: Biblo and Tannen, 1965), 59–70, and Henry Ansgar Kelly, "Inquisition and the Prosecution of Heresy: Misconceptions and Abuses," *Church History* 58 (1989): 439–51; rpt. in *Inquisitions and Other Trial Procedures in the Medieval West* (Burlington, Vt.: Ashgate, 2001), 439–51.

13. In 1255, Pope Alexander IV allowed the Dominican inquisitors of Paris to proceed "simply, plainly, and without the uproar and figures of speech of lawyers and judgments [*simpliciter et de plane et absque avocatorum ac judiciorum strepitu et figura*]," in his bull *Cupientes*, in Paul Frédéricq, ed., *Corpus documentorum inquisitionis haereticae pravitatis neerlandicae*, 5 vols. (Ghent: J. Vuylsteke, 1889–1906), 1, no. 130:123–24, and countless inquisitors later cited this phrase to justify their prohibition of lawyers in their trials. While Kelly acknowledges in "The Secrecy of Witnesses" that canonists interpreted Alexander's words to justify a prohibition of legal counsel, he nevertheless argues: "Persons accused of heresy had a right to be defended by legal counsel, just like persons accused of other crimes. Only actual heretics, that is, persons judicially convicted of heresy, were forbidden lawyers" (445). Nevertheless, the threat of being prosecuted for heresy oneself if one failed to prove that one's client was not a heretic would obviously deter most lawyers from taking on accused heretics' cases. See also Walter Ullmann, "The Defense of the Accused in the Medieval Inquisition," *Irish Ecclesiastical Record* 73 (1950): 481–89.

14. In 1199, Innocent III published the decretal *Vergentis in senium*, which asserted an equivalence between heresy and treason and which, given the Roman tendency to justify the use of torture in cases of treason, would later be used to justify the use of torture in cases of heresy as well. In 1252, Innocent IV published the bull *Ad extirpanda*, which explicitly allowed the *podestà* of certain northern Italian cities "to compel all heretics he has captured, without injury to their persons or danger of death, to confess their errors and to accuse other heretics they know, as thieves, murderers of souls, and robbers of the sacraments of God and the Christian faith [*omnes haereticos, quos captos habuerit, cogere citra membri diminutionem et mortis periculum, tamquam vere latrones, et homicidas animarum, et fures sacramentorum Dei, et Fidei Christianae, errores suos expresse fateri, et accusare alios haereticos, quos sciunt*]," *Bullarium diplomatum et privilegiorum sanctorum Romanorum pontificum*, ed. Aloysius Tomassetti (Turin: Seb. Franco et Henrico Dalmazzo editoribus, 1857; rpt. 1857), 3:556.

15. On Wazo of Liège (985–1048), see Albert Bittner, *Wazo und die Schulen von Lüttich* (Breslau: Breslauer Genossenschafts-Buchdruckerei, 1879) and C. Stephen Jaeger, *The Envy of Angels: Cathedral Schools and Social Ideas in Medieval Europe, 950–1200* (Philadelphia: University of Pennsylvania Press, 1994). As bishop, Wazo distinguished himself by his independence vis-à-vis the emperor. He refused to condemn Wigger, the archbishop of Ravenna, as the emperor demanded, because Wigger was an Italian and therefore subject to the pope rather than the emperor, and he denied that the emperor had the authority to fill the pontifical chair vacated by the Synod of Sutri in 1046. Wazo

may not have wanted bishops to release heretics to the secular arm because he did not want them to accept secular involvement in ecclesiastical affairs. Anselm of Liège (1008–c. 1056), canon and dean of the school at Liège, wrote this chronicle, continuing the work of Heriger, the abbot of Lobbes, who had died in 1007.

16. "Heretics at Châlons-sur-Marne and Bishop Wazo," in Wakefield and Evans, 89–93, at 90; "an terrenae potestatis gladio in eos sit animadvertendum, nec ne, modico fermento nisi exterminentur totam massam posse corrumpi," Anselm of Liège, *Gesta episcoporum Tungrensium, Traiectensium et Leodiensium*, ed. Rudolph Koepke, MGH SS, 8:134–234, at 226–27. Cf. 1 Cor 5:67.

17. On the history of interpretations of this parable, see Stephen L. Wailes, *Medieval Allegories of Jesus' Parables* (Berkeley and Los Angeles: University of California Press, 1987), 103–8. Jerome appears to have been the first to identify the cockle with heretical doctrines. He warns that Church leaders should not sleep, like the master in this parable, "lest, on account of this negligence, the Enemy sow cockle, that is, the doctrines of heretics [ne per illius negligentiam inimicus homo superseminet zizania, hoc est, haereticorum dogmata]," Jerome, *Commentariorum in Evangelium Matthaei*, PL 26, cols. 14–218, at col. 93.

18. "ne forte colligentes zizania eradicetis simul cum eis et triticum, sinite utraque crescere usque ad messem," Mt 13:29–30.

19. "Heretics at Châlons-sur-Marne and Bishop Wazo," 92. "specie severitatis," Anselm of Liège, *Gesta episcoporum*, 227.

20. "Heretics at Châlons-sur-Marne and Bishop Wazo," 92. "quia horum quoslibet, quos mundi huius ager zizania habet, messis illa forsitan triticum inveniet, et quos in via Domini adversarios nun habemus, possible omnipotenti Deo est in illa caelesti patria nobis facere etiam superiores," Anselm of Liège, *Gesta episcoporum*, 228.

21. "Heretics at Châlons-sur-Marne and Bishop Wazo," 92. "quem hic habuit persecutorem, utpote martir apostolum, illic se gaudet habere priorem," Anselm of Liège, *Gesta episcoporum*, 228.

22. "Heretics at Châlons-sur-Marne and Bishop Wazo," 92. "nec eos queramus per secularis potentiae gladium huic vitae subtrahere, quibus vult idem creator et redemptor Deus sicut novit parcere," Anselm of Liège, *Gesta episcoporum*, 227.

23. "Heretics at Châlons-sur-Marne and Bishop Wazo," 92. "Ad horum profecto servorum vos pertinere numerum, ardens in pectore vestro pro animabus diabolica fraude deceptis spiritualis zeli fervor indicat, quo ne a malis boni corrumpantur," Anselm of Liège, *Gesta episcoporum*, 227.

24. "Heretics at Châlons-sur-Marne and Bishop Wazo," 92. Translation modified. "ne dum iusticiam in puniendis praevaricatoribus nos exercere putamus . . . , ei praeiudicium faciamus, qui non vult mortem peccatorum, nec laetatur in perditione moriencium, sed per pacientiam et longanimitatem suam novit peccatores ad paenitentiam reducere," Anselm of Liège, *Gesta episcoporum*, 227.

25. "Heretics at Châlons-sur-Marne and Bishop Wazo," 92. Translation modified. "Sic, sic nimirum tales ultimae illius patris familias messi a nobis convenit reservari, quidque messores suos de his facere iubeat, sicut et de nobismet ipsis cum timore et tremore oportet expectari," Anselm of Liège, *Gesta episcoporum*, 228.

26. "Heretics at Châlons-sur-Marne and Bishop Wazo," 91. "imitata Salvatorem suum, qui mitis et humilis corde non venit clamare neque contendere, sed potius

obprobria, sputa, alapas, postremo crucis mortem subire," Anselm of Liège, *Gesta episcoporum*, 227. Cf. Mt 12:19 and Tim 2:24–26.

27. "Heretics at Châlons-sur-Marne and Bishop Wazo," 91. "iubetur interim tales quodammodo tollerare," Anselm of Liège, *Gesta episcoporum*, 227.

28. "Heretics at Châlons-sur-Marne and Bishop Wazo," 93. "qui . . . per pacientiam et longanimitatem suam novit peccatores ad paenitentiam reducere," Anselm of Liège, *Gesta episcoporum*, 227.

29. "Heretics at Châlons-sur-Marne and Bishop Wazo," 92. "ne a vobis immature, ne ante tempus fieri debeat," Anselm of Liège, *Gesta episcoporum*, 227.

30. Thomas Aquinas quotes St. John Chrysostom as writing of this parable, "Our Lord says this so as to forbid the slaying of men. For it is not right to slay heretics, because if you do so you will necessarily slay many innocent persons [*haec dixit dominus prohibens occisiones fieri. Nec enim oportet interficere haereticos, quia si eos occideritis, necesse est multos sanctorum simul subverti*]," Aquinas, *ST* 2a-2ae.10.8, obj. 1. Cf. St. John Chrysostom, *Hom. xlvi in Matth.*

31. "non est etiam contra mandatum domini, quod est in eo casu intelligendum quando non possunt extirpari zizania sine extirpatione tritici," *ST* 2a-2ae.11.3, ad 3. Citing Augustine, Aquinas explains that one need not fear uprooting Catholics along with heretics, "when a man's crime is known and appears execrable to all, so that he has no defenders, or none such as might cause a schism [*quando ita cuiusque crimen notum est et omnibus execrabile apparet ut vel nullos prorsus, vel non tales habeat defensores per quos possit schisma contingere*]," *ST* 2a-2ae.10.8. Cf. Augustine, *Contra Ep. Parmen.* 3.2.

32. "nescitis quia modicum fermentum totam massam corrumpit. Expurgate vetus fermentum," 1 Cor 5:6–7.

33. "resecandae sunt putridae carnes, et scabiosa ovis a caulis repellenda, ne tota domus, massa, corpus et pecora, ardeat, corrumpatur, putrescat, intereat," *ST* 2a-2ae.11.3. Cf. Gal 5: 9. Aquinas is quoting Jerome, *Commentariorum in epistolam Beati Pauli ad Galatas* 3.9, *PL* 26, col. 403.

34. "in iudicio Dei semper recipiuntur redeuntes, quia Deus scrutator est cordium, et vere redeuntes cognoscit," *ST* 2a-2ae.11.4, ad 1. Cf. Wis 1:6.

35. "Praesumit autem eos non vere reverti qui, cum recepti fuissent, iterum sunt relapsi," ibid.

36. "sed a periculo mortis eos non tuetur," ibid.

37. "Deus est principale obiectum caritatis, proximus autem ex caritate diligitur propter Deum," *ST* 2a-2ae.23.5, ad 1.

38. "Amor autem amicitiae quaerit bonum amici, unde quando est intensus, facit hominem moveri contra omne illud quod repugnat bono amici. Et secundum hoc, aliquis dicitur zelare pro amico, quando, si qua dicuntur vel fiunt contra bonum amici, homo repellere studet," *ST* 1a-2ae.28.4.

39. "zelus. . . . ex intensione amoris provenit," ibid. Cf. Augustine, *De diversis questionibus LXXXIII* (hereafter QQ 83), qu. 35.

40. "Manifestum est enim quod quanto aliqua virtus intensius tendit in aliquid, fortius etiam repellit omne contrarium vel repugnans. Cum igitur 'amor sit quidam motus in amatum,' ut Augustinus dicit in libro octoginta trium quaest., intensus amor quaerit excludere omne quod sibi repugnat," *ST* 1a-2ae.28.4. Cf. Augustine, QQ 83, qu. 35.

41. "Et per hunc etiam modum aliquis dicitur zelare pro Deo, quando ea quae sunt contra honorem vel voluntatem Dei, repellere secundum posse conatur," *ST* 1a-2ae.28.4.

42. "posset in praeiudicium salutis aliorum hoc esse, tum quia, si relaberentur alios inficerent; tum etiam quia, si sine poena evaderent, alii securius in haeresim relaberentur," *ST* 2a-2ae.11.4.

43. Aquinas does concede that, in the past, the Church has tolerated heretics "when there were a great number of unbelievers [*quando erat magna infidelium multitudo*]" and that it was right for it to do so "in order to avoid an evil, that is, in order to avoid the scandal or disturbance that could come forth from this or an impediment to the salvation of those who, if they were tolerated, might gradually be converted to the faith [*nisi forte ad aliquod malum vitandum, scilicet ad vitandum scandalum vel dissidium quod ex hoc posset provenire, vel impedimentum salutis eorum, qui paulatim, sic tolerati, convertuntur ad fidem*]," *ST* 2a-2ae.10.11.

44. "hereticum hominem post unam et secundam correptionem devita, sciens quia subversus est qui eiusmodi est et delinquit proprio iudicio condemnatus," Tit 3:10–11. Cf. Mt 18:17.

45. "si adhuc pertinax inveniatur, Ecclesia, de eius conversione non sperans, aliorum saluti providet, eum ab Ecclesia separando per excommunicationis sententiam; et ulterius relinquit eum iudicio saeculari a mundo exterminandum per mortem," *ST* 2a-2ae.11.3.

46. "si aliquid de huiusmodi bonis existens in uno impedire possit aeternam salutem in multis, non oportet quod ex caritate huiusmodi bonum ei velimus, sed potius quod velimus eum illo carere, tum quia salus aeterna praeferenda est bono temporali; tum quia bonum multorum praefertur bono unius," *ST* 2a-2ae.11.4.

47. "non solum septies, sed usque septuagies septies," *ST* 2a-2ae.11.4, ad 2. Cf. Mt 18:22.

48. "Non autem intelligitur de peccato in proximum vel in Deum commisso, quod non est nostri arbitrii dimittere," *ST* 2a-2ae.11.4, ad 2.

49. Cf. *ST* 2a-2ae.40.1, ad 2; 2a-2ae.108.1, ad 2; 2a-2ae.108.2, ad 2.

50. "Heretics at Châlons-sur-Marne and Bishop Wazo," 93; "ipsi eisque communicantes catholica communione priventur, caeterisque omnibus publice denuntietur, ut secundum propheticam ammonitionem exeant de medio eorum et immundissimam eorum sectam ne tetigerint, quoniam qui tetigerit picem, inquinabitur ab ea," Anselm of Liège, *Gesta episcoporum* 228. Cf. Is 52:11 and Eccles 13:1.

51. "Respondeo dicendum quod Ecclesia, secundum domini institutionem, caritatem suam extendit ad omnes, non solum amicos, verum etiam inimicos et persequentes, secundum illud Matth. V, *diligite inimicos vestros, benefacite his qui oderunt vos*," *ST* 2a-2ae.11.4.

52. "Et ideo non statim condemnat, sed *post primam et secundam correctionem*, ut apostolus docet," *ST* 2a-2ae.11.3.

53. See Henry Charles Lea, *A History of the Inquisition of the Middle Ages*, 3 vols. (New York: Harper & Bros., 1887; rpt. New York: The Harbor Press, 1955).

54. In addition to these studies, research on the medieval Inquisition has been prodigious in recent years. See, for example, Yves Dossat, ed., *Les Hérésies et l'Inquisition, XIIe-XIIIe siècle: Documents et études* (Aldershot: Variorum, 1990); Peter Segl, ed., *Die Anfänge der Inquisition im Mittelalter, mit einem Ausblick auf das 20. Jahrhundert und*

seinem Beitrag über religiöse Intoleranz im nichtchristlichen Bereich, Papers from the 8th Bayreuther Historisches Kolloquium held by the Facheinheit Geschichte, Universität Bayreuth (May 29-30, 1992) (Köln: Böhlau, 1993); Grado Giovanni Merlo, Contro gli eretici: La coercizione all'ortodossia prima dell'Inquisizione (Bologna: Il Mulino, 1996), a collection of five articles originally published between 1988 and 1995; Monique Zerner, ed., Inventer l'hérésie? Discours polémiques et pouvoirs avant l'Inquisition (Nice: Z'éditions, 1998); Agostino Borromeo, ed., L'Inquisizione, Comitato del Grande Giubileo dell'Anno 2000 Commissione Teologico-Storica, Atti del Simposio internazionale, Città del Vaticano (29-31 October 1998) (Vatican City: Biblioteca Apostolica Vaticana, 2003); Caterina Bruschi and Peter Biller, eds., Texts and the Repression of Medieval Heresy (Woodbridge, Suffolk: York Medieval Press, 2003); Praedicatores, Inquisitores, vol. 1: The Dominicans and the Medieval Inquisition; and Inquisition et pouvoir, Actes du colloque international tenu à la maison mediterranéene de sciences de l'homme (24-26 octobre 2002), ed. Gabriel Audisio (Aix-en-Provence: Publications de l'Université de Provence, 2004). For two short but useful introductions to the medieval Inquisition, see Bernard Hamilton, The Medieval Inquisition (New York: Holmes & Meier, Inc., 1981; rpt. 1989) and Albert Clement Shannon, The Medieval Inquisition, 2d ed. (Collegeville, Minn.: Liturgical Press, 1991). Discussions of heresy have often addressed the Inquisition as well. See Jacques Le Goff, ed., Hérésies et sociétés dans l'Europe pré-industrielle, 11e-18e siècles (Paris: Mouton, 1968); Willem Lourdaux and Daniel Verhelst, eds., The Concept of Heresy in the Middle Ages, 11th-13th Centuries, Proceedings of the International Conference, Louvain (May 13-16, 1973) (The Hague: Martinus Nijhoff, 1976; rpt. Leuven: University Press, 1976) and Malcolm Lambert, Medieval Heresy: Popular Movements from the Gregorian Reform to the Reformation, 3d ed. (Oxford: Basil Blackwell, 2002).

55. Edward Peters, Inquisition (New York: The Free Press, 1988, rpt. Berkeley and Los Angeles: University of California Press, 1989), 57.

56. James B. Given, Inquisition and Medieval Society: Power, Discipline, and Resistance in Languedoc (Ithaca: Cornell University Press, 1997), 167. See also Given, "Social Stress, Social Strain, and the Inquisitors of Medieval Languedoc," in Christendom and Its Discontents: Exclusion, Persecution, and Rebellion, 1000-1500, ed. Scott L. Waugh and Peter D. Diehl (Cambridge: Cambridge University Press, 1996), 67-85; "The Inquisitors of Languedoc and the Medieval Technology of Power," American Historical Review 94 (1989): 336-59; and "Les inquisiteurs du Languedoc médiéval: Les éléments sociétaux favorables et contraignantes," in Inquisition et pouvoir, Actes du colloque international tenu à la maison méditerranéenne de sciences de l'homme (24-26 October 2002), ed. Gabriel Audisio (Aix-en-Provence: Publications de l'Université de Provence, 2004), 57-70.

57. John H. Arnold, Inquisition and Power: Cathars and the Confessing Subject in Medieval Languedoc (Philadelphia: University of Pennsylvania Press, 2001), 12. See also Arnold, "Inquisition, Texts, and Discourse," in Texts and the Repression of Medieval Heresy, ed. Bruschi and Biller, 63-80.

58. R. I. Moore, Formation of a Persecuting Society: Power and Deviance in Western Europe, 950-1250 (Oxford: Basil Blackwell, 1987); rev. ed., Formation of a Persecuting Society: Authority and Deviance in Western Europe 950-1250 (Malden, Mass.: Wiley-Blackwell, 2007). Despite its title, Heresy and the Persecuting Society in the Middle Ages: Essays on the Work of R. I. Moore, ed. Michael Frassetto (Leiden: Brill Academic

Publishers, 2006) concentrates more on Moore's *The Origins of European Dissent* (London: Allen Lane, 1977; rpt. New York: Basil Blackwell, 1985) than on his later work.

59. Moore, *Formation of a Persecuting Society*, 194.

60. John Christian Laursen and Cary J. Nederman, eds., *Beyond the Persecuting Society: Religious Toleration Before the Enlightenment* (Philadelphia: University of Pennsylvania Press, 1999). See also Cary J. Nederman and John Christian Laursen, eds., *Difference and Dissent: Theories of Tolerance in Medieval and Early Modern Europe* (Lanham, Md.: Rowman & Littlefield, 1996).

61. Moore, "Bibliographical Excursus: Debating the Persecuting Society," in *Formation of a Persecuting Society*, 172–96, at 193.

62. Moore, *Formation of a Persecuting Society*, 195.

63. See Cary J. Nederman, *Worlds of Difference: European Discourses of Toleration, c. 1100-c. 1550* (University Park: Pennsylvania State University Press, 2000).

64. Cary J. Nederman, review of Frassetto, ed., *Heresy and the Persecuting Society in the Middle Ages*, in *The Catholic Historical Review* 94, no. 3 (July 2008): 545–46, at 546.

65. John Christian Laursen and Cary Nederman, "General Introduction: Political and Historical Myths in Toleration Literature," in *Beyond the Persecuting Society*, 1–10, at 4–5.

66. "salus extra ecclesiam non est." This saying originated with Cyprian of Carthage, in his Letter 72, *Ad Jubaianum de haereticis baptizandis*, in the third century, and was repeated by Pope Innocent III, in the profession of faith he required of Waldensians in 1208; by the Fourth Lateran Council, in its first canon, in 1215; and by Pope Boniface VIII, in his bull *Unam sanctam ecclesiam* of 1302.

67. Christine Caldwell Ames, in *Righteous Persecution: Inquisition, Dominicans, and Christianity in the Middle Ages* (Philadelphia: University of Pennsylvania Press, 2009), has argued for the religious basis of inquisitorial persecutions in the Middle Ages, as opposed to the primarily political, social, or economic bases that have tended to be privileged in recent scholarship. See also Ames's articles "Does Inquisition Belong to Religious History?" *The American Historical Review* 110, no. 1 (February 2005): 11–37 and "Dominican Inquisitors as 'Doctors of Souls': The Spiritual Discipline of Inquisition, 1231–1331," *Heresis* 40 (2004): 23–40. While Ames's research heads in the same direction as my own, her focus remains upon the general patterns she perceives among inquisitors rather than upon individual cases, as mine will be.

68. As Richard Kieckhefer points out in *Repression of Heresy in Medieval Germany* (Liverpool: Liverpool University Press, 1979), 3–5, and then in "The Office of Inquisition and Medieval Heresy: The Transition from Personal to Institutional Jurisdiction," *Journal of Ecclesiastical History* 46 (1995): 36–61, when Gregory IX first appointed Dominican friars to pursue heretics, he made no mention of the "Inquisition," but merely referred to the "inquests" (*inquisitiones*) these friars would be conducting. Though these inquisitors often collaborated with each other, making copies of their registers for each other and composing inquisitors' manuals for their benefit; though they joined together to judge the cases of particularly notorious heresiarchs; though they sought to give the impression of institutional solidarity during the general sermon, Kieckhefer stresses that they were appointed individually and that they worked individually and not as representatives of any institution. In the absence of such an institution, Peters proposes in *Inquisition*, "It may be more accurate to speak of medieval *inquisitors* rather than a medieval *inquisition*" (68). See, too, Kelly,

"Inquisition and the Prosecution of Heresy," 439, for this argument. These historians' refusal to refer to a medieval "Inquisition" has not gone uncontested. In *Inquisition and Power*, Arnold argues (rightly, in my view) that, by the early fourteenth century, medieval people did in fact perceive the office of the Inquisition as existing independently of individual inquisitors (70). He explains, "[O]ne might speak of the Inquisition with a capitalized letter, . . . not as the fictional 'institution' Kieckhefer rightly decries, but as a mechanism for producing 'truth,' using a particular kind of authority and language, that lays claim to continuity in its textual repetition. The inquisitorial process, and the texts it produces, extend beyond the individual inquisitor, who is himself constituted by them" (90).

69. As a roundtable in *The American Historical Review* 114, no. 3 (June 2009) addressed, biography, once regarded with suspicion by historians, has become increasingly respected in recent years. Whereas once the account of an individual's life was seen as belletristic, given its "old-fashioned" focus upon an autonomous subject, "the New Biography" is seen as scholarly, given its location of that subject within his or her social, political, and cultural context. If historians had once rejected biography because it seemed to enshrine a coherent, unified self, whose existence had long been disproved by Michel Foucault and Roland Barthes, among others, now many of them accept biography because it can explore how an individual performs a coherent, unified self, through the various social categories at his or her disposal. See Jo Burr Margadant, ed., *The New Biography: Performing Femininity in Nineteenth-Century France* (Berkeley and Los Angeles: University of California Press, 2000). Scholars of early modern history and literature especially have devoted studies to individual lives. See, for example, Carlo Ginzburg, *I Formaggio e i vermi: il cosmo di un mugnaio del '500* (Torino: G. Einaudi, 1976); Natalie Zemon Davis, *Le Retour de Martin Guerre* (Paris: R. Laffont, 1982); Stephen Greenblatt, *Renaissance Self-Fashioning: From More to Shakespeare* (Chicago: University of Chicago Press, 1983) and *Will in the World: How Shakespeare Became Shakespeare* (New York: W. W. Norton, 2004); and James Shapiro, *A Year in the Life of William Shakespeare: 1599* (New York: HarperCollins, 2005). On the traditions of medieval biography and modern biography of medieval people, see *Writing Medieval Biography (750–1250): Essays in Honour of Professor Frank Barlow*, ed. David Bates, Julia Crick, and Sarah Hamilton (Woodbridge: Boydell Press, 2006), especially the historiographical survey of these subjects in the introduction (1–13).

70. In recent years, increasing emphasis has been paid to the texts concerning medieval heresy and Inquisition. In *Texts and the Repression of Medieval Heresy*, Bruschi and Biller write, "There has been a seismic shift: the texts and the actions and mindsets which produced them have slowly become *themselves* also elements of the past reality which historians need to describe" (8–9).

71. Moore, *Formation of a Persecuting Society*, 170.

72. Daniel Ols, "La Spiritualité des inquisiteurs," *Angelicum* 58 (1981): 181–209, at 202. Merlo comments upon this article in *Contro gli eretici*, "Tuttavia non si può tacere la discutibile applicazione del termine 'spiritualità' a un'azione repressiva cruenta per quanto attuata 'avec conscience et conviction'" (11, n. 1).

73. Yves Dossat, "Une Figure d'inquisiteur: Bernard de Caux," *CF*, vol. 6, *Le Crédo, la morale et l'Inquisition*, 253–72, at 270.

74. See Laurent Albaret, ed., *Les Inquisiteurs: Portraits de défenseurs de la foi en Languedoc (XIIIe-XIVe siècles)* (Toulouse: Privat, 2001). William Thomas Walsh provides

a popular Catholic apology for the Inquisition in *Characters of the Inquisition* (New York: P. J. Kenedy & Sons, 1940). In addition to the individual studies of inquisitors considered in the coming chapters, see Walter L. Wakefield, "Friar Ferrier, inquisitor," *Heresis* 7 (1986): 33–41.

75. In *Tudor Autobiography: Listening for Inwardness* (Chicago: University of Chicago Press, 2008), Meredith Ann Skura furnishes a precedent for this approach. Insofar as literary critics have denied the existence of an inner life and by extension of autobiography in England before the seventeenth century, Skura argues, it is because they have recognized evidence of inner life only in personal revelations, of a kind which men and women of the sixteenth century generally hesitated to make. Despite this reticence, Skura asserts, people of this era did have inner lives, and they expressed these inner lives, not, perhaps, in *what* they wrote, but in *how* they wrote it. If we want to appreciate the inner lives of people from earlier time periods, she suggests, we need to recognize that inner lives can take more forms than we might expect.

76. See Moore, *Formation of a Persecuting Society*, 168.

CHAPTER ONE

1. Bernard of Clairvaux's writings have been collected in *Sancti Bernardi Opera*, ed. Jean Leclercq, Charles H. Talbot, and Henri Rochais, 8 vols. (Rome: Editiones Cistercienses, 1957–77): vol. 1, *Sermones super Cantica canticorum 1–35*; vol. 2, *Sermones super Cantica canticorum 36–86*; vol. 3, *Tractatus et opuscula*; vol. 4, *Sermones I*; vol. 5, *Sermones II*; vol. 6, *Sermones III*; vol. 7, *Epistolae I: Corpus epistolarum 1–180*; vol. 8, *Epistolae II: Corpus epistolarum 181–310* and *Epistolarum extra corpus 311–547*. For criticism of Bernard, see the writings of Jean Leclercq, many of which have been collected in *Recueil d'Études sur Saint Bernard et ses écrits*, 5 vols. (Rome: Edizioni di Storia e Letteratura, 1961–92) and others of which are available as *S. Bernard et l'esprit cistercien* (Paris: Editions du Seuil, 1966) and *Nouveau visage de Bernard de Clairvaux: Approches psycho-historiques* (Paris: Les Editions du Cerf, 1976). For other, relatively general treatments of this figure, see John R. Sommerfeldt, *Bernard of Clairvaux on the Life of the Mind* (New York: Newman Press, 2004); Adriaan H. Bredero, *Bernard van Clairvaux: Tussen cultus en historie* (Kampen: Kok/Agora, 1993); Brian Patrick Maguire, *A Difficult Saint: Bernard of Clairvaux and His Tradition* (Kalamazoo, Mich: Cistercian Publications, 1992); G. R. Evans, *The Mind of St. Bernard of Clairvaux* (Oxford: Clarendon Press, 1983); and Etienne Gilson, *La Théologie mystique de saint Bernard* (Paris: J. Vrin, 1934). There have been numerous important recent collections of studies on Bernard, including *Bernhard von Clairvaux: Rezeption und Wirkung im Mittelalter und in der Neuzeit*, ed. Kaspar Elm, Akten des Wolfenbürreler Symposiums (Oktober 23–27, 1990) (Wiesbaden: Harrassowitz, 1994); *Bernardus Magister: Papers Presented at the Nonacentenary Celebration of the Birth of Saint Bernard*, ed. John R. Sommerfeldt (Kalamazoo, Mich: Cisterican Publications, 1993); *Vies et légendes de saint Bernard: Création, diffusion, réception (XIIe-XXe siècles)*, ed. Jacques Berlioz, Patrick Arabeyre, and Philippe Poirrier, Actes des rencontres de Dijon (7–8 June 1991), (Saint-Nicolas-Les Citeaux: Abbaye de Citeaux: 1993); *Bernard de Clairvaux: Histoire, mentalités, spiritualité*, Actes du colloque de Lyon-Cîteaux-Dijon (juin 1990) (Paris: Cerf, 1992); *La Dottrina della vita spirituale*

nelle opere di san Bernardo di Clairvaux, Atti del convegno internazionale, Roma (11-15 settembre 1990) (Rome: Editiones Cistercienses, 1991); E. Rozanne Elder and John R. Sommerfeldt, eds., *The Chimaera of His Age: Studies on Bernard of Clairvaux* (Kalamazoo, Mich: Cistercian Publications, 1980); and *Bernard of Clairvaux: Studies Presented to Dom Jean Leclercq* (Washington, D.C.: Cistercian Publications, 1973).

2. See René Locatelli, "L'Expansion de l'ordre cistercien," in *Bernard de Clairvaux: Histoire, mentalités, spiritualité*, 103-40.

3. Bernard himself writes to Eugenius, "They say that you are not the pope, but that I am, and from everywhere those who have business to conduct come to me [*Aiunt non vos esse papam, sed me, et undique ad me confluunt qui habent negotia*]," Bernard of Clairvaux, *Epistola* 239.1.

4. See Walter Map, *De Nugis Curialium/Courtiers' Trifles*, ed. and trans. M. R. James, rev. C. N. L. Brooke and R. A. B. Mynors (Clarendon Press: Oxford, 1983), 88. See also Jacques Berlioz, "Saint Bernard dans les *exempla* (XIIIe-XVe siècles), in *Vies et légendes de saint Bernard*, 211-28, and "Saint Bernard dans la littérature satirique de *l'Ysengrinys* aux *Balivernes des courtisans* de Gautier Map (XIIe-XIIIe siècles)," ibid., 116-40.

5. "Erat enim 'vir potens, in opere et sermone' coram Deo ut creditur, et ut publice notum est, coram hominibus," John of Salisbury, *Historia Pontificalis/ Memoirs of the Papal Court*, ed. and trans. Marjorie Chibnall (London: Thomas Nelson and Sons, 1956; rpt. 1962), 20. Cf. Acts 7:22.

6. On Abelard, among the abundance of studies, see John Marenbon, *The Philosophy of Peter Abelard* (Cambridge: Cambridge University Press, 1997); M. T. Clanchy, *Abelard: A Medieval Life* (Oxford: Basil Blackwell, 1997); and D. E. Luscombe, "Peter Abelard," in Peter Dronke, ed., *A History of Twelfth-Century Western Philosophy* (Cambridge: Cambridge University Press, 1988), 279-307.

7. For this treatise, see Bernard of Clairvaux, *Opera*, 8:17-40. See also Jean Leclercq, "Les Formes successives de la lettre-traité de Saint Bernard contre Abélard," *Revue Bénédictine* 78 (1968): 87-105.

8. For Bernard's letters against Abelard, see Bernard, *Epistolae* 187-94, 327, and 330-38. The dossier on Abelard's trial at Sens includes letters from Bernard to William of Saint-Thierry (327); to the bishops of the archdiocese of Sens (187); to the bishops and cardinals in the curia (188); to Innocent (189, 239, and 330); to Cardinal Guy of Castello (192), to Cardinal Ivo (193); to Cardinal Stephen, Bishop of Palestrina (331); to a certain Cardinal G. (332); to Gregory, Cardinal Deacon of Saints Sergius and Bacchus (333); to Cardinal Guy of Pisa (334); to an unnamed cardinal priest (335); to an unnamed abbot (336); and to Cardinal Haimeric (338). For studies of Abelard and Bernard, among the multitude of possibilities, see A. Victor Murray, *Abelard and St. Bernard: A Study in Twelfth-Century 'Modernism'* (Manchester: Manchester University Press, 1967); Edward Little, "Bernard and Abelard at the Council of Sens," in *Bernard of Clairvaux: Studies Presented to Dom Jean Leclercq*, 55-71; and Jacques Verger, "Saint Bernard et les scholastiques," in *Vies et légendes de saint Bernard*, 210-10.

9. Perhaps because of Gilbert of La Porrée professed repentance of his alleged heresy, Bernard's discussion of his errors, in his *Cantica canticorum* 80.6-9 and in *De consideratione* 5.7, is relatively brief and restrained, in contrast to his discussion of Abelard's faults.

10. For Henry's activity in Le Mans, see *Ex gestis pontificum Cenomannensium*, Bouquet, 12:539-58, especially 547-52; Hildebert of Lavardin, *Epistolae*, PL 171, cols.

135–311, especially *Epistola* 24, col. 242; and Alberic des Trois-Fontaines, *Chronicon*, *MGH SS*, 23:839. For discussion of Henry, see Jeffrey Burton Russell, *Dissent and Reform in the Early Middle Ages* (Berkeley and Los Angeles: University of California Press, 1965), 68–78; R. I. Moore, *The Origins of European Dissent* (London: Alan Lane, 1977; rpt. Toronto: University of Toronto Press, 1994), 82–114; Malcolm Lambert, *Medieval Heresy: Popular Movements from the Gregorian Reform to the Reformation*, 3d ed. (Oxford: Basil Blackwell, 2002), 44–50; and Raoul Manselli, "Il monaco Enrico e la sua eresia," *Bullettino dell'Istituto storico italiano per il medio evo e Archivio Muratoriano* 65 (1953): 1–6.

11. For Bernard's letter to Alphonsus Jordan on Henry, see *Epistola* 241.

12. For Bernard's letter to the people of Toulouse on Henry, see *Epistola* 242.

13. In "'Les Albigeois': Remarques sur une dénomination," in *Inventer l'hérésie : discours polémiques et pouvoirs avant l'Inquisition*, ed. Monique Zerner (Nice: Z'éditions, 1998), 219–69, Jean-Louis Biget questions the tendency to assimilate the diffuse dissident movements of the mid-twelfth-century Midi into one, monolithic "Cathar" or "Albigensian" heretical sect, "plus ou moins fantasmatique" (235).

14. For the *Sermones super Cantica canticorum*, see Bernard, *Opera*, vols. 1 and 2, esp. Sermons 65 and 66, in 2:172–88. It has commonly been thought that Bernard composed these sermons in response to an appeal from Everwin, the prior of the Premonstratensian abbey of Steinfeld, who wrote to him in 1143, troubled by the recent discovery of two clusters of heretics near Cologne, one of which constituted the first "Cathar" sect in Western Europe. For Everwin's letter, see *Epistola ad S. Bernardum (Ep. 472)*, PL 182, cols. 676–80. For discussion of these sermons and Everwin's letter, see Jean Leclercq, *Recueil d'études sur saint Bernard et ses écrits*, vol. 1; Anne Brenon, "La lettre d'Evervin de Steinfeld à Bernard de Clairvaux de 1143: un document essentiel et méconnu," *Heresis* 25 (1995): 7–28; and Raoul Manselli, "Everino di Steinfeld e san Bernardo di Clairvaux," in *Studie sulle eresie del secolo XII*, 2d ed. (Rome: Istituto Palazzo Borremini, 1975), 145–56. In *Des contestataires aux 'Cathares': discours de réforme et propagande antihérétique dans les pays du Rhin et de la Meuse avant l'Inquisition* (Paris: Institut d'études augustiniennes, 2006), however, Uwe Brunn argues that the heretics Everwin describes were detected in 1147 or 1148, after Bernard had composed Sermons 65 and 66, and that the help Everwin sought against heretics would have therefore taken the form of a pastoral campaign, like that Bernard had undertaken against heretics in the Midi in 1145. Brunn maintains, furthermore, that neither of the groups of heretics that Everwin depicts should be identified as "Cathars."

15. In "Bernardo e i movimenti ereticali," in *Bernardo cisterciense*, ed. Enrico Menestò, Atti del XXVI Convegno storico internazionale, Todi (8–11 October 1989) (Spoleto: Centro di studi sulla spiritualità medioevale dell'Università degli Studi di Perugia, 1990), 165–86, Giorgio Cracco argues that Sermon 65 concerns Henry's followers in Toulouse and Sermon 66 the Cathars and other, unnamed heretics in Cologne, but Moore rightly notes that Bernard himself seems to make no distinction between these different sects, either here or in elsewhere.

16. "Tolosani," Bernard, *Cantica canticorum* 65: Preface.

17. While Bernard contrasts these "new heretics [*novi haeretici*]," *Cantica canticorum* 65: Preface, to the late antique "Manichaeans [*Manichaei*]" in *Cantica canticorum* 66.2 (who, he states, could name their founder, Manes), he refers to them as "Manichaeans [*Manichaei*]" in *Cantica canticorum* 66.7.

18. "textores et textrices," Bernard, *Cantica canticorum* 65.5.

19. For accounts of Bernard's journey to the Midi, see Geoffrey of Auxerre, in *Vita prima*, in *PL* 185, cols. 225- 466, at cols. 312–14 and 412–16. (The *Vita prima* was composed by several authors. The edition in the *Patrologia latina* includes Bk. 1, by William of Saint-Thierry, cols. 225–68; Bk. 2, by Arnold of Bonneval, cols. 268–301; Bk. 3, by Geoffrey of Auxerre, cols. 301–22; Bk. 4, also by Geoffrey of Auxerre, cols. 322–50; Bk. 5, also by Geoffrey of Auxerre, cols. 351–68; Bk. 6, Pt. 1, by Philip of Clairvaux, cols. 369–86; Bk. 6, Pt. 2, by various authors, cols. 385–94; Bk. 6, Pt. 3, by Geoffrey of Auxerre, cols. 395–416.) See also Geoffrey of Auxerre, *Epistola ad Archenfredum*, *PL* 185, cols. 410–16; and Conrad of Eberbach, *Exordium magnum Cisterciense, sive narratio de initio Cisterciensis Ordinis*, ed. Bruno Griesser (Rome: Editiones Cistercienses, 1961), 110–11. For critical studies of this voyage, see Beverly M. Kienzle, *Cistercians, Heresy, and the Crusade in Occitania, 1145–1229: Preaching in the Lord's Vineyard* (Woodbridge, England: York Medieval Press, 2001) and "Tending the Lord's Vineyard: Cistercians, Rhetoric, and Heresy: The 1143 Sermons and the 1145 Preaching Mission," *Heresis* 25 (1995): 29–61; Gilles Bounoure, "Saint Bernard et les hérétiques du Sarlandais," *Bulletin de la Société Historique et Archéologique du Périgord* 116 (1989): 277–92 and "Le dernier voyage de saint Bernard en Aquitaine: La Piété des Périgourdins, l'utilité des dimanches, et la vitesse du cheval du saint Bernard," *Bulletin de la Société Historique et Archéologique du Périgord* 115 (1988): 129–34; and R. I. Moore, "St. Bernard's Mission to the Languedoc in 1145," *Bulletin of the Institute for Historical Research* 47 (1974): 1–10. In "St. Bernard's Mission," Moore argues that Bernard's letters give no indication than he encountered any heretics other than the Henricans. Other sources, including Geoffrey of Auxerre, *Vita prima*; William of Puylaurens, *Chronique, 1145–1275*, ed. and trans. Jean Duvernoy (Paris: CNRS, 1976; rpt. Toulouse: Le Pérégrinateur, 1996), esp. 32–35; and Conrad of Eberbach, *Exordium magnum Cisterciense* 17, pp. 110–11, however, may complicate the situation.

20. On the Dominicans' appreciation of Bernard, see Alain Boureau, "La Présence de saint Bernard dans les légendiers dominicains du XIIIe siècle," in *Vies et légendes de saint Bernard*, 84–90.

21. See Jean Leclercq, "L'Hérésie d'après les écrits de s. Bernard de Clairvaux," in *The Concept of Heresy in the Middle Ages, 11th-13th Centuries*, ed. Willem Lourdaux and Daniel Verhelst (The Hague: Martinus Nijhoff, 1976; rpt. Leuven: University Press, 1976), 12–26.

22. Evans, *The Mind of St. Bernard of Clairvaux*, 98.

23. Dominique Iogna-Prat, *Ordonner et exclure: Cluny et la société chrétienne face à l'hérésie, au judaïsme et à l'Islam (1100–1150)* (Paris: Aubier, 1998), 131. In addition to these other studies, Pierre Riché provides a survey of Bernard's actions and writings against heretics in "Saint Bernard et l'hérésie," in *Saint Bernard et la recherche de Dieu, Actes du colloque organisé par l'Institut catholique de Toulouse (25–29 January 1991)*, *Bulletin de la Littérature Ecclésiastique* 93, fasc. 1 (1992): 17–25.

24. Kienzle, *Cistercians, Heresy, and the Crusade in Occitania, 1145–1229*, 11.

25. "subtilissima quaedam vitia specie palliata virtutum," Bernard, *Cantica canticorum* 64.6.

26. On the Cistercians' evolving relationship with this new learning, see Derek Baker, "Heresy and Learning in Early Cistercianism," in *Schism, Heresy, and Religious*

Protest, Papers Read at the Tenth Summer Meeting and the Eleventh Winter Meeting of the Ecclesiastical History Society, ed. Derek Baker (Cambridge: Cambridge University Press, 1972), 93–107.

27. On Bernard's contacts with these learned clerics, see Nikolaus Häring, "Saint Bernard and the *Litterati* of His Day," *Cîteaux: Commentarii Cistercienses* 25 (1974): 199–222.

28. On Bernard's relationship to contemporary learning, see Jacques Verger, "Le Cloître et les écoles," in *Bernard de Clairvaux: Histoire, mentalités, spiritualité*, 459–73. Jean Leclercq's *L'Amour des lettres et le désir de Dieu* (Paris: Éditions du Cerf, 1957), is also useful.

29. "si ignoras te, non habebis timorem Dei in tei, non humilitatem," Bernard, *Cantica canticorum* 36.7.

30. "Osculetur me osculo oris sui," ibid., 8.2. Cf. Sg 1:1.

31. "Merito proinde sponsa, quem diligit anima sua inquirens, non se suae carnis sensibus credit, non curiositatis humanae inanibus ratiociniis acquiescat," ibid., 8.6.

32. "Melius illi erat si, iuxta titulum libri sui, seipsum cognosceret, nec egrederetur mensuram suam," Bernard, *Epistola* 192.1.

33. "Nihil nescit omnium quae in caelo et quae in terra sunt, praeter seipsum," Bernard, *Epistola* 193.1.

34. "Nihil videt 'per speculum et in aenigmate, sed facie ad faciem' omnia intuetur," ibid., 192.1. Cf. 1 Cor 13:12 and Ps 130:1.

35. See, for example, Bernard's letters regarding his nephew Robert (*Epistola* 1), a certain Henry (*Epistola* 509), and Arnold, the abbot of the Cistercian monastery at Morimond (*Epistola* 5).

36. "It, et perit miser, non tam exsul ad patriam quam canis reversus ad vomitum. Et se perdidit infelix, et suorum acquisivit neminem," Bernard, *Cantica canticorum* 64.2. Cf. 2 Pet 2:22.

37. "supernae gratiae . . . irrorari," ibid., 64.3.

38. On the spread of wandering preachers in the wake of the Gregorian Reform, see Henrietta Leyser, *Hermits and the New Monasticism: A Study of Religious Communities in Western Europe, 1000–1150* (London: Macmillan, 1984); Jean Musy, "Mouvements populaires et hérésies au XIe siècle en France," *Revue historique* 253 (1975): 33–76; and Johannes Wilhelm von Walter, *Die ersten Wanderprediger Frankreichs: Studien zur Geschichte des Mönchtums*, 2 vols. (Leipzig: Deicherschen Verlagshandlung, 1903).

39. "Quomodo praedicabunt, nisi mittantur?" Bernard, *Cantica canticorum* 64.3. Rom 10:15 (Vg: Quomodo vero).

40. "voluntatem vestram, ecce nunc . . . magistram habetis, non me," ibid., 19.7.

41. "Homo apostata est, qui relicto religionis habitu—nam monachus exstitit—ad spurcitias carnis et saeculi, tamquam 'canis ad suum vomitum, est reversus," Bernard, *Epistola* 241.3. Cf. Prov 26:4.

42. "gyrovagus et profugus super terram," Bernard, *Epistola* 241.3. Cf. Lk 2:44. Benedict had defined gyrovagues as monks "who spend their entire lives drifting from region to region. . . . Always on the move, they never settle down, and are slaves to their own wills and gross appetites [*qui tota vita sua per diversas provincias ternis aut quaternis diebus per diversorum cellas hospitantur, semper vagi et numquam stabiles, et propriis voluntatibus et gulae illecebris servientes*]," *The Rule of Saint Benedict in Latin and English with Notes*, ed. Timothy Fry (Collegeville, Minn.: The Liturgical Press, 1981), 1:10–11.

43. "Cumque mendicare coepisset, posuit in sumptu Evangelium—nam litteratus erat—, et venale distrahens verbum Dei, evangelizabat ut manducaret," Bernard, *Epistola* 241.3.

44. "Quomodo . . . praedicabunt, nisi mittantur?" ibid., 242.3. Cf. Rom 10:15. In his original mission to Le Mans, Henry does seem to have been sent by Hildebert of Lavardin, the bishop of this town, but, due to the insurrection he aroused against this bishop, he soon lost that authorization.

45. See also Bernard, *Liber de gradibus humilitatis et superbiae* 14.42, in *Opera*, ed. Leclercq, 3:13–59, at 48–49. This chapter is entitled "De singularite."

46. "non habet callidus hostis machinamentum efficacius ad tollendam de corde dilectionem, quam si efficere possit, ut in ea incaute et non cum ratione ambuletur," Bernard, *Cantica canticorum* 19.7.

47. "Nihil ergo simile habent constantia martyrum et pertinacia horum, quia mortis contemptum in illis pietas, in istis cordis duritia operatur," Bernard, *Cantica canticorum* 66.13.

48. "Habemus in Francia monachum sine regula, sine sollicitudine praelatum, sine disciplina abbatem, Petrum Abaelardum, disputantem cum pueris, conversantem cum mulierculis," Bernard, *Epistola* 332.1.

49. "Homo sibi dissimilis est, intus Herodes, foris Ioannes, totus ambiguus, nihil habens de monacho praeter nomen et habitum," ibid., 193.1. See also Bernard, *Epistolae* 330 and 331.

50. "Frequenter siquidem post diurnum populi plausam, nocte insecuta cum meretricibus inventus est praedicator insignis, et interdum etiam cum coniugatis," ibid., 241:3.

51. "homo a Deo,' qui sic contraria Deo et facit, et loquitur," ibid., 241.2. Cf. Jn 9:16.

52. "Quotidie latus tuum ad latus iuvenculae est in mensa, lectus tuus ad lectum eius in camera, oculi tui ad illius oculos in colloquio, manus tuae ad manus ipsius in opere; et continens vis putari?" Bernard, *Cantica canticorum* 65.4.

53. "Ubi apostolica forma et vita quam iactatis?" ibid.

54. See Bernard, *Epistola* 89.2. See also Bernard, *Cantica canticorum* 12.8 and 76.10.

55. See Bernard, *Epistola* 48. See also Bernard, *Cantica canticorum* 22.2.

56. "Aut si idoneum crediderunt ob habitum religionis, quod induor, in habitu species est sanctitatis, non sanctitas," Bernard, *Epistola* 449.1. See also Bernard, *Cantica canticorum* 55.2.

57. "Clamat ad vos mea monstruosa vita, mea aerumnosa conscientia. Ego enim quaedam Chimaera mei saeculi, nec clericum gero nec laicum. Nam monachi iamdudum exui conversationem, non habitum," Bernard, *Epistola* 250.4.

58. Homer is the first to describe the chimera in the *Iliad* 6.181, where he represents her as a goddess with the head of a lion, the body of a goat, and the tail of a serpent, who breathed forth flames. Hesiod depicts her in *Theogony* 319 as a creature with three heads, one from each of these animals. Bernard was more likely to have encountered this monster in Ovid, *Metamorphoses* 9.648 or Isidore of Seville, *Etymologiae* 11.3.36. T. Alexander Heslop argues, in "Contemplating Chimera in Medieval Imagination: St. Anselm's Crypt of Canterbury," in *Raising the Eyebrow: John Onians and World Art Studies*, ed. Lauren Golden (Oxford: British Archaeological Reports, 2001), 153–68, that, at the turn of the eleventh and twelfth centuries, the chimera was perceived positively before it became defined by Bernard's negative characterization. For Anselm of Canterbury, for example, God

alone can conceive of creatures *ex nihilo*, but the human artist can patch together these creatures to make chimerical hybrids. The creation of such a hybrid is thus the closest an artist can come to godlike creation.

59. "ridicula monstruositas," Bernard, *Apologia ad Guillelmum abbatem* 12:29, in *Opera*, 3:82–108. For just a sampling of the criticism that has been devoted to this passage, see Thomas E. A. Dale, "The Monstrous," in *A Companion to Medieval Art: Romanesque and Gothic in Northern Europe*, ed. Conrad Rudolph (Malden, Mass.: Blackwell, 2006), 253–73; Conrad Rudolph, *"Things of Greater Importance": Bernard of Clairvaux's "Apologia" and the Medieval Attitude Toward Art* (Philadelphia: University of Pennsylvania Press, 1990); and Meyer Schapiro, "On the Aesthetic Attitude in Romanesque Art," in *Art and Thought: Issued in Honor of Dr. Ananda K. Coomaraswamy on the Occasion of His 70th Birthday*, ed. K. B. Iyer (London: Luzak, 1947), 130–50; rpt. Meyer Schapiro, *Romanesque Art* (New York: G. Braziller, 1977), 1–27, esp. 6–11.

60. Caroline Walker Bynum, "Monsters, Medians, and Marvelous Mixtures: Hybrids in the Spirituality of Bernard of Clairvaux," in *Metamorphosis and Identity* (New York: Zone Books, 2001), 113–62. Bernard's contemporaries were also drawn to such hybrids. Christine Ferlampen-Archer, in "Le Monstre dans les romans des XIIIe et XIVe siècles," in *Écriture et modes de pensée au Moyen Âge (VIIIe-Xve siècle)*, ed. Dominique Boutet and Laurence Harf-Lancner (Paris: École Nationale Supérieure, 1993), 69–87, maintains that it was precisely in the twelfth century, when Bernard was living, that hybrids became an important object of interest (in bestiaries, for example), disappearing in the early thirteenth century, and reappearing in the fourteenth century not as fixed, composite beings but as mobile shape-shifters. Constance Brittain Bouchard, in *"Every Valley Shall Be Exalted": The Discourse of Opposites in Twelfth-Century Thought* (Ithaca: Cornell University Press, 2003), similarly argues that it was in the twelfth century that opposites, such as the secular life and the religious life or the masculine and the feminine, came to be valued as opposites, while, in the thirteenth century, one pole was made to dominate the other or the two poles were made to meet in the middle.

61. See Henri de Lubac, *Exégèse médiévale: Les quatre sens de l'écriture*, 4 vols. (Paris: Auber, 1959–64), esp. vol. 2, chap. 8, "Le Fondement de l'histoire," 425–87. On Bernard's version of exegesis, see 2:571–620.

62. "pseudoprophetae," 1 Jn 4:1.

63. "seductores," 2 Jn 7.

64. "et hic est antichristus quod audistis quoniam venit, et nunc iam in mundo est," 1 Jn 4:3.

65. "draco ille magnus, serpens antiquus, . . . vocatur Diabolus, et Satanas, qui seducit universum orbem," Rev 12:9.

66. "sicut draco," Rev 13:11.

67. "pseudopropheta," Rev 19:20. Cf. Mt 24:11 and 24:24.

68. "Praecedit iam Petrus Abaelardus ante faciem Antichristi parare vias eius," Bernard, *Epistola* 336.1. Cf. Lk 1:76.

69. "Evasimus rugitum Petri Leonis, sedem Simonis Petri occupantem; sed Petrum Draconis incurrimus, fidem Simonis Petri impugnantem," Bernard, *Epistola* 330.1.

70. "virus suum," Bernard, *Epistolae* 330.1 and 332.1.

71. "iste vero, nova dogmata scribens, iam providit quomodo virus suum transfundat in posteros, quomodo noceat 'generationi omni quae ventura est," Bernard, *Epistolae* 330.1 and 332.1. Cf. Ps 70:18.

72. "tamquam draco, 'sedet in insidiis in occultis, ut interficiat innocentem," Bernard, *Epistola* 330.1. Cf. Ps. 9:28 (8) (Vg: insidiis . . . in).

73. "draconem . . . sedens in insidiis," ibid., 189.2.

74. "Attendite a falsis prophetis, qui veniunt ad vos in vestimentis ovium, intrinsecus autem sunt lupi rapaces," Mt 7:15.

75. "iter arripui ad has partes, quas potissimum singularis ferus depascitur, 'dum non est qui' resistat 'neque qui salvum faciat.' Quippe de tota Francia pro simili effugatus malitia, has solas sibi invenit expositas, in quibus fiducialiter sub tuo dominatu in gregem Christi toto furore bacchatur," Bernard, *Epistola* 241.2. Cf. Ps 79:14 and Ps 7:3.

76. "lupi . . . devorabant plebem vestram sicut escam panis, sicut oves occisionis," ibid., 242.1.

77. "Versatur in terra sub vestimentis ovium lupus rapax," ibid., 241.1.

78. "cogniscite in vestimentis ovium lupos rapaces," ibid, 242.3.

79. "qua arte diabolica persuasit populo stulto et insipienti, de re manifesta nec suis credere occulis," ibid., 241.2.

80. "Capite nobis vulpes parvulas, quae demoliuntur vineas," Bernard, *Cantica canticorum* 63.1. Cf. Sg 2:15.

81. For the history of this exegesis, see G. M. Dubarle, "Les Renards de Samson," *Revue du Moyen Âge latin* 7 (1951): 174–76; Lothar Kolmer, *'Ad capiendas vulpes': Die Ketzerbekämpfung in Südfrankreich in der ersten Hälfte des 13. Jahrhunderts und die Ausbildung des Inquisitionsverfahrens* (Bonn: Röhrscheid, 1982); Maddelena Scopello, "Le Renard symbole de l'hérésie dans les polémiques patristiques contre les gnostiques," *Revue d'histoire et de philosophie religieux* 71 (1991): 73–88; Jacques Voisenet, "Le Renart dans les bestiaires des clercs médiévaux," *Reinardus* 9 (1996): 179–88; and my own "Filz a putein, puant heirites': The Heterodoxy of Renart," *Reinardus* 16 (2003): 1–12. Origen, Ambrose of Milan, and Augustine are just three of the most important clerics who identify the scriptural foxes with heretics.

82. "Sola ista malignior ceteris versutiorque haeresibus, damnis pascitur alienis, proprie gloriae negligens," Bernard, *Cantica canticorum* 65.2.

83. "his malignissimis vulpibus . . . nocere quam vincere malunt," ibid.

84. "Versuta est valde, operta est iniquitate et impietate sua, plane tam pusilla atque subtilis, ut humanos quidem facile frustretur obtutus," ibid., 65.4.

85. "secretum prodere noli," ibid., 65.2.

86. "Iam quod ad vitam moresque spectat, neminem concutit, neminem circumvenit, neminem supergreditur. Pallent insuper ora ieiuniis, panem non comedit otiosus, operatur manibus unde vitam sustenat," ibid., 65.5. Cf. Lk 3:14, Prov 31:27, and 1 Thess 4:11.

87. "Ubi iam vulpis? Tenebamus eam: quomodo elapsa est manibus?" ibid., 65.5.

88. "aemulor enim vos Dei aemulatione, despondi enim vos uni viro virginem castam exhibere Christo," 2 Cor. 11:2.

89. "Ecclesiae maculat castitatem. . . . Maculavit Ecclesiam homo ille," Bernard, *Epistola* 338.1.

90. "familiarius," ibid., 330.1.

91. "Quantum desiderarem videre amicum Sponsi pro Sponsa zelantem in absentia Sponsi!" Ibid.

92. "Nam quia Sponsum diligis, Sponsam ad te clamantem non 'despicis in opportunitatibus, in tribulatione," ibid. Cf. Ps 9:22.

93. "Inter haec omnia genera hostium, quibus circumvallatur Ecclesia Dei, . . . nihil periculosius, nihil molestius est, quam cum ab eis, quos continet in gremio suo, et quos suis fovet uberibus, laceratur interius," ibid.

94. "Si filius eius es, defende uterum qui te portavit et ubera quae suxisti," ibid., 333.1.

95. "Si filius huius es, si materna ubera recognoscis, non deseras matrem in periculo, non subtrahas humeros tuos in tempore tribulationis," ibid., 334.1.

96. "si amas Dominum Iesum toto corde, tota anima, tota virtute tua, numquid, si videris eius iniurias contemptumque, ferre ullatenus aequo animo poteris? Minime," Bernard, *Cantica canticorum* 44.8.

97. "Nonne qui oderunt te, Domine, oderam, et super inimicos tuos tabescebam? Perfecto odio oderam illos, et inimici facti sunt mihi," ibid., 60.10 and 50.7. Cf. Ps. 138:21.

98. "de quo constat quod ad amorem Dei non sit deinceps rediturus, sapiat tibi necesse est, non prope iam nihili, sed nihili ex toto, utpote quod in aeternum nihili est. . . . Non modo iam non diligendus, insuper et odio habendus est," ibid., 50.7.

99. "qui diligunt, zelantur," Bernard, *De consideratione* 3.9, *Opera*, ed. Leclercq, 3:379–493.

100. "Diligite justitiam, qui judicatis terram," ibid. Cf. Wis 1:1.

101. "Amator iustitiae inquirit iustitiam et prosequitur eam; porro omnem iniustitiam persequitur," ibid.

102. "principes, . . . de clero, necnon et de ordine episcoporum, qui magis persequi eos debuerant, propter quaestum sustineant, accipientes ab eis munera," Bernard, *Cantica canticorum* 66.14.

103. " . . . osculis inhiare . . . , secretum quaerere sibi, fugitare publicum, declinare turbas, et curae ipsarum propriam praeferre quietem," ibid., 9.9.

104. "osculis contemplationis," ibid., 9.8.

105. "deliciis dulcis quietis tuae non longe antehac fruebare," Bernard, *De consideratione* 1.1.

106. "in mediis occupationibus, quoniam multae sunt, dum finem diffidis, frontem dures, et ita sensim te ipsum quodammodo sensu prives iusti utilisque doloris," ibid., 1.3.

107. "cor durum," ibid.

108. "exceditur et seceditur etiam a corporeis sensibus, ut sese non sentiat quae Verbum sentit," Bernard, *Cantica canticorum* 85.13.

109. "Hoc siquidem vera et casta contemplatio habet, ut mentem, quam divino igne vehementer succenderit, tanto interdum repleat zelo et desiderio acquirendi Deo qui eum similiter diligant, ut otium contemplationis pro studio praedicationis libentissime intermittat," ibid., 57.9.

110. "redeat divino amore vehementissime flagrans et aestuans iustitiae zelo, necnon et in cunctis spiritualibus studiis atque officiis pernimium fervens," ibid., 49.4.

111. "Itaque homo de Ecclesia exercitatus et doctus, si cum haeretico homine disputare aggreditur, illo suam intentionem dirigere debet, quatenus ita errantem convincat, ut et convertat," ibid., 64.8. (Vg: et operiet).

112. "haeretici capiantur . . . , non armis, sed argumentis, quibus refellantur errores eorum; ipsi vero, si fieri potest, reconcilientur Catholicae, revocentur ad veram fidem," ibid.

113. See Constant J. Mews, "Peter Abelard and the Enigma of Dialogue," in *Beyond the Persecuting Society: Religious Toleration Before the Enlightenment*, ed. John Christian Laursen and Cary J. Nederman (Philadelphia: University of Pennsylvania Press, 1999), 25–52.

114. "Itaque in praesentia omnium, adversario stante ex adverso, producta sunt quaedam capitula de libris eius excerpta. Quae cum coepissent legi . . . ," Bernard, *Epistola* 189.4.

115. "Responde mihi, . . . Dei est, an non, mysterium quod occultas?" Bernard, *Cantica canticorum* 65.3. Cf. Rom 12:3.

116. "An forte nec Paulum recipitis? De quibusdam ita audivi," ibid.

117. "Procedit Golias, . . . clamat adversus phalangas Israel exprobratque agminibus sanctorum, eo nimirum audacius quo sentit David non adesse," Bernard, *Epistola* 189.3.

118. "imparatus . . . et immunitus, nisi quod mente voluebam: 'Nolite praemeditari qualiter respondeatis; dabitur enim vobis in illa hora quid loquamini," ibid., 189.4. Cf. Lk 21:14.

119. "Dicebam sufficere scripta eius ad accusandum eum," ibid.

120. "Ego non eum accuso apud Patrem: est qui eum accuset liber suus," ibid., 192.1.

121. "Porro capitula, iudicio omnium examinata, inventa sunt fidei adversantia, contraria veritati," ibid., 189.4.

122. "disputationes . . . et pugnas verborum, quae magis ad subversionem quam ad inventionem proficiunt veritatis," Bernard, *De consideratione* 1.13.

123. "destruunt simplicitatem veritatis," ibid.

124. "Cumque totis ingenii viribus, quo non mediocriter callebat, asserere et defendere conaretur errorem, Malachia contra disputante et convincente, iudicio omnium superatus, de conventu confusus quidem exiit, sed non correctus," Bernard, *Vita Sancti Malachiae episcopi* 26.57, in *Opera*, 3:307–78.

125. "non ratione victum, sed episcopi pressum auctoritate," ibid.

126. "resipiscat," ibid.

127. "sanaretur," ibid.

128. "obstinatissimos," Bernard, *Cantica canticorum* 66.14.

129. "istos, nec rationibus convincuntur, quia non intelligunt, nec auctoritatibus corriguntur, quia non recipiunt, nec flectuntur suasionibus, quia subversi sunt," ibid., 66.12.

130. "potestas . . . non modo in corpora hominum, sed etiam in corda," ibid., 66.13.

131. "mori magis eligunt, quam converti. Horum finis interitus, horum novissima incendium manent," ibid., 66.12.

132. "Deus . . . fateri te veritatem faciat, vel ex necessitate," Bernard, *Vita Sancti Malachiae* 26.57.

133. "Infirmitas ista haud alia . . . quam ipsa mors est," ibid.

134. "Hoc autem non dixit a semetipso, sed pulchre Deus per insanum corripuit eum, qui sanis acquiescere noluit consiliis sensatorum," ibid.

135. "error magis confirmaretur, cum non esset qui responderet aut contradiceret," Bernard, *Epistola* 189.4.

136. "pro homine sic indurato, sed magis fidei dolens iniuriam," Bernard, *Vita Sancti Malachiae* 26.57.

137. "non est opus ... frustra multa adversus homines stultissimos atque obstinatissimos dicere," Bernard, *Cantica canticorum* 66.14.

138. "sufficit innotuisse illos, ut caveantur," ibid.

139. "Nam si haereticus non surrexit de faece, Ecclesia tamen confirmatur in fide; et quidem de profectibus Sponsae Sponsus sine dubio gratulatur," ibid., 64.9.

140. "factum non suademus, quia fides suadenda est, non imponenda," ibid., 66.12.

141. "Approbamus zelum," ibid.

142. "Dei enim minster ille est, vindex in iram ei qui male agit," ibid. Cf. Rom 13:4.

143. "melius procul dubio gladio coercentur, illius videlicet qui 'non sine causa gladium portat,' quam in suum errorem multos traicere permittantur," ibid. Cf. Rom 13:4.

144. "viros in litteris famosissimos, Petrum Abaielardum et prefatum Gislebertum, tanto studio insectatus est, ut alterum Petrum scilicet condempnari fecerit, alterum adhibita omni diligentia nisus sit condempnare," John of Salisbury, *Memoirs of the Papal Court*, 16.

145. "Set mihi persuaderi non potest quod homo tante sanctitatis non habuerit zelum Dei," ibid.

146. "In quo servus Dei, etsi nimietate forsitan excessit, piis certe mentibus non de nimietate, sed de fervore exemplum reliquit," William of Saint-Thierry, *Vita prima* 1.8, col. 251. Interestingly, in *Cantica canticorum* 49.5 and *De consideratione* 2.23, Bernard himself recognizes the importance of having zeal tempered by "discretion" (*discretio*), which prevents the zealot from abusing the weak and accusing the innocent.

CHAPTER TWO

1. In contrast to Bernard of Clairvaux, whose works spread out over eight volumes, Dominic Gúzman wrote little: all we possess from his pen are two letters regarding heretics (which we will consider) and a third letter offering spiritual guidance to the Dominican nuns of Madrid. The primitive constitutions of the Friars Preacher, drafted for the first general chapter of the order in 1220, are thought to reflect Dominic's views, but they are the product of many minds in addition to his. Given the paucity of Dominic's own writings, it is necessary for anyone seeking to understand this figure to turn to the numerous other Dominican and non-Dominican sources which make mention of him during the thirteenth and early fourteenth centuries. Jordan of Saxony, who became master general of the order after Dominic's death, provided the first account of Dominic's life in a small volume on the origins of the Friars Preacher composed between 1219 and 1221 and reedited in 1233, and, in doing so, established the foundation upon which subsequent lives would rest. The canonization proceedings of 1233–34 brought many contemporaries of Dominic to Bologna or Toulouse to testify in his behalf, adding their recollections to Jordan's corpus. Shortly after Dominic was proclaimed a saint in 1234, his friars began to prepare new lives of their founder, in recognition of his exalted status. Peter Ferrand contributed one such legend between 1237 and 1242, as did Constantine of Orvieto between 1246 and 1247 and Humbert of Romans around 1256. Gerard of Frachet collected a series of miracles and edifying tales about the Dominicans in his *Vitae fratrum* of 1259, devoting the first section of the work to Dominic. Other works from a variety of genres also addressed Dominic in the mid-years of the thirteenth century.

Thomas Agni of Lentini prepared a sermon about Dominic before 1255, and Stephen of Bourbon inserted anecdotes about him in his manual for preachers in the 1250s. Stephen of Salanhac began a history of the Dominican order which included pages about Dominic in the 1270s; given his roots in the Midi, it may be that he derived his information from a local tradition in this region. In the first decades of the fourteenth century, Berengar of Landorra, the current master general of the order, commissioned an account of Dominic's miracles, and Bernard Gui edited and expanded Stephen of Salanhac's account of Dominic, in addition to drafting his own narratives about the saint. Peter Calo, who died in the mid-fourteenth century, also wrote an account. In general, while the earlier lives of Dominic had tended to depict the saint as one of many individuals instrumental in the development of the order (including Diego of Azevedo, Fulk of Marseilles, and Reginald of Orleans), the later accounts tend to portray Dominic as a solitary founder. The earlier accounts are more distinctively historical, emphasizing the realistic details of his life, and the later ones more conventionally hagiographical, stressing the miracles associated with him. The Cistercian chronicler Peter of Les Vaux-de-Cernay (writing around 1218), the secular priest William of Puylaurens (writing around 1275), and the secular cleric William of Tudela (writing between 1210 and 1213) have little to nothing to say about Dominic in particular, but these three authors depict well the preaching mission against the heretics in the Midi of 1203–8, in which Dominic participated, and thus are relevant to our purpose. For criticism of Dominic, see especially Marie-Humbert Vicaire's numerous scholarly works, including *Histoire de Saint Dominique*, 2 vols. (Paris: Éditions du Cerf, 1957; rev. ed., 1982) and the essays collected in *Dominique et ses prêcheurs*, 2d ed. (Paris: Éditions du Cerf, 1979). For discussion of the sources of Dominic's life in particular, see Vicaire, *Saint Dominique et ses frères: Évangile ou croisade* (Paris: Éditions du Cerf, 1967), 31–43. On the ways in which Dominic's biography was transformed by his friars as their order developed, see Luigi Canetti, *L'Invenzione della memoria:. Il culto e l'immagine di Domenico nella storia dei primi frati Predicatori* (Spoleto: Centro italiano di studi sull'alto medioevo, 1996).

2. "noctem [impartiebatur] deo," Jordan of Saxony, *Libellus de principiis Ordinis Praedicatorum*, ed. H. C. Scheeben, MOPH, vol. 16 (Rome: Institutum historicum FF. Praedicatorum, 1935), pp. 25–88, at 105. See also Charles Peytavie, "La Figure de l'hérétique dans l'hagiographie de saint Dominique: L'exemple du *Libellus de principiis Ordinis Fratrum Praedicatorum* de Jourdain de Saxe, O.P.," *Heresis* 36–37 (2002): 239–52.

3. "Flendi pro peccatoribus, pro miseris, pro afflictis singularem gratiam tribuerat ei Deus, quorum calamitates in intimo gestabat compassionis sacrario, et estuantem interius per exitus oculorum foras ebuliebat affectum," Jordan of Saxony, *Libellus* 12.

4. See *Acta canonizationis s. Dominici*, ed. R. P. Angelus Walz, MOPH, vol. 16 (1935): Bologna Canonization Process, 118–67; Languedoc Canonization Process, 173–87, at (Bologna), 25. Even the torments of the damned souls in Hell are said to have caused him pain, as Ventura of Verona testifies, in *Acta canonizationis s. Dominici* (Bologna), 11.

5. "Diem impartiebatur proximis," Jordan of Saxony, *Libellus* 105.

6. "Tempore diurno cum fratribus sociisve nemo communior, nemo iucundior," ibid., 104.

7. "inerat cordi eius mira et pene incredibilis salutis omnium emulatio," ibid., 34.

8. On this campaign, see Etienne Delaruelle, "Paix de dieu et croisade dans la chrétienté du XIIe siècle," CF, vol. 4, *Paix de Dieu et guerre sainte* (Toulouse: Privat, 1969),

72–90, and Vicaire, "'L'Affaire de paix et de foi' du Midi de la France," ibid., 102–27; rpt. in *Dominique et ses prêcheurs*, 2d ed. (Paris: Editions du Cerf, 1979), 3–20.

9. "cum ordo noster specialiter ob predicationem et animarum salutem ab initio noscatur institutus fuisse, et studium nostrum ad hoc principaliter ardenterque summo opere debeat intendere, ut proximorum animabus possimus utiles esse," *Constitutiones antiquae ordinis Fratrum Praedicatorum (1215–1237)*, ed. A. H. Thomas (Leuven: Dominikanenklooster, 1965), Prologus, 15.

10. See Vicaire, "Saint Dominique et les inquisiteurs," *Annales du Midi* 79 (1967): 173–94; rpt. in *Dominique et ses prêcheurs*, 36–57, for this history of this linkage of Dominic and the Inquisition. See also Canetti, *L'Invenzione della memoria*, Appendix, "*Persequutor hereticorum*: Domenico e gli eretici," 221–66.

11. Christine Thouzellier provoked a debate with Vicaire when she referred to Dominic as displaying a "zèle précocement 'inquisitorial" in *Catharisme et Valdéisme en Languedoc à la fin du XIIe et au début du XIIIe siècle: Politique pontificale, controverses* (Paris: Presses Universitaires de France, 1966), 251. Vicaire refuted this accusation of Thouzellier's in "Saint Dominique et les inquisiteurs," to which Thouzellier replied in "*L'Inquisitio* et saint Dominique," *Annales du Midi* 80 (1968): 121–30, to which Vicaire once again responded, in "Note sur la mentalité de saint Dominique," *Annales du Midi* 80 (1968): 131–36, to which Thouzellier once more answered in "Réponse au M.-H. Vicaire," in *Annales du Midi* 80 (1968): 137–38. See also Vicaire, "*Persequutor hereticorum* ou les 'persecutions' de saint Dominique," CF, vol. 6, *Le Crédo, la morale et l'Inquisition* (Toulouse: Privat, 1971), 75–84; rpt. in *Dominique et ses prêcheurs*, 143–48. See Innocent III's bull of May 31, 1204, in *Monumenta diplomatica S. Dominici*, 8–11, to Arnold Amalric, Peter of Castelnau, and Ralph, where he grants these legates this authority.

12. Dominic refers to reconciling Pons Roger "by the authority of the Lord Abbot of Cîteaux [Arnold Amalric], legate of the apostolic see, who enjoined this function on us [*Auctoritate domini abbatis Cisterciensis, apostolice Sedis legati, qui hoc nobis iniunxit officium*]," *Monumenta Diplomatica S. Dominici*, ed. Vladimír J. Koudelka and Raymond J. Loenertz, MOFP, vol. 25 (Rome: Apud Institutum Historicum Fratrum Praedicatorum, 1966), Epistola 8. He warns, "Should he refuse to observe these directives, we command that he be deemed a perjurer and a heretic excommunicated from association with the faithful [*Quod si observare contempserit, tamquam periurum, hereticum et excommunicatum haberi precipimus et a fidelium consortio sequestrari*]," ibid. Dominic declared at least eleven other heretics reconciled during this time, according to testimony at the inquisitorial processes of 1243–44 and 1245–46.

13. Ibid., *Epistola* 61.

14. "Ipse enim fuit primus inquisitor per sedem apostolicam deputans et eius litteras duas legi, in quibus de hoc officio mentionem facit expressam," Peter Calo, *Legendae Sancti Dominici*, ed. Simon Tugwell, *MOPH*, vol. 26 (Rome: Apud Institutum Historicum Fratrum Praedicatorum, 1997), 127–296, at 271–72.

15. "Predicante aliquando viro Dei Dominico in partibus Tolosanis, contigit quosdam hereticos captos et per eum convictos, cum redire nollent ad fidem catholicam, tradi iudicio seculari," Constantine of Orvieto, *Legenda Sancti Dominici* 51, *MOPH*, vol. 26 (Rome: Apud Institutum Historicum Fratrum Praedicatorum, 1935).

16. "gerente inquisitionis officium contra labem hereticam," Bernard Gui, *Legenda sancti Dominici*, in Bernard Gui, *Scripta de Sancto Dominico*, ed. Simon Tugwell, *MOPH*, vol. 27 (Rome: Apud Institutum Historicum Ordinis Fratrum Praedicatorum, 1998), 272.

17. Tugwell, "Introduction: *Speculum Sanctorale*," 173.

18. When Dominic was living in Italy, the Dominican provincial prior Stephen locates him in "the cities of Lombardy, in which a great multitude of heretics were burned [*in civitatibus Lombarie, in quibus maxima multitudo hereticorum est combusta*]," *Acta canonizationis s. Dominici* (Bologna), 39, yet he does not attribute these burnings to Dominic. Stephen of Salanhac writes of Dominic, "He judged by the sword and fire spiritually and even corporally [*iudicavit quoque in gladio et igni spiritualiter et etiam corporaliter*]," *De quatuor in quibus Deus Predicatorum ordinem insignivit* 2.2, ed. Thomas Kaeppeli, *MOPH*, vol. 22 (Rome: Institutum Historicum Fratrum Praedicatorum, 1949), yet he provides no details about the corporeal judgments he ascribes to the saint.

19. Gui, *Scripta de Sancto Dominico*, ed. Tugwell, 172.

20. "Siquidem dum piis exhortationibus quendam infidelem ad fidele matris ecclesie gremium invitaret et ille responderet necessitudinem temporalium sibi provocativam societatis infidelium pro eo, quod eidem ab hereticis necessarie ministrabantur impense, quas aliunde habere non poterat," Jordan of Saxony, *Libellus* 35.

21. "quarundam feminarum nobilium, quas parentes earum ratione paupertatis erudiendas et nutriendas tradebant hereticis," ibid., 27.

22. "egestate compulsi," Peter Ferrand, *Legenda Sancti Dominici* 16.

23. "ex intimo mox ei compassus affectu se ipsum venumdare decrevit et pretio sui redimere anime periclitantis inopiam; quod et fecisset, nisi dominus, qui dives est in omnes, aliunde providisset, quo illius hominis resarciretur egestas," Jordan of Saxony, *Libellus* 35. Cf. Rom 10:12.

24. "Ad susceptionem autem quarundam feminarum nobilium . . . quoddam instituit monasterium, situm . . . nomen loci eiusdem Prulianum," ibid., 27.

25. "Ipsa nocte vero, qua in prefata civitate hospitati sunt, supprior ille cum hospite domus heretico multa disputatione et persuasione fortiter et ferventer agens, dum non posset hereticus resistere sapientie et spiritui quo loquebatur, ad fidem ipsum spiritu dei mediante reduxit," ibid., 15. Cf. Acts 6:10.

26. "Serve Dei, adjuva nos. Si vera sunt, que hodie predicasti, iam diu mentes nostras erroris spiritus excecavit. Nam istis, quos tu hereticos vocas, nos autem bonos homines appellamus, usque in hodiernum diem credidimus et adhesimus toto corde. Nunc autem in medio fluctuamus. Serve Dei, adiuva nos, et ora ad dominum Deum tuum, ut notam nobis faciat fidem suam, in qua vivamus, moriamur et salvemur," Constantine of Orvieto, *Legenda Sancti Dominici* 48, ed. H.-C. Scheeben, *MOPH*, vol. 16 (1935), 286–352. A certain Berengaria testifies about this incident at the canonization proceedings. See *Acta canonizationis s. Dominici* (Toulouse), 23.

27. "Constantes estote et exspectate intrepide; confido in Domino meo, quod ipse, qui neminem vult perire, iam ostendet vobis, quali domino hactenus adhesistis," Constantine of Orvieto, *Legenda Sancti Dominici* 49.

28. "Cumque essent incendio deputati, aspiciens inter alios quendam Raymundum, de Grossi nomine, ac si aliquem in eo divine predestinationis radium fuisset intuitus. 'Istum,' inquit officialibus curie, 'reservate, nec aliquomodo cum ceteris comburatur.'

Conversusque ad eum blandeque alloquens, 'Scio,' inquit, 'fili mi, scio, quod adhuc licet tarde bonus homo eris et sanctus," Constantine of Orvieto, *Legenda Sancti Dominici*, 51. Cf. Ez 11:33.

29. Tugwell, "Introduction: *Speculum sanctorale*," in Bernard Gui, *Scripta de Sancto Dominico*, MOPH, vol. 27 (1998), 237–94, at 234.

30. As such converts were expected to do, Raymond Gros shared his knowledge about his former co-religionists with the Dominican friars in order to assist them in their prosecutions, and he did so in a manner so thorough that he is said to have kept several clerics busy transcribing his confession for several days. Many heretics who heard of Raymond Gros's change of heart followed him, in despair, to the friars' house, where, instead of confessing themselves, they said merely, "My lords, know that it is all as Lord Raymond said [*Domini, sciatis quod totum est ita sicut dominus Raimundus dicit*]," William Pelhisson, *Chronique (1229–1244), suivie du récit des troubles d'Albi (1234)*, ed. and trans. Jean Duvernoy (Paris: CNRS, 1994), 94. For the numerous other sources on Raymond Gros's activities as a Cathar Perfect, see ibid., 92–93, n. 103. Strangely enough, a certain Peter Garcias of Bourguet-Nau testified to inquisitors in 1247 that "Brother R[aymond] Gros died in the faith of the heretics [*frater R. Gros obiit in fide hereticorum*]," *Documents pour servir à l'histoire de l'Inquisition dans le Languedoc*, ed. Célestin Douais, 2 vols. (Paris: Librairie Renouard, 1900), 2:105. There is no evidence to support Garcias's contention, however, and Tugwell for one rejects it in "Introduction: *Speculum sanctorale*," at 232–33.

31. Vicaire questions the veracity of Constantine's anecdote for several reasons. He notes that, while William Pelhisson describes Raymond Gros's conversion in detail, he omits any reference to Dominic's prophecy of this conversion, even though he would have been familiar with this prophecy from Constantine's text and, even more, from Humbert of Romans' retelling of it in his own legend of the saint. It was likely, Vicaire concludes, that Constantine, a hagiographer particularly interested in such marvels, invented the prophecy in order to explain, in retrospect, the surprising character of Raymond Gros's conversion but that Pelhisson rejected it as untrue. Tugwell, however, contests Vicaire's assumption that Pelhisson must have known of Constantine's or Humbert's texts at the time he wrote this chronicle and hypothesizes that Raymond Gros may have shared this information with the other friars only after he had established himself in the order. See Tugwell, "Raymund Gros and Dominic's Prophecy," *Bernardi Guidonis Scripta de Sancto Dominico*, MOPH, vol. 27 (1998), 228–36.

32. "tam affabili persuasione devincens quam irrefragabili rationum connexione," Peter Ferrand, *Legenda Sancti Dominici* 11, ed. Marie-Hyacinthe Laurent, MOPH, vol. 16 (1935): 209–60. Cf. Acts 6:10.

33. "benigna ... et evangelica persuasione," Constantine of Orvieto, *Legenda Sancti Dominici* 12.

34. "eos caritative ad penitentiam et conversionem fidei horabatur," John of Spain, *Acta canonizationis s. Dominici* (Bologna), 27.

35. "Nec certe deerat ei caritas, qua maiorem nemo habet, ut animam suam ponat quis pro amicis suis," Jordan of Saxony, *Libellus* 35. Cf. Jn 25:13.

36. "Karitatis quoque perfectione non vacuus pro salute proximorum animam suam ponere promptus erat," Peter Ferrand, *Legenda Sancti Dominici* 21.

37. "Omnes homines largo excipiebat caritatis sinu, et cum omnes dilligeret, ab omnibus amabatur," Jordan of Saxony, *Libellus* 107.

38. "Domne abbas, sciatis, quia caballus magistri nostri, qui tam malus vobis apparet, non ita cervicosus et pinguis est, sicut iste sonipes vester," Conrad of Eberbach, *Exordium magnum Cisterciense, sive narratio de initio Cisterciensis Ordinis*, ed. Bruno Griesser (Rome: Editiones Cistercienses, 1961), 17, p. 111.

39. "Verumtamen scire te convenit, quia iumentum istud, de quo mihi insultas, brutum est animal. . . . Quod si pro libitu suo comedit atque pinguescit, nihil inde iustitia laeditur, nihil Deus offenditur," ibid.

40. "Nunc igitur, si placet, respice collum meum et vide, et si grossius est collo magistri tui, inde me forsitan iuste reprehendere poteris," ibid.

41. "Impossible mihi videtur, homines istos solis ad fidem reduci verbis, qui potius innituntur exemplis," Jordan of Saxony, *Libellus* 20.

42. "Quod ergo das consilium, pater bone?" Ibid.

43. "Quod me videritis facere faciatis," ibid.

44. "Isti et suis similibus quomodo potestis credere, qui vobis predicant Christum humilem et pauperem cum tanto fastu, diviciis, sommariis et equitaturis?," Stephen of Bourbon, *Tractatus de diversis materiis predicabilis*, in *Anécdotes historiques, légendes et apologues*, ed. A. Lecoy de La Marche (Paris: Librairie Renouard, 1877), 2:83. So strongly did the Cathars believe that men of God should show "examples" of good, Christian behavior that, should their own Perfect ever fail in this regard, they held that the sacraments they celebrated would lose their efficacy.

45. The Cistercians were at first wary of Diego's proposal. According to Peter of Les Vaux-de-Cernay, "The legates did not themselves wish to take responsibility for such an initiative; instead, they promised that, if some acceptable authority were to set such an example, they would most willingly follow it [*Dicti vero legati, hec omnia quasi quandam novitatem per se arripere non volentes, dixerunt quod, si quis favorabilis auctoritatis eos sub hac forma vellet precedere, ipsum libentissime sequerentur*]," *The History of the Albigensian Crusade*, trans. W. A. Silby and M. A. Silby (Rochester, N.Y.: Boydell Press, 1998); *Hystoria albigensis*, ed. Pascal Guébin and Ernest Lyon, 3 vols. (Paris: Champion, 1926–39), 1:21. Diego immediately stepped forward in order to himself provide such an example. On November 17, 1206, Innocent III formally approved the preachers' adoption of mendicancy in a letter to Ralph of Fontfroide, *PL* 215, cols. 1024–25. Still, the Council of Paris in 1213 and the Council of Rouen in 1214 ordered ecclesiastical superiors to provide monks or canons with sufficient mounts and provisions for their travel, out of concern that it would be disgraceful for them to beg.

46. "ex eo deinceps tempore cepit non supprior, sed frater Dominicus appelari," Jordan of Saxony, *Libellus* 21.

47. "ceperunt pariter Christum pauperem pedes et pauperes predicare," Constantine of Orvieto, *Legenda Sancti Dominici* 14.

48. "dum quod lingue vox promeret, vite meritum confirmaret," ibid.

49. "Nos . . . huiusmodi alimentis non utimur modo. Panem nobis tantum et aquam frigidam exhibete," Peter Ferrand, *Legenda Sancti Dominici* 22.

50. "Non . . . in hac molitie sed super tabulas quiescemus," ibid.

51. "Cilicia. . . . Nemo sciat, servetur secretum," ibid.

52. "Aurum quidem cuius fulgore subornatur ypocrita, in publicum aliquatenus . . . proferebat," ibid.

53. "sancta quadam ypocrisi," ibid.

54. Ideo nonnunquam pater iste sanctus ammonebat fratres suos ut, cum apud seculares essent, . . . aliquantum virtutis apparenciam ostenderent in se ipsis, in abstinentiis, vigiliis, verborum ac gestuum disciplina," ibid., 23.

55. See Augustine, *De mendacio*, PL 40, col. 419. See also the discussion of lying in chap. 7.

56. "heretici, dum speciem preferunt pietatis, dum evangelice parsimonie et austeritatis mentiuntur exempla, persuadent simplicibus vias suas," Jordan of Saxony, *Libellus* 20.

57. "Deo autem manifesti sumus," 2 Cor 5:11.

58. "hominibus suademus," ibid.

59. "quod loquor, non loquor secundum Dominum, sed quasi in insipientia, in hac substantia gloriae," 2 Cor 11:17.

60. "Sic Paulus cogitur fieri insipiens, suas veras enumerando virtutes, austeritates et pericula proferendo, ut eorum tumorem refelleret, qui se de vite merito iactitabant," Jordan of Saxony, *Libellus* 20.

61. "hoc modo animas, quas heretici false virtutis imagine deludebant, ipsi vera sanctitas et religionis exhibitione ad veritatem fidei revocarent," Peter Ferrand, *Legenda Sancti Dominici* 13. Jordan of Saxony cites Diego as having bidden the Cistercian monks, "Make flee [the heretics'] feigned holiness with true religious life because the arrogance of false apostles can only be convicted by evident humility [*fictam santicatem vera religione fugate, quia fastus pseudoapostolorum evidenti vult humilitate convinci*]," Jordan of Saxony, *Libellus* 20.

62. "ut et ipse eas ostensione sanctitatis illiceret," Peter Ferrand, *Legenda Sancti Dominici* 13.

63. "ad proximorum edificationem . . . virtutis apparenciam ostenderent in se ipsis," ibid., 23.

64. "Vere isti homines boni sunt," ibid.

65. "Stupuerunt itaque admirantes tantam excellentiam sanctitatis et ceperunt magis ac magis allici ad fidem catholice veritatis," ibid., 22.

66. "mentes femineas, tanto tempore in errore fraudatus, facilius reducere potuit tam terribilis visio ipsis oculis foris exhibita, quam sola verborum quantalibet persuasio per aures infusa," Constantine of Orvieto, *Legenda Sancti Dominici* 49.

67. "secularium mentes exemplis pocius moveri quam verbis," Conrad of Trent, *Leggenda S. Dominici autore anonymo (Conrado de Trebensee)*, in *Der hg. Dominikus: Untersuchungen und Texte*, ed. Berthold Altaner (Breslau: G. P. Aderholz, 1922), 249–57, at 252.

68. For sources on the disputation of Lombers (which is not to be confused with an earlier encounter between Cathar heretics and ecclesiastics in this town in 1165), see William of Puylaurens, *Chronique*, 1145–1275=*Chronica magistri Guillelmi de Podio Laurentii*, ed. and trans. Jean Duvernoy (Paris: CNRS, 1976; rpt. Toulouse: Le Pérégrinateur, 1996), 4.

69. For sources on the disputation of Narbonne, see Bernard of Fontcaude, *Adversus Waldensium, sectam liber*, PL 204, cols. 791–840.

70. On the disputation at Carcassonne under Peter, see "Letter of Peter II of Aragon to All the Faithful of Christ, February, 1204," in *Bullaire du Bienheureux Pierre de Castelnau, martyr de la foi (16 février 1208)*, ed. Augustin Villemagne (Montpellier: Imprimerie de la Manufacture de la Charité, 1917), 407–9.

71. On the debate at Servian, see Peter of Les Vaux-de-Cernay, *Hystoria albigensis*, 22–23.

72. On the debate at Béziers, see ibid., 24.

73. On the debate at Carcassonne, see ibid., 24, 52, and 53.

74. On the debate at Verfeil, see William of Puylaurens, *Chronique*, 8.

75. On the debate at Lavaur, see Jordan of Saxony, *Libellus* 23 (if only for the mention of this city as one of the places where disputations were held).

76. On the debate at Montréal, see William of Puylaurens, *Chronique*, 9 and Peter of Les Vaux-de-Cernay, *Hystoria albigensis*, 26. See also Vicaire, "Saint Dominique à Prouille, Montréal et Fanjeaux," *CF*, vol. 1, *Saint Dominique en Languedoc* (Toulouse: Privat, 1966; rpt. 1987), 15–40.

77. On the debate at Fanjeaux, see Jordan of Saxony, *Libellus* 23.

78. On the debate at Pamiers, see ibid., 23 (though only, again, for the mention of this city as a place where disputations were regularly held); Peter of Les Vaux-de-Cernay, *Hystoria albigensis*, 48; and William of Puylaurens, *Chronique*, 8. See also Vicaire, "Rencontre à Pamiers des courants vaudois et dominicain (1207)," *CF*, vol. 2, *Vaudois languedociens et Pauvres catholiques* (Toulouse: Privat, 1967), 163–94. Dominic was said to have continued to dispute with Italian heretics in Bologna, Milan, Piacenza, and Modena in 1220 and 1221, though we possess no accounts of these meetings.

79. "veneno perfidie infectus," Peter of Les Vaux-de-Cernay, *Hystoria albigensis*, 23.

80. "eos sibi familiares fecerat et amicos," ibid.

81. "heretica pessima," ibid., 215.

82. "Ab sa mala doctrina n'i a mans convertitz," *Chanson de la Croisade Albigeoise*, ed. Eugène Martin-Chabot, 3 vols. (Paris: Les Belles Lettres, 1957), st. 145, v. 15, 2:48. On Esclarmonda, see J. M. Vidal, "Esclarmonde de Foix dans l'histoire et le roman," *Revue de Gascogne*, année 52, nouvelle série, vol. 11 (1911): 53–79.

83. "apud eum institerunt, ut cum suo heresiarcha habere colloquium dignaretur," William of Puylaurens, *Chronique*, 4.

84. "plus confundi episcopum quam hereticum confidentes," ibid.

85. Catholic chroniclers use either passive or weak active verbs when referring to these disputations. Jordan of Saxony writes, for example, that "There were frequently disputations [*frequenter disputationes fierent*]," Jordan of Saxony, *Libellus* 24. Peter Ferrand states in his *Legenda Sancti Dominici*, "There were at this time frequent conflicts of disputation [*Fiebant autem eo tempore frequentes . . . disputationum conflictus*]" (15) and "A contest of disputation was indicated [*esset indicta disputationis contentio*]" (15). Constantine of Orvieto affirms, similarly, in his *Legenda Sancti Dominici*, "There were frequently conflicts of disputation [*frequenter fierent disputationum conflictus*]" (15).

86. "Quodam die convenerunt omnes heresiarche apud quoddam castrum in Carcasonensi diocesi, quod dicitur Mons Regalis, disputaturi unanimiter adversus viros," Peter of Les Vaux-de-Cernay, *Hystoria albigensis*, 26.

87. "plurima hinc inde obiecta fuissent," William of Puylaurens, *Chronique*, 8.

88. "comes Valdenses die uno, predicatores nostros die altero, procuravit," Peter of Les Vaux-de-Cernay, *Hystoria albigensis*, 48.

89. "ficta humanitas," ibid.

90. "Nemo ascendit in celum," William of Puylaurens, *Chronique*, 8.

91. "Maledicat vos Deus, quia grossi heretici estis! Credebam quod subtilitatem aliquam haberetis," ibid.

92. "cum venerabilis episcopus dictum Theodoricum ad ima conclusionis disputando deduxisset, 'Scio,' inquit Theodoricus, 'scio cujus spiritus sis. Siquidem in spiritu Helye venisti'; ad hec sanctus, 'Et si ego in spiritu Helye veni, tu venisti in spiritu Antichristi," Peter of Les Vaux-de-Cernay, *Hystoria albigensis*, 23.

93. "meretricem," ibid., 52.

94. "magnates et milites et mulieres et populi fidei disceptationi interesse volentes," Jordan of Saxony, *Libellus* 23.

95. "conveniebat ad hoc spectaculum virorum ac mulierum, divitum ac nobilium et populi multitudo," Peter Ferrand, *Legenda Sancti Dominici* 15.

96. "judices de ipsis credentibus hereticorum," Peter of Les Vaux-de-Cernay, *Hystoria albigensis*, 26.

97. "clerico seculari, arbitro a partibus electo," William of Puylaurens, *Chronique*, 8.

98. "erat favens Valdensibus," Peter of Les Vaux-de-Cernay, *Hystoria albigensis*, 48.

99. "Ite, domina, filare colum vestram! Non interest vestra loqui in huiusmodi concione," William of Puylaurens, *Chronique*, 8.

100. "Proh dolor! quod inter christianos ad istam vilitatem status Ecclesie fideique catholice devenisset, ut de tantis opprobriis esset laicorum iudicio discernendum!" ibid., 9.

101. "hereticos confundebant," Peter of Les Vaux-de-Cernay, *Hystoria albigensis*, 24.

102. "Habita ibi disputatione cum Valdensibus, plane convicti sunt Valdenses et confusi," ibid., 48.

103. "mutus cum suis credentibus et confusus," William of Puylaurens, *Chronique*, 4. At Carcassonne, Peter of Aragon deemed the Waldensians "convicted [*convicti*]" of heresy and the Cathars "proven [*probati*]" to be heretics, *Bullaire du Bienheureux Pierre de Castelnau*, 108 and 109.

104. As Tugwell notes, "Dominic 'convicted' heretics in the sense that, whether they acknowledged it or not or whether anything was done about it or not, he demonstrated that they were, in fact, heretics," "Introduction: *Speculum sanctorale*," 170, n. 150.

105. "Discurrentes igitur predicatores sancti hereticosque disputando manifestissime convincentes, set, quia obstinati erant in malicia, convertere non valentes. . . . [P]arum aut nichil predicando sive disputando proficere potuissent," Peter of Les Vaux-de-Cernay, *Hystoria albigensis*, 51.

106. "quosdam clericos, qui vel imperitia, vel librorum inopia laborantes, hostibus veritatis non resistendo, facti sunt in offensionem et scandalum fidelibus quibus praesunt," Bernard of Fontcaude, *Adversus Waldensium*, PL 204, col. 793.

107. See the "disputation [*disputamen*]" between the Catholic Izarn, presumably a representative of the inquisitor Bernard of Caux, and the Cathar Perfect Sicart of Figueiras from 1242–44 in *Las novas del heretje*, ed. Peter T. Ricketts, in *Contributions à l'étude*

de l'ancien occitans: Textes lyriques et non-lyriques en vers (Birmingham, Ala., 2000), 75–113, v. 182 and the "disputation [*disputatio*]" between Jacques Fournier, the bishop of Pamiers, and the converted Jew Baruch from 1320 in *Le Registre d'Inquisition de Jacques Fournier, évêque de Pamiers (1318–1325), Manuscrit no. Vat. Latin 4030 de la Bibliothèque Vaticane*, ed. Jean Duvernoy, 3 vols. (Toulouse: Privat, 1965), 1:186. Peter Seila, one of Dominic's first followers, is said to have debated with Raymond Imbert, a Cathar Perfect, at the house of Arnold Roger, a Cathar believer, before Roger's household during the winter of 1217–18. See the testimony of Pons Steven of Baziège to Bernard of Caux and John of Saint-Peter on July 7, 1245, in MS 609 Toulouse, fol. 58v. Tugwell hypothesizes in "Notes on the Life of St. Dominic," *AFP* 65 (1995): 5–169, at 95–99 and 121–27 that this disputation would have occurred after the revolt of the Toulousans against Simon of Montfort and the return of their Raymond VI, in September 1217.

108. "Bernard Gui's Description of Heresies," Wakefield and Evans, 373–445, at 377–78. "Et ideo non expedit in tali casu contra hereticos sic astutos de fide coram laycis disputare," Bernard Gui, *Manuel de l'inquisiteur*, ed. Guillaume Mollat, 2 vols. (Paris: "Les Belles Heures" and Champion, 1926–27), 1:6.

109. Peter of Les Vaux-de-Cernay locates this miracle in Montréal, while Jordan of Saxony and Peter Ferrand trace it to Fanjeaux. Constantine of Orvieto situates the episode in Fanjeaux in one manuscript and in Montréal in another. As Peter cites Dominic himself as the source of his information, his account is generally followed here. Virtually all of the sources on Dominic provide accounts of this miracle, the only incident from his preaching campaign to have entered firmly into his hagiographic record.

110. "cuidam heretico tradidit cedulam illam, ut super objectis deliberaret," Peter of Les Vaux-de-Cernay, *Hystoria albigensis*, 54.

111. "dixerunt ei socii sui ut in medium ignem illam proiceret et, si cedula illa combureretur, vera esset fides ... hereticorum; si vero incombusta maneret, fidem quam predicabant nostri bonam esse faterentur," ibid.

112. "Domine, mitte manum tuam et tange eos' ... dum eis hunc saltem vexatio tribueret intellectum," Jordan of Saxony, *Libellus* 33.

113. "Multis iam annis cantavi vobis dulciter predicando, obsecrando, plorando, sed dicitur in terra mea vulgariter: Ubi non valet benedictio, valeat baculus," Stephen of Salanhac and Bernard Gui, *De quatuor in quibus Deus Praedicatorum ordinem insignivit* 2.3, p. 15. It is puzzling that Stephen cites Dominic as prophesying the advent of the Albigensian Crusade in August 1217, though the crusaders had already been in the Midi for eight years at that point. It may be that Stephen is transferring Diego's prophecy to Dominic. Bernard of Clairvaux is cited as expressing a similar frustration with heretics in Geoffrey of Auxerre, *Vita prima*, col. 414B and in William of Puylaurens, *Chronique*, 1, as is Berengar of Carcassonne in Peter of Les Vaux-de-Cernay, *Hystoria albigensis*, 99.

114. "Ecce concitabimus adversum vos principes et prelatos qui, heu, convocabunt adversus terram hanc gentes et regna et multos in ore gladii interficient, turres diruent, muros precipitabunt et destruent vosque omnes, pro dolor, in servitutem redignent et sic valebit *bagols*, idest baculi fortitudo, ubi non valuit benedictio et dulcedo," Stephen of Salanhac and Bernard Gui, *De quatuor in quibus Deus Praedicatorum ordinem insignivit* 2.3, pp. 15–16.

115. "Caedite eos. Novit enim Dominus qui sunt eius," Caesarius of Heisterbach, *Dialogus miraculorum*, ed. Jospeh Strange, 2 vols. (Coloniae: Sumptibus J. M. Heberle, 1851), 1:302.

116. "Eo tempore, quo ibi cruce signati fuerunt, mansit frater Dominicus usque ad obitum comitis Montisfortis verbi divini sedulus predicator," Jordan of Saxony, *Libellus* 34.

117. See Vicaire, "Les Clercs de la croisade," *CF*, vol. 4, *Paix de Dieu et guerre sainte en Languedoc au XIIIe siècle*, 260–80; rpt. as "Les Clercs de la croisade: L'Absence de Dominique" in *Dominique et ses prêcheurs*, 20–35.

CHAPTER THREE

1. "fidei zelatores," Gregory IX, *Dolemus et vehementi* (October 21, 1233), letter to Siegfried III, archbishop of Mainz; Conrad II, archbishop of Hildesheim; and Conrad of Marburg, in *Epistolae saeculi XIII e regestis pontificum romanorum*, ed. G. H. Pertz and Carolus Rodenberg, *MGH SS* (Berolini: apud Weidemannos, 1883), 1:451.

2. "Ubi est zelus Moysis?" Gregory IX, *Vox in Rama audita est* (June 11–14, 1233), letter to Siegfried, Conrad II, archbishop of Hildesheim, and Conrad of Marburg, ibid., 433. Cf. Num 25:1–6 and 9.

3. "Ubi est zelus Phinees? ... Ubi est zelus Elie?" ibid., 433–34. Cf. Num 25:6–13 and 1 Kg 18:40.

4. "non solum homines sed etiam ipsa elementa coniurarent in eorum excidium et ruinam ipsosque delerunt de terre facie, non parcentes sexui vel etati, ut essent cunctis gentibus in opprobrium sempiternum, ultio de ipsis sumi non posset sufficiens sive digna," ibid., 434.

5. We possess one text written by Conrad of Marburg, namely, the *Epistola examinatorum miraculorum sancte Elyzabet ad dominum papam* (February 1233), in Albert Huyskens, ed., *Quellenstudien zur Geschichte der hl. Elizabeth: Landgräfin von Thüringen* (Marburg: N. G. Elwert, 1908), 155–239. Aside from this letter, the records relating to Conrad fall into three categories. First, there are chronicles and annals, including Alberic of Trois-Fontaines, *Chronicon* (1241–42), ed. P. Scheffer-Boichorst, in *MGH SS*, 23:631–950; *Annales breves Wormatienses* (1165–1295), in *MGH SS*, 17:74–79; *Annales Erphordenses Fratrum Praedicatorum*, in *Monumenta Erphesfurtensia saec. XII. XIII. XIV*, ed. Oswaldus Holder-Egger, in *Scriptores rerum Germanicarum in usum scholarum ex Monumentis Germaniae Historicis separtim editi* (Hannover and Leipzig: Impensis Bibliopolii Hahniani, 1899), 72–116; *Annales Wormatienses* (1165–1295), in *MGH SS*, 17:34–73; *Acta imperii selecta: Urkunden deutscher Könige und Kaiser, mit einem Anhange von Reichssacken*, ed. Johann Friedrich Böhmer (Innsbruch: Wagner, 1870; rpt., Aalen: Scientia Verlag, 1967); *Gesta Treverorum*, in *MGH SS*, 24:400–402, translated in part as "Heretical Sects in Trier," in Wakefield and Evans, 267–69; and *Liber Chronicorum sive Annalis Erfordensis*, in *Monumenta Erphesfurtensia*, 724–83. Second, there are letters from Gregory IX in *Epistolae saeculi XIII e regestis pontificum romanorum*, ed. Pertz and Rodenberg, including *Sollicitudinem tuam* (June 12, 1227), to Conrad, 277; *Hospitale in Marburch* (Oct. 14, 1232), to Conrad, 389–90; *Ille humani generis* (Oct. 29, 1232), to Siegfried, 394–96; *O altitudo divitiarum* (June 10, 1233), to Conrad, 429–30; *Vox in Rama audita est* (June 11–14, 1233), to Siegfried and Conrad, 432–34; *Vox in Rama, id est tonitruo* (October 23, 1233), to the bishops, archbishops, abbots, and other prelates of Germany, 453–55; *Dolemus et vehementi* (Oct. 21, 1233), to Siegfried, Conrad II, and

Conrad of Marburg, 455–56; *Querit assidue perfidia* (Oct. 31, 1233), to Siegfried, Conrad II, and Conrad, the Dominican provincial of Germany, 455–56; *Vinee Domini cultores* (July 26, 1235), to Eberhard II, archbishop of Salzburg, and Conrad II, 544–46; and *Cum interfectores* (July 31, 1235), to Eberhard and Conrad II, 546–47. Third, there are accounts of the life of Elizabeth of Hungary which also address Conrad, as we shall see.

6. "Isti sunt heretici, nos deponimus manus ab ipsis," *Annales Wormatienses*, 39.

7. "misertus et timens," ibid.

8. "Quare sic proceditis?" ibid.

9. According to the Digest of Justinian, "It is better to let a guilty person go free than to condemn an innocent one [*satius enim esse impunitum relinqui facinus nocentis quam innocentem damnari*]," in *Corpus iuris civilis*, ed. Paul Krueger (Berolini, Apud Weidmannos, 1954), 48.19.5. This sentiment was reiterated at the Council of Narbonne of 1243–44.

10. "Vellemus comburere centum innocentes inter quos esset unus reus," ibid.

11. "et si quos culpabiles et infamatos inveneritis, ... procedatis contra eos iuxta statuta nostra contra haereticos noviter promulgata," Gregory IX, *Epistola* (October 11, 1231), *Analecta Hassiaca*, ed. Johann Philipp Kuchenbecker, 12 vols. (Marburgi: P. C. Müller, 1728–42), 3:73. The statutes to which Gregory is referring are presumably the decretal *Excommunicamus*, composed in February 1231, in *Les Registres de Grégoire IX*, ed. Lucien Auvray, 2 vols. (Paris, A. Fontemoing, 1896–1907), vol. 1, no. 539, cols. 351–52 and expanded upon in a letter to Dietrich II of Weid, archbishop of Trier, in June of that same year, in *Acta imperii selecta*, 665–67.

12. A few days after having composed this letter, Gregory wrote to Burchard of Ratisbon, the prior of the Dominican convent of Regensburg, and his colleague Dietrich and ordered them, similarly, "to seek out diligently those who are heretics or who are infamed of heresy ... [and] to proceed against them [*diligenti perquiratis sollicitudine de hereticis et etiam infamatis et, ... procedatis contra eos*]," Fearns, 73–75, at 74. This letter is often read as launching the Inquisition. In "Dominikaner und Inquisitoren in Heiligen Römischen Reich," in *Praedicatores, Inquisitores*, 1: *The Dominicans and the Medieval Inquisition*, ed. Wolfram Hoyer (Rome: Istituto Storico Domenicano, 2004), 211–48, Peter Segl argues that it constitutes more a pastoral exhortation of Dominican friars to collaborate with bishops than a judicial appointment of Dominican inquisitors. See also Dietrich Kurze, "Anfänge der Inquisition in Deutschland," in *Die Anfänge der Inquisition im Mittelalter, mit einem Ausblick auf das 20. Jahrhundert und seinem Beitrag über religiöse Intoleranz im nichtchristlichen Bereich*, ed. Peter Segl, Papers from the 8th Bayreuther Historisches Kolloquium held by the Facheinheit Geschichte, Universität Bayreuth (May 29–30, 1992) (Köln: Böhlau, 1993), 131–94.

13. "Heretical Sects in Trier," 267. "princeps et caput huius persecutionis," *Gesta Treverorum*, 400.

14. "per Alemanniam vero facta est tanta hereticorum conbustio, quod non possit numerus conprehendi," Alberic of Trois-Fontaines, *Chronicon*, 931.

15. "zelator catholice fidei et expugnator validissimus heretice pravitatis," Dietrich of Apolda, *Vita S. Elyzabeth*, in *Der Vita der heiligen Elisabeth*, ed. Monika Rener (Marburg: N. G. Elwert, 1993), 59.

16. See Alexander Patschovsky, "Zur Ketzerverfolgung Konrads von Marburg," *Deutsches Archiv für Enforschung des Mittelalters* 37 (1981): 641–93, esp. 651–65. This

article comprises three sections, the first of which addresses the judicial procedures Conrad used in prosecuting heretics, the second the relationship between the Passau Anonymous's *De secta Manicheorum* and Conrad's prosecutions, and the third Conrad's role as a judge of heretics, including in the trial of Heinrich Minnike, provost of a nunnery in Goslar.

17. "facta est confusio a seculis inaudita," Alberic of Trois-Fontaines, *Chronicon*, 932.

18. The most extensive studies of Conrad of Marburg date from the nineteenth or early twentieth centuries. See Ernst Ludwig Theodor Henke, *Konrad von Marburg: Beichtvater der heiligen Elisabeth und Inquisitor* (Marburg: N. G. Elwert, 1861); Balthasar Kaltner, *Konrad von Marburg und die Inquisition in Deutschland: Aus der Quellen bearbeitet* (Prague: F. Tempsky, 1882); and Paul Braun, *Der Beichtvater der heiligen Elisabeth und deutsche Inquisitor, Konrad von Marburg (+1233)* (Weimar: Druck der hof-buchdruckerei, 1909).

19. The primary sources on Elizabeth of Hungary, including her relationship with Conrad, are an anonymous letter regarding her death (November 17, 1231), in Huyskens, ed., *Quellenstudien zur Geschichte der hl. Elizabeth*, 148–49; a letter from Conrad to the pope (November 16, 1232), included with the *Epistola examinatorum miraculorum sancte Elyzabet ad dominum papam* (February, 1233), prepared by Conrad, Siegfried, and Raymond, abbot of Ebernach, which includes reports about one hundred and six miracles attributed to Elizabeth, in ibid., 155–239; the account of Elizabeth's life by her maids Guda, Isentrude, Elizabeth, and Irmengard (collected by the papal emissaries Conrad II, Hermann, the abbot of the Cistercian monastery of Georgenthal, on August 10, 1232 and on January 1, 1235), published as the *Libellus de dictis quatuor ancillarum S. Elisabethae sive Examen miraculorum eius*, in ibid., 110–40; another *Relatio miraculorum sancte Elizabeth* (January, 1235), compiled by the same authors, in ibid., 243–66; the *Processus et ordo canonizationis Beate Elyzabet propter quorumdam detractiones et calumpnias* (before May 27, 1235), prepared probably by the Dominican Raymond of Peñafort, in ibid., 142–46; the Cistercian Caesarius of Heisterbach's *Vita sancte Elyzabeth Lantgravie* (1236), ed. Albert Huyskens, in *Die Wundergeschichten des Caesarius von Heisterbach*, ed. Alfons Hilka (Bonn: Peter Hanstein Verlagsbuchhandlung, 1937), 3:344–81, which, prepared quickly after the canonization on May 27, 1235, constituted Elizabeth's official biography; Caesarius of Heisterbach's *Sermo de translatione beate Elyzabeth* (1237), which addressed the translation of Elizabeth's relics into the splendid new church of Saint Elizabeth in Marburg on May 1, 1236, ibid., 381–90; James of Voragine, *Legenda aurea* (c. 1260), ed. Giovanni Paulo Maggioni, 2d ed., 2 vols. (Tavarnuzze-Firenze : SISMEL, Edizioni del Galluzzo, 1998), 2:1156–79; and the Dominican Dietrich of Apolda's *Die Vita der heiligen Elisabeth* (1287), which relies upon Conrad's letter, the testimony of the four maids, and Caesarius's *Sermo de translatione beate Elyzabeth*. For some recent criticism, see Ernst Wilhelm Wies, *Elisabeth von Thüringen: Die Provokation der Heiligkeit* (Esslingen: Bechtle, 1993), esp. 89–99 and 191–97.

20. "Mortuus; mortuus est et michi mundus et omne, quod in mundo blanditur," Dietrich of Apolda, *Vita S. Elyzabeth*, 70. See also *Liber cronicorum sive annalis Erfordensis*, 761.

21. According to Dietrich of Apolda's account of the ceremony in the church, before the assembled crowd, as "an imitator of Christ [*imitatrix Christi*]," "She stripped herself

entirely and made herself naked, so that, naked, she followed the naked in the steps of poverty and charity [*omnino se exuit et nudavit, ut et nuda et nudum paupertatis et charitatis gressibus sequeretur*]," *Vita S. Elyzabeth*, 87–88. Dietrich's language recalls Jerome's claim that "Naked, I follow the naked Christ [*nudus nudum Christum sequi*]" (*Epistola* 52.5), where the nakedness assumed is not a literal absence of clothing but a metaphorical absence of property. At the same time, however, his language also recalls Francis's action when, having been accused before a bishop of stealing cloth from his merchant father, the saint did in fact remove all of his clothing, as a literal manifestation of the metaphorical poverty he was adopting. See Jean Châtillon, "*Nudum Christum Nudus Sequere*: A Note on the Origins and Meaning of the Theme of Spiritual Nakedness in the Writings of St. Bonaventure," *Greyfriars Review* 10, no. 1 (1996): 293–340. It is probable that Elizabeth stripped herself metaphorically rather than literally, but it is not impossible that, as she exchanged her court garb for the grey habit of the tertiary, she did humbly expose herself before these onlookers. See Philip Hermongenes Calderon's 1891 painting, *St. Elizabeth of Hungary's Great Act of Renunciation*, now at the Tate Gallery, which, following the account of this ceremony in Charles Kingsley's 1848 *The Saint's Tragedy*, represents Elizabeth kneeling naked before the altar in the presence of Conrad and some nuns. At the time of the painting's exhibition at the Royal Academy, Catholics expressed outrage at what they saw as Calderon's misinterpretation of the metaphorical language of the *vita* and consequent defamation of their religion.

22. As Alexander Patschovsky observes briefly, Conrad imagined a "Reich Gottes, repräsentiert auf Erden in seinen Heiligen," which he aspired to promote through the cultivation of Elizabeth's sanctity, and a "Reich Satans, verkörpert in den Ketzern," which he sought to destroy by crushing the heretics' wickedness. See "Konrad von Marburg und die Ketzer seiner Zeit," in *Sankt Elisabeth: Fürstin, Dienerin, Heilige: Aufsätze, Dokumentation, Katalog*, ed. Philipps-Universität Marburg with the Hessischen Landesamt für Geschichtliche Landeskunde (Sigmaringen: Thorbecke, 1981), 70–77, at 70. Patschovsky criticizes Conrad's failure to appreciate the fact that both Elizabeth's spirituality, as a *soror in saeculo*, and the Cathar heretics' spirituality, as Perfect, derived from the same reforming movement, which sought to enable Christians to achieve holiness in this world. See also Matthias Werner, "Die heilige Elisabeth und Konrad von Marburg," in *Sankt Elisabeth*, 45–69, which stresses the necessity of interpreting these figures' relationship in the context of its time, and "Elisabeth, Franziskus von Assisi, und Konrad von Marburg," ibid., 359–95, which examines the relation between these three figures.

23. "offensus," Isentrude, *Libellus de dictis quatuor ancillarum*, 118.

24. The Dominican hagiographer James of Voragine highlights the discrepancy between Elizabeth's perceived fault and Conrad's punishment when he writes, "Taking her disobedience with great displeasure, he would not unbend until he had her strongly beaten, stripped to her shift [*Quod ille egre ferens tantam eius inobedientiam relaxare noluit donec usque ad camisiam expoliatam . . . fortiter verberari fecit*]," *Legenda aurea*, 1160.

25. "Intret, si vult," Irmengard, *Libellus de dictis quatuor ancillarum*, 135.

26. "post tres ebdomadas habuit vestigia verberum et amplius beata Elizabet, que acrius fuerat verberata," ibid., 136.

27. The French poet Rutebeuf cites Conrad as saying not only that Elizabeth should enter the convent if she so wished but that "I want it well . . . that she enter [*Je wel bien . . .*

qu'ele i aille]," Rutebeuf, *La vie de sainte Elysabel* (1264), in *Oeuvres complètes*, ed. Michel Zink (Paris: Bordas, 1989), 635–751, at 730, so that, even more than in the original accounts, he appears to be encouraging her to commit the action for which he will punish her. Rutebeuf quotes Elizabeth as telling Irmengard, "Let God pardon him the misdeed when he abandons himself to such blows [*Que Dieux le meffait li pardone/ Puis que il au coz s'abandone*]," ibid., 732, vv. 1699–1700, so that the saint herself represents such beatings as a "misdeed" (*meffait*) on Conrad's part.

28. "magister Cunradus multipliciter temptavit eius constantiam, frangens eius in omnibus voluntatem," Isentrude, *Libellus de dictis quatuor ancillarum*, 126–27.

29. On the relations between male confessors and holy women, see John W. Coakley, *Women, Men, and Spiritual Power: Female Saints and Their Male Collaborators* (New York: Columbia University Press, 2006). In his study of nine confessional couples between 1150 and 1400, Coakley sees a positive partnership between the men, with their formal, institutional authority, as ordained priests or learned clerics, and the women, with their informal, spiritual authority, as mystics and prophets. He mentions Conrad and Elizabeth only once (on p. 18), to illustrate the obedience of female saints to male confessors, and the disturbing aspects of these figures' relationship bear little relation to the overall dynamic he is describing. For a more critical view of relations between male confessors and holy women, see Dyan Elliot, *Proving Women: Female Spirituality and Inquisitorial Culture in the Late Middle Ages* (Princeton: Princeton University Press, 2004).

30. "Sciens . . . Christum, qui est fortitudo Dei, dixisse: 'Non veni facere voluntatem meam, sed voluntatem eius, qui misit me' (Ioh 6:38), patris, sine murmure cordis et contradictione responsionis," Caesarius of Heisterbach, *Vita Sancte Elyzabeth Lantgravie*, 367–68.

31. "sibi necesse esse taliter contraria contrariis curare," Conrad of Marburg, *Epistola*, 158.

32. "Magister Cunradus, . . . , in multis beate Elyzabeth probavit constantiam, frangens in omnibus illius voluntatem, ut ex hoc ipsi obedienti amplius meritum accresceret. Propter quod, ut plus eam affligeret, contraria cordi eius precepit," Caesarius of Heisterbach, *Vita Sancte Elyzabeth Lantgravie*, 367.

33. "Oportet nos talia sustinere libenter, quia sic est de nobis, ut de gramine, quod crescit in flumine, fluvio inundante gramen inclinatur et deprimitur et sine lesione ipsius aqua inundans pertransit. Inundatione cessante gramen erigitur et crescit in vigore suo iocunde et delectabiliter. Sic nos quandoque oportet inclinari et humiliari et postmodum iocunde et delectabiliter erigi," Irmengard, *Libellus de dictis quatuor ancillarum*, 136.

34. "Nos sumus similes testudini, que tempore pluvie se retrahit in domum suam. Sic nos, ut obediamus, retrahamus nos a via, qua ire cepimus," ibid.

35. "Sed contra voluntatem Tuam Te teste nollem vitam eius uno crine redimere, nunc ipsum et me Tue gratie reconmendo, de nobis Tua fiat voluntas," Isentrude, *Libellus de dictis quatuor ancillarum*, 124.

36. "tanquam [pueros meos] proximum diligo," ibid., 126.

37. "nimis diligaret eum," Irmengard, *Libellus de dictis quatuor ancillarum*, 136.

38. "pour ce que ele entendoit que sa mère l'i avoit mainte foiz besié," Jean de Joinville, *Histoire de Saint Louis*, in *Historiens et chroniqueurs du Moyen Age: Robert de Clari, Villehardouin, Joinville, Froissart, Commynes*, ed. Albert Pauphilet and Edmond Pognon (Paris: Librairie Gallimard, 1952), 207–372, at 228.

39. "Et quia magister Cunradus omnem contemptum ei persuaserat," Isentrude, *Libellus de dictis quatuor ancillarum*, 126.

40. "dilectas vel amicas," Irmengard, *Libellus de dictis quatuor ancillarum*, 138.

41. "Deinde ut eam plus affligeret, singulos sibi dilectos de familia ab ea singulariter repulit, ut de quolibet per se doleret," ibid., 126.

42. "cum multo mentis gravamine et infinitis lacrimis," ibid.

43. "Et quia magister Cunradus omnem contemptum ei persuaserat, supplicavit Domino . . . ut . . . dilectionem puerorum ei tolleret," Isentrude, *Libellus de dictis quatuor ancillarum*, 126.

44. "Dominus audivit orationem meam. . . . Deo teste pueros meos non curo, tanqua alium proximum diligo, Deo commisi eos, faciat de eis, quod sibi placet," ibid.

45. "omnes mundanas possessiones, quas quondam dilexeri, stercora reputo. . . . nichil diligo, nisi pure solum Deum," ibid.

46. "Item beata Elysabeth puerum eius—anni et dimidii habens etatem—iussit omnino removeri a se, ne nimis diligaret eum et ne per illum inpediretur in servitio Dei," Irmengard, *Libellus de dictis quatuor ancillarum*, 136. Hermann was actually four years old at this time. It is possible that Irmengard is confusing Hermann with one of Elizabeth's daughters or Hermann's age with the age of one of these daughters.

47. "quia timebat aliquid de antehabita gloria sua nos secum tractare et ex hoc eam forsam temptari vel dolere," Isentrude, *Libellus de dictis quatuor ancillarum*, 126–27.

48. "subtraxit ei omne humanum solatium in nobis, volens eam soli Deo adherere," ibid., 127.

49. "ut per patientiam animam suam possideat," James of Voragine, *Legenda aurea*, 1166.

50. "omnia patientissime et gaudens sustinebat," Isentrude, *Libellus de dictis quatuor ancillarum*, 125–26.

51. "beata Elyzabeth . . . tribulationes sibi illatas cum multa . . . cordis letitia sustinuit," Caesarius of Heisterbach, *Vita sancte Elyzabeth Lantgravie*, 363–64.

52. "tribulatio cum patientia iustum letificat, probat, purgat et glorificat," ibid., 363. Cf. Eccl 2:5.

53. "seculariter indutus," Elizabeth, *Libellus de dictis quatuor ancillarum*, 131.

54. "O domina mea, cessate ab oratione, quia iam deficio," ibid.

55. "Sed ipsa studiosius orationi insistebat," ibid.

56. "In nomine Domini oro, quod cessetis ab oratione, quia iam igne consumor," ibid., 132.

57. "Ad minus de cetero cum huiusmodi capillis choreas non frequentabit," ibid.

58. "verberavit eam virgis, que quasi sompnolenta iacuit et pigra ad confitendum ammonitionem non attendebat," Isentrude, *Libellus de dictis quatuor ancillarum*, 129.

59. "Videris minus discrete Te habere et quare non servis creatori Tuo?" Ibid., 131.

60. "O domina mea, supplico Vobis, ut oretis pro me, ut Dominus det mihi gratiam suam ad serviendem ei," ibid.

61. "quo caritatis ardore fervet, que calore suo fluxum secularis concupiscencie siccat et ad amorem eternitatis inflammat," Dietrich of Apolda, *Vita S. Elyzabeth*, 106.

62. "Quam benigna animarum zelatrix virgis verberavit, et a sompno negligentie verberibus excitatam ad confessionem induxit," ibid., 102.

63. "His et aliis pietatis exercitiis . . . , mundi amatoribus displicuit, apud quosdam etiam pios reprehensibilis apparuit; nunc autem inter sanctos tanquam sol resplendet," ibid.

64. On heretics in Germany at this time, see also Ludwig Förg, *Die Ketzerverfolgung in Deutschland unter Gregor IX: Ihre Herkunft, ihre Bedeutung, und ihre rechlichen Grundlagen* (Berlin: Verlag D. Emil Ebering, 1932; rpt. Vaduz: Kraus Reprint, Ltd., 1965); Richard Kieckhefer, *Repression of Heresy in Medieval Germany* (Liverpool: Liverpool University Press, 1979), esp. 11–18; Daniela Müller, "Conrad de Marbourg et les cathares en Allemagne," *Heresis* 3 (1992): 53–80; and Lambert, *Medieval Heresy*, 3d ed., 116, 165–81.

65. "pestifera secta Luciferanorum," Alberic of Trois-Fontaines, *Chronicon*, 931.

66. Patschovsky has argued persuasively that these Catholic clerics were only misinterpreting Cathar doctrine, which did indeed represent the devil in an unconventional way. See Patschovsky, "Zur Ketzerverfolgung Konrads von Marburg," esp. 651–65, as well as *Der Passauer Anonymus: Ein Sammelwerk über Ketzer, Juden, Antichrist aus der Mitte des 13. Jahrhunderts* (Stuttgart: Hiersemann, 1968) and "Der Ketzer als Teüfelsdiener," in *Papsttum, Kirche und Recht in Mittelalter*, ed. H. Mordek (Tübingen: M. Niemeyer, 1991), 317–34.

67. Gregory refers to having heard from letters from the archbishop of Mainz, the bishop of Hildesheim, and Conrad of Marburg, of the Satanic practices of these heretics in *Vox in Rama audita est* (June 11–14, 1233), *Epistola . . . archiepiscopo Maguntino, . . . episcopo Hildesemensi et magistro Conrado de Marbuch, predicatori verbi Dei*, in Pertz and Rodenberg, eds. *Epistolae saeculi XIII e regestis pontificum romanorum*, 1:433. On the connection between Gregory's letter and Conrad's circle, see Bernd-Ulrich Hergemöller, *Krötenküß und schwartzer Kater. Ketzerei, Götzendienst, und Unzucht in der inquisitorischen Phantasie des 13. Jahrhunderts* (Warendorf: Fahlsbusch, 1996).

68. "Huius pestis initia talis perferuntur," Gregory IX, *Vox in rama*, 1:433.

69. "interdum," ibid.

70. "plerumque," ibid.

71. "que in scholis huiusmodi esse solet," ibid.

72. "sicut dicunt," ibid.

73. "accusatum oportuit confiteri se hereticum esse, buffonem, cattum, pallidum virum et huiusmodi monstra diffidentie pacis in osculo salutasse," Alberic of Trois-Fontaines, *Chronicon*, 931.

74. This letter is copied in Alberic of Trois-Fontaines, *Chronicon*, 931–32. "quedam femina vaga Aleydis annorum 20 . . . , fixit se hereticam, secte illius fuisse suum virum," ibid., 931.

75. "cognatos et notos et affines, qui eam exheredare videbantur," ibid.,

76. "Nescio quem accusare; dicite mihi nomina, de quibus suspicionem habetis," ibid.

77. "Heretical Sects in Trier," 267. Translation modified. "tantusque fuit omnium zelus, ut nullius, qui tantum propalatus esset, excusatio vel recusatio, nullius exceptio vel testimonium admitteretur, nec defendendi locus daretur," *Gesta Treverorum*, 400. Siegfried and Bernard concur, relating, "The master gave to no one, . . . a legitimate defense [*Et magister nulli quantumvis alte persone locum dedit legitime defensionis*]," Alberic of Trois-Fontaines, *Chronicon*, 931.

78. "nullo contradictente," *Annales breves Wormatienses*, 75.

79. "Et prevaluit ubique voluntas eorum," *Annales Wormatienses*, 39.

80. See Justin Martyr, *Apologia Prima*, in *Patrologiae cursus completus . . . series graeca*, ed. Jacques Paul Migne, 161 vols. (Paris: Garnier Frères, 1857–91), vol. 6, col. 327–440, at col. 369; Minucius Felix, *Octavius*, ed. and trans. Jean Beaujeu, 2d ed. (Paris: Société d'Edition 'Les

Belles Lettres,' 1974), 13; and Tertullian, *Apologétique*, ed. and trans. Jean-Pierre Waltzing and Albert Severyns, 3d ed. (Paris: Société d'Edition 'Les Belles Lettres,' 1971), chap. 7, p. 16.

81. See Paul of Saint-Père de Chartres, *Cartulaire de l'abbaye de Saint-Père de Chartres*, ed. Benjamin Edamé-Charles Guérard, 2 vols. (Paris: Crapelet, 1840), 1:109–15; Guibert of Nogent, *Autobiographie*, 430; and Walter Map, *De nugis curialium*, 118. On the history of this legend, see Norman Cohn, *Europe's Inner Demons: An Enquiry Inspired by the Great Witch-Hunt* (New York: Basic Books, Inc., 1975), 16–31.

82. "Et multos condempnabant qui in hora mortis dominum nostrum Iesum Christum toto corde invocabant, et auxilium sancte Dei genitricis et omnium sanctorum etiam in igne valido clamore implorabant. Audite quanta fuit hec miseria!" *Annales Wormatienses*, 39.

83. "iudex sine misericordia," ibid.

84. "frater Conrardus de Marburg . . . hereticos quoscumque volebat per totam Teutoniam . . . combussit," *Annales breves Wormatienses*, 75.

85. "magistro Conrado, . . . nimis ei credidit," Alberic of Trois-Fontaines, *Chronicon*, 931.

86. "iudicium fulminante," ibid.

87. "multi . . . a quodam fratre Cunrado ignis supplicio per diversa Teutonie loca, si fas est dici, nimis precipiti sententia sunt addicti. Nam eodem die quo quis accusatus est, seu iuste seu iniuste, . . . , est dampnatus et flammis crudelibus iniectus," *Annales Colonienses Maximi*, 843. If any accused party, having saved his life through a claim of repentance, was rumored to have relapsed into heresy, this chronicle states, "He was apprehended and without any reconsideration was burned [*absque ulla retractatione deprehensus cremabatur*]," "Heretical Sects in Trier," 268; *Gesta Treverorum*, 401.

88. "quidam catholici . . . maluerunt innocenter cremari et salvari, quam mentiri de crimine turpissimo, cuius non erant conscii, et suplicium promereri. Quibus ipse magister martirium promittebat," Alberic of Trois-Fontaines, *Chronicon*, 931.

89. "Et ego, Petre, quid feci mali, ut cum tantis opprobriis et contumeliis condemnarer ad crucem? disce ergo exemplo meo omnia aequanimiter ferre," Antoninus, *Chronicon*, in Ambrose Taegio, *Legenda Beatissimi Petri Martyris . . . ex multis legendis in unum compilata* 1.6, in *De S. Petro Martyre ex Ordine Praedicatorum*, in *Acta sanctorum*, ed. Daniel Papebroch (Antwerp: Ioannem Meursium, 1675), April, 3:679–719, at 689.

90. "Quis . . . dicere potest, Mundus sum a peccato ut non egeat venia?" Ibid.

91. "sacri martyrii desiderio maxime flagrens," Thomas of Celano, *Vita prima S. Francisci* 1.20, in *Analecta Franciscana*, ed. College of St. Bonaventure, 10 vols. (Florence: Ad Aquas Claras, Collegium S. Bonaventurae, 1895–41), 10 (1942), 1–115, at 42.

92. Francis of Assisi, "Fragments (1209–1223)," in *Francis of Assisi: The Early Documents*, trans. Regis J. Armstrong, J. A. Wayne Hellmann, and William J. Short, 4 vols. (New York: New City Press, 1999-2001), vol. 1, *The Founder*, 87-96, at 87. This passage is from a manuscript in the library of Worchester Cathedral, Worchester, England, Codex Q 27.

93. "In omnibus autem iniuriis et afflictionibus Deo gaudens gratias agebat, quod ipsam sic multipliciter dignabatur flagellare, quia, quem castigat Dominus, diligit," Isentrude, *Libellus de dictis quatuor ancillarum*, 126, n.a.

94. "accusatoribus et testibus resilientibus, aliis se coactos vel circumventos in comitem mala dixisse se fatentibus, aliis de odioso presumptive notatis," *Gesta Treverorum*, 402.

95. "Denuncio vobis, quod comes Seynensis hinc recedit pro homine catholico et inconvicto," ibid.

96. "magister Conradus submurmurando ait: 'Si convictus esset, alia ratio est," ibid.
97. "ut moderatius et discretius in tanto negotio se gereret," Alberic of Trois-Fontaines, *Chronicon*, 932.
98. "Ob quam causam frater Cunradus, huius persecutionis hereticorum minister, a quibusdam nobilibus, nullum locum venie vel gratie apud ipsum invenientibus, iuxta Marburg est occisus," *Annales Colonienses Maximi*, 843.
99. "quos ipsi tam in parentibus eorum quam in propriis personis infamaverant et dampnificaverant," *Annales Wormatienses*, 40.
100. "insuper de defuncti Cunradi factis clamosis vocibus miserabiliter querelantibus, tantus subito cepit oriri tumultus et turbatio, ut hi qui ex parte magistri Cunradi exstiterant se manus adversariorum desperarent evadere," *Annales Erphordenses*, 86.
101. "magistri Cunradi de Marburc formam . . . irritam," ibid., 85–86.
102. "flagitiosissimi et sceleratissimi homicide," Gregory IX, *Cum interfectores*, 546.
103. "virum consumate virtutis," Gregory IX, *Vox in Rama, id est tonitruo*, 454.
104. "perditionis filii," Gregory IX, *Vinee Domini cultores*, 544–45.
105. "ministrum luminis," Gregory IX, *Vox in Rama, id est tonitruo*, 454.
106. "tenebrarum filiis," ibid., 454.
107. "perditionis filii . . . dicti magistri sanguinem innoxium effuderunt," Gregory IX, *Vinee Domini cultores*, 544–45.
108. "viros sanguinum . . . predictum magistrum Conradum . . . sacrilegis tenere manibus et ferina mente perimere presumpserunt," Gregory IX, *Vox in Rama, id est tonitruo*, 454.
109. "humani generis inimicus . . . magistrum Conradum de Marburch . . . suorum manibus ministrorum extinexit," Gregory IX, *Querit assidue perfidia*, 455–56.
110. "contra se provocaverint celum et terram," Gregory IX, *Cum interfectores*, 546.
111. "Et gavisi sunt domini assistentes ipsis, et ducentes eos in civitates et villas suas, fodentes foveas et incidentes in eas," *Annales Wormatienses*, 39.
112. "domno Heinrico illustri comiti Seinensi, . . . vir christianus prepotens et dives et honestissime vivens," ibid.
113. "vir christianissimus, suam fidem catholicam volens toto posse defendere," ibid.
114. "murus pro domo Domini," *Gesta Treverorum*, 402.
115. "ad defendendum comitem ac dominos et totam Theutoniam ire ad curiam Romanam," *Annales Wormatienses*, 40.
116. "quos inter preminentes plantes ecclesie providit Dominus locum magnitudinis obtinere," Gregory IX, *Vinee Domini cultores*, 545.
117. "dum tanti sceleris patratores . . . immunes a stipendio meritorum evasisse conspiciunt," ibid.
118. "minoribus, . . . exemplum validum presumendi contraria devotioni conceditur," ibid., 544.
119. "ut pene immensitas, diffusa per orbem terreat pestilentes, non solum manus a similibus cohibens set etiam cogitationes avertens," Gregory IX, *Cum interfectores*, 547.
120. "Qui non acquievit, sed tandem contra nostram monitionem crucem publice predicavit Moguntie. Quo viso quidam ex illis interfecerunt eum prope Marbuch," Alberic of Trois-Fontaines, *Chronicon*, 932.
121. "Cumque multa contra defuncti Cunradi partem et aliqua pro ipso fuissent allegata, unus ex prelatis in hec prorupit verba, dicens magistrum Cunradum de Marburc

dignum fore extumulandum ac velut hereticum concremandum," *Annales Erphordenses*, 86.

122. "Exhinc procellosa illa persecutio cessavit, et periculosissima tempora, quibus a diebus Constantii imperatoris heretici et Iuliani apostate nulla alia fuere similia, sereniori ceperunt spirare clementia," *Gesta Treverorum*, 402.

123. "preconem fidei Christiane," Gregory IX, *Vox in Rama, id est tonitruo*, 454.

124. "preconem precipuum summi regis," Gregory IX, *Querit assidue perfidia*, 455.

125. "Cuius Dominici canis lingua maiori latratu terruit lupos graves?" Gregory IX, *Vox in Rama, id est tonitruo*, 454.

126. "incremento catholice fidei plurimum oportunus," Gregory IX, *Vinee Domini cultores*, 544.

127. "Christiane sanctificationis concusso pariete," Gregory IX, *Vox in Rama, id est tonitruo*, 453–54.

128. "in hoc et modicus fuerit zelus catholice fidei et exilis attentio sedem apostolicam reverendi," Gregory IX, *Vinee Domini cultores*, 544–45.

129. "Quid est igitur, o prelati, quod velut si commissorum dampna gregum minime curaretis, magistrum Conradum de Marburch, ecclesie paraninphum, . . . non defletis?," Gregory IX, *Vox in Rama, id est tonitruo*, 454.

130. See Albert of Huchelnheim's and Siboto of Hoingen's testimony, in Huyskens, ed. *Quellenstudien zur Geschichte der hl. Elizabeth*, 259. When asked whether Elizabeth or Conrad had fulfilled their prayers, both men profess ignorance, but Siboto adds, "He hopes that it was both of them [*Sperat autem, quod amborum*]," 260.

131. "Et sic divino auxilio liberata est Theutonia ab isto iudicio enormi et inaudito," *Annales Wormatienses*, 40.

132. On the later Inquisition in this region, see Klaus-Bernard Springer, "Dominican Inquisition in the Archdiocese of Mainz (1348–1520)," in *Praedicatores, Inquisitores*, 1:311–93; Kieckhefer, *Repression of Heresy in Medieval Germany*; and Herbert Grundmann, "Ketzerverföre des Spätmittelalters als quellenkritisches Problem," *Deutsches Archiv für Erforshung des Mittelaters* 21 (1965): 519–75.

133. "Et horum accusatio paulatim cepit ascendere a rusticis ad burgenses honorabiles et eorum uxores, et tandem ad milites et eorum uxores, inde ad castellanos et nobiles et in fine ad comites prope et longe positos," Alberic of Trois-Fontaines, *Chronicon*, 931.

134. "Heretical Sects in Trier," 267. "quique auctoritate apostolica fretus et animi constantia preditus, ita animosus factus est, ut neminem timeret, tantique esset ei rex vel episcopus quanti pauper laicus," *Gesta Treverorum*, 401.

135. "Heretical Sects in Trier," 268. "nec erat adeo pure quis conscientie, qui se huiusmodi tempestatem non timeret incurrere," *Gesta Treverorum*, 401.

136. "Attamen fratri Conrado durissimo iudici non suffecit, nec ipse cum suis ab eorum proposito desistebant, omnibus episcopis et clericis sibi reclamantibus," *Annales Wormatienses*, 39.

CHAPTER FOUR

1. On Giovanni di Balduccio's 1339 tomb for Peter of Verona, see Venturino Alce, "La Tomba di S. Pietro Martire e la Capella Portinari in S. Eustorgio di Milan: Noti-

zie storiche critiche," *MD* 69 (1952): 3-34; Gian Alberto dell'Acqua, ed., *La Basilica Sant'Eustorgio in Milano* (Cinisello-Balsamo [Milano]: Amilcare Pizzi, 1984); Formica Luciano, ed., *La Capella Portinari: Documenti, storici e lettere critice* (Milano: Cartaria G. Garanzine e C., 2001). For Peter's iconography more generally, see Alce, "Iconografia di S. Pietro da Verona, martire domenicano," *MD* 70 (1953): 3-36.

2. In chronological order, the most important medieval texts leading up to Peter's canonization are the following: a document in which the *podestà* of Milan increases penalties against heretics, which cites Peter as a motivating agent, edited in "Études sur les anciennes confréries dominicaines, 2 : Les Confréries de Saint-Pierre Martyr," ed. Gilles Meersseman, *AFP* 21 (1951): 51-196, at 113-16, from 1234; Pope Innocent IV's letter *Misercors et miserator*, Ripoll, vol. 1, no. 227, pp. 192-93, in which the pope appoints Peter inquisitor, from June 13, 1251; and records produced by the inquisitor Roger Calcagni in Florence, edited in *Quel che non c'è nella 'Divina Commedia' di Dante o l'Eresia con documenti e con ristampa della questioni dantesche*, ed. Felice Tocca (Bologna: Ditta N. Zanichelli, 1899), 34-57, which make mention of Peter's activity in anti-heretical circles, from November 27, 1244 to August 24, 1255. Several letters deplore Peter's assassination, including Innocent IV's letter *Gaudemus in Domino*, in *AD* (April 1889): 904-5, from May 18, 1252; Roderick of Atencia's letter to Raymond of Peñafort, edited in *AD* (April 1889): 901-3, from May 1252; and John of Colonna's epistle, edited in *AD* (April 1889): 908-10, from March 1253. Other texts record investigations into Peter's murderers, including the inquiry into his assassination by Raynier Sacconi and Guy of Sesto (or Friar Daniel), edited in *AD* (April 1889): 905-7, from September 2, 1252; the record of the examination Stephen Gonfanonerlo, one of the conspirators against Peter, edited by Luigi Fumi in "L'Inquisizione Romane e lo stato di Milano: Saggio di richerche nell'Archivio di Stato," *Archivio Storico Lombardo*, ser. 4, fasc. 15, vol. 13 (1910): 7-124 and 285-414 and vol. 14 (1910): 145-220, vol. 14, 197-220, from 1295; and "Processo per l'uccisione di s. Pietro martire," ed. J. S. Villa, *Archivio Storico Lombardo* 4 (1877): 790-94. The hagiographic works celebrating Peter's life and death begin with Innocent IV's bull *Magnis et crebris*, in which the pope declares Peter's canonization, edited in Ripoll, 1:228-30, from March 24 or 25, 1253. Because the three thirteenth-century *vitae* were written around the same time, it is difficult to determine in what order they were composed and in what ways they influenced each other. They are Thomas Agni of Lentini's *Vita* (or *Legenda*) *Santi Petri Martyris*, which was written between 1255 and 1270, in Ambrose Taegio's *Legenda Beatissimi Petri Martyris . . . ex multis legendis in unum compilata*, which was, in turn, included in the Bollandists' *Acta Sanctorum*, ed. Daniel Papebroch (Antwerp: Ioannem Meursium, 1675), April, 3:679-719; Gerard of Frachet's account of Peter's life in *Vitae fratrum* 6.1, ed. Benedictus Maria Reichert, *MOPH*, vol. 1 (Louvain: Charpentier & Schoonjans, 1896), 236-48, which was written between 1259 and 1260; and James of Voragine's similar account, in his *Legenda aurea*, ed. Giovanni Paulo Maggioni, 2d ed., 2 vols. (Tavarnuzze-Firenze: SISMEL, Edizioni del Galluzzo, 1998), 1:421-42, which was written between 1260 and 1263. The fourteenth-century *vitae* include Berengar of Landorra's *Miracula collecta*, edited in Taegio, *Legenda beatissimi Petri Martyris*, 23-29, 57, 61-66, 68-74, 85-90, 94-95, 97-98, 100-103, 105, and 113 and by Heribert Christian Scheeben in *Analecta sacro Ordinis Fratrum Praedicatorum* 34 (1926): 808-10, which was written between 1314 and 1316, and Peter Calo's *De Sancto Petro Martyre ex magno*

legendari, edited only in Taegio, *Legenda Beatissimi Petri Martyris*, 13–18, 20, 75–83, 104, and 106, which was written between 1323 and 1340. Also of interest are Galvano Fiamma's *Cronica Ordinis Praedicatorum ab Anno 1170 usque ad 1333*, edited by Benedikt Maria Reichert (Rome: In domo generalitia, 1897) and, in part, by Gundisalvo Odetto, in "La *Chronaca maggiore dell'Ordine domenicano* di Galvano Fiamma," *AFP* 10 (1940): 297–373, which was written in 1333, and Antoninus of Florence's *Chronicon partibus tribus distincta ab initio mundi ad MCCCLX*, again available in Taegio, *Legenda Beatissimi Petri Martyris*, 6, 19, 21–22, which was written between 1474 and 1479.

3. On Peter's work in Florence, see Stefano Orlandi, "Il Centario della Predicazione di S. Pietro Martire a Firenze (1245–1945)," *MD* 63 (1946): 26–41, 59–87, and Daniel R. Lesnick, *Preaching in Medieval Florence: The Social World of Franciscan and Dominican Spirituality* (Athens: University of Georgia Press, 1989).

4. Peter was long said to have founded two confraternities in Milan, one, the Society of the Virgin, which united Catholics under the banner of a figure denigrated by the heretics and revered by the Friars Preachers, and the other, the Society of the Faith (or the Faithful)—later renamed the Society of Saint Peter Martyr—which brought Catholics together to oppose the heretics and support the inquisitors in their struggles against them, but these facts are now disputed. In cities like Toulouse, Milan, and Florence, where heretics seem to have been widely tolerated by the civil authorities and the general population alike, such confraternities served as important meeting-places for those more rigorously Catholic in their orientation. Under Peter's guidance, the laymen who belonged to these organizations, in Florence as well as Milan, agitated for public authorities to take action against the heterodox and for their peers to elect leaders who would fulfill this religious duty. On these confraternities, see G. G. Meerssemann, "Études sur les anciennes confréries dominicaines, 2 : Les Confréries de Saint-Pierre Martyr," *AFP* 21 (1951): 51–196, and N. J. Housley, "Politics and Heresy in Italy: Anti-Heretical Crusades, Orders, Confraternities, 1200–1500," *Journal of Ecclesiastical History* 33 (1982): 193–208.

5. "arbitrantes se posse pacifice vivere si eorum tam validus persecutor de medio tolleretur," James of Voragine, *Legenda aurea*, 425.

6. "fidei pugil," ibid., 421, 425.

7. "contra illius diros hostes mente intrepida ferventique spiritu continuum certamen exercens suum tandem agonem," ibid., 422.

8. "urpote inter haereticos a puero conversatus, et qualiter sensum perverterent Scripturarum, et quibus verbis suam sauciatam conscientiam palliarent," Thomas Agni of Lentini, *Vita* 30.

9. See Bernard Montagnes, "Les inquisiteurs martyrs," in *Praedicatores, Inquisitores*, vol. 1: *The Dominicans and the Medieval Inquisition*, ed. Wolfram Hoyer (Rome: Istituto Storico Domenicano, 2004), 513–43.

10. On William Arnold and Stephen of Saint-Thibéry, see Yves Dossat, "Le Massacre d'Avignonnet," in *CF*, vol. 6, *Le Crédo, la morale et l'Inquisition*, 343–59.

11. Other inquisitors would be killed in coming years, including Bernard of Traversa, Pagan of Lecco, Peter of Cadiretta, Catalan Faure, Peter Pascal, and Anthony Pavoni.

12. "In novitiatu suo contra carnem nimio zelo succensus," Thomas Agni of Lentini, *Vita* 4.

13. "mensuram propriae fragilitatis excedens, fere civem perdidit," ibid.

14. Henry Charles Lea, *A History of the Inquisition of the Middle Ages*, 3 vols. (New York: Harper & Bros., 1887; rpt. New York: The Harbor Press, 1955), 1:239.

15. Ibid., 2:214.

16. Ibid.

17. Antoine Dondaine, "Saint Pierre Martyr: Études," *AFP* 23 (1953): 66–162 at 66.

18. Donald S. Prudlo, *The Martyred Inquisitor: The Life and Cult of Peter of Verona († 1252)* (Aldershot: Ashgate Publishing, 2008), 100–101.

19. See Sixtus V, "Invictorum Christi militum" (April 13, 1586), in Ripoll, 5:448.

20. Prudlo, *The Martyred Inquisitor*, 173.

21. "Beatus Petrus Martyr . . . ex parentibus haereticis originem traxit, ut tamquam lux de tenebris, rosa de spinis, flos exortus de sentibus," Thomas Agni of Lentini, *Vita* 9.

22. "Petrinus," James of Voragine, *Legenda aurea*, 422.

23. It appears to have been the Nicene Creed that Peter was studying, given his uncle's reference to "visible things." On the history of such creeds, see Jaroslav Pelikan, *Credo: Historical and Theological Guide to Creeds and Confessions of Faith in the Christian Tradition* (New Haven: Yale University Press, 2003).

24. "Credo in Deum omnipotentem creatorem celi et terre, et cetera," Gerard of Frachet, *Vitae fratrum* 6.3, p. 236.

25. "Noli dicere creatorem, cum ipse Deus non sit creator visibilium, sed dyabolus," ibid.

26. "auctoritates, more hereticorum," ibid., 237.

27. "Sed mirum valde, quod ita omnes illas auctoritates contra eum convertit, quod in nullo potuit resister," ibid., 236.

28. "hoc puerum bonae indolis unctio caelestis edocuit, ut venenosorum serpentum insultus fugeret, et lupos rapaces, licet contectos ovinis pellibus, inimicos agnosceret, ac eorum consortia devitaret," Thomas Agni of Lentini, *Vita* 1.

29. Donald Weinstein and Rudolph M. Bell, *Saints and Society: The Two Worlds of Western Christendom, 1000-1700* (Chicago: University of Chicago Press, 1982), 49 and 64.

30. "haereticorum opprobriorum," Thomas Agni of Lentini, *Vita* 8 and 32.

31. "ubi licet esset ab haereticorum instantia elognatus, non desuere tamen novae impugnationis genera," ibid., 3.

32. "Quis enim inter carnis illecebras, mundi fallacias, hostis insidias et lubricos sodalium comitatus, integritatem mentis et corporis sufficeret custodire?" ibid., 2.

33. "florem pudicitiae sua subripere decertantia, adolescentioris aetatis assueta," ibid., 3.

34. "Avertens etiam non esse tutum cum scorpionibus habitare, velut alter Joseph, pallium reliquit in manu Aegyptiae suo insidiantis pudori; et ad religionis refugium confugiens, mundum cum flore decidenti, parentes cum errore perimenti despiciens, mundus ipse Praedicatorum ordinem. . . . est ingressus," ibid.

35. "se velle pocius dicere sicut legerat, et ita credere sicut scriptum habebat," Gerard of Frachet, *Vitae fratrum* 6.3, p. 237.

36. See Walter Ong, *Rhetoric, Romance, and Technology* (Ithaca, N.Y.: Cornell University Press, 1971), 113–41; Ong, *Fighting for Life: Contest, Sexuality, and Consciousness* (Ithaca, N.Y.: Cornell University Press, 1981), 119–48; and Ong, *Orality and Literacy: The Technologizing of the Word* (London: Methuen & Co., 1982; rpt. London: Routledge, 1995), 112–15.

37. "in hoc articulo non desistens Symbolum fidei, quod propter blanditias patrui puer deserere noluerat, propter mortis angustias, velut praeco fide, nequaquam oblitus est confiteri," Thomas Agni of Lentini, *Vita* 38.

38. "ordinem predicatorem sub beato Dominico intrasset," Gerard of Frachet, *Vitae fratrum* 6.3, p. 237.

39. "per paupertatis et humilitatis vestigia beatum Patrem Dominicum ducem, virginem virgo sequens, magnum perfectionis apicem attigit; semper de virtute proficiens in virtutum et procedens quasi lux splendens usque ad perfectam diem," Thomas Agni of Lentini, *Vita* 3.

40. Gerard of Frachet recounts this story as something that happened to an unnamed Dominican friar in Germany in 1230 in the *Vitae fratrum* 5.23, 211–12.

41. "prudenti usis consilio, praetendit, se, propter ea quae ab illo audierat, quasi in parte rationabilia viderentur, aliquantulum titubare: dixitque illi, libenter se velle eos audire in eorum ecclesia; et siquid ei verbis rationabilibus aut signis ostenderent, eis fideliter adhaerere," Berengar of Landorra, *Miracula collecta* 26–27.

42. "Et quoniam qui vult jacentem erigere, debet se ad apprehendendum illum aliqualiter inclinare, imitatus Apostolum dicentem, 'Factus sum Judaeis Judeus, ut Judaeos lucrifacerem," ibid. Cf. 1 Cor 9: 20.

43. "Gaudent haeretici, beatos se reputantes, si illum possant habere propitium quem sic fortissimum habebant impugnantorem," ibid., 27.

44. "Noctem illam fere B. Petrus duxit insomnem, devotioni et obsecrationibus vacans, ut Christi pietas diaboli machinamenta ad honorem detegeret catholicae veritatis," ibid.

45. "Prime vero mane consurgens, quasi matutinas dicturus, exivit domum, et ad Catholicorum ecclesiam missam celebrans, duas consecravit hostias; quarum unum sumpsit, alteram vero clam sub [cappa] in pyxide portans," ibid.

46. "cumque omnes . . . convenissent haeretici," ibid.

47. "si es vere mater Dei, adora hunc filium tuum," ibid.

48. "venisset hereticus cum multitudine hereticorum," Gerard of Frachet, *Vitae fratrum* 6.3, p. 237.

49. "filii tenebrarum prudentiores filiis lucis, cum essent armis veritatis exuti, se multitudine armaverunt, ut quem ratione non poterant, saltem multiloquio superarent," Thomas Agni of Lentini, *Vita* 32.

50. "heretico acutissimi ingenii et eloquentie singularis, adtendens hastucias eius," Gerard of Frachet, *Vitae fratrum* 6.3, p. 237.

51. "vir clamosus garrulusque et malitiosis sermonum versutiis eruditus," Thomas Agni of Lentini, *Vita* 32.

52. "Insistente eo semel quibusdam disputacionibus et gravibus hereticorum conflictacionibus, cepit mens eius postea de aliquibus articulis propulsari," Gerard of Frachet, *Vitae fratrum* 6.3, pp. 238–39.

53. "aliquis titubationis motus in eo insurgeret," Antoninus, *Chronicon* 19.

54. "prosternens se coram altari cum multis lacrimis rogavit dominum, ut causam suam defenderet, et ut aut illi lumen vere fidei infunderet aut loquela privaret, qua ita contra Deum abutebatur," Gerard of Frachet, *Vitae fratrum* 6.3, p. 237.

55. "Sed ubi ille comperit suggestionem esse maligni, ad oracionem recurrit, et prostratus coram altari beate Marie virginis, cepit ipsam devotissime invocare per filium, ut temptacionem illam sibi sua pietate auferret," ibid., 6.3, p. 239.
56. "Ego rogari pro te, Petre, ut non deficiat fides tua," ibid., 6.3, pp. 238–39. Cf. Lk 22:32.
57. "At cuius vocem consurgens, sensit continuo illum ambiguitatis scrupulum penitus recessisse, nec post, . . . aliquem circa huiusmodi sensit motum," ibid., 6.3, p. 239.
58. "cum lacrymis," Antoninus, *Chronica* 2.19.
59. "ut defensioni verae fidei suae provideret," ibid.
60. "omni amota ambiguitate in fide solidari se sensit. Inde ergo confortatus," ibid.
61. "pluribus haereticis convocatis," Peter Calo, *De Sancto Petro Martyre* 2.18, p. 691.
62. "Cum autem populus miraculum hoc ejus enarrabit, ego è contrario me nullatenus infirmum extitisse asseram, vosque testimonium perhibebitis juratis, et per hunc modum nullus ejus miraculis fidem adhibebit amplius," ibid., 2.18, pp. 691–92. Gerard tells how a heretic went to Friar Theobald, another brother in residence at the convent of Saint Eustorgius who was renowned for his sanctity, and requested that he cure a feigned illness. Later, Peter Calo expanded this account and depicted the heretic as appealing to Peter, instead of the less famous Theobald.
63. "Utinam ego fuissem ibi, quia validius percussissem," Gerard of Frachet, *Vitae fratrum* 6.3, p. 240.
64. "Rogo Dominum meum Jesum Christum, ut si infirmus es, sanitatem tibi restituat; si autem infirmitatem fraudulenter simulas, corpori tuo ad animae salutem infirmitatem tribuat," Peter Calo, *De Sancto Petro Martyre* 2.18, p. 692.
65. devotione non ficta," ibid.
66. "per B. Petri orationem et merita ab infirmitate mentis et corporis liberatus," ibid.
67. "cum lacrymis," Roderick of Atencia, "Lettre," 902.
68. "in agnum utique lupus, ferus in mitem, impius in pium, furibundus in mansuetum, in modestum effrenis, profanus in sanctum," Innocent IV, quoted in James of Voragine, *Legenda aurea*, 425.
69. "Dei mortui et non viventis," *Annales minorum*, ed. Luke Wadding (Florentia: Ad Claras Aquas, 1931), 5:299–300.
70. Ibid.
71. "O ecclesia Romana, omnes habes plenas manus de sanguine martirum," quoted in Grado Giovanni Merlo, "Pietro di Verona—San Pietro martire, Difficoltà e proposte per lo studio di un inquisitore beatificato," in *Culto dei santi: Istituzioni e classi in età preindustriale*, ed. Sofia Boesch Gajano and Lucia Sebastiani (Roma: L'Aquila, 1984), 471–88, at 485.
72. Merlo, "Pietro di Verona—San Pietro martire," 484.
73. Christine Caldwell Ames, "Peter Martyr: The Inquisitor as Saint," *Comitatus* 31 (2000): 137–73, at 150.
74. Ibid., 173. See also Michael Goodich, "The Politics of Canonization in the Thirteenth Century: Land and Mendicant Saints," *Church History* 44 (1975): 302–7.
75. Christine Caldwell Ames, *Righteous Persecution: Inquisition, Dominicans, and Christianity in the Middle Ages* (Philadelphia: University of Pennsylvania Press, 2009), 67.
76. "Ego scio pro certo, quod heretici tractant mortem meam, et pro morte mea pecunia est deposita; sed faciant, quod volunt, quia deterius faciam eis mortuus quam vivus,"

Gerard of Frachet, *Vitae fratrum* 6.3, p. 239. Gerard dates this prophecy to a month before Peter's death, while James of Voragine ascribes it to Palm Sunday, which would have fallen on March 24, two weeks before his demise. Even well before the plot was afoot, Peter was said to have predicted his martyrdom. Thomas Agni of Lentini reports that Peter informed his brethren, "Know that I will not die except by the hands of the unfaithful [*Sciote, me nunquam nisi per manus infidelium moriturum,*"] *Vita* 30. Peter Calo cites him as having told the people of Cesena that "I will be killed for the faith by heretics after the next Resurrection of the Lord, for my death has been ordained by them [*post futuram Domini Resurrectionem proximam pro fide ab haereticis occidar, quoniam ab eis mors mea ordinata est,*]" *De sancto Petro Martyre* 2.15. By "Resurrection of the Lord," Peter is referring to Easter.

77. "Rogo vos quod permittatis me cantare solum et fratrum Dominicum, quia vos discordatis in cantu," Roderick of Atencia, "Lettre," 902.

78. "Si non poterimus ad domum fratrum pervenire, apud sanctum Simplicianum poterimus hospitari," James of Voragine, *Legenda aurea*, 426.

79. "nec in modico nec in magno ab hoc vigore justicie desinentes," Roderick of Atencia, "Lettre," 902.

80. "ut numquam permittat, me aliter mori quam pro fide Christi," Gerard of Frachet, *Vitae fratrum* 6.3, p. 237.

81. "attentis et crebris postulationibus . . . , quod non sineret eum ex hac luce migrare, nisi sumto pro illo calice passionis," James of Voragine, *Legenda aurea*, 423.

82. "non se defendens, non fugiens," Roderick of Atencia, "Lettre," 903.

83. "non divertentem ab hoste," Innocent IV, quoted in James of Voragine, *Legenda aurea*, 440.

84. "In manus tuas, Domine, commendo spiritum meum," ibid. Cf. Innocent IV, "in manus tuas, domine, commendo spiritum meum," *Gaudemus in Domino*, 905, and Ps 30:6 and Lk 23:46.

85. "fidei symbolum . . . innocentis sanguinis effusione subscripsit," John of Colonna, "Lettre," 909. Guy of Evreux, Ms. Vat. lat, 1252, fol. 193rb. Quoted in Dondaine, "Saint Pierre Martyr," 106, n. 114. Given the brutality of the first blow Peter seems to have received, still reflected in the skull preserved at Saint Eustorgius, Dondaine points out that the saint would have lost consciousness immediately, so that, whatever words he may have spoken prior to his death (if any) must have been uttered when he heard Carino's quick footsteps approaching behind him. Donald S. Prudlo suggests in "The Assassin-Saint: The Life and Cult of Carino of Balsamo," *Catholic Historical Review* 94 (January, 2008): 1–21 that, before delivering the blow that crushed Peter's skull, Carino struck his victim on the shoulder or on the side of his head, so that he would have been able to utter these words. See also Prudlo, *The Martyred Inquisitor*, 64–65.

86. "O beatum virum, cui ex praesenti vita jam futura inceperat, et cujus pedes jam in caelestis Jerusalem atriis stantes erant! et qui adhuc in carne corruptibili positus, jam gloriae incorruptibilis et laudis perpetuae primitias degustabat!" Thomas Agni of Lentini, *Vita* 30.

87. "faciant, quod volunt, quia deterius faciam eis mortuus quam vivus," Gerard of Frachet, *Vitae fratrum* 6.3, p. 239.

88. "ad gravissimas questiones," Roderick of Atencia, "Lettre," 903.

89. "quam plurimi errorem suum relinquerent et ad gremium sancte ecclesie convolarent ita ut civitas Mediolanum et comitatus eiusdem, ubi tot hereticorum conventicula residebant, adeo sit purgata ut aliis expulsis et aliis ad fidem conversis nullus ibidem auderet aliquatenus apparere," James of Voragine, *Legenda aurea*, 427.

90. In Villa, ed., "Processo per l'uccisione di s. Pietro martire," Manfred Chrono and Fazio of Giussano refer to Daniel as apprized of the plot against Peter. Fiamma describes Daniel as a "vir pulcerimus corpore verbis et scientia prefulgidus . . . Qui cum cognosceret hereticorum facta ac versutias, factus est inquisitor in diocesi Brixiensi," Fiamma, "La *Cronaca maggiore dell'Ordine domenicano* di Galvano Fiamma," 330.

91. Dondaine understandably rejects this reading as an impossibility, given the rapid progress which Daniel would have to have made within the order by the time of the inquest, merely five months after Peter's death, and the impropriety of a conspirator being charged with investigating the conspiracy. Still, given the Dominicans' encouragement of dramatic transformations of heretics into friars and persecutors into inquisitors, it is not inconceivable that a learned and respected collaborator in Peter's murder could have become an investigator of this crime. Pruldo suggests that Daniel may have served as an auditor during this trial, not as a judge. See Prudlo, *The Martyred Inquisitor*, 74, n. 14.

92. "Plures etiam ex his, haeresiarchae pessimi et famosi, Ordinem Praedicatorum ingressi, haereticos et fautores eorum mirabili fervore persecuti sunt," Thomas Agni of Lentini, *Vita* 40.

93. In "The Assassin-Saint," Prudlo writes, "The lack of documentary evidence for the remainder of Carino's life should give the historian pause" (9), but he concludes, seemingly on the basis of the evidence of Carino's cult, "Although Carino's conversion story was recorded very late, there seems little reason to doubt it" (11).

94. See Serafino Razzi, *Vite de i santi e beati, cosi huomini, come donne, del Sacro ordine de' Fratri Predicatori* (Firenze: Nelle Stamperia di Bartolomeo Sermatelli, 1572), 77; Giovanni Michele Piò, *Delle Vite degli huomini illustrati di S. Domenico, Libri quattro* (Bologna: Per Sebastiano Bonomi, 1620), 210; Tristano Calchi, *Historiae patriae libri viginti*, 7 vols. (Milano: Apud ber. Melchioris Malatestae, 1627); rpt. in Joannis Georgii Graevi, ed., *Thesaurus antiquitatum et historiarum Italiae* (Lugduni Batavorum: Petrus Vander, 1704), vol. 2, pt. 1, cols. 81–536, at col. 333; Peter Ribadeneyra, *The Lives of the Saints with Other Feasts of the Year According to the Roman Calendar*, trans. William Petre (St. Omers: English College Press, 1634; rpt. St. Omers: Ioachim Carlier, 1659), 288, originally published as *Flos sanctorum* in 1630; Giuliano Bezzi, *Il fuoco trionfante, racconto della traslatione della miracolo. imagine detta la Madonna del Fuoco, protettrice della Città di Forlì, solenizzata da essa Città sotto li XX. di ottobre in M. D. C. XXXVI.* (Forlì: Per Gio. Cimatti, 1637), 59; "Commentarius praevius: Petrus Martyr, Ordinis Praedicatorum," in *Acta sanctorum*, 3 (April 29): 682; Francesco Maria Merenda, *Brevi compendi dell' Ordine de Predicatori delle vite morienti e vive morti di quei Beati e Servi di Dio che nella chiesa di S. Dominico di Forlì gloriosamente riposano* (Forlì: Per li Cimatti, 1654), 68–87, and *Vita del Beato Carino*, nuova édizione (Forlì: Tip. Operaia Raffaelli, 1938); Paolo Bonoli, *Istorie della città di Forlì intrecciate di varii accidenti della Romagna e dell' Italia* (Forlì: Per li Cimatti, e Saporetti, 1661), 80 and 346 and *Storia di Forlì*, ed. and corr. (Forlì: Presso Luigi Bordandini, 1826), 1:214–15; 2:474; Ripoll, 1:230,

n. 5; and Pier-Tommaso Campagna, *Storia di S. Pietro-Martire da Verona del sagro ordine de' Predicatori* (Milano: Giuseppe Pichino Malatesta, 1741). I have relied upon Pier-Tommaso Campagna, "Saint Pierre Martyr: Prince de l'Inquisition romaine," in *AD* 29 (April 1889): 773–815.

95. This hospital (or hospice) presumably stood on the site of the Church of Saint Sebastian, which was built at the end of the fifteenth century adjacent to the Church of Saint James the Apostle. Antonio Calandrini and Gian Michele Fusconi point out, in *Forlì e i suei vescovi: Appunti e documentazione per una storia della chiesa di Forlì*, 2 vols. (Forlì: Tipografia Litografia Valbonesi, 1985–92), that Saint Sebastian was commonly invoked against the plague and ulcerous wounds (1:664, n. 88). This church (or, more properly speaking, oratory) now serves as an art gallery.

96. The ruins of the current church and convent reflect the considerable expansion of the complex during the early and mid-sixteenth century and the restoration of the complex in 1715–19, under the plans of Giuseppe Merenda. On the early history of Dominicans in Forlì, see Calandrini and Fusconi, *Forlì e i suei vescovi*, 1:660–62. Interestingly enough, in the thirteenth century, Dominican sisters also had a convent in Forlì known as Saint Mary Magdalene, which was presumably designed to receive penitents.

97. Campagna, "Saint Pierre Martyr," 806.

98. See Philip F. Mulhern, *The Early Dominican Laybrother* (Washington, D.C.: n.p., 1944). Mulhern writes, "The lay brotherhood formed a separate, quasi-autonomous group within each community, and besides its participation in the common life, it had its supervisor and observances" (29–30). The fact that Carino was known almost exclusively by a nickname, that he could be hired as an assassin for forty pounds, that he did not possess a horse of his own with which to carry out the assassination, and even that he relied upon a peasant's crude farming tool to perform the murder, all suggest that he was lower class and probably unlearned enough to fit among the other *conversi* of the convent. At the same time, lay brothers were often defined not only by their class origins but by their previous criminality. Allowed into the convent to do penance for their misdeeds, they were segregated from the friars proper on account of their notoriety and consequent unworthiness for sacred orders. See Stephen M. Donovan's article on "Conversi" in *The Catholic Encyclopedia*, vol. 4 (New York: Robert Appleton Co., 1908), www.newadvent.org/cathen/04346b.htm. Donovan writes, "[A]mong the *conversi*, there were not seldom those who were either entirely illiterate, or who in the world had led a life of public scandal, or had been notorious criminals, and while on the one hand it was unjust that such should be debarred from the means of doing penance in the cloister and from the other benefits of religious life, they were at the same time hardly to be considered fit subjects for the reception of Sacred orders." In "The Assassin-Saint," Prudlo suggests that Carino was not a formal lay brother but, rather, an "affiliate lay penitent" (11, n. 35).

99. See the document of December 13, 1255, in the Archivio Capitolare di Forlì, Perg. no. 54. The reference is to a Dominican church dedicated to Peter, but an altar at the church of Saint James the Apostle seems to be what is meant. In 1583, Sebastiano Menzocchi painted Carino killing Peter for the altar of Saint Peter Martyr in the Chiesa del Suffragio in Forlì.

100. Merenda, *Vita del Beato Carino*, 6.

101. Piò, *Delle Vite degli huomini illustrati*, 210.

102. Merenda, *Vita del Beato Carino*, 10.
103. Ibid., 8.
104. Ibid., 6.
105. Carino died perhaps on April 7, perhaps on August 3, and perhaps on November 12, the last of which days serves as his feast day. Razzi cites him as asking to be buried underneath a staircase, but Piò claims that he wanted to be interred in the cemetery for criminals. All later authors follow Piò.
106. The Dominican friars of Forlì attempted to have Carino recognized as a saint in the nineteenth century, under the pontificate of Pope Pius IV, but without success. In 1867, when this convent was closed and Carino's relics were transferred to the cathedral of Forlì, his cult seemed to have received a fatal blow. In 1934, however, Don Emilio Griffini, a parish priest of the Church of Saint Martin in Balsamo—now Cinisello Balsamo, a suburb of Milan—received permission to obtain the head and minor relics of his parish's native son. On April 2 of that year, an elaborate translation took place.
107. Razzi, *Vite de i santi e beati*, 77.
108. Ribadeneyra, *The Lives of the Saints*, 288.
109. Merenda, *Vita del Beato Carino*, 3.
110. This artwork appears to have first been described around the year 1760 by Allegranza, a monk of the convent of Saint Eustorgius, in his *Descrizione historica della basilica di S. Eustorgio*, a manuscript which was conserved in the parish archives of the church. Michele Caffi refers to this artwork briefly in *Della Chiesa di Sant' Eustorgio in Milano: Illustrazione storico, monumentale, epigrafica* (Milano: Tipografia da Giuditta Boniardi-Pogliani, 1841). He notes, after having observed the Church's recent refusal to confirm Carino's cult, due to the lack of necessary documentation, "Pure col titolo di beato (B. ACERINVS DE BALSAMO PETRICIDA) nella quale leggenda notisi l'errore di *Acerinus* anzichè *Charinus* come si ha dai processi, egli era stato effigiato a chiaro-scuro nell'anno 1505 con altri beati domenicani in uno degli stalli del coro dell'altar maggiore di questa basilica" (100–101). While Caffi refers to the artwork as a "chiaro-scuro," A. Moiraghi describes it, in "Il Beato Carino," *Rivista di scienze storiche* (1906): 47–61 and 193–211, as a "statua" (208). He writes, "Nel 1505 fu fatta scolpire in legno l'effigie de 34 Beati dell' Ordine con aureola intorno la fronte e il titolo di Beato apposto ai loro nomi: furono, qualche anno doppo, portate nel coro" (207–08). According to Moiraghi, the Congregation of Rites considered the evidence of this sculpture when attempting to determine the extent of the cults of the Blessed Reginald, Innocent V, John of Vercelli, Aimone, and Bartholomew the Martyr.
111. Though all texts agree that, in this artwork, an "A" obscures Carino's name, they differ as to the spelling. The name is cited as "Acerinus" in Caffi and "Acierinus" in Moriaghi. "Beatus" is at times spelled out, at times left abbreviated as "B."
112. Quoted in *Il Rosario: MD* 51 (1934), 138–39, at 139.
113. The summa against heretics attributed to Peter has survived in two manuscripts, namely, cod. 1065 (N. 16), Bibl. communale, Perugia, and cod. 1738. A. 9, Bibl. Nat., Florence, conv. soppr. I have consulted the Florence manuscript. Sections from the Perugia manuscript have been edited by Thomas Kaepelli, "Une *Somme contre les hérétiques* de s. Pierre Martyr (?)," in *AFP* 17 (1947): 295–335. Kaepelli hesitates to attribute this summa definitively to Peter, but Prudlo expresses more confidence in his authorship.

114. See Antoine Dondaine's edition of this letter in "Saint Pierre Martyr: Études," *AFP* 23 (1953): 66–162, at 91–93.

115. "corrigere ac punire delinquentes," Bibl. Nat., Florence, conv. soppr, p. viii.

116. "vesanias," Kaepelli, ed., "Une *Somme contre les hérétiques* de s. Pierre Martyr (?)," 331.

117. "delirant," ibid., 323, 324, 329, and 330.

118. "per . . . diabolicas fantasias," ibid., 326.

119. "Exhibe te Iohannem incestuosis, heu apostatis fornicantibus Finees, Petrum mentientibus, et blasphematibus Paulum, negociantibus Christum," Dondaine, ed., "Saint Pierre Martyr," 92.

120. "ego, adhuc, in valle sollicitudinis moror et pro aliis fere totam vitam meam expendi," ibid.

121. "Exi ergo, Petre galle, de medio babillonis, qui secundum doctrinam quam docuisti dampnatus es sine alicuius spei redemptione, et veni ad ecclesiasm dei," Kaepelli, ed. "Une *Somme contre les hérétiques* de s. Pierre Martyr (?)," 306.

122. "haereticorum opprobriorum," Thomas Agni of Lentini, *Vita* 8 and 32.

123. "fidei defensor," ibid., 8 and 32.

CHAPTER FIVE

1. Bernard Gui was the author of many works, which will be referred to as they arise. For the most complete list of his writings, see Thomas Kaepelli, *Scriptores Ordinis Praedicatorum Medii Aevi*, vol. 1 (Rome: Ad S. Sabinae, 1970), 205–25. On Bernard Gui, see Léopold Delisle, *Notice sur les manuscrits de Bernard Gui* (Paris: Imprimerie Nationale, 1879); Antoine Thomas, "Bernard Gui, frère Prêcheur," in *Histoire littéraire de la France*, Ouvrage commencé par les religieux bénédictins de la congrégation de Saint-Maur et continué par des membres de l'Institut (Académie des Inscriptions et Belles-Lettres), vol. 35 (Paris: n.p., 1921; Nendeln, Liechtenstein: Kraus Reprint, 1971), 139–232; Bernard Guenée, *Entre l'Église et l'état: Quatre vies de prélats français à la fin du Moyen Âge, XIIIe-XVe siècle* (Paris: Gallimard, 1987), trans. by Arthur Goldhammer as *Between Church and State: The Lives of Four French Prelates in the Late Middle Ages* (Chicago: University of Chicago Press, 1991), chap. 1, "Bernard Gui (1261–1331)," 37–70; *CF*, vol. 16, *Bernard Gui et son monde (1261–1331)* (Toulouse: Privat, 1981), including Paul Amargier, "Eléments pour un portrait de Bernard Gui," 19–37; Anne-Marie Lamarrigue, *Bernard Gui (1261–1331): Un historien et sa méthode* (Paris: Honoré Champion, 2000); and Agnès Dubreil-Arcin, "L'Inquisition de Toulouse: Bernard Gui (1314–1331), un inquisiteur méthodique," in Laurent Albaret, ed., *Les Inquisiteurs: Portraits de défenseurs de la foi en Languedoc (XIIIe-XIVe siècles)* (Toulouse: Privat, 2001), 105–13.

2. We know little about Gui's family. There was a maternal uncle by the name of Bertrand who left Gui some money in his will for the purpose of buying books when Gui was about thirty years old. There was also a nephew by the name of Peter Gui who also became a Dominican friar of some repute. Peter served as prior of the convent of Périgueux in 1333 and of Carcassonne in 1335, and he served as a provincial of the order between 1337 and 1343.

3. On Gui's work as a prior, see Yves Dossat, "Les Priorats de Bernard Gui," *CF*, vol. 16, *Bernard Gui et son monde*, 85–106.

4. Stephen of Salagnac and Bernard Gui, *De quatuor in quibus Deus Praedicatorum ordinem insignivit*, ed. Thomas Kaeppeli, *MOPH*, vol. 22 (Rome: Institutum Historicum Fratrum Praedicatorum, 1949).

5. Gui, *De fundatione et prioribus conventuum provinciarum Tolosanae et provinciae Ordinis Praedicatorum*, ed. Paul Amargier (Rome: ad S. Sabinae, apud Institutum historicum fratrum praedicatorum, 1961). See also Anne-Marie Lamarrigue, "Bernard Gui, historien du Midi," *Heresis* 38 (2003): 51–69.

6. In 1318, Gui prepared a life of Thomas Aquinas; in 1320, he catalogued the Angelic Doctor's works; and in 1324, with Aquinas canonized and new materials available from the canonization proceedings, he revised this life. For Gui's writings on Aquinas, including the relevant section from his *Catalogus magistrorum* and the *Legenda S. Dominici* from his *Speculum sanctorale*, see Gui, *Scripta de Sancto Dominico*. In addition to his universal writings, Gui attended to local history, composing accounts of the counts and the bishops of Toulouse, the saints and the bishops of Limoges, and the churches and the bishops of Lodève. He wrote a few theological works, namely, on the articles of faith, on original sin and the Immaculate Conception, and on the office of the Mass, all largely cobbled together from other sources. See Marie-Humbert Vicaire, "Positions scolaires et fonctions occasionnelles de Bernard Gui," *CF*, vol. 16, *Bernard Gui et son monde*, 55–83.

7. On Gui's work as a bishop, see Bernard Guillemain, "Le Milieu épiscopal et cardinalice de Bernard Gui," *CF*, vol. 16, *Bernard Gui et son monde*, 317–31 and Jean-Marie Carbasse, "Bernard Gui, évêque de Lodève (1234–1331)," *CF*, vol. 16, *Bernard Gui et son monde*, 333–59.

8. It was presumably Peter Gui, the compiler and copyist of his uncle's *Speculum sanctorale*, who composed a brief biography of Bernard Gui, edited by Delisle as "Vie de Bernard Gui écrite par un contemporain," in *Notices sur les manuscrits de Bernard Gui*, Appendix 25, 169–455, esp. 427–28. The author of this biography provides us with the few personal details which we possess about Gui, or indeed about any medieval inquisitor. As Dubreil-Arcin notes, "Cette biographie, fiable par ses origines, fait de Bernard Gui un des rare inquisiteurs des XIIIe et XIVe siècles à n'être pas connu exclusivement par des documents de l'Inquisition," "L'Inquisition de Toulouse," 106. See also Bernard Montagnes, "Bernard Gui dans l'historiographie dominicaine," in *CF*, vol. 16, *Bernard Gui et son monde*, 183–203.

9. "Sub hoc humili loco jacet frater Bernadus Guidonis, ordinis Fratrum Praedicatorum, post nonnullas per Italiam, Galliam et Flandriam legationes apostolicas, primum Tudensis in Gallaecia, deindi Lodovenis episcopus, in gallia Narbonensi, qui animam coelo reddit anno Salutis Domini MCCCXXXI, die XXX Decembris. Requiescat in pace. Amen," quoted in Delisle, *Notices sur les Manuscrits de Bernard Gui*, 185.

10. I refer to Bernard Guénée's chapter on Gui in *Between Church and State*.

11. I refer to *CF*, vol. 16, *Bernard Gui et son monde*, where Annette Pales-Gobilliard's "Bernard Gui, inquisiteur et auteur de la *Practica*" (253–64), Raoul Manselli's "Bernard Gui face aux 'spirituels' et aux apostoliques" (265–78), and Jacques Paul's "La Mentalité de l'inquisiteur chez Bernard Gui" (279–316) stand out among other articles devoted to Gui's service as a historian, as a prior, and as a bishop.

12. In "La Mentalité de l'inquisiteur chez Bernard Gui," Jacques Paul argues that Gui was moderate in his treatment of heretics, particularly in contrast to the anonymous author of the 1270s whose inquisitors' manual (included in vol. 36 of the Fonds Doat) he used as the foundation of the fourth section of his *Practica*. In "Bernard Gui, inquisiteur et auteur de la *Practica*," Annette Pales-Gobilliard writes, similarly, "Par rapport aux bûchers du siècle passé, le nombre de 42 personnes abandonnées au bras séculier sur 930 coupables examinés par Bernard Gui, ne fait pas apparaître celui-ci plus sévère que ses prédécesseurs" (262). While the earlier inquisitors Bernard of Caux and John of Saint-Pierre consigned one out of one hundred heretics to the stake, Gui, according to Pales-Gobilliard's current statistics, condemned roughly the same percentage of guilty parties to this fate.

13. *Le Livre des sentences de l'inquisiteur Bernard Gui: 1308–1323*, ed. Annette Pales-Gobilliard, 2 vols. (Paris: CNRS, 2002). The manuscript Pales-Gobilliard edited is Add. Ms. 4697, in the British Library, under the title *Liber sententiarum continens sententias et acta inquisitionis Tholosane ab 1307 ad 1323*. As A. E. Nickson explains in "Locke and the Inquisition of Toulouse," *The British Museum Quarterly* 36, no. 3–4 (1973): 83–92, this manuscript resurfaced in the seventeenth century in the possession of an English Quaker merchant in residence in Rotterdam by the name of Benjamin Furly. In 1687, the philosopher John Locke, then a political exile in Rotterdam and an associate of Furly, is known to have read the manuscript and to have transcribed large sections of it into his journal. In 1688, Philippus van Limborch borrowed Furly's manuscript, whose contents he included in his *Historia inquisitionis, cui subjungitur Liber sententiarum inquisitionis Tholosanae ab anno Christo 1307 ad annum 1323* (Amsterdam: Henricum Wetstenium, 1692). Until Nickson's article, it was widely assumed that Furly's manuscript had disappeared and that Limborch's edition of it constituted the only available access to Gui's sentences. Yet Furly's son John had brought the manuscript back to England, John's son Thomas had sold it to Bishop Secker in 1755, and Secker had given it to the British Library, where it was first catalogued in 1756 and where it remains to this day.

14. Gui's *Practica inquisitonis heretice pravitatis* consists of five books. The first three books contain collections of formulas used in delivering sentences in court, during the "general sermon," and on other occasions; the fourth book contains a collection of documents addressing inquisitors' powers, including papal bulls, imperial edicts, royal decrees, and conciliar decisions; and the fifth book—generally considered the most interesting—contains a summary of the beliefs and practices of Cathars, Waldensians, Pseudo-Apostles, and Beguins, as well as Jewish converts to Christianity who have reverted to Judaism and sorcerers or invokers of demons, together with advice on how to proceed against these deviants in the faith. When I cite the fifth book of the *Practica*, I will be alluding to Guillaume Mollat's edition of this section in *Manuel de l'inquisiteur*, 2 vols. (Paris: "Les Belles Heures" and Honoré Champion, 1926-27), vol. 1 and to Wakefield and Evans' translation of it in "Bernard Gui's Description of Heresies," 373-445, both of which I will reference by book, chapter, section, and page number. When I cite the first, second, third, or fourth books of the *Practica*, I will be alluding to Célestin Douais' complete *Practica inquisitionis heretice pravitatis* (Paris: A. Picard, 1886), which I will reference by book number and by section and subsection numbers, insofar as Douais makes them available.

15. For *De inquisitione hereticorum*, see "Der Tractat des David von Augsberg über die Waldesier," ed. Wilhelm Preger, *Abhandlungen der bayerischen Akademie der Wissenschaften* 14, no. 2 (1878): 183–235, at 203–35. The attribution to David of Augsburg is uncertain.

16. See Stephen of Bourbon's *Tractatus de diversis materiis praedicabilis*, in *Anécdotes historiques, légendes et apologues*, ed. A. Lecoy de La Marche (Paris: Librairie Renouard, 1877), , 2:290–99.

17. Antoine Thomas criticizes the organization of the *Practica*, attributing its overlapping sections to the evolution of the work over the course of its author's career, but he writes, also, "La *Practica* de Bernard Gui est une mine extrêmement riche où l'historien curieux de connaître les manifestations de la vie religieuse au XIIIe siècle et au commencement du XIVe a beaucoup à prendre" ("Bernard Gui, frère Prêcheur," 208). Molinier, who devotes a chapter of *L'Inquisition dans le Midi de la France au XIIIe et au XIVe siècle: Étude sur les sources de son histoire* (Paris: Sandoz et Fischbacher, 1880) to the *Practica*, states, "Ce n'est plus seulement l'Inquisition qui se révèle à nous dans son exercice, c'est l'inquisiteur lui-même qui nous livre à un certain point les secrets de sa pensée et de sa conscience" (197–236, at 236).

18. Gui's discussion of the Cathars relies heavily upon Peter Autier's confession, as well as upon Raynier Sacconi's *Summa de Catharis et de Leonistis*. Gui pursued the Cathars, first, in the Toulousain, where he served as principal inquisitor, and, later, in the Albigeois, where he aided Geoffrey of Ablis, the inquisitor of Carcassonne; John of Beaune, Geoffrey's successor; and Jacques Fournier, the bishop of Pamiers (and future Pope Benedict XII) in pursuing heretics. Geoffrey's registers have been edited by Annette Pales-Gobilliard, as *L'Inquisiteur Geoffroy d'Ablis et les cathares du comté de Foix (1308-1309)* (Paris: CNRS, 1984), and Fournier's registers by Jean Duvernoy, as *Le Registre d'inquisition de Jacques Fournier, évêque de Pamiers (1318-1325)*, 3 vols. (Toulouse: Privat, 1965).

19. Less familiar with the Waldensians than the Cathars, Gui relied heavily upon Stephen of Bourbon's *Tractatus de diversis materiis praedicabilis* and David of Augsburg's *De inquisitione hereticorum* for his description of members of this sect. Following Guillaume Mollat's example, when I cite the *Practica*, I will be placing those passages Gui has lifted from other authors in italics. For the position of Gui's *Practica* in the context of other thirteenth- and fourteenth-century inquisitors' manuals, see Antoine Dondaine, "Le Manuel de l'inquisiteur (1230–1330)," *AFP* 17 (1947): 85–194.

20. In the Toulousain and the Albigeois, there were few Pseudo-Apostles, and there is only one such heretic whose case is recorded in his *Liber sententiarum*. Nevertheless, Gui was sufficiently interested in these heretics, perhaps as a result of his encounters with them in Italy in 1317 and 1318, to have studied the anonymous Italian treatise on the sect; to have written his own tract on them, modeled upon this earlier treatise; and to have included a section on them in his *Practica*. For the anonymous text on the Pseudo-Apostles and for Gui's own text, see *Historia fratris Dulcini heresiarche di anonimo sincrono: e, De secta illorum qui se dicunt esse de ordine Apostolorum di Bernardo Gui*, ed. Arnaldo Segarizzi, 2 vols. (Città di Castello: Tipi della Casa Editrice S. Lapi, 1907). Gui's treatise is also included in Mollat, ed., *Manuel de l'inquisiteur*, 2:66–121, which will be cited here.

21. Gui appears to have been personally present at all but one of these sermons, when he was represented by subordinates. In addition, Gui presided over the burning of copies of the Talmud on November 28, 1319 and the reconciliation of the people of Cordes, who had earlier defied the authority of the Inquisition, on June 29, 1321.

22. James B. Given puts into question Gui's reputed leniency in "A Medieval Inquisitor at Work: Bernard Gui, 3 March 1308 to 16 June 1323," in *Portraits of Medieval Living: Essays in Memory of David Herlihy*, ed. Samuel K. Cohn Jr. and Steven A. Epstein (Ann Arbor: University of Michigan Press, 1996), 207–32. He compares the rate at which Gui had people executed with similar rates in secular courts in France, Italy, and England and finds him to be more severe than contemporaneous judges. Though Manselli finds in Gui "un volonté sincère de connaître, un besoin de vérité qui s'appuie sur des données certaines et dignes de foi" ("Bernard Gui faces aux 'spirituels' et aux 'apostoliques," 275), he also judges him to have emphasized the juridical side of the Inquisition, in contrast to Fournier, who stressed the pastoral aspect of this office. Whereas Gui aspired simply to prove the accused to be guilty in order to condemn them, Fournier, Manselli judges, aimed to uncover their beliefs in order to refute their errors.

23. I am using the word "performative" not in J. L. Austin's sense, to refer to utterances which bring about the actions they signify, but in the more everyday sense, to refer to actions, expressions, and utterances related to a dramatic performance.

24. In *Inquisition*, for example, Edward Peters claims that Eco's portrait of Gui resembles more a nineteenth-century representation of an inquisitor than any fourteenth-century original (307). See also Peter Biller, "Umberto Eco et les interrogations de Bernard Gui," in *Inquisition et pouvoir*, ed. Gabriel Audisio (Aix-en-Provence: Publications de l'Université de Provence, 2004), 257–68.

25. Umberto Eco, *Il Nome della rosa* (Milan: Bompiani, 1980), translated by William Weaver as *The Name of the Rose* (New York: Harcourt Brace & Company, 1983), 300–301.

26. Lay people obviously had access to devotional works such as psalters and books of hours. Occasionally, translations of Scripture would be produced for noble readers, but more as venerated additions to their libraries than as practical means of the dissemination of the Word of God to the people. Waldensians and Lollards were particularly active in producing and consuming translations of Scripture, Church Fathers, and theological texts and, as a result, were particularly prosecuted for doing so. See the collection of articles on *Heresy and Literacy, 1000–1530*, ed. Peter Biller and Anne Hudson (Cambridge: Cambridge University Press, 1996) and Margaret Deansely, *The Lollard Bible and Other Medieval Biblical Versions* (Cambridge: Cambridge University Press, 1920).

27. Heretical sects, as Gui represents them, are what Brian Stock has termed "textual communities," that is, groups of lay readers (or lay listeners) who, encountering Scripture and other religious texts directly, without the mediation of Catholic clerics, interpret them as they see fit. See *The Implications of Literacy: Written Language and Models of Interpretation in the Eleventh and Twelfth Centuries* (Princeton: Princeton University Press, 1987).

28. "Bernard Gui's Description of Heresies," 5.1.4, p. 384, trans. modified. "applicando et exponendo pro se et contra statum Romane ecclesie," Gui, *Manuel de l'inquisiteur* 5.4, p. 26. See note 14.

29. "Description," 5.2.6, p. 396. "Istud dicitur in evangelio vel in epistola sancti Petri aut sancti Pauli aut sancti Jacobi," *Manuel de l'inquisiteur* 5.2.6, p. 62.

30. "Description," 5.2.6, p. 396, trans. modified. "ut magis dicta eorum ab auditoribus acceptentur," *Manuel* 5.2.6, p. 62.

31. "Description," 5.2.1, p. 387, trans. modified. "cum essent *ydiote et illiterati*," *Manuel* 5.2.1, p. 34.

32. "Description," 5.2.1, p. 387, trans. modified. "cum essent *ydiote et illiterati*," *Manuel* 5.2.1, p. 34.

33. "Description," 5.3.4, p. 408. "Penitentiam agite, appropinquabit enim regnum celorum," *Manuel* 5.3.4, p. 94–96.

34. "Description," 5.3.4, p. 407, trans. modified. "*Dicunt enim* quedam que videntur aperte laudabilia, *ut sic* attrahant et *alliciant auditores*," *Manuel* 5.3.6, p. 94.

35. "Description," 5.3.4, p. 408, trans. modified. "pretendunt exterius quedam signa devotionis ad Deum, que omnia prima facie videntur auditoribus bona et pia," *Manuel* 5.3.4, p. 96.

36. "Description," 5.3.3, p. 407, trans. modified. "aliqua similitudine bonitatis vel pietatis, ut magis reddantur credibilia verba ipsorum," *Manuel* 5.3.3, p. 94.

37. "Description," 5.3.4, p. 407, trans. modified. "*Dicunt enim* quedam que videntur aperte laudabilia, *ut sic* attrahant et *alliciant auditores*," *Manuel* 5.3.4, p. 94. In a like manner, the Waldensians propound good and moral precepts only "so that they be listened to more easily by others and so that they secure a hold over their listeners [*ut sic facilius in aliis audiantur et capiant audientes*]," "Description," 5.2.6, p. 396, trans. modified; *Manuel* 5.2.6, p. 60.

38. "Description," 5.1.4, p. 383, trans. modified. "communiter dicent . . . ipsi tenent locum apostolorum," *Manuel* 5.1.4, p. 24–26.

39. "Description," 5.2.4, p. 391, trans. modified. "dicentes se esse successores apostolorum et jactantes se tenere et servare evangelicam et apostolicam paupertatem," *Manuel* 5.2.4, p. 46.

40. "Description," 5.3.3, p. 405. "apostolos seu *de ordine apostolorum*," *Manuel* 5.3.3, p. 88.

41. "Description," 5.4.5, p. 424. "ecclesiam spiritualam quantum ad viros quos vocant spirituales et evangelicos, qui vitam Christi et apostolorum servant," *Manuel* 5.4.5, p. 144.

42. "Description of Heresies," 5.2.6, p. 396, trans. modified. "*dicentes illos tantum esse apostolorum successores qui vitam eorum* imitantur et tenent," *Manuel* 5.2.6, p. 58.

43. "Description," 5.2.1, p. 387. "quorum apostolorum imitatores et successores . . . se esse temerarie asserebant," *Manuel* 5.2.1, p. 36.

44. "Description," 5.2.4, p. 391. "se ipso vite et perfectioni apostolice comparantes et meritis coequantes, in se ipsis inaniter gloriantur, dicentes se esse successores apostolorum et jactantes se tenere et servare evangelicam et apostolicam paupertatam," *Manuel* 5.2.4, p. 46.

45. "Description," 5.2.5, p. 393. "*frequentant ecclesias et predicationes et in omnibus se religiose* et *composite* exterius *gerunt* et student *habere verba quasi linita et cauta*," *Manuel* 5.2.5, p. 52.

46. "Description," 5.2.5, p. 393. "*aliquando se ingerunt simulate familiaritatibus religiosorum et clericorum, ut se contegant, et largiuntur eis munera* vel dona vel faciunt obsequia seu servitia," *Manuel* 5.2.5, p. 52.

47. "Description," 5.2.5, p. 393. "ut sibi et suis adquirant oportunitatem liberiorum latendi et vivendi et nocendi animabus," *Manuel* 5.2.5, p. 52.

48. "Revelatio autem divina ordine quodam ad inferiores pervenit per superiores. . . . Et ideo, pari ratione, explicatio fidei oportet quod perveniat ad inferiores homines per maiores," Aquinas, *ST* 2a-2ae.2.6.

49. "Description," 5.2.7, p. 399. "*se esse simplices aut nescire sapienter respondere,*" *Manuel de l'inquisiteur* 5.2.7, p. 70.

50. "Description," 5.4.5, p. 421. "*cum sint, ut aiunt, layci et homines simplices,*" *Manuel* 5.4.5, p. 136.

51. "Description," 5.2.7, p. 398. "*Et vos, domine, numquid ita creditis?*" *Manuel* 5.2.7, p. 66.

52. "Description," 5.2.7, p. 398. "*Ita omnino credo,*" *Manuel* 5.2.7, p. 66.

53. "Description," 5.2.7, p. 398. "*Credo quicquid vos et quicquid alii boni doctores me jubent credere,*" *Manuel* 5.2.7, p. 66.

54. "Description," 1.1, 381; "ut ita fallant simplices," *Manuel* 1.1, p. 16.

55. "ad . . . seducendum corda simplicium," Gui, *Practica* 5.8.8, p. 352.

56. "Description," 5.4.5, p. 421. "sunt tamen astuti, callidi et versuti," *Manuel* 5.4.5, p. 136.

57. "Description," 5.2.8, p. 400, trans. modified. "duplicitatibus verborum," *Manuel* 5.2.8, p. 72.

58. "Description," 5.2.8, p. 400, trans. modified. "fugas verborum," *Manuel* 5.2.8, p. 72.

59. "Description," 5.2.8, p. 400, trans. modified. "sophismata," *Manuel* 5.2.8, p. 72.

60. "Description," 5.2.7, p. 397. "fallacias," *Manuel*, 5.2.7, p. 64.

61. "Description," 5.3.5, p. 408, trans. modified. "tergiversationes," *Manuel* 5.3.5, p. 96.

62. "Description," 5.2.7, p. 398. "Et ego credo, intelligendo quod ipse credit me ita credere," *Manuel* 5.2.7, p. 64.

63. "Description," 5.2.7, p. 398. "*Illi boni doctores quibus vis credere sunt magistri secte tue cum quibus, si ego sentio, credis michi et illis,* set *aliter non credis,*" *Manuel* 5.2.7, p. 66.

64. "Description," 5.2.7, p. 398. "*Si homo simplex es, responde et age simpliciter, sine palliatione verborum,*" *Manuel* 5.2.7, p. 66.

65. "Description," 5.2.7, p. 398. "pavidus," *Manuel* 5.2.7, p. 68.

66. "Description," 5.2.7, p. 398. "contremiscens," *Manuel* 5.2.7, p. 68.

67. "Description," 5.2.7, p. 400. "in tali . . . anxietate," *Manuel* 5.2.7, p. 70.

68. "Description," 5.2.8, p. 401. "cum queritur ab aliquo si ita credat, respondet cum admiratione, quasi iratus: 'Quid crederem ego aliud, numquid debeo ego ita credere?" *Manuel* 5.2.8, p. 74.

69. "Description," 5.2.8, p. 401. "*Ego sum homo simplex et illiteratus et nescio istas questiones,* subtilitates, et de facili caperetis me et induceretis in errorem," *Manuel* 5.2.8, p. 74.

70. "Description," 5.2.7, p. 398. "*Si omnia que dico vultis aliter interpretari quam sane et simpliciter, tunc nescio quid* vobis *debeam respondere; simplex homo sum et illiteratus, nolite me capere verbis,*" *Manuel* 5.2.7, p. 66.

71. "Description," 5.2.7, p. 399. "*Cum autem vident astantes libenter eis compati quasi simplicibus quibus fiat injuria et in quibus nichil mali inveniatur, assumunt fiduciam et simulant se flere et miserabiles ostendere,*" *Manuel* 5.2.7, p. 70.

72. "Description," 5.2.8, p. 402, trans. modified. "intendunt . . . ut infametur inquisitor apud laycos, quod simples homines videatur infestare sine causa et querere occasionem perdendi eos nimis cautelose examinando," *Manuel* 5.2.8, p. 76.

73. "Description," 5, "Preface," p. 377. "Nimis enim est grave hereticos deprehendere ubi ipsi non aperte confitentur errorem seu occultant vel ubi non habentur certa et sufficientia testimonia contra ipsos," Manuel 5, "Instructio generalis," p. 6.

74. "Description," 5.3.3. p. 407. "aperte ... profiteri et defendere in omnibus et per omnia predictam doctrinam suam," Manuel 5.3.3, p. 94.

75. "Description," 5.3.8, p. 411. "Vidi ego et expertus sum de uno quod per duos fere annos detentus in carcere et sepius examinatus tergiversando veritatem noluit confiteri, quam tandem aperuit et detexit," Manuel 5.3.8, p. 106. Gui is referring to Peter of Galicia.

76. "Description," 5, "Preface," p. 377. "Angit enim conscientia, ex una parte, si non confessus nec convictus puniatur," Manuel 5, "Instructio generalis," 1:6.

77. "Description," 5, "Preface," p. 377. "ex altera vero parte, angit amplius animum inquirentis informatum de falsitate et calliditate et malitia talium per experientiam frequentem, si evadant per suam vulpinam astutiam in fidei nocumentum, quia ex hoc ipsi amplius roborantur et multiplicantur et callidiores efficiuntur," Manuel 5, "Instructio generalis," p. 6. As he puts it elsewhere, "Those heretics, glorying therein, are further encouraged by observing how they thus elude learned men, slipping cleverly out of their hands by the sly cunning and tortuous ambiguity of their replies [*ipsi heretici gloriantes per hoc amplius roborantur, videntes quod viris litteratis ita illudunt quod de manibus eorum per suas vulpinas, versutias et tortuosas responsionum ambages callide celabuntur*]," "Description," 5, "Preface," p. 377; Manuel 5, "Instructio generalis," p. 6.

78. "Description," 5, "Preface," p. 377. "layci fideles inde sumunt materiam scandali quod inceptum inquisitionis negotium contra aliquem quasi confuse relinquitur et quodam modo infirmantur in fide, videntes quod viri litterati sic a personis rudibus et vilibus illuduntur," Manuel 5, "Instructio generalis," p. 6.

79. "frater Bernardus Guidonis ordinis Praedicatorum, inquisitor heretice pravitatis in regno Francie auctoritate apostolica deputatus," Le Livre des sentences, ed. Pales-Gobilliard, 1:326.

80. "ipsum per diffinitivam sentenciam in hiis scriptis hereticum esse declaramus et pronunciamus et eundem tanquam talem relinquimus curie seculari," ibid., 1:330.

81. In "Les Sentences de Bernard Gui, Inquisiteur à Toulouse (1307–1328)," mémoire sous la direction de Henri Gilles, Université des Sciences Sociales, Toulouse I, 1980–81, Michel Barrère argues that Gui's *Practica* represents the Inquisition as a performance of ecclesiastical power. He writes, "Il y a, dans cette liturgie, une affirmation du pouvoir de l'Église et de sa supériorité intrinsèque et une supériorité qui n'est pas simplement celle du droit, mais celle de la force, qui montre le condamné abjurant à genoux, soumis, vaincu, bientôt marqué" (82).

82. See Jean Duvernoy, "Pierre Autier," Cahiers d'études cathares 21, no. 47 (Autumn 1970): 9–49, and Le Catharisme, vol. 2, L'Histoire des Cathares (Toulouse: Privat, 1979), 315–33, and Malcolm Lambert, The Cathars (Oxford: Wiley-Blackwell, 1998), chap. 10, "The Last Missionary," 230–71.

83. "Description," 5.1.1, p. 381; "ut ad conversionem sepius invitentur, quia conversio talium est plurimum utilis," Manuel 5.1.1, p. 16. See also Gui, Practica 4, p. 218.

84. "Description," 5.1.1, p. 381; "conversio hereticorum Manicheorum communiter vera est er raro ficta; et quando convertuntur, detegunt omnia et aperiunt veritatem et revelant omnes complices suos; unde sequitur magnus fructus," Manuel 5.1.1, p. 16.

85. For the sentence of Peter Autier, see Gui, *Practica* 3, pp. 129–31.

86. "Amelii de Perlis alias cognominati de Alta Rippa, dyocesis Appamiensis, capti et deprehensi in heresi in dyocesi Tholosana in qua plurima conmisit in heresi personas hereticando alias et fidem suo falso dogmate corrumpendo," *Le Livre des sentences*, ed. Pales-Gobilliard, 1:326.

87. "legitime ac evidenter nobis constat . . . per plures testes in inquisitione legitime receptos," ibid.

88. "legitime ac evidenter nobis constat . . . per confessionem seu magis professionem tam nepharium quam prophanam Amelii de Perlis," ibid.

89. "prout Petrus Auterii hereticus tenebat, quem coram nobis et aliis suum esse ancianum in secta heresis recognovit ac ambo unus alium mutuo coram nobis proni in terram modo hereticali adoraverunt et ejusdem secte esse se ipsos dixerunt et se alias pluries adorasse modo consimili ibidem recognoverunt," ibid., 328.

90. "The Chronicle of William Pelhisson," trans. Walter L. Wakefield, in *Heresy, Crusade, and Inquisition in Southern France,* 1100–1250 (Berkeley and Los Angeles: University of California Press, 1974), Appendix 3, 207–36, at 213. "Tunc commota est villa valde contra Fratres, et mine et verba multa fuerunt contra eos supra modum, et multi hereticales incitabant populum ut lapidaret Fratres, et domus eorum omnino diruerentur, quia probos homines, ut dicebant, et coniugatos accusabant iniuste de heresi," William Pelhisson, *Chronique (1229–1244), suivie du récit des troubles d'Albi (1234)*, ed. and trans. Jean Duvernoy (Paris: CNRS, 1994), 52.

91. "The Chronicle of William Pelhisson," 212. "adiutores eius remanserunt confusi. Benedictus Deus et beatus Dominicus servus eius, qui ita defendit suos," Pelhisson, *Chronique,* 50.

92. "The Chronicle of William Pelhisson," 214. "Per omnia benedictus Deus qui liberavit Frates qui erant in magno periculo, et magnificavit fidem suam coram inimicis suis. Unde gavisi sunt valde catholici, et hereticales confusi et confutati," Pelhisson, *Chronique,* 56.

93. "per confessiones etiam talium deteguntur sepius complices et errores et ex hoc invenitur veritas et falsitas detegitur et officium prosperatur," Gui, *Practica* 3.38, 144. While I recognize the qualms recent historians have expressed about rendering *officium inquisitionis* as "the Office of the Inquisition," given the nature of the "Inquisition" at this time as a function exercised by individuals rather than an institution staffed by a collectivity, I see no better translation. In "The Office of the Inquisition in Medieval Heresy," Richard Kieckhefer has acknowledged that *officium inquisitionis* can refer to such a collectivity "when the formidable tribunals were gathered and manifesting themselves to the public *qua* assemblies" (60). As we will see especially in this next chapter, Gui regularly employs "the Office of the Inquisition" (*officium inquisitionis*) or even, at times, "the Inquisition" (*inquisitio*) to refer to an entity, distinguished from "inquisitors" (*inquisitores*), committed to the prosecution of heretics, which can be supported or opposed by the populace.

94. "licet a nobis et multis aliis sepius monitus et requisitus fuerit, ut eam confiteretur et crederet ac teneret et a suis erroribus resiliret," *Le Livre des sentences*, ed. Pales-Gobilliard, 1:328.

95. "salutem animarum ac puritatem fidei intendit principaliter et inquirit, et ideo hereticos converti et redire volentes ad ecclesiasticam unitatem recipit ad penitentiam

prima vice; per confessiones etiam talium deteguntur sepius complices et errores, et ex hoc invenitur veritas et falsitas detegitur et officium prosperatur," Gui, *Practica* 3.38, 144.

96. "Sacerdos autem sit discretus et cautus, ut more periti medici superinfundat vinum et oleum vulneribus sauciati, diligenter inquirens et peccatoris circumstantias et peccati, per quas prudenter intelligat, quale illi consilium debeat exhibere et cuiusmodi remedium adhibere, diversis experimentis utendo ad sanandum aegrotum," *Omnis utriusque sexus*, Mansi, vol. 22, col. 1010.

97. On the connection between pastoral and inquisitorial confession, see Annie Cazenave, "Aveu et contrition: Manuels des confesseurs et interrogatoires d'inquisition en Languedoc et en Catalogne (XIIIe-XIVe siècles)," *La Piété populaire au Moyen Âge: Actes du 99e Congrès national des Sociétés savantes (Besançon, 1947)* (Paris: Bibliothèque Nationale, 1977), 333–52, and Nicole Bériou, "La Confession dans les écrits théologiques et pastoraux du XIIIe siècle: Médication de l'âme ou démarche judiciaire?" in *L'Aveu: Antiquité et Moyen Âge*, Actes de la Table Ronde, organisée par l'École française de Rome, avec le concours du CNRS et de l'Université de Trieste (Rome, 28–30 mars 1984) (Rome: École Française de Rome, 1986), 261–82.

98. "Description," "Preface," 378. "medicus animarum," *Manuel* 5, "Instructio generalis," p. 8.

99. "Description," "Preface," 378. "sicut non omnium morborum est eadem medicina, quin potius singulorum diverse sunt et singule medicine, sic nec ad omnes hereticos diversarum sectarum idem modus interrogandi, inquirendi et examinandi est servandus," *Manuel* 5, "Instructio generalis," pp. 6–8.

100. "esset reservandus et reddendus inquisitoribus et ab eis recipiendus," Gui, *Practica* 3.38, 144.

101. "rigori equitas preferatur," ibid.

102. See Pierre Michaud-Quantin, *Sommes de casuistique et manuels de confession au Moyen Âge (XII-XVIe siècles)* (Louvain: Editions Nauwelaerts, 1962); Thomas N. Tentler, *Sin and Confession on the Eve of the Reformation* (Princeton: Princeton University Press, 1977); and Leonard E. Boyle, "Summae Confessorum," in *Les genres littéraires dans les sources théologiques et philosophiques médiévales: Définition, critique et exploitation* (Louvain-la-neuve: Institut d'Études Médiévales, 1982), 227–37.

103. "debet pio, dulci ac suavi alloquio inducere ipsum ad compunctionem et confessionem, proponens ei beneficia quae contulit sibi Deus," Raymond of Peñafort, *Summa de Paenitentia*, ed. Xaverio Ochoa and Aloisio Diez (Rome: Commentarium pro religiosis, 1976), col. 831.

104. "Si vero non vult confiteri, proponat ei terrores iudicii, poenas inferni," ibid.

105. "Dies illa dies irae, calamitatis et miseriae, dies tribulationis et angustiae tenebrarum et caliginis, dies nebulae et turbinis, dies tubæ et clangoris," ibid., cols. 831–32. Cf. Zeph 1:15–16.

106. "ut in hoc rigori equitas preferatur et evitetur etiam scandalum pusillorum si petenti sacramentum penitentie ab Ecclesie negaretur," Gui, *Practica* 3.38, 144.

107. "Nec ab eadem secta discedere, nec fidem Romane ecclesie credere, nec ore fateri voluit," *Le Livre des sentences*, ed. Pales-Gobilliard, 328.

108. "preffatum Amelium presentem et ad fidem catholicam converti nolentem," ibid.

109. "Quin immo ad cumulum dampnationis sue tanquam perditionis filius et gehenne mortem corporalem sibi accelerans et properans ad eternam, ab eo tempore quo captus extitit, noluit comedere nec bibere tanquam sui ipsius proprius homicida," ibid.

110. "aut pro fide, seu magis perfidia sua, mori pocius eligunt quam converti," Gui, *Practica* 4.3.2, p. 220.

111. "Description," 5.1.1, 381, trans. modified. "Postquam autem sepius fuerint invitati et expectati ad conversionem, si redire noluerint et apparuerint indurati," *Manuel* 5.1.1, p. 16.

112. "Description," 5.2.1, p. 387, trans. modified. "essent *pertinaces*," *Manuel* 5.2.1, p. 36. "stubbornly refuse to swear," "Description," 5.4.8, p. 437. "*pertinaciter jurare recusaverint,*" *Manuel* 5.4.8, 178. "with a stubborn mind," "Description," 5.4.11, p. 438. "*animo pertinaci*," *Manuel* 5.4.11, p. 188. See also 5.4.8, p. 182.

113. "Description," 5.3.8, p. 411. "*ad confitendum veritatem in unum obstinati*," *Manuel* 5.3.8, p. 106.

114. "Description," 5.4.2, p. 413, trans. modified. "imbuti et . . . indurati," *Manuel* 5.4.2, p. 114. "with a hardened mind," "Description," 5.4.8, p. 437, trans. modified. "*animo indurato*," *Manuel* 5.4.8, p. 180.

115. "expectatus predicta omnia contempnens perseverat adhuc in sua perfidia animo indurato," *Le Livre des sentences*, ed. Pales-Gobilliard, 1:328.

116. "Inquisitor igitur velut justus judex, sic teneat in condemnationibus penalibus rigorem justicie quod non solum in mente servet interius, set etiam in facie ostendat exterius compassionem, ut per hoc vitet notam indignationis et iracundie que argumentum et notam crudelitatis inducit," Gui, *Practica* 4.3.2, 233.

117. "servet interius juditii severitatem, quod pretendat in facie exterius justicie veritatem, quia hoc faciens coactus justicie necessitate, non allectus cupiditate avancie," ibid.

118. "Sic etiam misericordia et veritas que mentem judicis non debent deserere ejusdem faciem precedant," ibid.

119. Eco, *The Name of the Rose*, 394.

CHAPTER SIX

1. We possess no writings by Délicieux. For studies on this figure, see Alan Friedlander, *The Hammer of the Inquisition: Brother Bernard Délicieux and the Struggle against the Inquisition in Fourteenth-Century France* (Leiden: Brill, 2000), as well as Friedlander's articles on this figure, including "Bernard Délicieux, le 'marteau des hérétiques,'" *Heresis* 34 (Spring/Summer 2001): 9–34, and "Jean XXII et les Spirituels: Le cas de Bernard Délicieux," *CF*, vol. 26, *La Papauté d'Avignon et le Languedoc*, 1316–1342 (Toulouse: Edouard Privat, 1991), 221–36; Jean-Louis Biget, "Autour de Bernard Délicieux: Franciscanisme et société en Languedoc entre 1295 et 1330," *Revue d'histoire de l'Église de France* 70 (1984): 75–93; Michel de Dmitrewski, "Fr. Bernard Délicieux, O.F.M.: Sa Lutte contre l'Inquisition de Carcassonne et d'Albi, son procès, 1297–1319," *Archivum Franciscanum Historicum* 17 (1924): 183–218, 313–37, and 457–88 and 18 (1925): 3–32; and Bernard Hauréau, *Bernard Délicieux et l'Inquisition albigeoise (*1300–1320*)* (Paris: Hachette, 1877; rpt. Portet-sur-Garonne: Loubatières, 1992).

2. Relatively little has been written about the Franciscans' role in the Inquisition. John Moorman, in *A History of the Franciscan Order from its Origins to the Year 1517* (Oxford: Clarendon Press, 1968), devotes only two pages to this topic (302–3). Given their prominence in Italy, most studies on Franciscan inquisitors have focused upon their activities against heretics in this country. See Mariano d'Alatri, *L'Inquisizione francescana nell'Italia centrale nel secolo XIII* (Rome: Istituto storico dei Fratri Minori Cappuccini, 1954); "San Bonaventura, l'eresia e l'inquisizione," *Miscellanea francescana* 75 (1975): 305–22; and *Eretici e inquisitori in Italia: Studi e documenti*, esp. vol. 1, *Il Duecento*, chap. 7, "I Francescani e l'eresia," 91–112, which echoes the article on Bonaventure.

3. On the strife between the Dominicans and Franciscans as a backdrop to Bernard Délicieux's career, see Yves Dossat, "Les Origines de la querelle entre prêcheurs et mineurs provençaux: Bernard Délicieux," *CF*, vol. 10, *Franciscains d'Oc, cc. 1280–1324* (Toulouse: Privat, 1975), 314–54.

4. See Jean Marx, *L'Inquisition en Dauphiné: Étude sur le développement et la répression de l'hérésie et de la sorcellerie du XIVe siècle au début du règne de François Ier* (Paris: Champion, 1914; rpt., Genève: Slatkine Reprints, 1978), 7–10.

5. There is some evidence that Franciscan inquisitors may have been more lenient toward heretics than their Dominican counterparts. William of Puylaurens recounts how the Dominican inquisitor Peter Seila came to be replaced by the Franciscan John of Notoire (who sent Stephen of Saint-Thibéry in his stead): "Since people were inclined to be afraid of the Friars Preacher as being too harsh, it was arranged that a member of the Order of Minors should join them so that this harshness might be seen to be moderated by his more gentle approach [*Adhuc quia Predicatores magis ut rigidiores timebant, de Fratrum Minorum ordine collega additur, qui videretur rigorem mansuetudine temperare*]," William of Puylaurens, *Chronique, 1145–1275*, ed. and trans. Jean Duvernoy (Paris: CNRS, 1976; rpt. Toulouse: Le Pérégrinateur, 1996), chap. 41, p. 160. While there has been little research to establish whether Franciscan inquisitors were in fact gentler than their Dominican counterparts, Jean-Louis Biget argues that, at least in regard to sodomites, they did show themselves to be more inclined to assimilate marginal populations into the Church than to expel them from it.

6. See M. Michèle Mulchahey, *"First the bow is bent in study—": Dominican Education Before 1350* (Toronto: Pontifical Institute of Mediaeval Studies, 1998) and "*Summae inquisitorum* and the Art of Disputation: How the Early Dominican Order Trained its Inquisitors," in *Praedicatores, Inquisitores*, vol. 1: *The Dominicans and the Medieval Inquisition*, ed. Wolfram Hoyer (Rome: Istituto Storico Domenicano, 2004), 145–56. While Mulchahey finds no specific training for inquisitors in Dominican convents, she does find a general training for friars, which included instruction on hearing confessions, assigning penances, and judging cases in accordance with canon law, which would have been useful to pursuers of heretics. In 1272 the General Chapter of the Franciscan Order in Lyon ordered that ministers in whose provinces the Friars Minor are pursuing heretics should appoint "discreet and mature men [*viros discretos et maturos*]" as inquisitors. Franz Ehrle, "Die ältesten Redactionen der Generalconstitutionen des Franziskanerordens," *Archiv für Literatur- und Kirchengeschichte des Mittelalters* 6 (1892): 1-137, at 44. On the formation of Franciscan inquisitors, see also Marx, *L'Inquisition en Dauphiné*, 58–59.

7. "duce et vexillario iniqui exercitus contra fratres et officium inquisitionis," Bernard Gui, *De fundatione et prioribus conventum provinciarum Tolosanae et Provinciae Ordinis Praedicatorum,* ed. Paul Amargier (Rome: ad S. Sabinae, apud Institutum historicum fratrum praedicatorum, 1961), 104. The full passage within which this phrase appears reads: "incentore malorum fr. Bernardo Deliciosi de ordine Minorum, duce et vexillario iniqui exercitus contra fratres et officium inquisitionis Helya Patricii de Carcassona, qui regulus Carcassonensis videbatur proditur veri regis." Duvernoy interprets the reference to "the commander-in-chief and standard-bearer of the army of the forces of evil" as applying to Eli Patrice (*Le Procès de Bernard Délicieux,* 1319, trans. Jean Duvernoy [Toulouse: Le Pérégrinateur, 2001], 223), but there are several reasons to interpret it as applying to Délicieux instead. First, syntactically, as the second part of the passage mentions Patrice and then identifies him as "the little king of Carcassonne," one would expect the first part of the passage to mention Délicieux and then identify him as "commander-in-chief and standard bearer." Second, historically, Délicieux is commonly represented as the leader of the people of Carcassonne at this moment, while Patrice is depicted as his deputy. See Friedlander, *The Hammer of the Inquisition,* 3 n. 6. Gui appears to envision Patrice as playing a regal role and Délicieux a military one.

8. Six Dominican friars served as inquisitor of Carcassonne during the period with which we are concerned: John Galand (1278–86), William of Saint-Seine (1286–92), Bertrand of Clermont (1293–1304), Arnold Jean (1298), Nicholas of Abbeville (1300–1303), Sicart Faure (1303), and Geoffrey of Ablis (1303–16).

9. The text of these registers is preserved, in part, in vol. 26 of the Collection Doat in the Bibliothèque Nationale.

10. By the turn of the thirteenth and fourteenth centuries, Carcassonne was already divided between the City and the *Bourg*. The City was composed of a walled settlement set on a hill overlooking the Aude River. With its fortifications and its fine vantage point on the countryside, it served militarily as a royal fortress and administratively as the capital of the local seneschalsy. During the wars which marked the first half of the thirteenth century in this region, the suburbs of the City (or *Bourg*) were purposefully destroyed by royal troops; after 1248, this outlying district was reconstituted across the river on flatter ground. By the time of Délicieux's activities, the *Bourg* had established itself economically as one of the major cloth centers of the Midi. Its citizens were enriched from their production of the rough fabric used for the lower classes' clothing as well as the more refined *camelin de Carcassonne*. See *Histoire de Carcassonne,* ed. Jean Guilaine and Daniel Fabre (Toulouse: Editions Privat, 2001), especially Jean-Marie Carbasse, "Des Carolingiens à la Croisade (fin 8e-13e siècle), 43–62; Jean Blanc, "Les coeurs et les pierres (9e-14e siècle)," 63–80, and "La ville royale: De la prospérité au déclin (13e-14e siècle)," 87–108.

11. The prisoners of the Inquisition were kept in a prison between the City and the river, while the records of this Office were stored in the Tower of Justice inside the walls, where the hooks that kept them aloft from rats can still be observed. See Antoine Sarraute, *Le Logis de l'Inquisition, maison historique* (Toulouse: Imprimerie du centre, 1914).

12. See Jean-Marie Vidal, "Querimoniae Carcasssonensis civitatis contra Fratrem Johannem Galandi, inquisitorem," *Un Inquisiteur jugé par ses 'victimes': Jean Galand et les Carcassonais (1285–1286)* (Paris: Alphonse Picard, 1903), 38–43, at 40. See also

Friedlander, *Hammer of the Inquisition*, 20–21. Other evidence suggests that not all prisoners of the Wall experienced such bleak conditions.

13. For the text of the Accord of 1299, see *Processus Bernardi Delitiosi: The Trial of Fr. Bernard Délicieux, 3 September-8 December 1319*, ed. Alan Friedlander (Philadelphia: American Philosophical Society, 1996), 313–18. For discussion of the Accord, see Friedlander, *Hammer of the Inquisition*, 30–35.

14. For the transcripts of these prisoners' trials, see *The Inquisition at Albi, 1299–1300: Text of Register and Analysis*, ed. Georgene W. Davis (New York: Columbia University Press, 1948). On Bernard of Castenet, see Julien Théry, "L'Évêque d'Albi, Bernard de Castenet (v. 1240–1317), une politique de la terreur," in *Les Inquisiteurs: Portraits de défenseurs de la foi en Languedoc (XIIIe-XIVe siècles)*, ed. Laurent Albaret (Toulouse: Privat, 2001), 71–87, and, "Les Albigeois et la procédure inquisitoire: Le procès pontifical contre Bernard de Castenet, évêque d'Albi et inquisiteur (1307–1308)," *Heresis* 33 (2000): 7–48.

15. On other uprisings against inquisitors during these years, see James B. Given, *Inquisition and Medieval Society: Power, Discipline, and Resistance in Languedoc* (Ithaca: Cornell University Press, 1997), 111–40.

16. On these figures, see Alan Friedlander, "Les Agents du roi face aux crises de l'hérésie en Languedoc, vers 1250-vers 1350," *CF*, vol. 20, *Effacement du Catharisme? (XIII-XIV siècle)* (Toulouse: Privat, 1985), 199–220.

17. On Geoffrey of Ablis, see Charles Peytavie, "L'Inquisition de Carcassonne, Geoffroy d'Ablis (1303–1316), Le Mal contre le mal," in *Les Inquisiteurs*, ed. Albaret, 89–100, and *L'Inquisiteur Geoffroy d'Ablis et les cathares du comté de Foix*, ed. and trans. Annette Pales-Gobilliard (Paris: CNRS, 1984).

18. Friedlander confirms that Délicieux was likely to have been involved in a conspiracy upon Benedict's life. See *Hammer of the Inquisition*, 273–87.

19. "rabies Carcassonensis," Gui, *De fundatione et prioribus*, "Priores in Conventu Carcassonensi," 100–108, at 103; cf. 104.

20. "beguini et fratres spirituales ordinis minorum, quorum omnium fuit caput et rector dyabolicus," Pierre Botineau, "Les tribulations de Raymond Barrau, O.P. (1295–1338): Les Durant et les Frédol. L'hérésie dans le diocèse de Béziers (env. 1315–1330)," *Mélanges d'archéologie et d'histoire, École française de Rome* 76 (1965): 475–528, at 504. On Délicieux's involvement with the Spiritual Franciscans and his ensuing trial and death, see Angelo of Clareno, *A Chronicle or History of the Seven Tribulations of the Order of Brothers Minor*, trans. David Burr and E. Randolph Daniel (St. Bonaventure, N.Y.: Franciscan Institute Pubs., 2005), 206–12, and Angelo of Clareno, *Liber chronicarum, sive, Tribulationum Ordinis Minorum*, ed. Giovanni M. Boccali (Santa Maria degli Angeli, Perugia: Porziuncola, 1999). See also David Burr, *Spiritual Franciscans: From Protest to Persecution in the Century After Francis* (University Park: Pennsylvania State University Press, 2001), esp. 191–96.

21. Because Délicieux was tried according to the "ordinary" procedures of canon law instead of the "extraordinary" procedures of the Inquisition, he was tried by bishops, namely, the archbishop of Toulouse, the bishop of Saint-Papoul, and the bishop of Pamiers (the latter the celebrated Jacques Fournier, later Benedict XII) and not by inquisitors like Gui. In

accordance with "ordinary" procedures, Délicieux was informed of the names of the witnesses being heard and the nature of their testimony. Indeed, he was commonly present during their depositions. He was tortured twice, but with consideration of his advanced age and frailty, and he confessed nothing under the torments. It was a prelate—perhaps Délicieux's old antagonist Bernard of Castenet, now cardinal of Porto, in residence at Avignon—who drafted the first set of articles against the accused party, forty-four in number, which served as the basis of the inquiry into his case in this papal city. It was a pope, John XXII, who, in his bull *Etsi cunctorum*, of July 16, 1319, assigned this case to the three bishops.

22. During the trial, three court notaries took minutes of what was being said. In early 1320, royal notaries joined these minutes with other relevant documents (including the witnesses' testimony, Délicieux's confession, and the final sentence) to make the trial transcripts, which were entered into the records of the seneschalsy of Carcassonne. In the seventeenth century, a certain Etienne Baluze made a copy of these transcripts, a text now preserved in 310 folio pages in the Bibliothèque Nationale as BN Ms. Lat. 4270. Given the loss of the original transcripts, Baluze's copy provides the only surviving record of the trial. Friedlander has furnished the standard edition of the *Processus Bernardi Delitiosi*. Jean Duvernoy has provided a French translation and commentary of the trial in *Le Procès de Bernard Délicieux*.

23. See Gui, *De fundatione et prioribus*, "Priores in Conventu Carcassonensi," esp. 101–102, and "Fundatio Conventus Albiensis," 197–206, esp. 204.

24. Though there is no direct reference to Gui in the trial transcripts, Délicieux refers to having at one point been read "the headings that the inquisitor of Toulouse produced against me [*capitula quae contra eum reddebat inquisitor Tolosanus*]," *Processus Bernardi Delitiosi*, ed. Friedlander, 166, in an unmistakable allusion to this figure. As Michel de Dmitrewski has observed in "Fr. Bernard Délicieux, O.F.M.: Sa lutte contre l'Inquisition de Carcassonne et d'Albi, son procès, 1297-1319," *Archivum Franciscanum Historicum* 17 (1924): 183–218, 313–37, 457–88; 18 (1925): 3–32, at 17:486–88, the language of these articles recalls Gui's accounts of Délicieux's activities in *De fundatione et prioribus*, as well as the forty-fifth formula of the third section of his *Practica*.

25. "si inquisitoribus videtur testibus deponentibus periculum imminere ex publicatione nominum eorumdem, possunt coram aliquibus personis eorumdem testium nomina exprimere non publice, set secrete," Gui, *Practica inquisitionis heretice pravitatis*, ed. Célestin Douais (Paris: A. Picard, 1886), 4.2.4, p. 189. Gui cites Innocent IV as authorizing this shift in Roman law, but Gregory IX had allowed this change earlier.

26. "Possunt etiam tales heretici per questionum tormenta 'citra membri diminutionem et mortis periculum, tanquam vere latrones et homicide animarum et fures sacramentorum Dei et fidei christiane," ibid., 4.3.2, p. 218.

27. "Bernard Gui's Description of Heresies," 5.4.8, in Wakefield and Evans, 373–445, at 437. "de consilio peritorum, prout qualitas negocii et persone conditio exegerit," Gui, *Le Manuel de l'inquisiteur*, ed. Guillaume Mollat, 2 vols. (Paris: "Les Belles Heures" and Champion, 1926–27), 5.4.8 (1:182).

28. "condemnaverant quosdam . . . pro crimine heresis, de quo confessi fuerant et convicti," Gui, *De fundatione et prioribus*, "Fundatio Conventus Albiensis," 201.

29. "sicut per inquisitionem legitimam et deprehensionem ipsorum hereticorum et credentium eorumdem postea patuit evidenter," ibid., 204. Cf. "sicut per legitimam

inquisitionem postmodum est inventum; et multi heretici capti fuerunt et combusti et credentes ipsorum," *Processus Bernardi Delitiosi*, ed. Friedlander, 78.

30. "si hodie viverent beati Petrus et Paulus et contra eos impingeretur quod hereticos adorassent, si procederetur contra eos super huiusmodi adoratione sicut per aliquos inquisitores istarum partium aliquando contra multos fuit processum, nec pateret eis via deffensionis," ibid., 174.

31. "si etiam quaererent nomina testium . . . non darentur eis," ibid.

32. "nihil eis diceretur per quod notitia dictorum hereticorum qui dicuntur adorati haberi posset," ibid.

33. "non est qui posset exprimere . . . ipsi apostoli qui tam sancti sunt a tali macula coram hominibus se possent deffendere," ibid.

34. "si sanctus Petrus et sanctus Paulus essent coram inquisitoribus, quantumcumque fuerint et sint boni Christiani, inquisitores eos ita male tractarent quod facerent eos heresim confiteri," ibid., 72.

35. "fuerant confessi se hereticos adorasse per vim tormentorum," ibid., 194.

36. "temporibus et annis istis insurrexerunt multi hereticales aut de genere hereticalium de Albia et de Cordua, confederati cum Carcassonensibus in malum," Gui, *De fundatione et prioribus*, "Fundatio Conventus Albiensis," 201.

37. "pretendentes iniquitatem inquisitorum et episcopi ac processuum eorumdem, condempnatos vero iustificantes et catholicos asserentes," ibid.

38. "ceperuntque ex tunc hereticales cornua erigere ac sevire gravius et amplius insanire," ibid.

39. "credebat processus predictos esse malos et iniustos et illos condemnatos fuisse condemnatos iniuste et ipsos esse veros catholicos et fideles," *Processus Bernardi Delitiosi*, ed. Friedlander, 195.

40. "nunquam dixit eos esse bonos nec catholicos quia nunquam eorum notitiam habuit . . . [A]liquando dixit referendo sicut audiverat quod per tormenta coacti fuerant confiteri ea pro quibus erant condemnati," ibid., 189.

41. "dixit ibidem quod ipse certus erat quod a quadraginta annis citra non fuerat hereticus vel hereticalis inventus in terra illa, videlicet Carcassonensi, Albiensi et Tolosana," ibid., 71.

42. "quod in tota lingua occitana non erant heretici nisi quadraginta vel quinquaginta et quod illi erant circa Albiam, Corduam et Carcassonam vel circa ad duas leucas," ibid., 177.

43. "Legitur quod semel erant multi arietes in quodum pulcherrimo prato viridi quod diversis rivis et fontibus rigabatur, et omni die exibant duo carnifices de civitate et capiebant arietes, modo unum, modo duos, singulis diebas," ibid., 78–79.

44. "Domini, qui sunt arietes pingues nisi homines de prato, id est de burgo Carcassonensi, viridi per fidem Catholicam Romanam, quod rigatur divitiis temporalibus et spiritualibus? Sed qui sunt arietes nisi homines divitis de villa Carcassonensi divites et pingues, qui excoriantur per carnifices, id est per inquisitores, qui capiunt divites, modo unum, modo duos, propter divitias suas?" ibid., 79.

45. "Domini, noveritis quod semel multi columbi comedebant grana in quodam campo, et Nisus, rapax avis, venit subito et rapuit unam columbam et apportavit et comedit, et in crastinum aliam et similiter tertia die alia," ibid., 254. Friedlander notes that

this *exemplum* is not original to Délicieux. The classical Latin author Phaedrus tells how a kite persuaded a flock of doves to crown him king and then devoured them, one by one. The early thirteenth-century preacher Jacques de Vitry recounts how an owl became the ruler of a flock of larks but then failed to protect them against hawks, who, again, ate the weaker birds. See Friedlander, *Hammer of the Inquisition*, 195–97.

46. "aliquis vellet vos facere hereticos et non sitis heretici," *Processus Bernardi Delitiosi*, ed. Friedlander, 75.

47. "quod inquisitores faciebant hereticum N'Embri de Limoso et quod non remaneret aliquis dives de Limoso in tota villa nec in terra quem non facerent dicti inquisitores hereticum, nisi fortiter resisteretur eis," ibid., 236. "Making" heretics, Délicieux contends, the inquisitors "unmake" Catholics. He is cited in the trial transcripts as "justifying the condemned people, declaring them Catholic and saying that the bishop [of Albi] and these inquisitors decatholicize Catholics [*condemnatos per eos iustificando et esse catholicos asserendo et dicendo quod dicti episcopus et inquistores decatholicabant catholicos*]," ibid., 201.

48. "Dixit tamen se aliquando dixisse pluribus et diversis personis quod si sentiebant se reos de crimine heresis, esto quod non possit hoc probari, confiterentur inquisitori," ibid., 176.

49. "si quis vero sentiat se hereticum talis retrahat se contribuere ad praedicta," ibid., 75.

50. "conceptus malus qui non transit in actum non debeat per hominem puniri sed a solo Deo," ibid., 133.

51. "Et quia scire malum vel videre non est malum sed potius operari, cum ipse nunquam eo usus fuerit nec ei fidem adhibuerit, . . . culpam ex videndo et legendo in eo non habuit," ibid., 138.

52. "calumpniantes et impugnantes multipliciter sententias et iudicium eorumdem," Gui, *De fundatione et prioribus*, "Fundatio Conventus Albiensis," 201.

53. "dictus frater Bernardus Delitiosi diffamavit publice et private inquisitores praedictos et processus eorum et sententias datas per eos contra personas culpabiles de heresi ac etiam per praefatum dominum episcopum Albiensem," *Processus Bernardi Delitiosi*, ed. Friedlander, 65.

54. "quosdamque falsos rotulos nomine inquisitorum et episcopi conflictos divulgaveront per villas et castella, in quibus dicebantur multorum vivorum ac defunctorum nomina contineri qui erant innocentes et innoxii, in multitudine incredibili et alias inaudita," Gui, *De fundatione et prioribus*, "Fundatio Conventus Albiensis," 201. Cf. *Processus Bernardi Delitiosi*, ed. Friedlander, 77.

55. "Et multa quae non continebant veritatem exposuit . . . contineri in dicto instrumento," *Processus Bernardi Delitiosi*, ed. Friedlander, 69.

56. "multum exagerans verbum abiurationis," ibid.

57. "cum veritate vel falsitate debebant in tantum facere et procurare quod saltem fratres Praedicatores perderent officium inquisitionis heretice pravitatis," ibid., 59.

58. "isti Predicatores . . . contra tantam communitatem ita magnam calumniam et falsitatem commiserunt," ibid., 171.

59. "patria quae hactenus fuerat diffamata testimonio ipsorum inquisitorum," ibid., 174.

60. "ista infamia vestra dilatata erat ad diversas partes mundi, ita quod nullus extra diocesim vadens audebat se fateri esse de Albigesio," ibid., 75.

61. "de inquisitoribus autem quod diu antequam ipse frater Bernardus haberet aliquid facere cum eis multis annis et per multos fuerant diffamati," ibid., 166.

62. "multis falsis suggestionibus et diffamationibus," Gui, *De fundatione et prioribus*, "Fundatio Conventus Albiensis," 197–206, at 201.
63. "Totamque patriam contra ipsos inquisitores et episcopum . . . concitarunt," ibid. Cf. *Processus Bernardi Delitiosi*, 77.
64. "ad concitandum corda ipsorum sub specie boni," ibid.
65. "ad concitandum eos contra officium inquisitionis et episcopum Albiensem et inquisitores," ibid., 75.
66. "ut assumerent [causam] contra praefatos episcopum et inquisitores," ibid., 66.
67. "qui inquisitionis officium impediunt et eius executione se opponunt," Gui, *Practica inquisitionis* 4.3.2, p. 228.
68. "impedimenta quae frater Bernadus Delicitiosi procuravit et pertractavit fieri contra officium inquisitionis et inquisitores heretice pravitatis concitando villas et populos contra eos," *Processus Bernardi Delitiosi*, 77.
69. "principalis adversarius et impeditor et detractor inquisitorum," ibid., 67.
70. "Contigit semel quod in quadam villa erat quidam probus homo qui vix aut nunquam, prout communiter dicebatur, potuit irasci seu ad iram concitari. Et tunc dixerunt aliqui trufatores seu adulatores: Nos faciemus tantum quod iste probus homo concitabitur ad iram," ibid., 238.
71. "Tu es homicida," ibid.
72. "Deus parcat tibi," ibid.
73. "Tu es latro, tu es adulter, tu es homicida," ibid.
74. "Deus indulgeat tibi," ibid.
75. "motus ad iram dixit quod ipse mentiebatur per gulam et fortiter percussit illum qui sibi hoc dixerat cum pugno," ibid.
76. "nos vero habemus cornua; insurgamus omnes simul contra carnifices et cum cornibus nostris percutiamus eos et sic expellemus eos de prato et vitam nostram et nostrorum observabimus," ibid., 79.
77. "quod homines Carcassonenses non concitavit adversus inquisitores, sed falsum instrumentum quod inquisitores contra universitatem burgi Carcassonae fecerant, . . . dictam universitatem concitavit," ibid., 167.
78. "et cum usque ad tempus verborum suorum huiusmodi inquisitor Carcassonensis suo libere ac pacifice officio uteretur, ex tunc, . . . concitata nimium et scandalisata communitate praedicta, non processit inquisitionis officium sicut prius, sed fuit ex hoc multipliciter impeditum," ibid., 207. Cf. ibid., 77–78.
79. "nunquam fuit intentionis quod faceret aliquid contra officium inquistionis, imo semper fuit voluntatis ad honorem dicti officii promovendum," ibid., 200.
80. "insurrexerunt multi hereticales aut de genere hereticalium . . . contra officium inquisitionis et contra inquisitores heretice pravitatis necnon contra d. Bernardum de Casteneto, episcopum Albiensem," Gui, *De fundatione et prioribus*, "Fundatio Conventus Albiensis," 201.
81. "Feceruntque in populo seditionem maximam," ibid.
82. "seditiones et concitationes populorum contra praefatos episcopum et inquisitores pluries," *Processus Bernardi Delitiosi*, 66.
83. "multitudine seditiosa," ibid., 68.
84. "venenosa verba et seditiosa," ibid.

85. "mala vero que faciebant et inferebant inquisitioni et fratribus et amicis, melius puto hic reticere quam per singula scribere propter honorem multitudinis, que tamen omnino non poterat excusari. . . . Alia pudet dicere," Gui, *De fundatione et prioribus*, "Priores in Conventu Carcassonensi," 100–108, at 103.

86. "Videns civitatem flevit super illam," Lk 19:41.

87. "fidei vestrae et famae vestrae quam vobis aliqui abstulerunt, scilicet duo proditores qui portant habitum Praedicatorum, videlicet frater Falco et frater Nicolaus," *Processus Bernardi Delitiosi*, 78.

88. "Sed noveritis quod ego inveni unum instrumentum proditiosum in quo aliqui proditores villae confitentur pro se et pro tota villa quod sunt heretici et se ipsos et totam villam in praedicto instrumento tanquam hereticos a fratre Falcone de heresi fecerunt absolvi," ibid.

89. "proditores inquisitores et proditores consules," ibid.

90. "Ego video hic aliquos proditores," ibid., 289.

91. "Ecce, illi quorum fracta sunt hospitia petunt emendam de quatuor tegulis fractis, et non deberent petere emendam sed deberent petere misericordiam a communitate villae et unire se cum eis, quod si facerent ego facerem posse meum quod reciperentur ad misericordiam," ibid., 242–43.

92. "frater Bernardus prosecutus est annis multis negotium assumptum per Carcassonenses, Albienses et Corduenses et quosdam alios contra praefatos episcopum et inquisitores . . . , et recipiebat stipendia et sumptus magnos a praedictis pro prosecutione dicti negotii et pecunias multas," ibid., 66.

93. "stipendiarius Carcassonensium et Albiensium et Corduensium," Gui, *De fundatione et prioribus*, "Fundatio Conventus Albiensis," 204.

94. "se fieri procuravit procuratorem, deffensorem et prosecutorem dictorum hominum contra dictos episcopum et inquisitores per dictos habitatores," *Processus Bernardi Delitiosi*, 64.

95. "Potestas etiam inquisitorum in puniendo fortis est et excellens: possunt si quidem punire . . . in substantia bonorum aut rerum," Gui, *Practica inquisitionis* 4.2.3, p. 179.

96. "ut ab eis pecunias extorquerent," *Processus Bernardi Delitiosi*, 58.

97. "totus ordo manuteneret processus et facta dictorum inquisitorum qualiacumque essent . . . ut dominaretur in partibus in quibus inquisitionem habebat," ibid., 166.

98. "Si inquisitor recedit nos non erimus appretiati nec timebimur in istis partibus, et ideo oportet ut inveniamus viam per quam timeamur in istis partibus et per consequens honoremur," ibid., 162.

99. "inquisitores hoc faciebant quia volebant dominari terram, et episcopus pro eo quia volebat contra illos cives procedere ad vindictam propter quamdam causam quam duxerant contra ipsum," ibid., 276.

100. "Dixit etiam quod per malas herbas intelligebat hereticos quod hortabatur si invenirentur exterminandos," ibid., 195.

101. "vocabat malas herbas aliquos homines de burgo Carcassonae qui communiter reputabantur favere officio inquisitionis et aliquos alios qui consenserant ordinationi contentae in instrumento," ibid., 288.

102. Even in the monition for Délicieux, the judges represent themselves as "having compassion for him, seeking and desiring the salvation of his soul [*compatientes* . . .

eidem fratri Bernardo et quaerentes et affectantes animae ipsius salutem]" and as having hope that "he repent and ask to be reconciled to the unity of the Church [*poenitet et ecclesiasticae unitati reconciliari se petit facere*]," ibid., 180.

103. "deberent petere misericordiam a communitate villae et unire se cum eis, quod si facerent ego facerem posse meum quod reciperentur ad misericordiam," ibid., 242–43.

104. "deberemus procedere eos capiendo et occidendo et destruendo ipsos et totam radicem eorum, ita quod de caetero nullus ipsorum nec de eorum genere essent in isto burgo," ibid., 245.

105. "Sic ego sum Jesus Christus; quantum ad officium Jesus, id est salvator vester, Christus id est unctus gratia Spiritus Sancti qui me incitavit multi anni sunt elapsi ad deffentionem fidei vestrae et famae vestrae," ibid., 78.

106. "apud Tolosam, praesente domino rege cum consiliariis suis et nobilibus et praelatis, dixit quod ipse multis annis laboraverat ut negotium et facta inquisitionis venirent in lucem, nec poterat, et tamen tantum clamaverat quod raucae factae fuerant eius fauces," ibid., 71.

107. "Si ego expendam de pecunia vestra non videtur esse mirum quia omnia quae habebam, sive sint libri sive alia, iam expendi pro dicto negotio prosequendo, et factus sum nihil habens, sed hoc nihil appretior quia paratus sum corpus meum exponere," ibid., 74.

108. "quia Frater Bernadus volebat esse primus martir," ibid., 73.

109. This is the opinion of Friedlander, in *The Hammer of the Inquisition*, 48–54 and 294–99 and "Bernard Délicieux, 'le marteau des hérétiques,'" 9–11 et passim, and Biget, in "Autour de Bernard Délicieux," 89–93. Biget writes of Délicieux, "Il n'ignore sûrement pas les liens de ses amis avec le catharisme mais son rapport à l'hérésie dépasse infiniment le cadre institutionnel et canonique par un effort de sympathie et de compréhension qui saisit parfaitement les parentés spirituelles. Il ne considère pas les cathares comme des ennemis diaboliques mais comme des chrétiens qui cherchent avec ferveur la voie de leur salut et dont les choix, tous comptes faits, ne sont pas tellement éloignés des siens" (90).

110. Yves Dossat, in "Les Origines de la querelle entre prêcheurs et mineurs provençaux: Bernard Délicieux," emphasizes to what degree the conflict during Délicieux's time was a conflict between Dominicans and Franciscans.

111. "Taceo de nominibus plurium aliorum religionis eiusdem, propter religionis honorem, qui in plurimis nocuerunt et male se habuerunt et plures personas contra inquisitionis officium concitarunt," Gui, *De fundatione et prioribus*, "Fundatio Conventus Albiensis," 204.

112. On the debates about poverty at this time, see David Burr, *Olivi and Franciscan Poverty: The Origins of the Usus Pauper Controversy* (Philadelphia: University of Pennsylvania Press, 1989) and Malcolm Lambert, *Franciscan Poverty: The Doctrine of the Absolute Poverty of Christ and the Apostles in the Franciscan Order, 1210–1323* (London: Franciscan Institute, 1961).

113. See Annie Cazenave, "La Vision eschatologique des Spirituels Franciscains autour de leur condamnation," in *The Use and Abuse of Eschatology in the Middle Ages*, ed. Werner Verbeke, Daniel Verhelst, and Andreas Welkenhuysen (Louvain: Leuven University Press, 1988), 393–403.

114. "si aliquis vocat vos hereticos, deffendatis vos si vultis quia vos habetis bonum ius ad deffendendum," *Processus Bernardi Delitiosi*, 239.

115. "frater Bernardus dixit eisdem consulibus quod semper volebant remanere in luto sicut porci," ibid., 305. See also the similar testimony of Peter Gaytou, ibid., 304, and Michael Sartre, ibid., 307.

116. "a magistro Raymundo Lulio, catalano de Maioricis," ibid., 88. On Délicieux's relation to Lull, see Friedlander, *Hammer of the Inquisition*, 240.

117. "quemdam librum quem portabat secum in quo est tabula generalis ad omnes scientias et quaedam propositiones super principiis scientiarum, et quidam libellus in quo probantur articuli fidei catholicae per necessarias rationes," *Processus Bernardi Delitiosi*, 88.

118. On Lull, see *CF*, vol. 22, *Raymond Lulle et le Pays d'Oc* (Toulouse: Privat, 1987) and Jocelyn N. Hillgarth, *Ramon Lull and Lullism in Fourteenth-Century France* (Oxford: Clarendon Press, 1971).

119. On Lull's attitude toward Muslims, see Cary J. Nederman, *Worlds of Difference: European Discourses of Toleration, c. 1100-c. 1550* (University Park: Pennsylvania State University Press, 2000), 30–36.

120. For some of Lull's remarks on heretics and other unbelievers, see *Libre de contemplació*, in *Obres essencials*, ed. Miquel Batllori et al., 2 vols. (Barcelona: Editorial Selecta, 1957-60), vol. 2, pp. 85-1269, at 2, 16, 77; 4, 36, 240; and 5, 39, 346. For Nicholas Eymerich's condemnation of these remarks, see "De Raymundo Lullo et eius erroribus," in *Directorium inquisitorum F. Nicolai Eymerici Ordinis Praedicatorum: cum commentariis Francisci Peniae sacrae theologiae ac iuris vtriusque doctoris: in hac postrema editione iterum emendatum et auctum, et multis litteris apostolicis locupletatum, ad exemplar Romanum diligenter denuo editum: accessit haeresum, rerum et verborum multiplex, et copiosissimus index* (Venice: Marcus Antonius Zalterium, 1595), pp. 255–60, at 260.

121. "unum amicum vocatum magistrum Arnaldum de Villanova aliter Catalani," *Processus Bernardi Delitiosi*, 97. On Délicieux's relation to Arnold, see Friedlander, *Hammer of the Inquisition*, 241–43.

122. See Raoul Manselli, "Arnaldo da Villanova e i papi del suo tempo tra religione e politica," *Studi Romani* 7 (1959): 146–51.

CHAPTER SEVEN

1. Printed in Barcelona in 1503 and 1536, the *Directorium inquisitorum* soon became the definitive work on the Inquisition, copies of which could be found in the collections of popes, cardinals, and the Inquisition of Venice. The edition I will be using is *Directorium inquisitorum F. Nicolai Eymerici Ordinis Praedicatorum: cum commentariis Francisci Peniae sacrae theologiae ac iuris vtriusque doctoris: in hac postrema editione iterum emendatum et auctum, et multis litteris apostolicis locupletatum, ad exemplar Romanum diligenter denuo editum: accessit haeresum, rerum et verborum multiplex, et copiosissimus index* (Venice: Marcus Antonius Zalterium, 1595). Hereafter, *Directorium inquisitorum* refers to Eymerich's work, and Peña, *Commentarium*, to Peña's commentary on it in this edition. In "Le Manuel de l'inquisiteur," *AFP* 17 (1947): 85–194, Antoine Dondaine cites Eymerich's work as marking the end of the tradition of medieval inquisitors' manuals, insofar as it turns from the practical orientation of its predecessors to a more theoretical approach to its topic (124).

2. The definitive discussion of Eymerich's career can be found in Claudia Heinmann, *Nicholaus Eymerich (vor 1320–1399)—'praedicator veridicus, inquisitor intrepidus, doctor egregius': Leben und Werk eines Inquisitors* (Münster: Aschendorff, 2001). Heinmann attributes much of the opposition Eymerich encountered in his role as inquisitor to the conflict between royal and papal powers in fourteenth-century Aragon. On Eymerich's seemingly obstinate and rigid character, she emphasizes his sense of duty as a guardian of the Catholic faith: "Eymerichs Standhaftigkeit in seinem Positionem und Ansichten kann man je nach Interpretation als blozße Sturheit bzw. dogmatische Starrheit oder aber als ein Zeichen von Pflechtbewußtein, Treue und Zuverlåssigkeit eines Hüters der Orthodoxie bezeichnen" (160). For other general studies, see also Josep Brugada i Gutiérrez-Ravé, *Nicolau Eimeric (1320–1399) i la polèmica inquisitorial* (Barcelona: Rafael Dalmau, 1998) and Thomas Kaepelli, *Scriptores Ordinis Praedicatorum Medii Aevi*, vol. 1 (Rome: Ad S. Sabinae, 1970), 156–65. In addition to the *Directorium inquisitorum*, Eymerich composed numerous works, including treatises against the Lullists, such as *Tractatus contra doctrinam Raymundi Lulli*, and writings in defense of the Avingonese papacy, such as *Tractatus de potestate papali*. For the complete listing of his works, see Heinmann, *Nicholaus Eymerich*, 161–210.

3. Peña's edition was published in Rome in 1578, 1585, 1587, and 1597 and in Venice in 1591, 1595 and 1607. See Edward M. Peters, "Editing Inquisitors' Manuals in the Sixteenth Century: Francisco Peña and the *Directorium inquisitorum* of Nicholas Eymerich," *Library Chronicle* 40, no. 1 (1974): 95–107. Peters situates Peña's edition within the context of the papacy's effort to produce printed editions of classic Catholic texts, such as the Vulgate, the Roman breviary, and the *Corpus iuris canonici*, in the post-Tridentine era. Agostino Borromeo, "A Proposito del *Directorum inquisitorum* di Nicolás Eymerich e delle sue editioni cinquecentesche," *Critica storica* 22, no. 4 (1983): 499–547, largely consists of a critique of Louis Sala-Moulin's partial translation of the *Directorium inquisitorum* as *Le Manuel des inquisiteurs* (La Haye: Mouton Editeurs, 1973). See also Emilie van der Verkené, *Zur Bibliographie des 'Directorium inquisitorum' des Nicolaus Eymerich* (Luxemburg: B.W.U., 1961).

4. "le plus révoltant," André de Morellet, *Mémoires l'abbé Morellet de l'Académie Française sur le dix-huitième siècle et sur la Révolution*, ed. Jean-Pierre Guicciardi (Paris: Mercure de France, 1988), 80. See also André Morellet, ed., *Abrégé du Manuel des inquisiteurs*, ed. Jean-Pierre Guicciardi (Grenoble: Editions Jérôme Millon, 1990; rpt. 2000).

5. "Je m'interdis toute réflexion, parce que le text seul suggéreait assez celles que j'aurais pu faire," Morellet, *Mémoires*, 80.

6. "ce monument d'atrocité et de ridicule qui rend tout à la fois l'humanité si odieuse et si à plaindre," Jean Le Rond d'Alembert, Letter to Voltaire, January 27, 1762, in Voltaire, *Oeuvres complètes*, ed. Jean-Michel Moreau, 52 vols. (Paris: Garnier Frères, 1877–85), 42:22–24, at 22.

7. "Je lis toujours avec édification le manuel de l'inquisition, et je suis très faché que Candide n'ait tué qu'un inquisiteur," Voltaire, Letter to Etienne Noël Damilaville, February 4, 1762, ibid., 36.

8. Edgar Allen Poe, "The Fall of the House of Usher," in *The Fall of the House of Usher and Other Writings* (Harmondsworth: Viking Penguin, 1986), 138–57, at 149. This story was first published in *Burton's Gentlemen's Magazine* in 1839. In recent years,

Eymerich has continued to enjoy a reputation for diabolic evil and intelligence through the Italian science fiction author Valerio Evangelisti's popular series of novels about him.

9. On the controveries Eymerich encountered in his later years as an inquisitor, see Jaume de Puig i Oliver, "Nicolás Eymerich, un inquisidor discutido," in *Praedicatores, Inquisitores*, vol. 1: *The Dominicans and the Medieval Inquisition*, ed. Wolfram Hoyer (Rome: Istituto Storico Domenicano, 2004), 545–93, which addresses especially the inquisitor Bernard Ermengol's 1386 commission of Dominican and Franciscan theologians, which defended the Lullists against Eymerich's attacks, and John of Vera's 1388 complaint on the part of the city of Valencia, which charged him with a dozen wrongdoings. De Puig i Oliver suggests that this latter complaint was motivated by concerns about inquisitorial procedure itself (589).

10. In 1238, under the influence of the Dominican Raymond of Peñafort, Gregory IX asked the mendicant orders to appoint inquisitors in Aragon, and in 1242 an important council was held at Tarragona to work out the procedures such judges would follow, but there is little evidence of heretics actually being prosecuted in this region during these decades. Indeed, through the end of the thirteenth century, there are almost as many reports of inquisitors being killed by heretics or their supporters (such as Pons of Blanes, Bernard Travesser, and Peter Cadreyta) as there are reports of heretics being killed by inquisitors. In the early fourteenth century, several *autos-da-fé* were held and numerous heretics were burned at the stake, but this spate of activity does not appear to have been sustained.

11. In addition to editing Eymerich's *Directorium inquisitorum*, Peña provided commentaries on Ambrose Vignate's, Paul Grilland's, and Bernard of Como's treatises on heresy and Inquisition and authored several studies of his own on the topic, including, in 1575, *De poenis hereticorum, apostatorum eorumque credentium, receptatorum, defensorum ac fautorum*, Biblioteca apostolica Vaticana, Vat. Lat. 6982; in the beginning of the seventeenth century, *De tempore gratiae quod ab haeresi ad catholicam [fidam] redeuntibus interdum concedi solet*, Biblioteca apostolica Vaticana, Barb. Lat. 998; and, in 1605, *Introductio seu praxis inquisitorum*, Biblioteca apostolica Vaticana, Reg. Lat. 388.

12. Peters, "Editing Inquisitors' Manuals in the Sixteenth Century," 103.

13. "ut pacatior et magis quietus sit animus," Peña, *Commentarium*, 422.

14. "quando Inquisitor videt haereticum cavillosum, versutum et astutum, ut nolit detegere errorem suum, sed circunducat negotium per cavillosas responsiones, et tergiversationes: tunc ipse Inquisitor ut clavuus clavo retundatur, debet etiam uti cautelis, ut in errore haereticum comprehendat," Eymerich, *Directorium inquisitorum*, 433. In the margin of the text, it is observed, "Adagio est de quo Plata lib. delictorum," c. 37 nu. 3. Cf. Gui, *Manuel de l'inquisiteur*, ed. and trans. Guillaume Mollat, 2 vols. (Paris: "Les Belles Heures" and Honoré Champion, 1926–27), 5.2.8, p. 74.

15. "cum essem astutus, dolo vos cepi," 2 Cor 2:16.

16. "credo in unam sanctam ecclesiam,' intelligendo de sua, et suorum complicium congregatione, quam vocat ecclesiam, et non de Ecclesia nostra," Eymerich, *Directorium inquisitorum*, 430. Cf. Gui, *Manuel de l'inquisiteur* 5.2.7, p. 64.

17. "Et ubi delatus petat gratiam, . . . , dicatur sibi, quod amplius fiet sibi quam ipse petat, et quaedam verba generalia, taliter," Eymerich, *Directorium inquisitorum*, 434.

18. "ut possim te citius vel statim liberare, et gratiam facere, ut vadas vias tuas ad domum," ibid., 433.

19. "Et Inquisitor . . . promittet sibi facere gratiam, et faciat: nam totu[m] est gratiosum, quod sit pro conversione haereticorum, et penitentiae sunt gratiae, et medelae," ibid., 434.

20. "Cum vero Inquisitores hanc se facturos gratiam reis spoponderit, de his poenis solum intelligitur, quae in eorum arbitrio positae sunt, quales sunt multae poenae poenitentiales," Peña, *Commentarium*, 437.

21. "si Deo placet, ego bene credo," Eymerich, *Directorium inquisitorum*, 430. Cf. Gui, *Manuel de l'inquisiteur* 5.2.8, p. 74.

22. "intelligendo *quod Deo non placet*, quod ipse hoc credat," Eymerich, *Directorium inquisitorum*, 430. Cf. Gui, *Manuel* 5.2.8, p. 74.

23. "clarum est, quod non dicis verum, et quod ita fuit discut dico ego; dicas ergo veritatem negotii clare," Eymerich, *Directorium inquisitorum*, 425.

24. "quasi admirans," ibid., 425.

25. "et quomodo tu potest negare, nonne clare est mihi?" ibid.

26. "et tunc legat in cedula sua, et pervertat eam," ibid.

27. "loquetur sibi blande, et mansuete, dando sibi innuere, quod iam scit eius factum," ibid., 433.

28. "Observa hic non dicere Eymericum, quod Inquisitor cum utitur hac cautela, dicat reo, se iam scire eius factum: quoniam si nesciret, et se scire diceret, peccaret; quod nullo modo fieri debet, etiam si inde veritas detegenda speraretur: sed dicit, quod det sibi innuere se scire factum eius," Peña, *Commentarium*, 435.

29. "caute enim potest Inquisitor ita loqui, ut reus quasi credat omnia iam scire inquisitorum: et hoc licitum est, et valde etiam accommodatum," ibid.

30. "o domine, ego sum homo simplex, et illitteratus, qui in simplicitate mea servio Deo, et nescio istas quaestiones, nec istas subtilitates; de facili caperetis me, et induceretis me in errorem," Eymerich, *Directorium inquisitorum*, 430. Cf. Gui, *Manuel* 5.2.8, p. 74.

31. "videas, ego compatior tibi, quia sic es delusus tua simplicitate, et perdis animam quadam bestialitate: et licet habeas aliquam culpam, maiorem habet, qui te de talibus instruxit; non facias peccatum alterius, tuum; nec facias te magistrum, ubi fuisti discipulus. . . . [Q]uis est ille, qui docuit te (qui nihil mali sciebas) hos errores?," Eymerich, *Directorium inquisitorum*, 433.

32. "dolor nimius invadit me, parcatis, pro Deo, vado ad lectum," ibid., 431.

33. "videas, ego compatiebar tibi, et volebam quod mihi diceres veritatem, ut expedirem te, et factum tuum, et non remaneres sic captus, quia delicatus es, et posses leviter incurrere aegritudinem," ibid., 434.

34. On the history of Catholic teachings on lying, see Peter Zagorin, *Ways of Lying: Dissimulation, Persecution, and Conformity in Early Modern Europe* (Cambridge, Mass.: Harvard University Press, 1990), esp. 1–37; Julius A. Dorszynski, *Catholic Teaching about the Morality of Falsehood* (Washington, D.C.: The Catholic University of America Press, 1948); and "Mensonge," in *Dictionnaire de théologie catholique*, ed. A. Vacant, E. Mangenot, and E. Amann (Paris: Librairie Letouzey et Ané, 1928), vol. 10, pt. 1, cols. 555–69. For general discusions of the ethics of lying, see Sissela Bok, *Lying: Moral Choice in Public and Private Life* (New York: Pantheon Books, 1978), and Jacques Derrida, "History of the Lie: Prologomena," in *Without Alibi*, trans. Peggy Kamuf (Stanford: Stanford University Press, 2002), 28–70. Derrida addresses Immanuel Kant's contention that a lie

always harms, if not an individual human being, then humanity as a whole. He interprets Kant as suggesting that, in lying, "You have renounced language because all language is structured by th[e] promise of veracity," commenting, "A very strong proposition, difficult to refute, unless one thinks otherwise the specter of the possible, of the possible lie that must continue to haunt veracity" (45).

35. "Non enim omnis qui falsum dicit mentitur, si credit aut opinatur verum esse quod dicit," Augustine, *De mendacio* 3.3, in *PL* 40, cols. 487–518, at 488.

36. "de re propria ad rem non propriam verbi alicuius ... translatio," Augustine, *Contra mendacium ad Consentium*, 10.24, in *PL* 40, cols. 518–58, at 533.

37. "vel respondeat verbum aliquod aequivocum, ut, puta, 'non est hic,' id est, non comedit hic, vel aliquod simile," Raymond of Peñafort, *Summa de Paenitentia*, ed. Xaverio Ochoa and Aloisio Diez (Roma: Commentarium pro religiosis, 1976), col. 385.

38. "verum dixit, sed aequivoce," ibid.

39. "tunc transferat se, si potest, ad aliam materiam, quasi interrogando eum de aliquo facto vel simile," ibid.

40. On casuistry and lying, see Albert R. Jonsen and Stephen Toulmin, *The Abuse of Casuistry: A History of Moral Reasoning* (Berkeley and Los Angeles: University of California Press, 1988), esp. chap. 10, "Perjury: The Case of Equivocation," 195–215; and Zagorin, *Ways of Lying*, 153–85; Johann P. Sommerville, "The 'New Art of Lying': Equivocation, Mental Reservation, and Casuistry," in *Conscience and Casuistry in Early Modern Europe*, ed. Edmund Leites (Cambridge: Cambridge University Press, 1988), 159–84; and Kenneth E. Kirk, *Conscience and Its Problems: An Introduction to Casuistry* (New York: Longmans, Green and Co., 1927; rpt. 1948), esp. 337–54 and 392–95.

41. "Humanae aures verba nostra talia judicant qualia foris sonant; divina vero judicio talia ea audiunt qualia ex intimis proferuntur. Apud homines cor ex verbis, apud Deum vero verba pensantur ex corde," Gregory the Great, *Moralium Libri, sive Expositio in Librum B. Job* 26.10, in *PL* 76, col. 357.

42. "cum benedictissimus et omniscius Deus noster nosceret eam esse mixtam, et compositam ex illis duabus partibus, novit etiam totam illam fuisse veram coram eo, et in foro conscientiae," Martin of Azpilcueta, *Commentarius in cap. Humanae Aures*, in *Opervm Martini ab Azpilcveta, doct. Navarri* (Romae: Ex Typographia Iacobi Tornerij, 1590), 453–65, at 454.

43. Zagorin, *Ways of Lying*, 176.

44. Augustine does seem to disapprove of strict mental reservations. He writes, "When something is said to God, then truth is embraced in the heart; when it is said to man, it is be proferred by the mouth of the body, because man is not an inspector of the heart [*Cum enim Deo tantum dicitur, tunc tantum in corde veritas amplectenda est: cum autem homini dicitur, etiam ore corporis verum proferendum est; quia homo non est cordis inspector*]," Augustine, *De mendacio* 17.36, in *PL* 40, col. 511.

45. "nam totum est gratiosum, quod sit pro conversione haereticorum, et paenitentiae sunt gratiae, et medelae," Eymerich, *Directorium inquisitorum*, 434.

46. "ut ... hereticus convertatur," ibid.,

47. "ad peccatores convertendos valdes est laudabile," Peña, *Commentarium*, 435.

48. "quoniam hic dolus bonus est, et ad publicam pertinet utilitatem, ut intellecta veritate rei, condemnentur, ne delicta maneant impunita," ibid., 437.

49. "ad fraudes detegendas, ad vitia praecavenda, et ad peccatores convertendos valdes est laudabile," ibid., 435.

50. "pertinet assumere vias non veras, sed simulatas et apparentes, ad aliquem finem prosequendum vel bonum vel malum," Aquinas, ST 2a-2ae.55.4. Aquinas also wrote that "craftiness" was when, "in order to obtain a certain end, whether good or evil, a man uses means that are not true but fictitious and counterfeit [inquantum aliquis ad finem aliquem consequendum vel bonum vel malum, utitur non veris viis, sed simulatis et apparentibus]," ST 2a-2ae.55.3.

51. "contrarium ejus quod in eo est," Aquinas, ST 2a-2ae.111.1.

52. "Si vero finis intentus non sit contrarius caritati, nec mendacium secundum hanc rationem erit peccatum mortale. Sicut apparet . . . in mendacio officioso in quo intenditur etiam utilitas proximi," Aquinas, ST 2a-2ae.110.4, trans. modified.

53. "Patet autem quod quanto bonum intentum est melius tanto magis minuitur culpa mendacii," Aquinas, ST 2a-2ae.110.2.

54. See Antonio Carcaterra, *Dolus bonus, dolus malus. Esigesi di D.* 4.3.1.2–3 (Naples: E. Jovene, 1970).

55. "deserviant et tuentur vel sua vel aliena," ibid., 4.3.1.2.

56. "dolum . . . bonum," ibid., 4.3.1.3.

57. "sollertia . . . , maxime si adversus hostem latronemve quis machinetur," ibid.

58. See Martin of Azpilcueta, *Commentarius in cap. Humanae Aures*, 463.

59. "duo sunt cautelarum genera: Quaedam deceptoria, et in malum finem directe, et ad decipiendum aptae, quae nusquam usurpari debent, et has iura detestantur. Alie sunt laudabiles et iudiciariae pro veritate investiganda, in quibus non iniquitas, sed ratio, iudicium, et utilitas versatur, ad bonum finem ordinatae," Peña, *Commentarium*, 435.

60. "quoniam longe aliud est fingere seu simulare, . . . ac mentiri, et decipere," ibid., 436.

61. On the history of torture, see Lisa Silverman, *Tortured Subjects: Pain, Truth, and the Body in Early Modern France* (Chicago: University of Chicago Press, 2001); Edward Peters, *Torture* (New York: B. Blackwell, 1985; rev. ed., Philadelphia: University of Pennsylvania Press, 1996); John H. Langbein, *Torture and the Law of Proof: European and England in the Ancien Régime* (Chicago: University of Chicago Press, 1977); Piero Fiorelli, *La Tortura giudiziara nel diritto comune*, 2 vols. (Milan: Giuffré, 1953–54); and Henry Charles Lea, *Superstition and Force: Essays on the Wager of Law, the Wager of Battle, the Ordeal, the Torture* (Philadelphia: Henry C. Lea, 1866; rpt. as *Torture*, Philadelphia: University of Pennsylvania Press, 1973).

62. "Solent a nostris gradus torturæ quinque numerari, eo ordine quo infligutur," Peña, *Commentarium*, 593.

63. See Paul Grilland, *De quaestionibus et tortura* (Venetiis: Franciscus Ziletus, 1584–86), q. 4, n. 11, pp. 295v–296r and Julius Clarus, *Opera omnia sive practica civilis atque criminalis* (Francofurti: Bassaeus, 1576; rpt. Venetiis: Ex typographia Baretiana, 1626), qu. 64, pp. 527–54. While the accused party who is exposed to Grilland's five stages of torture is subjected to the strappado in increasingly painful ways, the accused party who is exposed to Clarus's five stages is, first, threatened with torture, then shown the torture chamber, then stripped and tied to instruments of torture, then stretched on the rack, and, finally, subjected to squassation (that is, hung by the strappado, with weights attached to his feet).

64. "licet corpus vere non torqueatur, animus tamen bene torquetur, et timoris patitur cruciatum, et sic largo modo dici potest tortura," Grilland, *De quaestionibus et tortura*, 295v.

65. "iste ultimus gradus, et modus torquendi perraro sit, et iudex haud facile ad illum deveniet, nisi in certis casibus, et criminibus attrocissimis ut est haeresis, et crimine laesae maiestatis, eversionis status, aut similis prodit . . . ubi de totius patriae, aut multorum salute tractatur," ibid., 296r.

66. Before long the awkwardness of turning the interrogations over to laymen during the torture sessions became apparent, especially given the secrecy under which such interrogations were supposed to be conducted. In 1256, Pope Alexander IV permitted inquisitors to supervise torture sessions, though only tacitly, by allowing them to absolve each other of irregularities they incurred in pursuing their role. See Eymerich, *Directorium inquisitorum*, 553; cf. 132–33.

67. The Council of Auxerre of 573–603 and the Council of Toledo of 675, while recognizing torture as a necessary evil, stated that priests and deacons may not attend its sessions. Gratian, writing around 1140, again accepted torture as a necessary evil in certain circumscribed cases, namely, when the magistrate is dealing with slaves, the lowest of freemen, and accusers of a bishop, but he again insisted, in *Decretum magistri Gratiani*, in *Corpus iuris canonici*, ed. Aemilius Ludwig Richter, 2 vols. (Leipzig: B. Tauchnitz, 1879), vol. 1, Pars 1, Dist. 86 c. 25, that clerics should not apply it. See also Pars 2, Causa 15, q. 6, dict. 1.

68. For one of the most important modern perspectives on torture, see Elaine Scarry, *The Body in Pain: The Making and Unmaking of the World* (Oxford: Oxford University Press, 1987), esp. chap. 1, "The Structure of Torture: The Conversion of Real Pain into the Fiction of Power," 27–59. While, philosophically, Scarry's book remains compelling, historically, its conclusions are somewhat anachronistic for the Middle Ages and the early modern period. Though the infliction of pain might seem to be an eternally negative sensation, it may be experienced differently in a society where it is part of an expected, publicly accepted judicial procedure, as was the case in medieval and early modern Europe, and in a society where it represents a violation of human rights and, hence, a violation of a taboo, as is the case in the modern world. However agonizing torture may have been in the fourteenth century, it was not experienced as an outrage. See Silverman's critique of Scarry in *Tortured Subjects*, 20–22.

69. "Et ideo si confiteri noluerit veritatem quam dicere tenetur, vel si eam mendaciter negaverit, mortaliter peccat," Aquinas, *ST* 2a-2ae.69.1.

70. "si talis steterit in negativa firmiter, et nullatenus . . . fateri voluerit veritatem," Eymerich, *Directorium inquisitorum*, 480.

71. "quaestionatus decenter, noluerit fateri veritatem," ibid., 481.

72. "dicendo quod oportet eum transire per omnia, nisi prodat veritatem," ibid.

73. "melius sustinent quaestiones, quia statim brachia trahuntur et firmanter," ibid.

74. "sunt ita pertinaces, quod quantumque; vexentur, ab eis veritas non habetur," ibid.

75. "hominibus multum facinorosis, et robustis," Peña, *Commentarium*, 484.

76. "hominibus facinorosis, quibus familiare est uti fraudibus ad occultandam veritatem," ibid., 595.

77. "in corporis fortitudine duraverit," ibid., 484.

78. See Aristotle *Rhetoric* 1.15; Quintilian *Institutio oratoria* 5.4; and *Rhetorica ad Herrenium* 2.7. Ulpian writes, "There are a number of people who, by their endurance and toughness under torture, are so contemptuous of it that the truth can in no way be squeezed out of them [*nam plerique patientia sive duritia tormentorum, ita tormenta contemnunt, ut exprimi ab eis veritas nullo modo possit*]," quoted in Peña, *Commentarium*, 483. On the rhetorical origins of torture, see Jody Enders, *The Medieval Theater of Cruelty: Rhetoric, Memory, Violence* (Ithaca: Cornell University Press, 2002), esp. 25–57.

79. Aristotle *Rhetoric* 1.15, trans. W. Rhys Robert (New York: Modern Library, 1954).

80. "Aliquis sunt etiam maleficiati, et in quaestionibus maleficiis utuntur, quia ante morerentur, quam aliquid faterentur: efficiuntur enim quasi insensibiles," Eymerich, *Directorium inquisitorum*, 481.

81. "maleficatos . . . ut non sentiant saevitatiam tormentorum," Peña, *Commentarium*, 483.

82. "in aliqua secreta corporis parte," ibid.

83. "in quibus inusitati quidam erant circuli, characteres, et figurae prorsus admirandae, et valde superstitiosae," ibid.

84. "Ubi autem decenter quaestionibus et tormentis expositus noluerit detegere veritatem, amplius non vexetur, sed abire libere dimittatur," Eymerich, *Directorium inquisitorum*, 481.

85. "per torturam indicia sint purgata," Peña, *Commentarium*, 485.

86. "de tali crimine, de quo fuit delatus, . . . non invenitur probatum aliquid legitime contra eum," Eymerich, *Directorium inquisitorum*, 481.

87. On medieval attitudes toward cruelty, see Daniel Baraz, *Medieval Cruelty: Changing Perceptions, Late Antiquity to the Modern Period* (Ithaca, N.Y.: Cornell University Press, 2003), and Luigi de Anna, "Elogio della crudelità: Aspetti della violenza nel mondo antico e medievale," in *Crudelitas: The Politics of Cruelty in the Ancient and Medieval World*, ed. Toivo Viljamaa, Asko Timonen, and Christian Krötzl, Proceedings of the International Conference, Turku (Finland), May 1991 (Krems: Medium Aevum Quotidianum, 1992), 81–113. The thirteenth-century *Tractatus de tormentis* attributed to Guido of Suzzara cautions judges to avoid excessive torture, especially given the liability they might incur if they do not. Later works based on the *Tractatus*, up to the fifteenth century, express no greater concerns. For a history of moral responses to torture from the classical period throught the sixteenth century, see Fiorelli, *La Tortura giudiziaria*, 2:205–31.

88. "Crudelis, quae nihil aliud est quam atrocitas animi in exigendis poenis," Seneca, *De clementia*, in *Moral Essays*, trans. John W. Basore, Loeb Classical Library, 3 vols. (London: William Heinemann, 1928), 1:346–449, at 436–37.

89. "Illos ergo crudeles vocabo, qui puniendi causam habent, modum non habent, sicut in Phalari, quem aiunt non quidem in homines innocentes, sed super humanum ac probabilem modum saevisse," ibid.

90. "austeritatem animi, per quam aliquis fit promptus ad poenas augendas," Aquinas, *ST* 2a-2ae.159.1, ad 1.

91. As Baraz writes in *Medieval Cruelty*, "Seneca was concerned with excessive punishment, which could be appraised according to external standards of judiciary procedure. Aquinas, conversely, is concerned only with the subjective psychology of the topic. The

external action belongs to a different category altogether, and he explicitly declines to deal with it in the context of his discussion of cruelty" (21).

92. Judith N. Shklar argues in *Ordinary Vices* (Cambridge: Belknap Press, 1984), chap. 1, "Putting Cruelty First," 7–44, that medieval thinkers, with the exception of Aquinas, appear relatively untroubled by cruelty in comparison with Renaissance humanists like Michel de Montaigne and Enlightenment *philosophes* like Montesquieu, and that even Aquinas appears relatively untroubled by the act of cruelty in comparison with the intention of its perpetrator. As she sees it, scholastics were fairly indifferent toward cruelty because they identified the human being less with the body than with the soul and because they saw this soul as tested and proven strong in the fire. In contrast, the *philosophes* felt horror upon contemplating torture, not because they possessed more refined sensibilities than their medieval and early modern predecessors, but rather because they possessed a different philosophical framework for making sense of the relation between the body and the self. In the Enlightenment, Silverman argues similarly in *Tortured Subjects*, torture was seen as essentially cruel, even when applied moderately and dispassionately, because it was no longer thought that truth could be attained by overcoming the self, the will, and bodily desires and by giving voice to an otherness within the self. She states, "When pain ceased to produce meaning, torture became a meaningless activity—cruel and inhuman because it was pointless" (68).

93. Fiorelli and Langbein have both argued that, insofar as Western Europe turned away from torture during the Enlightenment, it was not because changing moral norms made this practice repugnant but because changing judicial norms made it unnecessary. In the medieval and early modern eras, jurists were unwilling to condemn an accused party without "full proof" of his guilt, at a time when only the eyewitnesses testimony of two reputable witnesses or the confession of this accused party fulfilled this criterion. Given that many crimes are committed without being observed by two eyewitnesses, judges commonly needed to obtain confessions in order to secure a conviction, and they needed to resort to torture to secure those avowals. In the modern period, jurists are willing to condemn an accused party on the basis of what would have earlier been considered "partial proof," including circumstantial evidence, and as a result do not need to secure a confession and hence to resort to torture in the same way that their predecessors did. Whereas Fiorelli and Langbein point to a judicial shift as bringing about the end of torture, Silverman points to an epistemological shift as producing this result.

94. "furore nimio repletus . . . ,, omnem indignationem et iram sui animi furibundi convertit," Angelo of Clareno, *Liber chronicarum, sive, Tribulationum Ordinis Minorum*, ed. Giovanni M. Boccali (Santa Maria degli Angeli, Perugia: Porziuncola, 1999), 606.

95. "omnem sui officii auctoritatem et potestatem ad crudelitatem," ibid., 604.

96. "iratus," ibid., 608.

97. "amenti furore insaniens," ibid., 610.

98. "insano furore vexatus," ibid., 610–12.

99. "omnibus a maligno spiritu agitatus videretur, quam humano sensu vel arbitrio regi," ibid., 602.

100. "quamvis hodie de sanguinariorum quorundam iucidum consuetudine, facile non expectatis aliis probationibus ad torturam protinus accedatur," Peña, *Commentarium*, 592.

101. "non laeti, sed quasi turbati," Eymerich, *Directorium inquisitorum*, 481.

102. Seneca had already characterized as cruel the individual who "searches out new kinds of torture [and] calls ingenuity into play so that he thinks up instruments by which the pain can be varied and prolonged [*nova supplicia conquirit, ingenium advocat ut instrumenta excogitet per quae varietur atque extendatur dolor*]," Seneca, *De clementia*, 422–25, trans. modified.

103. "modis, et . . . novis, . . . exquisitus," Eymerich, *Directorium inquisitorum*, 481.

104. "Non tamen defuerunt qui plura excogitaverint tormentorum genera," Peña, *Commentarium*, 593–94.

105. "caeterum, ut ingenue dicam quod sentio; haec tractatio de novis tormentis excogitandis carnificum est potius et crudelium, quam iureconsultorum et theologorum," ibid., 594. Peña is echoing Clarus, *Opera omnia*, 546.

106. "nam hoc praeterquam quod nulla certa lege cavetur, crudele etiam nimis, et inhumanum videtur," ibid., 485.

107. See Aristole *Rhetoric* 1.15; Cicero *Pro Sulla oratio* 28.78; *Ad Herrenium* 2.7; Augustine *De civitate dei* 19.6; Jerome *Epistola* 45; and Nicholas I, *Epistola* 99. Ulpian writes, in a passage quoted by Peña, "Others have so little endurance that they would rather tell any kind of lie than suffer torture, so that they speak in various ways, incriminating not only themselves but others also [*Alii tanta sunt impatientia, ut quoduis mentiri quam pati tormenta velint ita sit, ut etiam vario modo fateantur: ut non tantum se, verum etiam alios comminentur*]," Peña, *Commentarium*, 483.

108. "quod per tormenta coacti fuerant confiteri ea pro quibus erant condemnati," *Processus Bernardi Delitiosi: The Trial of Fr. Bernard Délicieux, 3 September–8 December 1319*, ed. Alan Friedlander (Philadelphia: American Philosophical Society, 1996), 189.

109. "Deposition of Ponsard of Gizy (27 November 1309)," in *The Templars: Selected Sources Translated and Annotated*, ed. Malcolm Barber and Keith Bate (Manchester: Manchester University Press, 2002), 289–92, at 290. "sunt falsa et quecumque ipse vel alii fratres dicti ordinis fuerunt confessi . . . erant falsa et quod predicta dixerunt per vim et propter periculum et timorem, quia torquebantur . . . inimicis eorum," "Ponzardi de Gysiaco depositio," in *Le Dossier de l'affaire des Templiers*, ed. Georges Lizerand (Paris: Librairie Ancienne Honoré Champion, 1923), 154–62, at 154–56.

110. "Nam aliqui sunt ita molles corde et vercordes, quod ad levem torturam omnia concederent quaecunque falsa," Eymerich, *Directorium inquisitorum*, 481.

111. "saepe enim contingit ob saevitiam tormentorum multos fateri quae non commiserunt," Peña, *Commentarium*, 484. Peña also states, "It often happens that, in order to evade the savagery of the torments, he says that he has done what he has not done, and he admits his guilt with a lie [*plane multo magis tunc contingeret, quando ad evadendam saevitiam tormentorum id diceret quod non commisit: nam tunc culpam mendacii admitteret*]," ibid., 527.

112. "tortura enim non tam adhibetur ad investigandum factum, quam ad habendam veritatem ex ore ipsiusmet delinquentis, cum factum vel dictum quod dicitur esse commissum, diffitetir," ibid., 593.

113. "meditatio frequens, et carceris calamitas, et replicata informatio proborum virorum," Eymerich, *Directorium inquisitorum*, 481.

114. "Non sit tamen Inquisitor multum voluntarius ad quaestionandum aliquem; nam quaestiones et tormenta non inferuntur, nisi in defectum aliarum probationum; et ideo perquirat alias probationes," ibid.

115. "quaestionent eum moderate, sine tamen effusione sanguinis," ibid.

116. "quaestionetur consuetis modis, et non novis, nec exquisitus," ibid.

117. "si . . . non est decenter quaestionatus, poterit (ut dictum est) iterum supponni quaestionibus et tormentis, not iterando, sed continuando," ibid.

118. Leah Otis-Cour, in "Les Enjeux de la torture: Une affaire d'homicide à Pamiers aux années 1330," in *La Douleur et le droit*, ed. Bernard Durand, Jean Poirier, and Jean-Pierre Royer (Paris: Presses Universitaires de France, 1997), 211–17, maintains that, though no one in the mid-fourteenth century, including the accused party, questioned whether torture should be used, there was disagreement about the manner of the torture, the duration of the torture, and the basis upon which the torture could be repeated. Jean-Marie Carbasse and Bernadette Auzary-Schmaltz, in "La Douleur et sa réparation dans les registres du Parlement médiéval (XIIIe-XIVe siècles)," in *La Douleur et le droit*, 423–37, demonstrate that, if the accused party was tortured either without sufficient cause or excessively, that is, *crudeliter et inhumaniter*, so that his limbs were mutilated or unusable, he could complain and receive financial compensation for his suffering. Jean-Marie Carbasse, in "Les Origines de la torture judiciaire en France du XIIe au début du XIVe siècle," in *La Torture judiciaire: Approches historiques et juridiques*, ed. Bernard Durand and Leah Otis-Cour, 2 vols. (Lille: Centre d'histoire judiciaire, 2002), 1:382–419, addresses excesses in applying torture and protests against these excesses, especially on 403–09.

119. "Ubi ergo praecedentes regulae fuerint observatae, ad torturam erit deveniendum, iuxta eum ordinem et ritum, que accuratissime praescripsit Eymericius," Peña, *Commentarium*, 593.

120. "Haec tot et tanta mala non deputat esse peccata; non enim haec facit sapiens iudex nocendi voluntate, sed necessitate nesciendi," Augustine *De civitate dei* 19.6, *CC*, 48:671.

121. "non potest iudex interiorem conscientiam accusati cognoscere," Aquinas, *Opera Omnia*, ed. Stanislaus Edward Fretté and Paul Maré, 34 vols., vol. 15: *Summa theologica, continuatio partis tertiae* 15.2 (Paris: Ludovicum Vivés, 1871–80).

122. Paulette L'Hermite-LeClercq, "La Torture judiciare chez Thomas d'Aquin," in *La Torture judiciaire*, 1:332–60, at 355.

123. Ibid.

124. It has frequently been observed that, in a time before anaesthesiacs and other modern medicines, pain was not only a more common experience in Western society than it is now but was often a healthful experience. As Bernard Durand observes in "Réflexion préliminaire: Une histoire juridique de la torture est-elle possible?" in *La Torture judiciaire*, 1:1–37, torture instruments were in part inspired by early medical instruments, such as the forceps used for removing a stillborn child from the mother's womb or the cords used for applying tourniquet. The chairs used by dentists, bonesetters, and surgeons resembled those employed by torturers, as both kinds needed to restrain the sitter's movement in order to apply pain to his or her body. As Ariel Glucklich notes in *Sacred Pain: Hurting the Body for the Sake of the Soul* (Oxford: Oxford University Press, 1981), esp. chap. 7, "The Tortures of the Inquisition and the Invention of Modern Guilt," 153–78, "The point then is not that life was painful so that the Inquisition did not seem

so horrible. The point, rather, was that pain was prevalent and familiar, and so it was meaningful, easily coopted by a positive ideology" (159).

125. "Et nos N. Episcopus et Inquisitor praefati, assignamus tibi tali, diem talem ad quaestiones continuandum, ut a tuo ore proprio veritas eruatur," Eymerich, *Directorium inquisitorum*, 481.

126. "This truth is lodged in the matter of the body: judges were required to draw it out (*tirer*) or extract it (*arracher*) from the body, just as tears and teeth are drawn. Truth resists in the flesh itself and must be torn out of that flesh piece by piece. It is a physical as much as a metaphysical property. As a result, any attempt to reach the truth must occur through a physical process of discovery. Because of its physical location, truth must be discovered by physical means. . . . Only torture can satisfy the demand for the real truth, hidden in the flesh, perhaps unknown even to its possessor," Silverman, *Tortured Subjects*, 65.

127. Ibid., 9.

128. On the history of Catholic teachings on capital punishment, see James J. Megivern, *The Death Penalty: An Historical and Theological Survey* (Mahwah, N.J.: Paulist Press, 1997), esp. 51–129, and E. Christian Brugger, *Capital Punishment and the Roman Catholic Moral Tradition* (Notre Dame, Indiana: University of Notre Dame Press, 2003), esp. 96–123. On the history of public execution during the medieval and early modern eras, see Pieter Spierenburg, *The Spectacle of Suffering: Executions and the Evolution of Repression: From a Preindustrial Metropolis to the European Experience* (Cambridge: Cambridge University Press, 1984), and Esther Cohen, *The Crossroads of Justice: Law and Culture in Late Medieval France* (Leiden: E. J. Brill, 1993), esp. chap. 11, "Power and Death: Public Executions," 181–201. Michel Foucault's *Surveiller et punir* (Paris: Gallimard, 1975) remains the reference point for all such discussions.

129. "stant ne ista omnia in veritate sicut lecta sunt?," Eymerich, *Directorium inquisitorum*, 504.

130. "Vis tu . . . eas abnegare et abiurare, ut possit animam tuam salvare et vitam corporalem preservare?," ibid.

131. "Deo inspirante," ibid., 515.

132. "in sua pertinacia, et impoenitentia," Peña, *Commentarium*, 499.

133. "igni in conspectu populi combusti," ibid.

134. "non . . . , per se in correctionem, et bonum eius qui punitur, sed in bonum publicum, ut alii terreantur, et a malis committendis avocentur," ibid., 432. Peña is speaking of the inquisitor's treatment of madmen here, but his words are generally applicable.

135. Maureen Flynn writes, "The *auto-da-fé* was considered by the public no more a human creation than was the Mass in the Catholic religion. Like the Mass, the *auto* re-enacted in the present an original cosmic event in the historic course of Christianity. As the Mass reactualized the sacrifice of Christ that had occurred once in the past, the *auto-da-fe* re-enacted a moment of cosmic judgment that would occur in the future . . . The *auto-da-fé* unveiled in time the divine plan that would be realized at the end of time," "Mimesis of the Last Judgment: The Spanish *Auto-da-fé*," *Sixteenth Century Journal* 22, no. 2 (1991): 281–97.

136. As Glucklich writes in *Sacred Pain*, "Foucault failed to take note that the state, in the form of its court officials and executioners, was not just applying brute force to the body of its victim. It was, rather, executing a formal procedure, a ritual imbued with

meaningful religious elements, in which the accused was expected to play an active and willing part" (156). Glucklich describes Damiens, the regicide put to death in Foucault's book, "not as a passive object that registered the signs of a technology of power, but as a subject of some consolation and potential redemption" (156).

137. "in carcere . . . duro, et obscuro," Eymerich, *Directorium inquisitorum*, 514.

138. "nam vexatio frequenter aperit intellectum, et calamitas carceris," ibid.

139. "Episcopus, et Inquisitor debeant esse summopere diligentes, et per se, et per alios facere, ut relapsos poeniteat et ad fidem catholicam revertatur," ibid., 512.

140. "Proviso tamen solerter, ne simulata conversione abiuret, et sub agni specie gerat lupum," ibid., 515. Cf. "proviso tamen soleter, ne simulata fictione redeat fraudulenter, et Episcopum et Inquisitorum, immo seipsum fallendo, sub agni specie lupum gerat," ibid., 503.

141. "quia illa conversio et abiuratio praesumuntur esse factae plus metu mortis, quam amore veritatis," ibid., 515.

142. "populus scandalizaretur," ibid., 504.

143. "gravissimum inde posset nasci incommodum. si n. reus malo spiritu agitatus, coram populo negaret ea ita se habere, in dubium revocarentur quae magno labore sunt inventa, et inquisita," Peña, *Commentarium*, 507.

144. "bene conversus," Eymerich, *Directorium inquisitorum*, 504.

145. "tales a principio sunt multum ferventes, ut combutantur," ibid., 514

146. "credendo se pati pro iustitiae, et quod sit martyr: . . . credentes statim evolare ad coelos," ibid.

147. "cum vivi cremantur, hec est omnino praecipiendum, ut lingua eorum alligetur, et impium os obstruatur, ne si libere loqui possint, audientes . . . impiis blasphemis offendant," Peña, *Commentarium*, 331.

148. "quemadmodum enim graviter peccaret, qui de eo crimine alterum infamaret; ita quoque peccaret qui infamaret seipsum," ibid., 527.

149. "ferat id aequo animo, ac laetetur, quod pro veritate mortem patiatur," ibid., 525.

150. "memineritque, se si patienter eam iniuriam et supplicium toleret, velut martyrem esse coronandum," ibid., 527.

151. We are also told that the Templars, "like martyrs for Christ, have died from torture with the palm of martyrdom for upholding the truth [*tamquam Christi martires, in tormentis pro veritate sustinenda cum palma martirii decesserunt*]," "Defense of the Order by a Group of Templars (7 April, 1310)," in *The Templars*, ed. Barber and Bate, 297–301, at 299; in "Templariorum quorumdam defensio," *Le Dossier de l'affaire des Templiers*, ed. Lizerand, 176–88, at 180.

152. "boni autem precantur et laudant," Augustine, *De civitate dei* 1.8., *CC*, 47:8.

153. "probat, purificat, eliquat," ibid.

154. "Tantum interest, non qualia, sed qualis quisque patiatur," ibid.

155. "Unde si flagella, quae pro peccatis a Deo infliguntur, fiant aliquo modo ipsius a Deo infliguntur, fiant aliquo modo ipsius patientis, rationem satisfactionis accipiunt. Fiunt autem ipsius, inquantum ea acceptat ad purgationem peccatorum, eis utens patienter," Aquinas, *Opera Omnia*, ed. Fretté and Paul, *Summa theologica, continuatio partis tertiae* 15.2.

156. "tamen quantum ad aliquid sunt, prout scilicet eis patienter utimur; et sic homo facit de necessitate virtutem; unde et meritoria et satisfactoria esse possunt," ibid., 5.2, Reply Obj. 1.

157. Philippe Ariès, *Essais sur l'histoire de la mort en Occident: Du Moyen Age à nos jours* (Paris: Editions du Seuil, 1975), trans. by Patricia M. Ranum as *Western Attitudes toward Death: From the Middle Ages to the Present* (Baltimore: Johns Hopkins University Press, 1974), 36–37. See also *L'Homme devant la mort* (Paris: Editions Seuil, 1977), trans. by Helen Weaver as *The Hour of our Death* (New York: Alfred A. Knopf, 1981).

158. Merback, *The Thief, the Cross, and the Wheel*, 143–44.

159. "l'un pour avoir parlé, et l'autre pour l'avoir écouté avec un air d'approbation," Voltaire, *Candide, ou l'optimisme*, ed. Christopher Thacker (Geneva: Librairie Droz, 1968), 121.

160. "Ils marchèrent en procession ainsi vêtus, et entendirent un sermon très pathétique, suivi d'une belle musique en faux-bourdon. Candide fut fessé en cadence, pendant qu'on chantait . . . , et Pangloss fut pendu, quoique ce ne soit pas la coutume," ibid.

CONCLUSION

1. "'Numquid non horres mortem? Quid acturus fuisses, si comprehendissemus te?'" Jordan of Saxony, *Libellus de Principiis Ordinis Praedicatorum*, ed. H. C. Scheeben, *MOPH*, vol. 16 (Rome: Institutum historicum FF. Praedicatorum, 1935), 34.

2. "'quo maiorem coronam martyrii protactione mererer,'" ibid.

3. "tamquam cui mortis illatione obsequerentur potius quam nocerent," ibid. Cf. Ps 93:21.

INDEX

Abelard, Peter, 17, 33, 36–39, 43, 214n6; conflict with Bernard of Clairvaux, 31, 44–45, 47; *Historia calamitatum*, 48; rationalism, 34–35, 45; resemblance to dragon, 40, 42, 57
action. *See* contemplation versus action
Ad abolendam (1184), 6
Ad extirpanda (1252), 151, 206n14
adulterers, 36–37, 159, 183
Alan of Lille, 32
Albaret, Laurent, 212n74
Alberic of Trois-Fontaines, 76, 86, 233n5, 239n74
Albi, 32, 124, 154, 155; imprisonment of inhabitants from, 147, 153, 186; revolt against Inquisition in, 140, 152, 162–63
Albigensian Crusade, 26, 56, 73–74, 94, 232n113
Albigensians. *See* Cathars
Albigeois, 26, 125, 147, 154, 158, 255n20
alchemy, 168
Alexander IV (pope), 206n13, 278n66
Alphonsus Jordan (count of Toulouse and Saint-Gilles), 32, 35, 41, 215n11
Amalric, Arnold (abbot of Cîteaux and papal legate), 25, 54–55, 74, 225nn11–12
Ames, Christine Caldwell, 15, 18–19, 113–14, 211n67
Amiel of Perles, 138–44
Anacletus II (antipope), 30, 40
Annales breves Wormatienses, 88–89
Annales Colonienses Maximi, 89, 92
Annales Erphordenses, 92, 95
Annales Wormatienses, 76, 88–89, 92, 94, 97–98

Anselm of Liège, 8
Antichrist, 39, 69, 72; forerunners of, 14, 40, 66
Antoninus (archbishop of Florence), 109, 244n2
Apostles, 41, 121, 153; as models for Dominic Guzmán, 63; as models for heretics, 37, 128–30, 229n61
Apostolic Succession, 129
Aquinas, Thomas, 124, 132, 181, 253n6; *Expositio in librum beati Iob*, 188–89
Aragon, 67; Inquisition in, 27, 146, 169–71, 274n10; resistance to Inquisition in, 28, 170, 273n2
Arians, 39, 96
Ariès, Philippe, 194–95
Aristotle, 34, 182, 186
Arnold, John H., 15–16, 212n68
Arnold, William, 101
Arnold of Villanova, 149, 168
asceticism: of Catholics, 36, 38, 62–65, 167, 102–3; of heretics, 33, 36, 62, 100
Augustine, 37, 39, 178–79; *Contra epistulam Parmeniani*, 208n31; *Contra mendacium*, 176; *De civitate dei*, 186, 188–89, 194; *De diversis questionibus LXXXIII*, 12, 208nn39–40; *De mendacio*, 64, 176, 276n44
Autier, Peter, 125, 138, 255n18
auto-da-fé, 2, 196, 274n10, 283n135. *See also* general sermon
Avignon, 124, 169–70, 266n21

Beguins: Bernard Délicieux and, 149; Bernard Gui on, 125, 128–29, 132, 143, 254n14. *See also* Franciscans, Spiritual
Benedict XI (pope), 149

287

Benedict XII (pope). *See* Fournier, Jacques (bishop of Pamiers)
Benedictines, 19, 30, 37, 112, 126. *See also* Peter the Venerable (abbot of Cluny)
Berengar of Landorra, 102, 107–8, 223–24n1, 243n2
Bernard (abbot of Clairvaux), 26–28, 30–52, 198, 232n113; campaign against heretics in the Midi, 32, 38, 47–48, 54, 62, 66; conflict with Gilbert of La Porrée, 31, 214n9; contrasted with Conrad of Marburg, 87; contrasted with Dominic Guzmán, 56–57, 61, 66; contrasted with Peter of Verona, 102, 107; *De consideratione*, 45, 214n9; *Epistolae*, on Peter Abelard, 31, 34–44, 47, 51, 214n8; on Henry of Lausanne, 31–32, 35–39, 41–42, 44, 47; *Sermones super Cantica canticorum*, 32–34, 36–37, 41–42, 44, 48–49, 51, 214n9, 215n14; *Vita Sancti Malachiae episcopi*, 49–51
Bernard (abbot of Fontcaude), 71
Bernard of Castenet (bishop of Albi), 265n14; defamed by Bernard Délicieux, 157; involvement in Bernard Délicieux's trial, 266n21; people aroused against, 158–59, 161–64; prosecution of heretics by, 25, 147
Bernard the Penitentiary, 77, 87–90, 97
Béziers, 74, 149, 167, 230n73; disputation with heretics in, 67, 70
biography, 212n69
bishops, involvement in prosecutions of heresy, 5–7, 10, 25, 44–46, 49
Blanche of Castile (queen regent of France), 82
Bologna, 118, 223, 230; university of, 99, 105
Boniface VIII (pope), 211n66
Brethren of the Free Spirit, 26
Bynum, Caroline Walker, 38–39, 219n60
Burci, Salvo, 114
burning of heretics. *See* public execution of heretics

Caesarius of Heisterbach, 80–81, 84, 232n115, 235n19
Calcagni, Roger, 100–101, 243n2
Calo, Peter, 55, 102–3, 110–11, 224n1, 243n2, 247n62, 248n76
Canso de la Crozada, 74
Carcassès, 147, 154
Carcassonne, 124, 146, 159; Accord of 1299, 147–48, 158, 162, 165, 265n13; Bernard Délicieux in, 27, 146, 163, 166, 264n7; Bernard Gui in, 27, 124, 150; *Bourg*, 147, 155, 160–61, 165, 264n10; burghers from, hanged, 149; citizens defamed for heresy, 147, 157, 162–63; *City*, 147, 264n10; disputation with heretics in, 67–68, 230n70, 231n103; Inquisition in, 155, 160, 164, 186–87, 264n8; Peter Gui in, 252n2; Ramon-Roger Trencavel, viscount of Albi, Béziers, and, 67; revolt against Inquisition in, 140, 147–50, 152–54, 160–63, 167, 187
Carino of Balsamo, 112–20, 249n94; assassination of Peter of Verona, 112–13, 115–16, 123, 248n85; beatification and cult, 119, 251n106, 251n110; conversion and admission into Dominican order, 118–20, 199, 249n93, 250n98; death, 251n105; torture and flight from prison, 117
Castile, 54, 71, 82, 170
Castres, 124, 148, 150
casuistry, 178, 180, 276n40
Catalan, Arnold, 101
Catalonia, 149, 167–68, 170
Cathars, 7, 32, 215n13; Bernard of Clairvaux and, 32, 215n14–17 (*see also* "Toulousans," as heretics); Bernard Délicieux and, 154, 271n109; Bernard Gui and, 127–29, 132, 138–39, 142–43, 147, 151, 254n14, 255n18; Conrad of Marburg and, 86, 98, 236n22, 239n64, 239n66; Dominic Guzmán and, 60, 64–67; in Germany, 86, 239n64, 239n66; in Italy, 114; in the Midi, 67–68, 70, 125, 138, 152; Nicholas Eymerich and, 170; Perfects, 55–56, 138–39, 228n44, 231n107, 232n107, 236n22; Perfects, admission into Dominican order, 60, 100, 117; Perfects, appointment as inquisitors, 100, 117; Perfects, conversion of, 60, 100, 117, 122, 138–39, 142–43; Peter of Verona and, 100–101, 112, 121–22; in Spain, 170. *See also* Amiel of Perles; Autier, Peter; Robert *le Bougre*; Daniel of Giussano; Esclarmonda of Foix; Gros, Raymond; Sacconi, Raynier
cathedral schools, 31, 34–35, 37, 39
Cauchon, Pierre (bishop of Beauvais), 25
charity, 5–6, 20, 198–200, 204n1; Bernard of Clairvaux as charitable, 33; Bernard Délicieux as charitable, 28; Dominic Guzmán as charitable, 27, 56–57, 61, 72–74; Eliza-

beth of Hungary as charitable, 85, 236n21; heretics as charitable, 27; Peter of Verona as charitable, 27, 101; shift from charity to zeal, 14, 27–28; Thomas Aquinas on, 11–14, 179; Wazo of Liège as charitable, 7, 9
Chrysostom, John (saint), 208n30
Cistercians, 30–35, 38, 137, 228n45; and the Albigensian Crusade, 74; as pursuers of heretics, 26, 28, 54–57, 62–63, 65; and scholasticism, 216n26. *See also* names of individual Cistercians
Clareno, Angelo, 185, 265n20
Clarus, Julius, 180, 277n63, 281n105
Clement V (pope), 149
Como, 100, 112, 114
confession, combination of judicial and penitential, 1–2, 78, 188–89, 192–93, 261n97
confession, judicial, 131, 135–36, 139–42, 174, 183, 280n93; under torture, 151–52, 187
confession, judicial, false, 187; considered as a possibility by Nicholas Eymerich, 186–88; elicited by Conrad of Marburg, 88–89, 92; elicited by inquisitors of Carcassonne, 153, 186–87, 200; elicited by prosecutors of Templars, 187; ignored as a possibility by Bernard Gui, 144–45
confession, penitential, 111, 140–42, 155–56, 261n102; friars trained to hear, 19, 263n6
confiscation of heretics' property, 22, 94, 143–44, 163–65
confraternities, 100, 244n4
Conrad of Marburg, 26–28, 75–98, 99–101, 121, 198, 235n18; contrasted with Peter of Verona, 107; letter on Elizabeth of Hungary, 233n5; murder of, 91–92; murder of, aftermath of, 92–97; prosecution of heretics, 76–77, 86–91, 97–98; relationship with Elizabeth of Hungary, 78–86, 88–91, 97–98; sanctity, alleged, 97
Conrad of Speyer, 91, 93
Conrad of Trent, 66
Constantine of Orvieto, 53, 55–56, 59–61, 63, 66, 223n1
contemplation versus action, 30–31, 33, 44–46, 54–55
conversion of heretics, 1–2, 7, 195; Thomas Aquinas on, 10–14; Bernard of Clairvaux on, 57; Bernard Gui on, 138, 141–43; Dominic Guzmán on, 61, 66, 73; Nicholas Eymerich on, 173, 178, 190–91, 193; Peter of Verona on, 27, 117–20; Wazo of Liège on, 8–9. *See also* Robert *le Bougre*; Carino of Balsamo; Daniel of Giussano; Gros, Raymond; Sacconi, Raynier
conversion of heretics, false, 11, 141, 191–93
Cordes, 148, 153–54, 163
Corpus iuris canonici, 171, 273n3
Counter-Reformation, 104, 120
Creed, 104, 106, 116, 245n23
criminals, heretics as, 119, 121–22, 151–52, 182, 195
cruelty, 24, 204n2, 205n11, 279n87, 280n92, 282n118; Conrad of Marburg as cruel, 79, 82, 84, 89, 92; Thomas Aquinas on, 184, 280n92; Bernard Gui on, 143–44; Nicholas Eymerich on, 184–86, 187; Seneca on, 184, 279n91, 281n102
crusades, 76–77, 93, 95; Second, 31; Sixth, 78. *See also* Albigensian Crusade

d'Alembert, Jean Le Rond, 169
Daniel of Giussano, 117, 243n2, 249nn90–91
David of Augsburg, 125, 255n19
defamation, 156–59
Délicieux, Bernard, 27–28, 146–68, 185–87, 199–200; book of necromancy of, 156; like Jesus Christ, 166; leader of revolt against Inquisition, 146–49, 159; leader of Spiritual Franciscans, 149, 166–67; mistress of, 167; plotter against Benedict XI, 149; plotter against Philip the Fair, 149, 156; prosecution of, 149
devil: allied with Bernard Délicieux, 149; allied with Catholics, according to heretics, 69, 185; allied with heretics, 8–9, 14, 93; according to Bernard of Clairvaux, 33, 40–41, 50, 57, 198; according to Conrad of Marburg, 86–89, 198, 239n67; according to Dominic Guzmán, 59, 66; according to Gregory IX, 86–89, 93, 239n67; according to Nicholas Eymerich, 192; according to Peter of Verona, 104–5, 108–9, 114, 121; Cathar teachings on, 104, 239n66; on san-benitos, 196
Diego of Azevedo (bishop of Osma), 54, 72, 107, 224n1; cursing heretics, 72–73; disputing with heretics, 68–73, 131; preaching to heretics, 67–68; proposing poverty to fellow preachers, 62–65
Dietrich of Apolda, 77, 85–86, 235n19, 235n21

disputations with heretics: Bernard of Clairvaux's rejection of, 46–51; Bernard Gui's rejection of, 72, 131; Catholic clerics' practice of, 66–71, 231n107; Catholic clerics' rejection of, 71–72; Dominic Guzmán's practice of, 46, 59, 67–73, 230n78, 230n85; Peter of Verona's practice of, 109, 131

Dominic Guzmán, 26–28, 53–74, 199; contrasted with Bernard Gui, 131; contrasted with Conrad of Marburg, 87; compared to Peter of Verona, 101; contrasted with Peter of Verona, 102, 107; disputing with heretics, 67–73; not participating in Albigensian Crusade, 73–74; performing miracle at Montréal, 72–73; preaching to heretics, 54–55, 62–63; receiving Peter of Verona into order, 107; serving as "inquisitor," 55–56

Dominicans, 54, 104, 100, 113–14, 118; conflicts with Franciscans, 148–49, 166, 185, 263n3, 271n110; lay brothers, 76, 118, 250n98; order founded by Dominic Guzmán, 26, 28, 54–55; not serving as inquisitors, 19; revolt against in Carcassonne, 147–49; serving as inquisitors, 7, 18–19, 28, 146, 164, 205n10, 234n12; training as inquisitors, 263n6. *See also names of individual Dominicans*

Eco, Umberto, 29, 126, 144
Elizabeth of Hungary (landgravine of Thuringia), 78–91, 89–91, 97–98, 102, 107
England, 6, 74, 235n22
Enlightenment, 171, 180–81, 280nn92–93
Esclarmonda of Foix, 68, 70
Eugenius III (pope), 31, 45, 214n3
Excommunicamus (1232), 234n11–12
excommunication of heretics, 13–14, 92, 143, 162, 172
execution. *See* public execution of heretics
Eymerich, Nicholas, 26, 28–29, 170, 189; *Directorium inquisitorum*, 169–70; Enlightenment rejection of, 169–70; on interrogation of accused parties, 172–80; on public execution, 190–95; on torture, 180–90

Fanjeaux, 58–59, 65, 67, 72, 230n77, 232n109
Ferdinand II (king of Aragon), 170
Ferrand, Peter, 58, 61, 64–65, 70, 223n1
Ferrand of Majorca, 149, 167

Ferrer, Vincent, 170
Florence, 100, 244nn3–4; Santa Maria Novella, 100, 110–11
Foix, 67, 125, 146
Forlì, 118, 250nn95–96, 350n99, 251n106
Foucault, Michel, 212n69, 283n128, 283n136
Fournier, Jacques (bishop of Pamiers), 25, 154, 232n107, 255n18, 256n22, 265n21
Fourth Lateran Council (1215), 7, 68, 140–41, 211n66
France, 26, 38, 54, 74, 82, 164
Francis of Assisi, 90, 105, 113–14, 128, 236n21
Franciscans: alleged leniency as inquisitors, 263n5; conflicts with Dominicans, 148, 166, 185, 263n3, 271n110; heretical offshoots, 7; protection of Bernard Délicieux, 149; rebelling against Dominican inquisitors, 20, 28–29, 166–67; serving as inquisitors, 18–19, 146–47, 166, 263n2, 263nn5–6; tertiaries, 79. *See also names of individual Franciscans*
Franciscans, Spiritual, 125, 149, 167, 170, 185, 265n20
Frankfurt, Diet of (1234), 92, 95–96
Fraticelli, 170
Frederick II (emperor), 25, 77
Free Spirit, Brethren of the, 26
Friars Minor. *See* Franciscans
Friars Preachers. *See* Dominicans
Fulk of Marseilles (bishop of Toulouse), 54, 68, 74, 224n1
Fulk of Saint-Georges, 148, 157, 162

Galand, John, 147
Gaucelin, Bernard (archbishop of Narbonne), 66
general sermon, 2, 125–26, 137–43, 190–95, 198. *See also* public execution of heretics
Geoffrey of Ablis, 148, 255n18, 264n8, 265n17
Geoffrey of Auxerre, 34, 216n19, 232n113
Gerard of Frachet, 102, 104, 107–10, 115, 223n1, 246n40, 247n62, 248n76
Germany: Conrad of Marburg's effect upon, 26, 76, 89, 92; early inquisitors in, 26; heretics in, 75, 86, 239n64; later inquisitors in, 97, 242n132; response to Conrad of Marburg in, 27, 77, 94–95
Gesta Treverorum, 76, 87, 91, 94–98
Gilbert of La Porrée, 31, 52, 214n9
Ginzburg, Carlo, 212n69
Given, James B., 15–16, 256n22, 265n15

grace, 9, 14, 195; Bernard of Clairvaux as filled with, 47–48; Bernard of Clairvaux on, 27, 33–35, 50, 57; Bernard Délicieux as filled with, 166; Dominic Guzmán as filled with, 53–54, 59; Elizabeth of Hungary as filled with, 85; Nicholas Eymerich on, 173–74; Bernard Gui on, 129; Peter of Verona as filled with, 110, 123; Wazo of Liège on, 9
Gratian, 171, 278n67
Gregorian Reform, 31, 67, 217n38,
Gregory IX (pope), 25, 80; commissioning of inquisitors, 7, 77, 211n68, 274n10; on Conrad of Marburg, 92–96; on Luciferian heretics, 86–87, 239n67; on the need for zeal against heretics, 75–77
Gregory XIII (pope), 171
Gregory the Great (pope), 39, 177, 179, 204n2
Grilland, Paul, 180, 181, 185, 274n11, 277n63
Gros, Raymond, 56, 60, 100, 227nn30–31
Gui, Bernard, 26–29, 55, 72, 124–47, 198, 224n1; *De fundatione et prioribus conventum provinciarum Tolosanae et Provinciae Ordinis Praedicatorum*, 150, 152, 157, 159, 161; *De quatuor in quibus Deus Praedicatorum ordinem insignivit* (with Stephen of Salanhac), 73, 124, 226n18; involvement in Bernard Délicieux's trial, 149–51, 156–66, 166n24; *Liber sententiarum*, 125, 135, 137–43; *Practica inquisitionis heretice pravitatis*, 125–26, 135–138, 141, 143–44, 159, 164
Gui, Peter, 125, 252n2, 253n8
Guy (abbot of Les Vaux-de-Cernay), 74
Guy of Evreux, 116

Henry II (count of Sayn), 91, 94
Henry II (king of England), 6
Henry VII (king of Germany), 77, 94
Henry of Lausanne, 6, 31–33, 35–40; preaching, 35–36, 214n10, 215n15, 217n42; resemblance to wolf, 41–42, 57
Henry of Marcy (abbot of Clairvaux and bishop of Albano), 28
heretics. *See* Arians; Beguins; Brethren of the Free Spirit; Cathars; Fraticelli; Hussites; Lollards; Lullists; Nestorians; Pelagians; Protestants; Pseudo-Apostles; public execution of heretics; Spiritual Franciscans; Waldensians

Hussites, 26, 171
hypocrisy, 64–65

imprisonment of heretics, 126, 264n11; desire of prisoners to leave prison, 173–75; harsh conditions in prison, 2, 147, 191; as inducement to confess, 187, 191; liberation of prisoners in Carcassonne, 148
Innocent II (pope), 30
Innocent III (pope), 25, 94, 206n14, 211n66, 228n45
Innocent IV (pope), 151, 205n12, 206n14; support of Peter of Verona, 100, 102, 113, 116, 243n2
Innocent XI (pope), 177
inquisitio, 7, 211n68, 260n93
inquisitio heretice pravitatis, 7
Inquisition: episcopal, 6–7, 25; pontifical, 7, 25; Portuguese, 195–96; Roman, 19, 29, 104, 171; Spanish, 19, 29, 104, 170–71; Venetian, 272n1
inquisitors' manuals, 19, 21–23; Passau Anonymous, *De secta Manicheorum*, 235n16; *Processus inquisitionis*, 205n12. See also David of Ausburg: *De inquisitione hereticorum*; Eymerich, Nicolas: *Directorium inquisitorum*; Gui, Bernard: *Practica inquisitionis heretice pravitatis*; Peter of Verona: *Contra patarinos*; Stephen of Bourbon: *Tractatus de diversis materiis predicabilis*
interrogation, 1–2, 131–37, 172–80, 198; equivocations during, 113, 175–80
Isabella (queen of Castile), 170
Italy: Bernard Gui in, 126, 230n78, 255n20; Dominic Guzmán in, 55, 86, 228n18; heretics in, 125–26, 263n2; inquisitors sent to, 26, 146; Peter of Verona in, 99–100, 103, 121–22. *See also* Lombardy

James (saint), 128
James II (king of Majorca), 149, 167
James of Voragine: on Elizabeth of Hungary, 83–84, 236n24; on Peter of Verona, 100, 102–3, 115, 117, 248n76
Jerome (saint), 11, 186, 207n17, 208n33
Jesus Christ: appealed to by those being burned, 89; commandments, 5; as model for bishops, 10; as model for the Church, 43; as model for Bernard Délicieux, 162,

Jesus Christ (cont.)
  166; as model for Dominic Guzmán, 63; as model for Elizabeth of Hungary, 80; as model for Francis of Assisi, 112–14; as model for heretics, 63, 128–29, 168, 190; as model for inquisitors, 113–16, 121; as model for Peter of Verona, 90, 114–16; as model for those unjustly accused, 90, 190
Jesus Christ, parable of the wheat and the cockle, 8, 207n17; used to justify expulsion of heretics, 10–11; used to justify expulsion of supporters of the Inquisition, 165; used to oppose expulsion of heretics, 8–9, 208n30
Jews, 8, 108, 122, 157, 168; pursued by inquisitors, 232n107, 254n14, 256n21
John (Conrad Tors's companion), 76, 88, 94, 97, 101, 144
John I (king of Aragon), 170
John XXII (pope), 149, 167, 266n21
John of Colonna, 116, 243n2
John of Joinville, 82
John of Picquigny (vidame of Amiens), 148, 153
John of Salisbury, 17, 31, 52
John of Spain, 61
John the Baptist, 37, 121
Jordan of Saxony, 53, 58–59, 61, 63, 69, 73–74, 199, 223n1, 232n109
judgment of God. See trial by God

Kelly, Henry Ansgar, 15, 19, 211n68
Kieckhefer, Richard, 15, 19, 211n68, 239n64, 260n93
Kienzle, Beverly Mayne, 32
Kramer, Henry (Institoris), 29

Lacan, Jacques, 22
Laursen, John Christian, 17–18
Lavaur, 67, 230n75
lawyers, 2, 7, 49, 197, 206n13
Lea, Henry Charles, 15, 103, 277n61
Leneveu, Richard (archdeacon of Auge), 148, 153
lepers, 16, 31, 79
Limoux, 148, 149, 155, 167
Locke, John, 254n13
Lollards, 26, 171, 256n26
Lombardy, 26, 99; heretics in, 118, 138, 140, 226n18
Lombers, 66, 68, 70, 229n68
Louis IX (king of France), 25
Luciferians, 86–87

Lucius III (pope), 6, 25
Ludwig IV (landgrave of Thuringia), 78–79, 81–82
Lull, Raymond, 18, 167–68, 170, 273n2
Lullists, 170, 273n2, 274n9
Lutzelkob, Gerard, 80, 91, 107
lying, 176, 178–79, 189, 195, 275n34; Cathar Perfects as opposed to, 139. See also casuistry; mental reservation

madmen, 184, 283n134; heretics as, 49–50, 66, 84, 121–22; inquisitors as, 184–85
Mainz, 76–77, 86, 91, 95
Mainz, Council of (1234), 92
Mainz, Synod of (1233), 91, 94–95, 98
Majorca, 146, 149, 167–68
Malachy (archbishop of Armagh), 49–51
"Manichaeans," 6, 32, 93, 138, 215n17. See also Cathars
Map, Walter, 88, 214n4, 240n81
Marburg, 79, 80, 84–85, 91–92, 95, 97
martyrs, 36, 78, 90, 115, 200; Conrad of Marburg as creating, 27; Bernard Délicieux as, 166; Dominic Guzmán (hypothetically) as, 199; heretics as, 36, 114, 192–93; innocent condemned parties as, 90, 192–94; inquisitors as, 114, 123, 199; Peter of Verona as, 28, 101, 112–20, 247–78n76; Templars as, 284n151
mental reservation, 177, 276n44
Merback, Mitchell B., 195
mercy, 54, 163, 165; inquisitors as merciful, 23, 89, 144, 172, 176–77, 191–93; inquisitors as merciless, 89, 91, 137
Merlo, Grado Giovanni, 113–14, 205n7
Michael (saint), 40
Midi: 21, appearance of heretics in, 31–32, 55, 58–60, 63–64, 86; Bernard of Clairvaux in, 26, 32, 36, 39, 47–48, 54, 224n1; Bernard Délicieux in, 146–49; Bernard Gui in, 124, 137–40; Dominic Guzmán in, 26, 54–55, 62–63, 66–68, 73–74; reappearance of heretics in, 125, 137–40, 154. See also Albigensian Crusade
Milan, 100, 112, 115–17, 119, 121, 244n4; Basilica of Saint Eustorgius, 99, 117, 251n110
miracles, 7, 183; caused by Bernard of Clairvaux, 31; caused by Dominic Guzmán, 59, 72–74; caused by Elizabeth of Hungary or Conrad of Marburg, 97; caused by Peter of Verona, 110–11, 117

monsters, 33, 38–39, 87–88
Montpellier, 54, 63, 146, 167
Montréal, 67–68, 230n76, 232n109; miracle at, 72–74
Moore, R. I., 15–18, 20–21, 25
Morellet, André, 169
mortification of the flesh, 36; of Bernard of Clairvaux, 62; of Carino of Balsamo, 119; of Dominic Guzmán, 53–54, 56–57, 64; of Elizabeth of Hungary, 79–80, 91; of heretics, 62; of Peter of Verona, 101–3
Moses, 75, 204n2
murder: of Conrad of Marburg, 91–97; of Dominic Guzmán (hypothetical), 199; heresy as equivalent to, 151, 206n14; libelous accusation of, 159; of other inquisitors, 101; of Peter of Verona, 99, 112–20; whether to prevent, through lying, 176
Muslims, 31, 61, 90, 168, 272n119

Narbonne, 146, 149, 167; disputation with heretics in, 66–68, 71
Narbonne, Council of (1244), 205n12, 234n9
Navarrus, Doctor (Martin of Azpilcueta), 177, 179
necromancy, 108, 149, 156
Nederman, Cary J., 17–18, 20
Nestorians, 39
Nicholas I (pope), 186
Nicholas IV (pope), 113
Nicholas of Abbeville, 147, 148, 162
Nicholas of Cusa, 17–18

obedience, 35, 78, 80–83, 90, 167, 181
Ong, Walter, 106

pain: changing attitudes toward, 181, 278n68, 280n92, 282n124; as pleasurable to cause, 184–86; as redemptive, 45, 79, 82–84, 181–82
Pamiers, 58, 125, 138; disputation with heretics in, 67–70; revolt against inquisitors in, 152, 230n78
Paris: cathedral school of, 37; university of, 26, 124, 170
Pascal, Blaise, 177
Patarines. *See* Cathars
patience, 10, 78, 83–84, 90, 167, 194
Patschovsky, Alexander, 77, 78, 236n22, 239n66
Paul (saint): Acts 7:58, 8; cited by heretics, 128; 1 Cor 3:3, 204n2; 1 Cor 5:6–7, 11; 1 Cor 9:19–21, 65; 1 Cor 9:20, 108; 1 Cor 13:1–13, 204n1; 1 Cor 13:12, 34–35; 2 Cor 2:16, 173; 2 Cor 5:11, 64–65; 2 Cor 11:2, 42; and hermeneutic tradition, 34–35, 39; as hypothetical victim of Inquisition, 152–54; in favor of cunning, 64–65, 173; in favor of expelling sinners from the Church, 11–13; in favor of waiting before expelling sinners from Church, 12; in favor of zeal, 52, 121, 198; as model of unbeliever converted to the faith, 8, 142; opposed to unauthorized preachers, 35–36; opposed to zeal, 204n2; paired with Saint Peter, 120; rejected by heretics, 48; Rom 10:2, 204n2; Rom 10:15, 35–36; Rom 13:4, 52, 198; on simple people, 132; 1 Tim 1:20, 121; Titus 3:10–11, 12–14
Pegg, Mark Gregory, 15
Pelagians, 39, 129
Pelhisson, William, 60, 139–40, 227n31
Peña, Francis, 171–72; commentary on Nicholas Eymerich's *Directorium inquisitorum*, 169; on interrogation of accused parties, 174–75, 178–80; on public execution, 190–95; on torture, 180–90
penance, 194; advocated by heretics, 128, 132; Carino of Balsamo as penitent, 119–20; Conrad of Marburg's murderers as penitents, 92–94; Dominic Guzmán as penitent, 54, 56–57; Dominican lay brothers as penitents, 250n98; Elizabeth of Hungary as penitent, 78–84, 98; friars trained to give, 263n6; Peter of Verona as penitent, 101–4, 112; and torture, 181
penance, given to repentant heretics, 1–2; abused by unrepentant heretics, 11, 141, 191–92; assigned by Conrad of Marburg, 77–92, 94; assigned by Dominic Guzmán, 55; Thomas Aquinas on, 11; Bernard of Clairvaux on, 46–47; Bernard Délicieux on, 155–56, 165; Nicholas Eymerich on, 178, 190–92; Bernard Gui on, 126, 140–42, 145
persecution, 8, 16–18, 21, 200; Bernard of Clairvaux as agent of, 44; Conrad of Marburg as agent of, 27, 76, 92–93, 96–97, 100; Dominic Guzmán as agent of, 225n11; inquisitors as agents of, 150, 156–57, 167; Peter of Verona as agent of, 100, 118; Peter of Verona as victim of, 114, 118, 249n91
Peter (saint), 40, 57, 120–21, 128–29, 142; as hypothetical victim of Inquisition, 152–54

Peter II (king of Aragon), 67
Peter IV (king of Aragon), 170
Peter of Castelnau (papal legate), 25, 54, 67, 225n11
Peter of Les Vaux-de-Cernay, 67–72, 74, 223–24n1, 232n109, 232n113
Peter of Verona, 26–28, 90, 97, 99–123, 199; *Contra patarinos*, 120–22, 251–52n113; heretical origins, 100–101; as inquisitor, 100; letter to prioress of Convent of Saint Peter, Campo Sancto, Milan, 121–22; as martyr, 28, 101, 112–20, 247–78n76; as penitent, 101–4, 112; as preacher, 99–100
Peter the Venerable (abbot of Cluny), 32
Peters, Edward, 15–16, 171, 205n11, 211n68, 256n24, 277n61
Philip Augustus (king of France), 94
Philip the Fair (king of France), 148–49, 156, 187
Phinehas, 75, 121, 204n2
Pisa, Council of (1135), 31
Poe, Edgar Allen, 169
poverty, 81; adopted by Dominic Guzmán, 63, 107, 228n45; adopted by Elizabeth of Hungary, 79, 81, 236n21; adopted by Francis of Assisi, 113–14; adopted by heretics, 62–64, 127, 130–31, 167; as an inducement to heresy, 58–59; initially rejected by Cistercians, 228n45; as religious ideal, 62–65, 172, 271n112
preachers, 99–100, 103, 128, 146; Bernard of Clairvaux as, 32, 38, 47–48, 54, 62, 66; Conrad of Marburg as, 76, 96; Bernard Délicieux as, 146, 156, 166; Dominic Guzmán as, 54, 62–63, 65–66; heretics as, 31–32, 35–36, 138; Peter of Verona as, 99–100
prostitutes, 16, 37
Protestants, 114, 171
Prouille, 58, 100
Provence, 124–25, 146
Prudlo, Donald S., 103, 118, 248n85, 249n91, 249n93
Pseudo-Apostles, 125–27, 129, 132, 135, 143, 170, 254n14, 255n20
public execution of heretics, 2, 6, 20, 198; beneficial to innocent parties, 90, 193–94; Bernard Gui's involvement in, 126, 131, 136–44; Conrad of Marburg's involvement in, 76, 89, 93; defended, 11, 25, 171; Dominic Guzmán's involvement in, 56, 60; Nicholas Eymerich's writings on, 171–72, 190–95; history of Catholic teachings on, 283n128; not objective of Inquisition, 2, 140–44, 174; opposed, 9–10, 17–18, 272n120; possibility of repentance during, 141, 191, 195; possibility of subversion of Inquisition during, 191–92; sought by heretics, 36, 50, 143, 145. *See also auto-da-fé*; general sermon
Publicans. *See* Cathars

Ralph of Fontfroide (papal legate), 54, 67, 225n11, 228n45
Raymond VI (count of Toulouse), 67, 94, 232n107
Raymond of Peñafort, 141–42, 176–77, 235n19, 243n2, 274n10
Raymond-Roger (count of Foix), 67–70
Reims, Council of (1148), 31
Rhetorica ad Herrenium, 182, 186
Robert II the Pious (king of France), 6
Robert *le Bougre*, 19, 100
Roderick of Atencia, 115–16, 243n2
Roger II (bishop of Châlons-sur-Marne), 8–11, 13
Roland of Cremona, 101
Rome, 18, 31, 92, 118, 169, 171
Rutebeuf, 236–37n27

Sacconi, Raynier, 19, 100, 117, 243n2, 255n18
saint, inquisitor as, 102–3, 105
saints' lives, 22, 25
Saracens. *See* Muslims
scandal, 71, 136, 142, 160–61, 192, 209n43
Scarry, Elaine, 278n68
scholasticism, 31, 34–35, 52, 180, 216n26, 280n92. *See also* cathedral schools
Seneca, 184, 279–80n91, 281n102
Sens, Council of (1140), 31, 47–48, 51
Servian, 67, 69, 230n71
Shklar, Judith N., 280n92
Siegfried III of Eppenstein (archbishop of Mainz), 77, 87–91, 95, 97
Silverman, Lisa, 189–90, 277n61, 278n68, 280n92, 283n126
Simon of Montfort, 74, 232n107
simplicity, 49, 132–34, 137, 175–76
Skura, Meredith Ann, 213n75
sodomites, 16, 36, 89
sorcerers. *See* witches
Spain, 77, 169–71, 223n1. *See also* Aragon; Castile; Catalonia; Diego of Azevedo (bishop

of Osma); Dominic Guzmán; Eymerich, Nicholas; Ferdinand II (king of Aragon); Inquisition: Spanish; Isabella (queen of Castile); Peña, Francis; Raymond of Peñafort; Thomas of Torquemada
Spiritual Franciscans, 125, 149, 167, 170, 185, 265n20
Stephen (saint), 8
Stephen of Bourbon, 63, 65, 125, 223–24n1, 255n19
Stephen of Saint-Thibéry, 101, 263n5
Stephen of Salanhac, 73, 124, 224n1, 226n18, 232n113
suicides, heretics as, 36, 50, 138, 143, 145
Summa theologica (Aquinas): on charity, 11–14; on cruelty, 184, 279n91, 280n92; on the duty to respond under interrogation, 181; on lying, 178–79, 277n50; on suffering, 188–89, 194; on the treatment of heretics, 10–13, 20, 127, 208nn30–31, 209n43; on zeal, 12
superstition, 36, 183

Templars, 187, 284n151
terror, 95, 103, 138, 190
testimony, 1–2; necessary before torture, 187, 280n92; necessary in heresy prosecutions, 135, 144, 151–52, 280n93; provided by converted Cathar Perfects, 138; provided for Amiel of Perles, 138–39; required from converted heretics, 1, 140, 142
testimony, false, 87–88, 92–93, 97, 144, 151–53, 193; in the registers in Carcassonne, 147, 157–58
testimony, secret, 1–2, 7, 151–53, 205–6n12, 206n13; not in Bernard Délicieux's case, 266n21
Thomas Agni of Lentini, 101–2, 104–7, 109, 116–17, 123, 223–24n1, 243n2, 247–78n76
Thomas of Aversa, 185
Thomas of Celano, 142
Thomas of Torquemada, 170
Thouzellier, Christine, 55, 225n11
toleration, religious, 17–18, 155–56, 160, 166–68
Tors, Conrad, 19, 76, 88, 93–94, 97; former heretic, 100; murdered, 101, 144
torture, 2, 171–72, 198; accused party's agency during, 181–84; of Carino of Balsamo, 117; danger of producing false confession during,
152–53, 186–88; of Bernard Délicieux, 266n21; five stages of, 180–81, 188, 277n63; history of, 152, 180–81, 277n61; initial approval for slaves, 278n67; later approval for accused heretics, 7, 151–52, 206n14, 278n66; legal recourses for those maimed, 282n118; prohibition against causing death or maiming, 151; prohibition of inquisitor's pleasure during, 184–86, 188; prohibition of unusual methods during, 185–86, 188; regulation of repetition of, 187–88; resemblance to medical procedures, 282n124; resemblance to trial by ordeal, 183; sufficient eyewitness testimony required to justify, 187, 280n92
Toulousain, 26, 125, 154, 255n20
"Toulousans," as heretics, 32–33, 36–42, 45, 48–51, 57
Toulouse: during Albigensian Crusade, 74; Bernard of Clairvaux in, 32, 41, 62; Bernard Délicieux in, 152, 166; Dominic Guzmán in, 55, 59, 64–65; Bernard Gui in, 124–26, 137, 253n6; heretics in, 32, 55, 59, 64, 137–40, 244n4; Inquisition in, 139–40, 146; resistance to Inquisition in, 139–40, 152
treason, 150, 161–65, 181; heresy as, 206n14; support of accused heretics as, 161–65; support of Inquisition as, 162–65
trial by God, 6, 183; trial by combat, 131, 183; trial by oath, 6–7, 183; trial by ordeal, 6–7, 183
Tugwell, Simon, 55–56, 60, 227nn30–31, 231n104, 232n107

Ulpian, 179, 182, 186, 279n78, 281n107

Verfeil, 47, 66–69, 230n74
Vicaire, Marie-Humbert, 56, 74, 224n1, 225nn10–11, 227n31
Virgin Mary, 53, 89, 107–8, 110, 112
Voltaire, 169, 195–96

Waldensians, 7, 211n66, 256n26; in Aragon, 170; in Germany, 86; Bernard Gui and, 127–30, 132–33, 143, 254n14, 255n19; Dominic Guzmán and, 67; in the Midi, 67–71, 125; Peter of Verona and, 121
Wazo (bishop of Liège), 7–12, 20, 206–7n15
William (abbot of Saint-Thierry), 34, 52, 107
William (bishop of Albi), 66, 68, 70–71

William of Puylaurens, 47, 68–71, 224n1, 232n113
William of Saint-Seine, 147
William of Tudela, 74
witches, 126, 171, 182–83, 187, 254n14
women: as accused heretics, 58, 67–68, 97; as accusers of heretics, 87; as audience members at disputations with heretics, 69–70; the Church as bride and mother, 42–43, 58; Dominic Guzmán's attitude toward, 58–60, 64–68, 72–73; and male confessors, 237n29; as wives or companions of accused heretics, 38, 191; as wives or mothers of potential Cistercian monks, 30. *See also* Elizabeth of Hungary (landgravine of Thuringia); Esclarmonda of Foix
Worms, Synod of (1233), 94

zeal, 5–7, 9, 27–28, 198–200, 204n2; Thomas Aquinas on, 12–14; Bernard of Clairvaux as zealous, 33, 39–40, 44–47, 51–52, 57, 223n146; Conrad of Marburg as zealous, 76–77, 87, 96–98, 101; Bernard Délicieux as zealous, 150, 166; Dominic Guzmán as zealous, 225n11; Elizabeth of Hungary as zealous, 85–86; Gregory IX on, 75–76, 96–97; Bernard Gui as zealous, 126, 130, 136; shift from charity to zeal, 14, 27–28

www.ingramcontent.com/pod-product-compliance
Lightning Source LLC
Chambersburg PA
CBHW021937290426
44108CB00012B/867